HENRY BRADSHAW SOCIETY

ffounded in the year of Our Lord 1890
for the editing of Rare Liturgical Texts

VOLUME CXIII

ISSUED TO MEMBERS FOR THE YEARS 1999–2000
AND
PUBLISHED FOR THE SOCIETY
BY
THE BOYDELL PRESS

THE LEOFRIC MISSAL I

INTRODUCTION, COLLATION TABLE
AND INDEX

Edited by

Nicholas Orchard

LONDON
2002

© Henry Bradshaw Society 2002

First published for the Henry Bradshaw Society 2002
by The Boydell Press
an imprint of Boydell & Brewer Ltd
PO Box 9, Woodbridge, Suffolk IP12 3DF, UK
and of Boydell & Brewer Inc.
PO Box 41026, Rochester, NY 14604–4126, USA
website: www.boydell.co.uk

ISBN 1 870252 17 9

ISSN 0144–0241

A catalogue record for this book is available
from the British Library

Library of Congress Cataloging-in-Publication Data
The Leofric Missal / edited by Nicholas Orchard.
    p. cm. — (Henry Bradshaw Society, ISSN 0144-0241 ; v. 113–114)
    Includes bibliographical references and index.
    Contents: v. 1. Introduction, collation table, and index — v. 2 Text.
    ISBN 1-870252-17-9 (alk. paper)
    1. Catholic Church—Liturgy—History—Middle Ages, 600–1500—Sources. 2.
Manuscripts, Latin (Medieval and modern)—England—Exeter. 3. Exeter
(England)—Church history—Sources. 4. Leofric, Bp. of Exeter, d. 1072. I. Orchard,
Nicholas, 1963– II. Henry Bradshaw Society (Series) ; v. 113–114.
BX2037.A3 L37 2002
264'.023—dc21   2002023217

This publication is printed on acid-free paper

Printed in Great Britain by
St Edmundsbury Press Ltd, Bury St Edmunds, Suffolk

TABLE OF CONTENTS

PUBLICATION SECRETARY'S PREFACE

Among the many liturgical manuscripts which have survived from Anglo-Saxon England, none is more complex than the 'Leofric Missal', now preserved in the Bodleian Library in Oxford as MS. Bodley 579. The book's complexity derives from the fact that it underwent three distinct phases of composition. The nucleus is a sacramentary written *c.* 900 for the use of an English archbishop, perhaps Plegmund, archbishop of Canterbury (890–923), but drawing on liturgical sources of continental, especially north Italian and Flemish, origin (Leofric A); substantial amplifications made in England, during the first half of the tenth century, apparently for the use of archbishops of Canterbury including Dunstan, who took the opportunity to have incorporated liturgical materials he had brought with him to Canterbury from Glastonbury (Leofric B); and finally additions made from the *Romano-German Pontifical* at Exeter in the time of Bishop Leofric (Leofric C), who bequeathed the book to his cathedral chapter on his death in 1072. But these three principal parts received annotations and additions of many kinds during the nearly two centuries in which the book was used in Anglo-Saxon England. The problem for an editor of this complex manuscript, therefore, is to distinguish the various phases of growth while not losing sight of the overall liturgical function which the book was designed to perform. The manuscript was first edited in 1883 by F. E. Warren (*The Leofric Missal* [Oxford]), who was to become one of the members of the Society's first Council on its establishment in 1890. For over a century Warren's edition has been an indispensable tool for students of English liturgy, but there are many ways in which its utility is limited: Warren did not number the individual prayers in the manuscript, making any kind of cross-referencing or comparison immensely cumbersome, and he did not fully distinguish the various campaigns of accretion. Inevitably, too, there have been huge advances in our knowledge of Anglo-Saxon palaeography and liturgy during the past century. The time is therefore ripe for a new edition which takes account of these scholarly advances. The Society is proud to welcome the publication of the present two-volume edition of the 'Leofric Missal' by Nicholas Orchard, the first volume of which, containing Introduction, Collation Table and Indexes, is issued as vol. CXIII against subscriptions for the years 1999–2000, with the second volume, containing Text, issued simultaneously as vol. CXIV for the years 2001–2002.

Michael Lapidge,
for the Publications Committee
June 2001

PREFACE

In the course of preparing this edition I have had much help. I owe an enormous debt of gratitude to Martin Kauffmann and Sabina Pugh of the Bodleian Library for making it possible (at exceedingly short notice) for me to examine the 'Leofric Missal' in its present disbound state – the book has been in the Department of Conservation since 1985; to Richard Pfaff and Peter Kidd for reading and commenting on a number of preliminary drafts; to Ron Baxter, John Lowden, Zoë Opačić, Achim Timmermann, Jonathan Vickers and Philip Ward-Jackson, all colleagues at the Courtauld Institute of Art in London, for their constant encouragement and advice; and to the respective staffs of the Bodleian, British and London Libraries, not to mention the Parker Library at Corpus Christi College, Cambridge, for their generous assistance. Last, not least, I should like to thank Michael Lapidge for inviting me to undertake the work in the first place. It has been immensely enjoyable. All errors, it hardly need be said, are my own.

ABBREVIATIONS

AB	*Analecta Bollandiana.*
ASE	*Anglo-Saxon England.*
Bede, *HE*	Bede, *Historia Ecclesiastica Gentis Anglorum*, ed. Bertram Colgrave and R. A. B. Mynors (Oxford, 1969, repr. with corrections, 1991).
Bischoff, *Katalog*	B. Bischoff, *Katalog der festländischen Handshcriften des neunten Jahrhunderts*, 3 vols (Wiesbaden, 1998 and forthcoming).
CCSL	Corpus Christianorum Series Latina.
CLLA	K. Gamber, *Codices latini liturgici antiquiores*, 2 vols, Spicilegii Friburgensis Subsidia 1 and 1A, 2nd ed. (Fribourg, 1969), with Supplement (Fribourg, 1988).
DACL	*Dictionnaire d'archaéologie chrétienne et de liturgie*, ed. F. Cabrol and H. Leclercq, 30 vols in 15 (Paris, 1907–53).
Delisle, 'Mémoire'	'Mémoire sur d'anciens sacramentaires', *Mémoires de l'Institut National de France, Académie des Inscriptions et Belles-Lettres* 32.i (Paris, 1886).
Drage, *Leofric*	E. Drage, 'Bishop Leofric and the Cathedral Chapter of Exeter: a reassessment of the manuscript evidence' (unpubl. Oxford DPhil. thesis, 1978).
Ebner, *Quellen*	A. Ebner, *Quellen und Forschungen zur Geschichte und Kunstgeschichte des Missale Romanum im Mittelalter: Iter Italicum* (Freiburg-im-Breisgau, 1896).
EEMF	Early English Manuscripts in Facsimile.
EK	*English Kalendars before AD 1100*, ed. F. Wormald, HBS 72 (London, 1934).
EL	*Ephemerides Liturgicae.*
Franz, *KB*	A. Franz, *Die kirchlichen Benediktionem im Mittelalter*, 2 vols (Freiburg-im-Breisgau, 1909).

Gerbert, *Monumenta*	M. Gerbert, *Monumenta veteris liturgicae Alemmanicae*, 2 vols (Sankt-Blasien, 1777–8).
HBS	Henry Bradshaw Society Publications.
Hohler, 'Books'	C. Hohler, 'Some service-books of the later Saxon Church', *Tenth-Century Studies*, ed. D. Parsons (Leicester, 1975), 60–83, 217–27.
JTS	*Journal of Theological Studies.*
Le sacramentaire grégorien	*Le sacramentaire grégorien: ses principales formes d'après les plus anciens manuscrits*, ed. J. Deshusses, 3 vols, Spicilegium Friburgense 16, 24 and 28, 2nd ed. (Fribourg, 1979–88).
Leroquais, *Notes*	The notebooks of Victor Leroquais, now Paris, Bibliothèque nationale de France, nouv. acq. 3160.
Leroquais, *Les sacramentaires*	V. Leroquais, *Les sacramentaires et les missels manuscrits*, 4 vols (Paris, 1924).
Leroquais, *Les pontificaux*	V. Leroquais, *Les pontificaux manuscrits*, 3 vols (Paris, 1937).
LM	*The Leofric Missal as used in the Cathedral of Exeter during the Episcopate of its First Bishop, A.D. 1050–72, together with some account of the Red Book of Derby, the Missal of Robert of Jumièges, and a few other Early Manuscript Service Books of the English Church*, ed. F. E. Warren (Oxford, 1883).
LQF	Liturgiewissenschäftliche Quellen und Forschungen.
Martène, *AER*	E. Martène, *De antiquis ecclesiae ritibus*, 4 vols, 2nd ed. (Antwerp, 1736–8).
Martimort, *La documentation*	A. G. Martimort, *La documentation liturgique de Dom Edmond Martène*, Studi e Testi 279 (Vatican City, 1978).
MGH SS	Monumenta Germaniae Historica, Scriptores.
Netzer, *L'introduction*	V. Netzer, *L'introduction de la messe romaine en France sous les Carolingiens* (Paris, 1910).
OR	*Les ordines romani du haut moyen âge*, ed. M. Andrieu, 5 vols, Spicilegium Sacrum Lovaniense 11, 23, 24, 28 and 29 (Louvain, 1931–65).
PL	*Patrologia Latina*, ed. J. P. Migne, 221 vols (Paris, 1844–66).

PRG	*Le pontificale romano-germanique du dixième siècle*, ed. C. Vogel and V. Elze, 3 vols, Studi e Testi 226, 227 and 269 (Rome, 1963–72).
Rasmussen, *Les pontificaux*	*Les pontificaux du haut moyen âge. Genèse du livre de l'évêque*, Spicilegium Sacrum Lovaniense 49 (Louvain, 1998).
RB	*Revue bénédictine.*
Robertson, *Saint-Denis*	A. W. Robertson, *The Service Books of the Royal Abbey of Saint-Denis* (Oxford, 1991).
RS	Rolls Series.

INTRODUCTION

Oxford, Bodleian Library, Bodley 579, the so-called 'Leofric Missal', is a hugely complex book. For the most part it is not really a missal at all, though the name has stuck, but a late-ninth or early-tenth-century combined sacramentary, pontifical and ritual with cues for the sung parts of various masses noted in its margins by the original, possibly French or Lotharingian, scribe. Now that colour reproductions of the manuscript in its entirety have been made available in digital form on the World Wide Web, one can easily determine how these annotations stand in relation to the main text page by page.[1] So far, so good. But, as I have indicated, there is a good deal more. For over the course of a hundred and forty or so years the sacramentary-pontifical-ritual was massively and sometimes randomly augmented: first, it seems, for the successors of Plegmund, archbishop of Canterbury (890–923), the man for whom, in my view, the book was originally compiled; then later, at Exeter for the man who eventually gave it its name: Bishop Leofric (1050–72). Leofric's bilingual 'donation' inscription survives on what is now fol. 1v:[2]

> Hunc missalem LEOFRICVS episcopus dat ẹcclesiẹ sancti petri apostoli in exonia ad utilitatem successorum suorum. Si quis illum inde abstulerit, ẹternẹ subiaceat maledictioni. FIAT. FIAT. Confirma hoc deus quod operatus es in nobis.

> Ðas boc leofric bisceop gef sancto petro, 7 eallum his aeftergengum into exancestre gode mid to þenienne, 7 gif hig aenig man ut abrede haebbe he godes curs and wraedde ealra halgena.

Since this is couched in the present tense, Leofric was presumably still alive at the time of its writing. The additions made during his episcopacy are easily identifiable. The 'Missal's' later medieval history,

---

[1] http://www.image.ox.ac.uk/pages/bodleian/Bodl579/main.htm
[2] For a photograph of fol. 1v, see F. Rose-Troup, 'Exeter manumissions and quittances of the eleventh and twelfth centuries', *Transactions of the Devonshire Association* 69 (1937), 417–45, fig. 1.

however, is nowhere near as interesting: the manuscript simply remained at Exeter, attracting few further additions, until 1602, when the Dean and Chapter gave it and numerous other volumes then in their possession to Thomas Bodley.[3] Some time later the book was assigned the shelfmark Super D. 1 Art. 76, and described in 1697 by Edward Bernard as no. 2675:[4]

> *Missale* antiquum Ecclesiae S. Petri Apostoli in Exonia, a Leofrico Episcopo donatum. In quo occurrunt: 1) *Historia* quaedam paginis 4 vel 5 primis. 2) Catalogus Sanctarum *Reliquiarum* quae habentur in Exoniensi Monasterio S. Mariae et S. Petri Apostoli, quarum partem maximam Rex Aethelstanus eius Fundator dedit, p. 6.

So far as one can tell, one of the first scholars to have taken an interest in the 'Missal' at Oxford was Humfrey Wanley. In a letter to Samuel Pepys dated 30th October 1702 he noted:[5]

> In the meantime, Be pleas'd Sir, to accept the Oldest Form of Bidding Prayer, that I ever met with. 'Tis as you will see in Latin, and I found it in a manuscript in the Bodleian Library (there inscrib'd Super D. etc. Art 76). ''Tis one of those very Missals which Bishop Leofric (who liv'd before and after the Conquest) gave to his new Cathedral Church of Exeter. 'Tis a thick book, and was written and fill'd up by a great many Hands. That part which follows was written about 700 years ago (as I judg'd by the Hand) is extant fol. 13 and is in the following words . . .'

He then went on to quote the text of three of the four prayers beginning with the word *Oremus*. But these did not find their way into print at the time. A year later, though, the manumissions in Old English on fols 8 and 377 caught the eye of George Hickes, and the pieces in question duly appeared in the fourth part of his *Thesaurus Grammatico-Criticus*

---

[3]   For the lists, see G. Oliver, *Lives of the Bishops of Exeter* (Exeter, 1861), pp. 301–10, 317–19 and 366–75; and W. D. Macray, *Annals of the Bodleian Library, Oxford*, 2nd ed. (Oxford, 1890), pp. 28–9. See also, F. Madan and H. E. Craster, *A Summary Catalogue of the Western Manuscripts in the Bodleian Library at Oxford*, 7 vols in 8 (Oxford, 1895–53) II.i, 487–9.

[4]   E. Bernard, *Catalogi Librorum Manuscriptorum Angliae et Hiberniae*, 2 vols (Oxford, 1697) I (part i), p. 143.

[5]   *Letters of Humfrey Wanley, Palaeographer, Anglo-Saxonist, Librarian, 1672–1726*, ed. P. L. Heyworth (Oxford, 1989), pp. 195–6. I owe this reference to Peter Kidd.

et Archaeologicus with Latin translations.[6] Hickes's work seems initially to have had the effect of inspiring a good deal of interest in the 'Missal'. For we find early in July 1711 a certain 'learned gentleman' from Pontefract by the name of Fothergill asking Thomas Hearne, the antiquary, to provide him with a transcript of the manuscript. On 15th August Hearne wrote a fascinating but rather gloomy reply:

> The Book of Offices that you referr me to is very ancient, and is one of those given to the Church of Exeter by Leofric the first Bishop of that see after 'twas translated from Crediton. 'Tis a thick Book in 4to or rather 8vo, and is accounted for in the Catalogue of Septentrional MSS printed with Dr Hickes's Thesaurus. And Dr Hickes himself hath printed some things out of it. I wish this venerable old Book (by which 'tis probable we might discover some Errors of the Romish Church), notwithstanding it's being imperfect in divers Places, were transcrib'd and printed exactly but I cannot meet with any Person in this University that is either qualify'd or indeed willing to undertake to transcribe it. I try'd a young lad, who is newly entred and of good Parts, and has a fair Reputation for his Scholarship, but the mistakes he has made (though the MS^t is generally fair) are so many that there will be more trouble in comparing his Transcript than in writing over anew. There is not the least Encouragement in this Place for reading and transcribing old MSS^{ts}. I will however try further about this Affair, and 'tis probable you may heare more hereafter. I am too much engag'd in Business, otherwise I would transcribe it myself, and oblige you with my copy.

Later in the correspondence it transpires that Fothergill thought that the whole of the book was in Old English. In 1712 Hearne was again approached for a transcript, this time by a friend, Hilkiah Bedford; and he replied in similar fashion:

> As for what you say about Leofrick's Missal or Book of Holy Offices, it is a thick Book in vellam of 377 Leaves or 754 Pages. A learned Gentleman not long since writ to me about it out of Yorkshire, and desir'd me to get it transcrib'd. Accordingly I try'd a Lad, but he was not capable of doing it. Nor do I yet know of any one that is either able or willing to write it out. For tho' we have so many young scholars at Oxford, yet there is so little encouragement for reading, studying and transcribing old MSS

---

[6]   G. Hickes, *Linguarum Veterum Septentrionalium, Thesaurus Grammatico-Criticus et Archaelogicus*, 5 parts (Oxford, 1703–5) Part IV, 12–14.

that I do not know one of them at present that applys himself that way: so y^t 'tis much to be fear'd that this part of usefull knowledge will in some time be quite neglected amongst us.

Nothing evidently came of the request. But in the summer of 1713, Bedford set about inveigling Hearne into making for William Talbot, then Bishop of Oxford and Dean of Worcester, a transcript of 'Leofric's' mass for St Maurice's day (nos 1730–34):

> . . . much out of order, he [the Dean] desires y^o to see whether ye commemora'on office for St Mauritius and ye rest of ye *Theban Legion* be in Leofrick's Missal, and if so to compare it wth y^e *Codices Sacramentorum 900 annis Vetustiores* 4o *Romae* 1680 and in *J. Mabillon de Liturgia Gallicana Lib.* 3 4to *Par.* 1685 . . .

The Dean's intended comparision was presumably with Cardinal Tommasi's edition of the text of the mass for the saint given in Vatican City, Biblioteca Apostolica Vaticana, Vat. Reg. lat. 317, the so-called 'Missale Gothicum', a 'Gallican' sacramentary now generally thought to have been written at Autun sometime in the first half of the eighth century.[7] At any rate, on 25th June, Hearne gave notice of his willingness to proceed with the work:

> Pray give my humble service to the Good Dean of Worcester and tell him I have found the Office for St Mauricius and the others martyred with him in the Missal of Leofrick. I will write it out and send it within three or four Days Time. 'Tis short and not so long as that in Mabillon de Liturgia Gall.

Bedford duly passed on the Dean's thanks.[8] For Hearne we are probably better informed than for most other scholars of the period. His notebooks have long been accessible in print. But it would be wrong, I think, not to suspect that many of his contemporaries also looked at Bodl. Super D. 1 Art 76 and made notes of their own. As far as printed comment is concerned, however, we next hear of the 'Missal' in the Victorian era, that is to say well over a century after Hickes had published his extracts: in 1846 William Maskell edited and discussed the

---

[7] *CLLA*, no. 210. For the various pre-twentieth-century editions and re-editions of this book, see *Missale Gothicum*, ed. H. M. Bannister, 2 vols, HBS 52 and 54 (London, 1917–19) I, xi–xx. The standard edition now, however, is *Missale Gothicum*, ed. L. C. Mohlberg, Rerum Ecclesiarum Documenta, Series Maior, Fontes 5 (Rome, 1960).

[8] See *Remarks and Collections of Thomas Hearne*, ed. C. E. Doble, D. W. Rannie and H. E. Salter, 10 vols, Oxford Historical Society 2, 7, 13, 34, 42, 43, 48, 50, 65 and 67 (Oxford, 1885–1915) III, 191, 205, 223–4, 268, 349–50, and IV, 203–6.

nature of the prayers to be said on the occasion of the archbishop's receiving his pallium; between 1849 and 1853 Daniel Rock gave numerous formulae, all carefully referenced and annotated, at various relevant points in his *Church of Our Fathers*, providing too, a short account of the book's character and possible origins; and in 1875 William Henderson published the pontifical and 'ritual' portions of the 'Missal'.[9] But in 1883 all these were largely rendered redundant by the appearance of Frederick Warren's handsome edition of the manuscript in its entirety.[10]

In order to aid his discussion of Bodley 579, Warren hit upon the idea of assigning a letter to each of the three parts of the book that in his view warranted separate discussion. He designated the original late-ninth or early-tenth-century sacramentary Leofric *A*; the three gatherings containing what he took to be a Glastonbury calendar and computus Leofric *B*; and a variety of other additions Leofric *C*. In general terms, the system is a useful one. However, as numerous scholars have found to their cost, Warren's *C* encompasses material that is clearly older than the material embodied in *B*. Some readjustment is therefore necessary: *A* can stand; but *B* will be extended in the commentary and edition given below to cover all the additions made in the period *c*. 920–1000; and *C* will be reserved solely for the material incorporated at Exeter. The three strata have been distinguished typographically.[11] It is probably well to say at this point too that Warren was not always as scrupulous as he should have been in giving the text of the manuscript itself. His 'preferred' readings, which surface here and there without warning, were not only taken to be 'genuine' by Henry Wilson, who collated *A*'s text with that of Vatican City, Biblioteca Apostolica Vaticana, Vat. Reg. lat. 316, the so-called 'Old' or 'Vatican Gelasian' sacramentary, and with books later edited for the Henry Bradshaw Society; they have also found

---

[9] W. Maskell, *Monumenta ritualia Ecclesiae Anglicanae*, 3 vols (Oxford, 1846–7) III, 299–300; D. Rock, *The Church of Our Fathers*, 4 vols (London, 1849–50); W. G. Henderson, *Liber pontificalis Christopher Bainbridge archiepiscopi Eboracensis*, Surtees Society 61 (Durham, 1875), pp. 301–57, and *Manuale et Processionale ad usum insignis ecclesiae Eboracensis,* Surtees Society 63 (Durham, 1875), pp. 129*–31*, 158*–9*, 173*–80*, 215* and 219*. Henderson's transcripts were bequeathed to the Henry Bradshaw Society in the 1920s and later donated to the Bodleian, where they are now Bodleian, Lat. lit. c. 4.

[10] Warren at the time was rector of the church of Frenchay, near Bristol. A short biography of his life and work is given by Henry Chadwick in Jane Stevenson's new edition of Warren's *Liturgy and Ritual of the Celtic Church* (Woodbridge, 1979), p. vii.

[11] *A* is in normal type, *B* finer, and *C* `monospaced`.

their way into the three great series of liturgical formulae edited by Dom Edmond Moeller: the *Corpus Benedictionum Pontificalium, Corpus Prefationum* and *Corpus Orationum*.[12]

But although Warren was not as careful an editor as one might have hoped, he seems to have been streets ahead of the competition when it came to the matter of *A*'s possible origins. In summary, his contention was that the main body of the sacramentary, which he dated early tenth century, had been produced in Lotharingia, and probably at Arras or Cambrai since the name of St Vedastus (6 Feb.), patron of Arras, had been picked out in red and green capitals in the book's litany: not an unreasonable conclusion to have reached. But at some point an element of doubt seems to have taken root in his mind. For although he stated quite rightly that *A* must have been prepared for a bishop or an arch-bishop, he seems not to have felt confident enough to suggest that *A*'s owner ought then to have been the bishop of Cambrai since there was no such person as the bishop of Arras at the time, the diocese of Arras having been united with that of Cambrai, and governed from Cambrai, as early as *c.* 700.[13] But Warren also seems to have thought that *A* was a Benedictine book, citing in favour of this secondary proposition the fact that proper prefaces had been provided for the two masses in honour of St Benedict (deposition: 21 March; translation: 11 July). Proper prefaces are normally a mark that a feast was of special significance.[14] But the two propositions as Warren framed them are impossible to square: both Arras and Cambrai were served by secular canons throughout the middle ages. If his idea was that the man who originally owned *A* might have been obliged to officiate from time to time in a nearby monastery, perhaps Saint-Vaast's, he did not say so. However, he did explain how he thought *A* had come to England: it had been brought over from Lotharingia by Leofric in 1042, whereupon an old Glastonbury calendar and computus had been inserted, and a series of additions made to its

---

[12] H. A. Wilson, *The Gelasian Sacramentary* (Oxford, 1894), and, for instance, *The Benedictional of Archbishop Robert*, HBS 24 (London, 1902), pp. 168–98. Dom Moeller's publications are: *Corpus Benedictionum Pontificalium*, 4 vols, CCSL 162 and 162A–C (Turnhout, 1971–9); *Corpus Prefationum*, 3 vols, CCSL 161A–C (Turnhout, 1980–1); and *Corpus Orationum*, 10 vols, CCSL 160 and 160A–I (Turnhout, 1992–8), continued after his death by B. C. 'T Wallant and J. M. Clement.

[13] Successive bishops of the diocese are always termed 'of Cambrai'. See for instance the *Historia Remensis Ecclesiae* of Flodoard of Reims, ed. M. Stratmann, MGH SS 36 (Hannover, 1998), pp. 211–12, 276, 390–2 and 417.

[14] *LM*, p. xl.

body 'in over thirty different handwritings'. We will come to these additions in a moment.

By and large, Warren's picture of *A*'s origins seem to have engendered little adverse comment. His views are repeated by Madan and Craster in the Bodleian's Summary Catalogue; by Otto Pacht and Jonathan Alexander in their description of *A*'s decoration, and numerous others; and Eleanor Drage has even gone so far as to suppose that *A* was prepared for Dodilo, bishop of Cambrai (887–901), by the community at Saint-Vaast to mark his elevation to the see.[15] Dodilo, by all accounts, had formerly been the abbey's prior, and he was later remembered at Saint-Vaast as the man who oversaw, in 893, the return of the relics of St Vedastus from Beauvais, the house to which they had been sent for safekeeping (in 879–80) during the Viking incursions.[16] Yet for all that, the best account of *A* to have found its way into print, and one which dispensed pretty effectively with Saint-Vaast (and Cambrai) as possible first homes for the book, has met with what can only be described as a sort of uneasy silence. In 1975 Christopher Hohler proposed that *A* had been written in England for use in England by a foreign scribe, a view he had been advocating privately for years in letters to scholars and friends throughout Europe. He stated that:[17]

The original core of this book, Leofric *A*, which Mr Ker dates ninth to tenth century is, as I have already said, written in a foreign hand, and has more than once been irresponsibly claimed as purely Lotharingian text. Anyone wishing to establish that

[15] Madan and Craster, *Summary Catalogue* II.i, 487–9; O. Pacht and J. J. G. Alexander, *Survey of Illuminated Manuscripts in the Bodleian Library, Oxford I: The German, Dutch, Flemish and French Schools* (Oxford, 1966), no. 422; D. N. Dumville, *English Caroline Script and Monastic History. Studies in Benedictinism A. D. 950–1030* (Woodbridge, 1993), p. 94; *idem, Liturgy and the Ecclesiastical History of Late Anglo-Saxon England* (Woodbridge, 1995), p. 42; and Drage, *Leofric*, p. 95.

[16] See *Monumenta Vedastina Minora*, ed. O. Holder-Egger, MGH SS 15.i (Hannover, 1887), pp. 402–4, with *Annales Vedastini* 879–80, ed. B. de Simson, *Annales Xantenses et Annales Vedastini*, MGH Scriptores rerum Germanicarum in usum Scholarum 12 (Hannover, 1909), p. 46, and *Annales Elnoneses minores* 881, ed. G. Waitz, MGH SS 5 (Hannover, 1844), p. 19. For the great fire at Beauvais, which destroyed most of the goods sent from Arras for safekeeping, see *Annales Vedastini* 886, ed. de Simson, p. 62. The 'feast of the return', that is to say the *relatio*, was celebrated on 15 July. The earliest surviving mass for the day is the one preserved in Laon, Bibliothèque municipale, 226, a twelfth-century sacramentary from Amiens. See Leroquais, *Les sacramentaires* I, 226. For the mass prescribed in Arras, Bibliothèque municipale, 444, a thirteenth-century missal from the abbey, see L. Brou, *The Monastic Ordinal of St Vedast's Abbey, Arras*, 2 vols, HBS 86–7 (London, 1956–7) I, 85.

[17] Hohler, 'Books', p. 78.

should produce another Lotharingian book with a separate sanctoral, St Mark on 18 May, the English coronation oath and an invocation of St Guthlac in the litany. When he does, I shall say it is derived from an English book. The Leofric Missal is patently English.

As we shall see, he was almost certainly right. There are compelling reasons for associating *A* not only with England, but with a particular Englishman: Plegmund, archbishop of Canterbury, as I have already indicated.

One of the first scholars to detect that something was amiss in Warren's account of how *A* had come to England was Henry Bannister. Noting that the words *et archiepiscopo nostro* had been written by an English scribe over an erasure in *A*'s Exultet preface for Holy Saturday, Bannister suggested that *A* had once been at Canterbury: when someone other than the pope, *antistes noster*, and the king is mentioned in this prayer, he or she is normally the head of the house at which the book was used.[18] Since this addition is datable to the mid tenth century, as David Dumville has pointed out, *A* must have remained at Canterbury.[19] That brings us neatly to the late-tenth-century calendar, which Warren, in company with Edmund Bishop, Francis Wormald and Hohler, attributed to Glastonbury.[20] This attribution has always seemed difficult. Indeed, one gets the feeling that Warren was not really convinced of it; and in recent years further doubts, all sound so far as they go, have been expressed in print by Dumville and Patrick Conner.[21] But it is much to be regretted that the clues to the calendar's real provenance provided by Daniel Rock in 1849 and Bishop in 1907 seem never to have attracted the attention they deserve.

In short Bishop discovered that *B*'s calendar and that of London, British Library, Additional 37517, the so-called 'Bosworth Psalter' (Canterbury, *c.* 1000) were based upon a common model: the sanctoral of a sacramentary now lost; and on the grounds that both calendars contained entries for saints said to be *in Glaestonia*, he proposed that this underlying sacramentary had been drawn up at Glastonbury and that *B* had also been produced there, since in his view there seemed to be no

---

[18] Madan and Craster, *Summary Catalogue* II.i, p. 489.

[19] Dumville, *English Caroline Script*, pp. 94–5.

[20] F. A. Gasquet and E. Bishop, *The Bosworth Psalter* (London, 1908), pp. 15–27; *EK*, pp. 43–55; Hohler, 'Books', pp. 69–70.

[21] Dumville, *Liturgy,* pp. 39–65, 82; P. Conner, *Anglo-Saxon Exeter. A Tenth-Century Cultural History* (Woodbridge, 1993), pp. 18–19.

other clear evidence for localisation. 'Bosworth', on the other hand, struck him as pretty certainly containing the late-tenth-century calendar of Christ Church Canterbury. In actual fact, the 'Glastonbury' feasts in *B* and 'Bosworth' are likely to be 'second-hand' since Glastonbury itself is named, a point recently stressed by Dumville, but apparently grasped by Rock when he noted that:[22]

> . . . while August 31st, 'In Glastonia, Sancti Aidani Episcopi', is carefully noticed, as well as 'In Glastonia, Sancti Ceolfrithi Abbatis' on the 25th September. Such a circumstantial mention of Glastonbury would incline us to think that this missal, if not the penmanship of a monk of that far-famed house itself, must have been copied for the use of and in some monastery of the west of England.

But Rock seems to have thought that *A* and *B* were coeval, thus rather spoiling the effect of his suggestion; and Canterbury evidently never crossed his mind. As we shall see, the calendars of *B* and 'Bosworth' must have been compiled with reference to a sacramentary brought by St Dunstan (d. 988) from the west country to Canterbury and later modified. In other words, both derive from a Christ Church book not Dunstan's original. It is also well to add, *pace* Bishop, that 'Bosworth' is pretty certainly from St Augustine's, not the cathedral.

That the new gatherings containing the calendar and computus were added to *A* soon after they had been written is confirmed by the fact that the scribe who wrote them wrote elsewhere in the book (fol. 210r, for instance): *B* was undoubtedly produced with a view to bringing *A*, an older Canterbury book, up to date. But when was the calendar's scribe at work? In order to deal with this question properly, we must go back to what Warren said in 1883. He stated:[23]

> The tables for finding the date of Easter Day range from 969–1006, comprising the fifty-second and fifty-third of the Dionysian cycles of nineteen years (no. 296), acquaintance with which was popularized in England by Bede. One or more of these cycles was often appended to a kalendar in its entirety. There is no certain ground for assigning the date of writing to the first year, but there are reasonable grounds for assigning it to one of the years and probably to one of the earlier years, in the first cycle. Another and less usual table gives the number of weeks and days which

22 Dumville, *Liturgy*, pp. 47–9; Rock, *The Church of Our Fathers* I, 84.
23 *LM*, p. liii.

elapsed between Christmas Day and Ash Wednesday, from A.D. 979 to A.D. 1011. Taking all these foregoing facts into consideration we may assign the latter part of the century as the date of Leofric B.

Now if the tables are at all relevant, the calendar's *terminus ante quem* will be 987, the last year of the first decennovenal cycle encompassed, and its *terminus post quem* sometime close to 969, for the reasons given by Warren, or 979, the year with which the table dealing with the interval between Christmas and Ash Wednesday begins. However, there is nothing to say that either table was fully up to date when the scribe wrote them, a point which we will come to later. Most art historians unfortunately have accepted the dating suggested by Warren without question and taken the drawings accompanying the computus to be the work of Glastonbury artists.[24]

C, by contrast, has been approached very differently. Eleanor Drage and T. A. M. Bishop have studied the palaeography; Neil Ker, Frances Rose-Troup and Patrick Conner the 'historical' matter; but the liturgical matter embodied in the twenty-one new gatherings, matter it should be said that seems for the most part to have been added at the express request of Leofric, has not been considered in nearly as much detail.[25] As we shall see, *C* contains formulae gathered from a wide variety of sources; and it is worth stating too that there is no reason whatsoever to think that *A* and *B* had found their way to the west country before Leofric's time. It will be best now, however, to turn to the manuscript itself.

Codicological and Palaeographical Description

Bodley 579 is a surprisingly small book, its leaves rarely more than 195mm high and 145mm wide. It will therefore have been easily portable. Among the 120 or so sacramentaries and missals described by Leopold Delisle in 1886, only three are of a comparable size:

Rouen, Bibliothèque municipale, 566 (275): a composite volume of fragments of sacramentaries from the ninth, tenth and eleventh centuries, probably assembled at the abbey of Saint-Denis for

---

[24] E. Temple, *Anglo-Saxon Manuscripts 900–1066*, A Survey of Manuscripts Illuminated in the British Isles 2, ed. J. J. G. Alexander (London, 1976), pp. 44–5, no. 17.

[25] See below, p. 206.

itinerant priests or monks. As Eric Palazzo has recently suggested, Part I (fols 1–8v) was probably written at Saint-Amand under Abbot Gozlinus, who ruled over both houses in the 870s.[26] Measures 170 × 130mm.

St Petersburg Public Library, Q. v. I. 41: a sacramentary probably written at some point in the 860s for the community serving the former cathedral of Tournai since St Piat (1 Oct.), patron of the house, is invoked in the prayer *Libera nos* in the book's Canon.[27] Measures 197 × 144mm.

and Paris, Bibliothèque nationale de France, lat. 10500: the sacramentary of Hughes de Salines, archbishop of Besançon (1030–66). Measures 200 × 153mm. As Bernard de Vrégille has shown, the book was written *c.* 1037–9.[28]

The others are either tall and thin or proportionately larger. Hughes de Salines, like *A*'s owner, presumably took his sacramentary about with him.

As Warren saw, *A* was written by a single scribe in an even, rounded, continental minuscule. But opinions as to the script's date have varied. Warren thought it early tenth century; Neil Ker favoured s. ix–x, that is to say, *c.* 880–920; Pacht, Alexander and Drage thought the second half of the ninth century; and more recently, Dumville has stated that:[29]

Leofric A, the original sacramentary, was written in what is understood to be a regional type of Continental Carolingian minuscule (profoundly influenced by Insular features): it is broadly datable in the century 850–950.

Unfortunately he did not take his palaeographical analysis further. But he seems generally to have agreed with the others since he went on to

---

[26] See Delise, 'Mémoire', p. 281; Leroquais, *Les sacramentaires* I, 144–5; Robertson, *Saint-Denis*, pp. 405–6; and E. Palazzo, 'Un *libellus missae* du scriptorium de Saint-Amand pour Saint-Denis', *RB* 99 (1989), 286–92. For more on Gozlinus, see below, p. 24.

[27] *CLLA*, no. 926; Delisle, 'Mémoire', pp. 396–400, with A. Staerck, *Les manuscrits latins conservés a la bibliothèque impériale de Saint-Petersbourg*, 2 vols (St Petersburg, 1910) I, 74–127. The book's text is partially ed. *Le sacramentaire grégorien* under the siglum T5.

[28] See Delisle, 'Mémoire', pp. 292–3, Leroquais, *Les sacramentaires* I, 138–41, and B. de Vrégille, 'Le rituel de saint Prothade et *l'ordo canonicorum* de Saint-Jean de Besançon', *Revue du moyen âge latin* 5 (1949), 97–114.

[29] N. R. Ker, *Catalogue of Manuscripts containing Anglo-Saxon* (Oxford, 1957), pp. 378–9; Dumville, *Liturgy*, p. 42.

suggest that *A* had first been added to in the 920s. The date reached by consensus is therefore *c.* 860–920. Perhaps sensing the need for some sort of context, Drage likened the scribe's work to that of three mid-ninth-century books from Corbie and one from Reims.[30] Her Corbie books are:[31]

Paris, Bibliothèque nationale de France, lat. 13909: a copy of Paschasius Radbertus's *Epitaphium Arsenii* written sometime in the period 836–51.

Paris, Bibliothèque nationale de France, lat. 12294: a copy of Paschasius's *Expositio in Threnos* written *c.* 845.

and Paris, Bibliothèque nationale de France, lat. 11532–3: a Bible with the short treatise *Chronicon de sex aetatibus mundi* written *c.* 855–69.

and her Reims book:

Cambridge, Pembroke College, 308: a copy of Hrabanus Maurus's commentary on the Catholic Epistles probably written at Reims in the mid ninth century. An inscription states that the book was given by Archbishop Hincmar (844–82) to the cathedral.[32]

But none of these comparisons are particularly telling. Perhaps closer in general aspect are:

Paris, Bibiliothèque nationale de France, lat. 2290: a sacramentary produced at Saint-Amand *c.* 878–86 for the abbey of Saint-Denis.[33]

and that of one of the many sets of additions to London, British Library, Additional 36678: the so-called 'Lothar Psalter', the body of which is generally thought to have been written *c.* 850. The additions that concern us are the ones made by a single scribe on fol. 169, a leaf

---

[30] Drage, *Leofric*, p. 92.

[31] Illustr. respectively, *Catalogue de manuscrits en écriture latine portant des indications de date, de lieu ou de copiste*, ed. C. Samaran and R. Marichal, 7 vols (Paris, 1959–84) III, pls X.i, X.ii and XII.i.

[32] For a description, see M. R. James, *A Descriptive Catalogue of the Manuscripts in the Library of Pembroke College, Cambridge* (Cambridge, 1905), pp. 275–6. Illustr. *New Palaeographical Society*, 1st Series, pl. 236, and P. R. Robinson, *Catalogue of Dated and Datable Manuscripts c. 737–1600 in Cambridge Libraries*, 2 vols (Cambridge, 1988) II, pl. 4. Bischoff, *Katalog*, no. 834.

[33] *CLLA*, no. 760; text partially ed. *Le sacramentaire grégorien* under the siglum R. See also Robertson, *Saint-Denis*, pp. 383–6. Illustr. Delisle, 'Mémoire', pls V and VI.

originally left blank. His, or possibly her, work seems datable to the last third of the ninth century.[34]

Richard Gameson, in his forthcoming study of Bodley 579's palaeography, will set *A* squarely in context.

As well as writing the whole of the main text, *A*'s scribe also provided most of his own rubric and the cues for the chant, which were presumably envisaged from the start, as the book's margins seem uncommonly generous. As we shall see, most books arranged in this way stem, like *A*, from cathedrals rather than monasteries.[35] A second scribe, probably to be identified with the artist who painted the major initials on fols 67v, 115v, 128r and 131v, appears to have 'helped out' by writing the lines of text in capitals following those initials; the first lines of text for St Stephen's day on fol. 158r, St Peter's day on fol. 176v and All Saints' day on fol. 198r; the display capitals on fol. 60r; the headings to the bidding prayers on fols 262r–3v; all the headings for the ordination services on fols 268r–81v; and the headings for the prayers for sins on fol. 324r.

The Structure of the Book

Although Drage was primarily interested in *C*, she did a good deal towards sorting out how Bodley 579 as we have it today had been assembled. Her collation is only wrong in two minor respects, which have been asterisked:[36]

C.		*B.*	
iv–7v	1^8	17r–v	Singleton.
8	Singleton.		
		C.	
A.		18r–25v	4^8
9r–12v	2^4	26–33v	5^8
13r–16v	3^4	34r–37v	6^4

---

[34] See E. K. Rand, *Studies in the Script of Tours. A Survey of the Manuscripts of Tours*, 2 vols, Medieval Academy of America Publications 3 (Cambridge, Mass., 1929) II, pl. CL. 2, and W. Koehler and F. Mütherich, *Die karolingische Miniaturen*, 10 vols in 5 (Berlin, 1930–82) IV (text), 35–46, and IV (illustr.), pl. 7A.

[35] See below, pp. 125–6.

[36] Drage, *Leofric*, pp. 73–82.

B.

38r–45v	7^8
46r–53v	8^8
54r–59v	9^6

A.

60r–67v	10^8
68r–75v	11^8
76r–83v	12^8
84r–91v	13^8
92r–99v	14^8
100r–107v	15^8 (3 and 6 are singletons)
108r–115v	16^8
116r–123v	17^8
124r–130v	18^8 (lacks 6)
131r–138v	19^8
139r–146v	20^8
147r–154v	21^8

C.

| 155r–157v | 22^4 |

A.

158r–65v	23^8
166r–73v	24^8
174r–81v	25^8
182r–89v	26^8
190r–97v	27^8
198r–205v	28^8
206r–13v	29^8
214r–23v	30^{10}
224r–31v	31^8
232r–41v	32^{10}
242r–53v	33^{12}

B.

| 254r–60v | 34^8 (2, 3 and 7 are singletons). |
| 261r–v | Half leaf inserted in the late tenth century. |

A.

| 262r–63v | *Singletons. |

B.

| 264r–65v | *Singletons. |

A.

| 266r–73v | 36^8 |

B.

| 274r–77v | 37^4 |

A.

278r–85v	38^8 (fol. 278 erased and rewritten in the early tenth century).
286r–93v	39^8
294r–303v	40^{10}
304r–13v	41^{10}
314r–23v	42^{10}
324r–35v	43^{12}

A and *B.*

| 336r–v | Singleton. *A* ends on fol. 336r. The verso was written on in the early tenth century. |

C.

337r–44v	44^8
345r–52v	45^8
353r–60v	46^8
361r–70v	47^8
371r–77v	48^8

A number of tenth-century additions written on pages or spaces originally left blank in *A* are not indicated in the collation given above. These will be dealt with in detail in the sections on *B*, below.[37] Two points concerning *B* warrant mention here, however. First, two gatherings seem to have been inserted in the early to mid tenth century: gathering 22, which was partially renewed in the late eleventh century, and gathering 37.[38] That is indication enough that the book had been unbound, probably at Canterbury, early in the tenth century; and given that further new gatherings were certainly brought in there in the late tenth century (*B*), and at Exeter in the mid eleventh (*C*), it may never have been properly re-sewn. Second, most of the early tenth-century additions were made either on spaces originally left blank throughout *A* or over erasures. It is unusual to find 'gaps' in the texts of sacramentaries, but *A*'s scribe seems to have gone to some trouble to start new sections on a new gathering or, at least, on the recto of a new leaf.[39] The divisions between the sections break down as follows:

I. 9r–16v: *Benedictiones ad lectorem* and Ordinary of the Mass.

II. 60r–154r: Temporal. Fol. 154v originally left blank.

III. 158r–253v: Sanctoral to the end of the *ordo defunctorum*. Various gaps originally divided one 'section' from another. The sanctoral ends on fol. 210r; the *commune sanctorum* begins on fol. 212r; the votive masses for the dead end half-way down fol. 245v; and the *ordo defunctorum* begins on fol. 246r. Fols 210v–211v and 253v were blank.

IV. 266r–73v, and 278r–336r: Litany to the end of *A*. Fol. 336r is a singleton, the verso of which was originally left blank. The *ordo ad visitandum infirmum* begins on fol. 319r, the preceding text ending half-way down fol. 318v.

---

[37] See below, p. 132.

[38] For the material on gathering 22, see below pp. 140–5 and 233–4.

[39] On 'brochures', see N. K. Rasmussen, 'Unité et diversité des pontificaux latins', *Liturgie de l'église particulière et liturgie universelle. Conférences Saint-Serge XXIIe semaine d'études liturgiques, Paris, 30 juin – 3 juillet, 1975*, ed. A. Pistoia, C. M. Triacca and A. M. Triacca, Biblioteca Ephemerides Liturgicae Subsidia 7 (Rome, 1976), 393–410, esp. 399.

Decoration

A's decoration is best dealt with in two parts: first, the pages at the beginning of the Canon on fols 60r–62r; and second, the major and minor initials which occur throughout the book. To begin then with the Canon.

60r: display page with the text of the introduction to the common preface. A large capital *P* in gold edged with red; in its bowl wavy lines of gold, turquoise and red. Beside and beneath, the text itself written alternately in lines of pinkish-red and brownish-black majuscules. The brownish-black majuscules are flecked with turquoise, red, pinkish-orange, green and white.

60v: the opening of the common preface of mass *Vere dignum*. A stylised letter *V* apparently formed from two confronted headless *J*'s with interlace tops and curling bowls that issue bird's heads and a central interlace design, set under a round-headed arch supported on two columns, both with fleshy acanthus on their bases and capitals. Four panels with cable interlace decorate the flat faces of the uprights and the arch itself. Above the *V*, directly beneath the apex of the frame, is the rest of the word *Vere* in large majuscule; below, the word *Dignum*, also in majuscule on a panel of light green hatching; and beneath that, in gold minuscule on a deep purplish-blue ground, the next few words of the prayer's text: *et iustum est aequuum*. As for the colours of the main initial and its frame, outlines are in brown and red, in that order; the infilling of gold; and the strands of cable interlace in the panels white on a brown background. The interstices of the central interlace design are filled with dark blue, green and yellow.[40]

61r: the remaining text of the common preface. An arched frame similar to the one on the preceding page, but with slightly fleshier capitals and looser interlace, surrounding the text of the prayer, written in gold on purple panels. The colours of the frame are generally as above. Its capitals, however, have been flecked with yellow.

61v: the opening of the prayer *Te igitur*. The letter *T*, with its interlace bar, curling ram's horn terminals, panels of interlace, and stylised

---

[40] Illustr. in Pacht and Alexander, *Survey of Illuminated Manuscripts in the Bodleian Library, Oxford I*, pl. XXXIV.

dragon heads (in blue and red) at its base, almost fills the rectangular frame in which it is set. To its right sits the smaller stylised E of the word *Te* in a panel with a light blue hatched background, and beneath in majuscules, the word *igitur*. The colours are again as fol. 60v.[41]

62r: the rest of the text of the prayer *Te igitur*. A rectangular frame similiar to the one on fol. 61v, but with the designs in the square corner-terminals re-arranged. The text again is written in gold minuscule on purple panels.

The closest parallels for the general design and layout of these pages are to be found in sacramentaries produced at the abbey of Saint-Amand in the ninth century. The style has sometimes been called 'Franco-Saxon style of Arras'; but more recently, André Boutemy has termed it the 'Franco-Saxon style of Saint-Amand'.[42] In approximate date order the books in question are:

Le Mans, Bibliothèque municipale, 77: possibly written for Aldric, bishop of Le Mans (832–57) in the early 850s.[43]

New York, Pierpont Morgan Library, Glazier 57: almost certainly produced for the abbey of Chelles *c.* 855.[44]

St Petersburg Q. v. I. 41: written sometime in the 860s for the community serving the former cathedral of Tournai.[45]

---

[41] Illustr. R. Deshmann, 'The Leofric Missal and tenth-century English art', *ASE* 6 (1977), 145–73, pl. Ia.

[42] A. Boutemy, 'Le style franco-saxon de Saint-Amand', *Scriptorium* 3 (1949), 260–4, and *idem*, 'Quel fut le fôyer du style franco-saxon?', *Miscellanea Tournacensia. Mélanges d'archéologie et d'histoire, Congrès de Tournai 1949*, 2 vols (Brussels, 1951) II, 749–73.

[43] *CLLA*, no. 743; its text is partially ed. *Le sacramentaire grégorien* under the siglum J. See also DACL 10.ii, cols 1545–8. The *Vere* monogram is illustr. A. Boinet, *La miniature carolingienne* (Paris, 1913), pl. CIV. Photographs of the Canon are available in the Conway Library of the Courtauld Institute of Art, London.

[44] *CLLA*, p. 356; text partially ed. *Le sacramentaire grégorien* under the siglum T1. For illustrations of the *Vere* monogram and brief accounts of the book's history, see J. Plummer, *Liturgical Manuscripts for the Mass and Divine Office* (New York, 1964), pp. 11–12, pl. I, and *idem*, *The Glazier Collection of Illuminated Manuscripts* (New York, 1968), pp. 10–11, no. 8, pl. 2.

[45] For a synopsis of the book's contents and a photograph of the pages, see Staerck, *Les manuscrits latins conservés a la bibliothèque impériale de Saint-Petersbourg* I, 74–127, II, pls LIII and LIV, though the wrong folio numbers are given. The *Te* monogram is also illustr. A. de Laborde, *Les prinicipaux manuscrits à peintures conservés dans l'ancienne bibliothèque impériale publique de Saint-Petersbourg*, 2 vols (Paris, 1936), pl. 1. A microfilm of the manuscript is available in the Manuscripts Students' Room of the British Library (Micro 703/3).

Reims, Bibliothèque municipale, 213: perhaps originally commissioned by Ragenelmus, bishop of the united dioceses of Noyon-Tournai (860–79) since the names of SS Medard and Eligius (8 June and 1 Dec.), patrons of Noyon, the episcopal seat, appear in the canon of the mass. The book may later have been given to Hincmar, archbishop of Reims (845–82).[46]

Stockholm, Kungligla Biblioteket, Holm A. 136: written for Ansegis, bishop of Sens (871–83).[47]

BNF lat. 2290: produced for Saint-Denis, almost certainly during the abbacy of Gozlinus (878–86).[48]

Vienna, Österreichische Nationalbibliothek, lat. 958: a late-ninth-century *libellus* for ordinations (rather than a sacramentary) perhaps written for the bishop of Liège. The manuscript later found its way to Bobbio.[49] For the most part, the decoration follows that of the Le Mans book page for page.

Boutemy also included in his list:

Cambrai, Bibliothèque municipale, 162–3: a sacramentary, now in two volumes, either from the abbey of Saint-Vaast at Arras, or possibly Cambrai, the provenance favoured by Edmund Bishop. Probably written shortly after 875.[50] The Canon-decoration which appears in the first volume seems simply to be a copy, less lavishly treated perhaps, of the decoration normal at Saint-Amand.

---

[46] *CLLA*, no. 762; text partially ed. *Le sacramentaire grégorien* under the siglum T2. The *Vere* and *Te* monograms are illustr. Leroquais, *Les sacramentaires* IV, pls XI and XII.

[47] *CLLA*, no. 763; text partially ed. *Le sacramentaire grégorien* under the siglum T4. On Ansegis, see *DACL* 15.i, cols 1207–10.

[48] See note 33 above. The *Vere* monogram is illustr. Leroquais, *Les sacramentaires* IV, pl. X. Photographs of the Canon are available in the Conway Library of the Courtauld Institute.

[49] *CLLA*, no. 764; ed. in facsimile, F. Unterkircher, *Karolingisches Sakramentar-Fragment*, Codices Selecti phototypice impressi 25 (Graz, 1971). See also *idem*, 'Interpretatio Canonis Missae in codice Vindobonensia 958', *EL* 91 (1977), 32–50. Since copies of Unterkircher's facsimile are extremely scarce, it is well to say that photographs of the Canon are given by R. Beer, *Kaiserliche Königlische Hof-Bibliothek in Wien. Monumenta palaeographica Vindobonensia. Denkmaler der Schreibkunst aus der Handschriften-sammlung des Habsburg-Lothringischen Erzhauses* (Leipzig, 1910), pls 39–46, and pp. 55–73, figs 11–15, for comparative material.

[50] *CLLA*, no. 761; Leroquais, *Les sacramentaires* I, 36–8; ed. *Le sacramentaire grégorien* under the siglum S; E. Bishop, 'On some early manuscripts of the Gregorianum', in his *Liturgica Historica* (Oxford, 1918), pp. 62–76, at 66, no. 3. On the decoration, see Boutemy, 'Quel fut le foyer de le style franco-saxon', pp. 756–65. Photographs of the *Vere* and *Te igitur* pages are available in the Conway Library.

A glance at any of the published photographs will show just how con-
sistent Saint-Amand's artists generally seem to have been.[51] A glance is
enough to show too that *A*'s decoration is clearly related. However,
certain economies of scale are apparent (*A* is considerably smaller than
the 'Saint-Amand' books). We have four decorated pages instead of
eight, a 'new' type of *Vere dignum* monogram, and an *E* in the *Te igitur*
page that has been entirely disengaged from the *T*. Such rearrangements
may have come naturally to a later artist: the same combination of a
large *T* and small separate *E* with arrow points as terminals occurs in
Paris, Bibliothèque nationale de France, lat. 9432, an early-tenth-century
sacramentary from Amiens; and a similar approach was taken by the
artist who worked on Chartres, Bibliothèque municipale, 577 (4), an
early-tenth-century sacramentary from Chartres, now lost. Thankfully
photographs of the latter were made and published by Canon Delaporte
in the 1920s.[52]

 A's artist also departed from the general scheme of the 'Saint-Amand'
books in a further respect: two frames have arched tops, a feature only to
be found in the Noyon sacramentary. But at Noyon the (single)
round-headed frame seems not to have been planned as part of the cycle
of Canon-decoration proper, for the page in question, fol. 10r, precedes
the page containing the preface to the sacramentary *In nomine domine
incipit liber sacramentorum* and bears no text.[53] The closest parallel to
the first of *A*'s frames, that is to say, the one surrounding the opening
words of the preface *Vere dignum* on fol. 60v, is to be found in Paris,
Bibliothèque nationale de France, lat. 12051, the so-called 'Missale
sancti Eligii', which is in actual fact, a late-ninth-century sacramentary-
cum-pontifical written at Corbie for some northern French bishop,
possibly Odo of Beauvais (861 × 862 – 881).[54] However, the inspiration
for this type of frame may well have come not from a sacramentary, but
a model akin to Arras, Bibliothèque municipale, 1045, a fragment of a

---

[51] So far as one can tell, the 'style' never spread to Italy or Germany. See the illustrations
in Ebner, *Quellen*, for instance.
[52] See Y. Delaporte, *Les manuscrits enluminés de la Bibliothèque Municipale de Chartres*
(Chartres, 1929), pp. 8–9 and plate III; and Leroquais, *Les sacramentaires* I, 75–8, with
G. L. Micheli, *L'enluminaire du haut moyen age et les influences irlandaises* (Brussels,
1939), pl. 247. For descriptions of the Amiens book, see Delisle, 'Mémoire', 159–62;
Netzer, *L'introduction*, pp. 103–5; Leroquais, *Les sacramentaires* I, 38–43; *CLLA*, no. 910.
[53] A photograph of the page is held by the Conway Library of the Courtauld Institute of
Art, London.
[54] Illustr. Boinet, *La miniature carolingienne*, pl. CXI. See further, pp. 25–6, below.

sumptuously decorated lectionary produced at Arras in the late ninth century.[55] A's design, for instance, is essentially a simpler version of the latter. The dragons at the apex of the arch have been reduced to simple interlace, the leaves on the capitals further schematised, and the internal foliate banding of the frame replaced by chain-interlace. But the similiarities in conception are unmistakeable, right down to the coloured text-band stretching from one column foot to the other; and in view of the fact that A's text has a number of variants peculiar to Cambrai BM 162–3, the late-ninth-century sacramentary probably from the abbey of Saint-Vaast at Arras mentioned above, it seems reasonable to suppose that A's decoration too, major and minor initials included, all by the same artist, depends on that of some book from the house. That leaves us to wonder a) whether the artist was a Frenchman living and working in France; a Frenchman working in England; or an Englishman working in England in an unfamiliar idiom; b) to what extent he reproduced faithfully what he had before him, or any model at all; and c) how great a say A's prospective owner had in how the book looked. Further work will probably only shed light on the first of these questions.

Initials

Warren helpfully divided A's initials into three classes. His scheme is as follows:

Class 1: those infilled with gold, edged in red and black; the opening lines of the prayer written in gold uncials. This type of initial occurs at:

67v: Christmas Day.	128r: Ascension Day.
115v: Easter Sunday.	131v: Pentecost Sunday.

To these should probably be added the D provided on fol. 177v for St Peter's day (29 June), which Warren reluctantly set among those of the second class, noting that:[56]

> The initial letter here belongs to the first class and is followed by a line of large black uncials, ornamented with red and green patches

---

[55] *CLLA*, no. 1045; Bischoff, *Katalog* I, number 107. For black and white reproductions, see L. V. Delisle, *L'évangelaire de Saint-Vaast d'Arras et la calligraphie franco-saxonne du IXe siècle* (Paris, 1888), and for a slightly garish picture in colour, *L'art du moyen âge en Arras. Catalogue de l'exposition, Musée d'Arras, Palais Saint-Vaast, 15 avr. – 30 juin, 1951*, ed. G. Mollet (Arras, 1951), frontispiece.

[56] *LM*, p. xxxv.

then by a line of rustic capitals similarly ornamented. This treatment marks special regard for St Peter, but does not quite elevate his festival into the first class.

Leaving aside the matter of its 'class', the feast is obviously important, as Warren saw. Indeed, Edward Nicholson and Cornelius Bouman both took its apparent prominence to be a sign that *A* had been produced at or for the abbey of St Peter at Leuze in the diocese of Cambrai.[57] Unfortunately both seem to have overlooked two significant facts: first, St Peter's day is often picked out in books from houses that were never, even for a single moment in their history, dedicated to the saint; and second, *A*, as has already mentioned, is a bishop's book. Leuze, as an abbey, must therefore be put to one side. But that leaves us to explain why the apostle's feast should have been given more attention than those of the Assumption and Nativity of the Virgin. If we assume for a moment that *A* had been drawn up with Canterbury in mind, one possible answer presents itself. Throughout the early middle ages Christ Church, that is to say the cathedral, was dedicated to the Trinity, not to the Virgin or any particular saint; and that remained the case until well after the Conquest. St Augustine's, on the other hand, had St Peter as its secondary patron. Little more than half a mile separates the two houses. If one had no principal saint of one's own, what better than to acknowledge a neighbour's, especially when in this case he stood for Rome, the Pope and St Augustine's mission in 597? Alternatively it may simply be that the emphasis given to the initial reflects the emphasis given in *A*'s Artesian model. A church of St Peter lay a short distance to the north of Saint-Vaast's.[58]

Although precise stylistic comparisions for the four principal initials listed above are hard to come by, the *D* provided for Easter Sunday does have the same sort of stylised *A* in its bowl as the *P* added to the 'Lothar Psalter' in the last third of the ninth century.[59] However, the letter forms in this part of the psalter are, generally speaking, somewhat differently conceived.

---

[57] Madan and Craster, *Summary Catalogue* II.i, 488–9, and C. A. Bouman, *Sacring and Crowning*, Bijdragen van het Instituut voor middeleeuwse Geschiedenis der Rikjs-Universiteit te Utrecht 30 (Groningen, Djakarta, 1957), pp. 10–11.
[58] See Brou, *The Monastic Ordinal of the Monks of St Vedast's Abbey* I, 36–44, with the plan opposite p. 26. The abbey, the castle and the churches of St Peter and St Mary were put to the torch by the Vikings in 887. See the *Annales Vedastini*, ed. de Simson, p. 71.
[59] Illustr. Koehler and Mutherich, *Die karolingische Miniaturen* IV, pl. 7A.

Class 2: smaller, less elaborate initials infilled with gold, edged in red, but not black; opening lines generally in black rustic capitals flecked with red and green. The opening line of the first prayer for St Stephen's day at the beginning of the sanctoral, however, is done in gold. The initials in question occur at:

65r: Vigil of the Nativity.
71r: Epiphany.
76r: Purification of the Virgin (2 Feb.).
94r: Fourth Sunday after Lent.
102r: Sixth Sunday after Lent.
106r: Maundy Thursday.
114v: Vigil of Easter.
118r: Wednesday after Easter Sunday.
120v: Octave of Easter.
130v: Vigil of Pentecost.
135v: First Sunday after Pentecost.
158r: St Stephen (26 Dec.).

170r: Invention of the Cross 3 May.).
175r: Nativity of John the Baptist (24 June).
186r: Assumption of the Virgin (15 Aug.).
189v: Nativity of the Virgin (8 Sept.).
191r: Exaltation of the Cross (14 Sept.).
194r: St Michael (29 Sept.).
198r: All Saints (1 Nov.).
199v: St Martin (11 Nov.).
202v: St Andrew (30 Nov.).

The initial *O* on fol. 108r, and the *O* marking the beginning of the votive masses on fol. 212r should be added to this list.

Class 3: simple initial letters of red or green, not ornamented with gold; followed by one line of rustic capitals in black, flecked with red and green.

77r: Annunciation (25 Mar.).
78r: Septuagesima Sunday.
82v: First Sunday in Lent.
149v: First Sunday in Advent.
159r: St John the Evangelist (27 Dec.).
160r: Innocents (28 Dec.).
169r: SS Philip and James (1 May).

180r: Translation of St Benedict (11 July).
181r: St Peter's Chains (1 Aug.).
184r: St Lawrence (10 Aug.).
187v: St Bartholomew (25 Aug.).
192v: St Matthew (21 Sept.).
197r: SS Simon and Jude (28 Oct.).
203v: St Thomas (21 Dec.).

The *E* of the Exultet on fol. 110r should be added. A number of initials have decorative infilling in their bowls, as, for instance, in the case of those provided on fols 184r and 187v for the feasts of St Lawrence and St Bartholomew. All other initials are generally done alternately in red and some shade of brown, or black. Green is used sparingly.

LEOFRIC A

General Liturgical Character of A

For Klaus Gamber and Abbé Emmanuel Bourque, *A* seemed little more than a 'fused' or 'mixed' Gregorian-Gelasian sacramentary, that is to say, a sacramentary containing elements drawn from three main sources: a copy of the book sent from Rome by Pope Hadrian to Charlemagne in the late 780s (the so-called Hadrianic Gregorian, or *Hadrianum*); the Supplement to the *Hadrianum* compiled by Benedict of Aniane in the early ninth century; and an 'Eighth-Century Gelasian' sacramentary, a type of book popular throughout Europe in the eighth century, as its name, first coined by Edmund Bishop, helpfully suggests.[1] Gamber therefore classed it with the great sacramentaries of Fulda and a number of others in his *Codices Liturgici Latini Antiquiores*.[2] Unfortunately *A* is nothing so simple.

As Warren saw, *A* is a bishop or archbishop's book. Fifty-one masses have episcopal benedictions, entered for the most part before the postcommunion prayer, which is where they should be, but on occasion after, as in certain 'Gallican' books; and an extensive pontifical, that is, a collection of services and other material expressly arranged for the use of a bishop or an archbishop, occupies the bulk of fols 246r–306v. Books with benedictions in their proper places seem at all times to have

---

[1] *CLLA*, no. 950; E. Bourque, *Étude sur les sacramentaires romaines*, 2 vols in 3 (Rome, 1948–58) II.ii, 266–7. For the *Hadrianum* and Supplement, see *Le sacramentaire grégorien* I; and for the 'Eighth-Century Gelasian' books, the study by B. Moreton, *The Eighth-Century Gelasian Sacramentary* (Oxford, 1976), though a number of his conclusions now need modification. On the fragment of an 'Eighth Century Gelasian' written in the early eighth century by an Anglo-Saxon scribe that turned up relatively recently in Münster University Library (Universitätsbibliothek, Fragmentensammlung IV. 8), see B. Bischoff, V. Brown and J. John, 'Addenda to *Codices Latini Antiquiores* II', *Medieval Studies* 54 (1992), 286–307, at 298, plate Vb; *CLLA* Suppl., no. 415. For arguments in favour of England as the true home of 'Eighth-Century Gelasians', see A. Baumstark and K. Mohlberg, *Das älteste erreichbare Gestalt des* Liber sacramentorum anni circuli *der römischen Kirke*, Liturgiegeschichtliche Quellen und Forschungen 11–12 (Münster-im-Westfalen, 1927), pp. 134*–76*. It is much to be regretted that Baumstark's views have regularly been overlooked by later writers.
[2] *CLLA*, nos 901–90. See also E. Palazzo, *Les sacramentaires de Fulda*, LQF 77 (Aschendorff Munster, 1994).

been particularly uncommon.[3] Those written in France in the period
c. 800–1000 are as follows:

Paris, Bibliothèque nationale de France, lat. 9428: the sacramentary
of Drogo, archbishop of Metz (c. 831–55).[4]

Stockholm Holm A. 136: the sacramentary written at Saint-Amand
c. 870–80 for Ansegis, bishop of Sens.[5]

Paris, Bibliothèque nationale de France, lat. 2291: a sacramentary
and gradual written at Saint-Amand for Gozlinus, abbot of Saint-
Germain-des-Pres (867–86), Saint-Amand (871–86) and Saint-Denis
(878–84), presumably shortly after it had become known that he had
been elected bishop of Paris (884-6). The book may even have been
commissioned by him. At the front, on fols 5–7, we have, in several
late-ninth or early-tenth-century hands, responses from an office in
honour of St Germanus (28 May); a mass in honour of St Germanus
with an episcopal benediction; a series of monastic *preces;* and a list
of the bishops of Paris originally ending with Gozlinus. The presence
of the benediction is highly suggestive. Later, further formulae for
St Germanus' day were added on fol. 17, together with a list of
monks and familiars of his abbey.[6] Three possibilities therefore
suggest themselves; first, that the additions were made either for or
by Gozlinus, who remained abbot of the house during his time as
bishop; second, that Gozlinus's successor at Notre-Dame took an
interest in the community of Saint-Germain and had the material
added; and last, that the book was owned by the community of
Saint-Germain, but reserved for the use of the visiting bishop. For the
moment, however, it seems best to leave the matter open. The
palaeographical character of these additions will probably turn out to
be crucial. As Victors Netzer and Leroquais saw, the attached gradual
is neither that of Notre-Dame nor Saint-Germain, but Saint-Amand.[7]

---

[3] A number of *A*'s benedictions have been transl. R. Tatlock, *An English Benedictional
translated and adapted from the Leofric Missal* (London, 1964).
[4] *CLLA*, no. 912; ed. in summary, F. Unterkircher, *Zur iconographie und Liturgie des
Drogo-Sakramentars* (Graz, 1977).
[5] See above, n. 37.
[6] See Delisle, 'Mémoire', pp. 148–9; Leroquais, *Les sacramentaires* I, 56–8; and best of
all, A. Wilmart, 'Un sacramentaire à l'usage de Saint-Germain-des-Prés. Mentions nécrologiques relatives a ce monastère', *Revue Mabillon* 17 (1927), 379–94. On Gozlinus, see
now *Recueil des actes de Charles le Chauve*, ed. A. Giry, M. Prou and G. Tessier, 3 vols
(Paris, 1943–55) III, 42–9.
[7] The sacramentary is partially ed. *Le sacramentaire grégorien* under the siglum T3, and
the gradual ed. Netzer, *L'introduction*, pp. 283–355. *CLLA*, no. 925. See also Robertson,
Saint-Denis, pp. 385, 434–5. The book was probably later at Saint-Denis.

Paris, Bibliothèque nationale de France, lat. 12051: the 'Missale sancti Eligii', according to a thirteenth-century inscription on its last page. But the book is not a missal at all, rather a late-ninth-century sacramentary-cum-pontifical written at Corbie, and still in its original binding. Later additions and a seventeenth-century ex-libris show that the volume remained at the house in subsequent centuries, and was probably used at some point either during or before the thirteenth-century in the parish church dedicated to St Eligius in the town, hence its name.[8] But BNF lat. 12051 cannot have been drawn up originally for Corbie, for it contains a substantial pontifical in the shape of extensive *ordines* for Wednesday, Thursday, Friday and Saturday of Holy Week, and for the dedication of a church: and if that that is not telling enough, we also have the presence throughout the volume of episcopal benedictions in their proper places on select feasts; no less than five masses for a dead bishop; a mass *pro episcopo uel congregatione* composed of prayers that in countless other books normally go under the superscription *pro abbate vel congregatione*; and no formulae of any sort for St Benedict, though his name does follow those of SS Hilary, Martin, Augustine, Gregory and Jerome in the standard northern French *Communicantes* of the Canon of the Mass. The same order of invocations also occurs in Paris, Bibliothèque nationale de France, lat. 12048, the so-called sacramentary of Gellone, an 'Eighth-Century Gelasian' written for Hildoard, bishop of Cambrai, but which passed soon thereafter to the abbey of Saint-Guilhem-le-Désert (Gellone), and in most of the books produced for export at Saint-Amand.[9] Only if one assumes that some member of the Corbie community thought himself a bishop can the book have been useful. That leaves us with the question of why the 'Missale sancti Eligii' exists at all. Hohler and Turner, seeing the impossibility of Corbie, suggested, albeit tentatively, Soissons.[10] Soissons, however, seems unlikely since no emphasis is given to the

---

[8]   See Delisle, 'Mémoire', pp. 64, 175–8; Leroquais, *Les sacramentaires* I, 63–4; D. Ganz, *Corbie in the Carolingian Renaissance*, Beihefte der Francia 20 (Sigmaringen, 1990), p. 146; and J. Vezin, 'Les relieures carolingiennes de cuir', *Bibliothèque d'École des Chartes* 128 (1970), 81–112, pls III–IV. *CLLA*, no. 901.

[9]   The portions of BNF lat. 12051 mentioned are ed. PL 78, cols 27, 79–92, 152–52, 214–16 and 236. BNF lat. 12048, is ed. A. Dumas and J. Deshusses, *Liber Sacramentorum Gellonensis*, 2 vols, CCSL 159 and 159A (Turnhout, 1981), and the literature surrounding it noted in *CLLA*, no. 855. For variants in the Canons of a number of early sacramentaries, see *Le sacramentaire grégorien* I, 87–92, nos 5–19 and notes, and Ebner, *Quellen*, pp. 407–8.

[10]   See C. Hohler, 'The type of sacramentary used by St Boniface', *Sankt Bonifatius: Gedenkgabe zum zwölfhundertjährigen Todestag* (Fulda, 1954), pp. 89–93, at 90–1 and D. H. Turner, *The Missal of the New Minster, Winchester*, HBS 93 (London, 1962), p. xviii.

mass for SS Gervase and Protase (19 June), twin patrons of the cathedral, provided in the sanctoral of the sacramentary; nor do their names appear anywhere in the Canon. By the same token one might also rule out other northern French cathedrals which had relics of major non-apostolic patrons, notably: Cambrai with St Gaugericus; Noyon with St Eligius; Amiens with St Firminus; and Beauvais with SS Lucianus and Justus. If, on the other hand, the scribe had no instructions to copy in material 'proper' to the house for which the sacramentary was intended, the one house that seems more likely than any other is Beauvais, which was ruled over by Odo (861 × 862 – 881), formerly abbot of Corbie (851 – 861 × 862): all of which would be to assume, of course, that the book never got sent out.[11] A modern edition of BNF lat. 12051's text is badly needed.

Paris, Bibliothèque nationale de France, lat. 1238: an early-tenth-century sacramentary probably from Reims.[12]

London, British Library, Loans 36 (14) (formerly Phillipps 3340): a late-tenth-century sacramentary from the cathedral of Noyon. A tall, thin and exceptionally interesting book. Arranged more or less as BNF lat. 12051, but its text is different and several benedictions are out of place, as in *A*. Its text is thoroughly 'harmonised'. SS Hilary and Martin, Medard, and Eligius, patron of the house, are named in the *Communicantes* of the Canon of the Mass, p. 22; the final section of the Exultet preface of Holy Saturday reads: *Precamur ergo te domine, ut nos tui ministros altaris, omnesque beati eligii confessoris tui . . .*, pp. 153–4; the prayers of the mass *in ecclesia cuiuslibet martyrum uel confessorum* name Eligius as the saint whose relics are possessed, pp. 344–5, which suggests that this was the mass that was regularly used; and the collect of the mass to be said for an abbot and congregation, p. 357, reads, like *A*'s: *Omnipotens sempiterne deus qui facis mirabilia magna solus, praetende super famulum tuum ill.*, not *abbatem nostrum* as in monastic books. The sacramentary was later augmented with further pontifical material, notably prayers for the bishop when vesting, benedictions, and an anathema against those despoiling the church and its property, pp. 7–16. As Turner notes, Noyon became monastic in 986 under Bishop Liudulfus (977–88). That explains why we have on pp. 29–30, pages originally

---

[11] On Odo see Ganz, *Corbie*, p. 34, and L. Duchesne, *Fastes episcopaux de l'ancienne Gaule*, 2nd ed., 3 vols (Paris, 1907–22) III, 121.

[12] See Leroquais, *Les sacramentaires* I, 81–3, and Netzer, *L'introduction*, pp. 122–3.

left blank, prayers *ad abbatem faciendum* naming St Benedict as especial patron.[13]

Paris, Bibliothèque nationale de France, lat. 12052: a sacramentary-cum-pontifical written to the order of Ratoldus, abbot of Corbie (d. 986).[14] As Christopher Hohler has shown, the book underlying BNF lat. 12052 is essentially a sacramentary of Saint-Denis that found its way first to Dol, probably in the early tenth century, then, when the clergy fled Dol in the 930s, to Orléans, from Orléans to Arras, and from Arras finally to Corbie, where the clean copy that we have today was made. Somewhere *en route*, perhaps at Dol, but more likely Orléans, an English pontifical was worked in, containing among other things: a mass for St Cuthbert (20 Mar.); a copy of a form of episcopal profession originally used by Herewine, bishop of Lichfield sometime between 814 and 816; a benedictional; and a coronation order. But Ratoldus could only have used BNF lat. 12052 with great trouble, for its sanctoral is not that of Corbie; nor are its temporal, votives and occasional services like those of any other surviving Corbie manuscript. His interest must have been purely scholarly.[15]

London, British Library, Harley 2991, fols 1r–37v: late-tenth and early-eleventh-century additions bringing a late-ninth or early-tenth-century sacramentary of the abbey of St Columba at Sens into line with the use of Nevers Cathedral.[16]

Tours, Bibliothèque municipale, 196: an early-eleventh-century sacramentary from the collegiate church of St Martin at Tours drawn up for the use of the archbishop of the cathedral of St Maurice.[17]

---

[13] For a short description, see D. H. Turner, 'A C10–C11 Noyon Sacramentary', *Studia Patristica* 5 (1962), 43–51.

[14] See Delisle, 'Mémoire', pp. 188–91, and Leroquais, *Les sacramentaires* I, 79–81.

[15] See Hohler, 'Books', pp. 64–9, for an account of the book's travels; on its benedictions, A. Prescott, 'The text of the benedictional of St Aethelwold', *Bishop Aethelwold: His Career and Influence*, ed. B. Yorke (Woodbridge, 1988), pp. 119–47, at 135–43; and on the form of profession, M. Richter, *Canterbury Professions*, Canterbury and York Society 67 (London, 1973), pp. xlviii–xlix, and no. 9. The coronation order is ed. R. A. Jackson, *Ordines Coronationis Franciae. Texts and ordines for the Coronation of Frankish and French Kings and Queens in the Middle Ages*, 2 vols (Philadelphia, 1995–2000) I, 177–200. A new edition of the book as a whole is to be issued by the Henry Bradshaw Society.

[16] For a description, see Netzer, *L'introduction*, pp. 123–7.

[17] According to Leroquais, the manuscript later found its way to Marmoutiers. See Leroquais, *Les sacramentaires* I, 145–7, with A. Dorange, *Catalogue descriptif et raisonné des manuscrits de la Bibliothèque de Tours* (Tours, 1875), pp. 108–9, and *DACL* 15.ii, cols 2671–2.

Even fewer sacramentaries from German and Italian cathedrals seem to have been prepared in this way. Indeed, the only example I have been able to find from the same period is the sacramentary of Wolfgang, bishop of Regensburg (972–94), now Verona, Biblioteca Capitolare, 87.[18] Warmund of Ivrea (1001–10), in company with numerous others, preferred his benedictional separate.[19]

That *A* cannot have been made for the bishop of the united diocese of Arras-Cambrai, as Warren apparently felt, seems clear on four principal counts. First, its litany is not of Cambrai: SS Gaugericus (11 Aug.) and Autbertus (13 Dec.), the two principal saints of the city are not invoked, as they are for instance, in the litany added in the late ninth or early tenth century to Cambrai, Bibliothèque municipale, 164, the sacramentary of Bishop Hildoard (780–816) and the earliest and best copy of the *Hadrianum* to have survived complete, and in the litanies of all later books from the cathedral.[20] Second, as has already been said, there was no such person as the bishop of Arras. The diocese established by St Vedastus in the sixth century was administered from Cambrai until 1093. Third, *A* cannot have been made for the exclusive and occasional use of any bishop (let alone Dodilo) either at the monastery of Saint-Vaast or the former cathedral, which may still have been served by a small body of canons in the ninth and tenth centuries, for the the the propers for St Vedastus composed by Alcuin for the communities at Arras sometime close to the year 796 – a fixture in books from the city of all dates, Cambrai BM 162–3 included – do not figure in *A*'s sanctoral.[21] Fourth, viewed as a

---

[18] Ed. K. Gamber and S. Rehle, *Das Sakramentar-Pontifikale des Bischofs Wolfgang von Regensburg*, Textus Patristici et Liturgici 15 (Regensburg, 1985); *CLLA*, no. 940.

[19] Warmund's sacramentary, now Ivrea, Biblioteca Capitolare, 31, is ed. in facsimile, F. dell'Oro, *Sacramentarium episcopi Warmundi* (Ivrea, 1990). Warmund's benedictional is now Ivrea, Biblioteca Capitulare, 10.

[20] Cambrai BM 164 is ed. H. Lietzmann, *Das Sacramentarium Gregorianum nach dem Aachener Urexemplar*, LQF 3 (Münster-im-Westfalen, 1921), and *Le sacramentaire grégorien* I. *CLLA*, no. 720; Bischoff, *Katalog*, no. 774. Its litany is ed. in summary by Leroquais, *Les sacramentaires* I, 11; and M. Coens, *Recueil d'études Bollandiennes*, pp. 280–1.

[21] Ed. *Le sacramentaire grégorien* I, 690–1, nos 55*–63*; and II, 303, nos 3478–82. See also, J. Deshusses, 'Les anciens sacramentaires de Tours', *RB* 89 (1979), 281–302, at 287–8. Copies of the mass spread quickly. For other early examples, see Leroquais, *Les sacramentaires* I, 79–80, and 100; PL 78, col. 408; Turner, 'A C10–C11 Noyon Sacramentary', pp. 144–5; and L. Gjerløw, *Adoratio Crucis* (Oslo, 1961), pp. 45–6. A proper preface for St Vedast's day was added in the early tenth century to Cambrai BM 164. See E. Bishop, 'On the early texts of the Roman Canon', in his *Liturgica Historica* (Oxford, 1918), pp. 77–115, at 99, n. 5.

whole, *A* is quite unlike any other northern French or German sacramentary, as will become clear.

So we have a bishop or archbishop's book with a litany that seems, on the face of things, to have some connexion with Arras. The name of St Vedastus is the only one to have been written in red and green rustic capitals; and as Hohler pointed out, the main text of the sacramentary has a number of variants there are only otherwise to be found, among the early books edited by Deshusses, in Cambrai BM 162–3.[22] But these 'Artesian symptoms' are purely superficial. For *A* probably began life as some sort of 'Eighth-Century Gelasian' sacramentary – most likely an early one from central or northern Italy – that was later transformed into *A* as we have it today with the help of a ninth-century sacramentary from Arras: but transformed not for use at any house in northern France, but for use at Canterbury. Quite aside from the English features mentioned by Hohler, we have numerous formulae that only otherwise appear in Anglo-Saxon books; others that only otherwise appear in books from northern Spain, central and northern Italy and the diocese of Mainz; and an order for the dedication of a church that expressly names St Andrew (30 Nov.) as patron. That church is pretty clearly Wells.

As Warren realised, however, *A* could be used on certain occasions by its owner in a house or houses served by monks. The proper masses provided for the two major feasts of St Benedict, his deposition and translation, are both fitted out with prefaces, and two masses in honour of monastic communities are provided among *A*'s votives: one *pro abbate et congregatione* (nos 1996–8) and the other a *missa monachorum propria* (nos 2051–3): The collect of the former runs:

> Omnipotens sempiterne deus, qui facis mirabilia magna solus, pretende super famulum tuum, abbatem .ill. et super cunctam congregationem illi commissam spiritum gratiae salutaris, et ut in ueritate tibi complaceant, perpetuum eis rorem tuę benedictionis infunde. Per dominum nostrum.

and that of the latter:

> Familiam huius cenobii, quesumus, domine, intercedente beata maria semper uirgine et omnibus sanctis perpetuo guberna

---

[22] Hohler, 'Books', p. 79. Cambrai BM 162–3 are ed. *Le sacramentaire grégorien* under the siglum S. *CLLA*, no. 761; Bischoff, *Katalog*, no. 773. The contents of the other ninth-century Gregorians consulted by Deshusses are listed *Le sacramentaire grégorien* III, 19–59.

moderamine, ut adsit eis et in securitate cautela, et inter aspera fortitudo. Per.

The presence of the word *eis* in both prayers, rather than *nobis*, is telling. So the mass *pro abbate et congregatione* presumably served as a 'general' mass, that is to say, one that might be read in any church, not necessarily a monastery, and whenever seemed appropriate. All the celebrant would have to do is supply the names of the (absent) abbot and congregation for whom the prayers were intended. The mass *missa monachorum propria*, on the other hand, will have been for the visit itself. The opening words, *Familiam* huius *cenobii*, are proof enough of that.

That further English pontifical material was added to *A* in a variety of English hands dateable to the period *c.* 930–1000 is a clear sign that *A* remained in the possession of later archbishops; and in the mid eleventh century, at Exeter, Leofric had excerpts from the Romano-German Pontifical copied in. We will come to *B* and *C* in due course. It will be best now, however, to look in detail at what *A* contains.

Benedictiones ad lectorem (nos 52–108)

A provides 24 short formulae for the blessing of the reader of the lessons at night office (matins). These are likely to have been copied in at the request of the man for whom the book was produced, for they are normally the preserve of episcopal collectars and breviaries, as the following list of books in which pre-eleventh-century examples survive will show:

Vienna, Österreichische Nationalbibliothek, Vindob. ser. nov. 2762: the combined collectar and pontifical of Baturich, bishop of Regensburg (817–48).[23]

Freiburg-im-Breisgau Universitätsbibliothek, 363: a mid-ninth-century pontifical and collectar from Basel.[24]

---

[23] F. Unterkircher, *Das Kollektar-Pontifikale des Bischofs Baturich von Regensburg* (817– 48), Spicilegium Friburgense 8 (Fribourg, 1962), pp. 78–84, nos 243–57, 265–365; *CLLA*, no. 1550.

[24] Ed. M. J. Metzger, *Zwei karolingische Pontifikalien vom Oberrhein*, Freiburger Theologische Studien 17 (Freiburg-im-Breisgau, 1914), pp. 61*–2*. *CLLA*, no. 1551; Bischoff, *Katalog* I, no. 1289.

Rome, Biblioteca nazionale, 1565 (Sessorianus 96): additions made in the late ninth or early tenth century to pages originally left blank in a late-ninth-century manuscript of Biblical commentaries. The book as a whole, which is made up of three distinct parts, was at Nonantola by the eleventh century.[25]

and Durham Cathedral Library, A. IV. 19: a collectar (the so-called 'Durham Collectar') written in southern England in the early-tenth-century and acquired by the community of Chester-le-Street while at Woodyates in Sussex, c. 970. The benedictions were added in the late tenth century.[26]

Surprisingly few of *A*'s formulae appear in the three continental books however. Baturich's collectar has twelve; the Nonantola manuscript and the Freiburg pontifical three each. But the Durham collectar, on the other hand, encompasses the whole series. This is highly suggestive. The Chester-le-Street community was a community of canons in the tenth century, and its books will therefore have been arranged according to the secular cursus. Indeed, the first group of blessings in both the collectar and *A* are designed for a matins service of nine lessons, the number normally read on feasts of the highest grade in secular houses; and two further groups are designed for a matins of three, the number standard for secondary feasts. This had been spotted by Bäumer as long ago as 1895, but he seems not to have known of *A*.[27] For *A*, however, the implication is clear: it must have been owned by someone used to the secular office too.

The series of blessings ends with five of the six ancient *benedictiones ante cybum*, which are common enough in ninth and tenth-century sacramentaries; one long and three short blessings *ad cybum*, which may be reworkings of older forms; and one long and two short blessings *ad*

---

[25] Ed. A. Wilmart, 'Séries de bénédictions pour l'office dans un recueil de Nonantola', *EL* 45 (1931), 354–61.

[26] Ed. A. Lindelöf, *Rituale ecclesiae Dunelmensis*, Surtees Society 140 (London, 1927), pp. 126–7. See also the facsimile, ed. T. J. Brown, *The Durham Ritual*, EEMF 16 (Copenhagen, 1969), 61v–2v. The collectar (but not the benedictions) is ed. A. Corrêa, *The Durham Collectar*, HBS 107 (London, 1992).

[27] S. Bäumer, *Histoire du Bréviaire*, trans. R. Biron, 2 vols (Paris, 1905) I, 384–6, at 385. For further sets of benedictions, see J. Leclercq, 'Une série de bénédictions pour les lectures de l'office', *EL* 59 (1945), 318–21; *idem*, 'Fragmenta Reginensia', *EL* 61 (1947), 289–96; *idem*, 'Bénédictions pour les leçons de l'office dans un manuscrit de Pistoie', *Sacris Erudiri* 8 (1956), 143–6; A. Olivar, 'Série de *benedictiones lectionum officii* d'après un document de Montserrat aux environs de 1500', *EL* 63 (1949), 42–56; and P. Salmon, 'Bénédictions de l'office des matins. Nouvelles séries', in his *Analecta Liturgica*, Studi e Testi 273 (Vatican City, 1974), 47–66. All contain references to a wider literature.

potum, which again may be reworkings. A third was erased in the eleventh century to make way for the addition of material in Anglo-Saxon.[28]

The Ordinary of the Mass (nos 113–16, 119–23 and 127–30)

Immediately after the blessings we come to what remains of *A*'s Ordinary, that is, the invariable framework of prayers and blessings said by the celebrant during his preparations for mass and during mass itself. Unfortunately a number of these prayers (and whatever rubric accompanied them) seem later to have been damped out – there is no sign of abrasion – to make way for new material, principally episcopal benedictions. These additions will be dealt with shortly. What survives, however, skeletal though it may be, is of the greatest interest. We have four bidding prayers (nos 113–16) which are similar in style to the prayers preceding the litany (nos 2277–80) and apparently unique. Then, after a gap, we have four apologiae all beginning with the words *Suscipe sancta trinitas* (nos 119–22), presumably to be said as the chalice and paten were brought to the altar. In the early-tenth-century sacramentary from Amiens, BNF lat. 9432, these go under the rubric: *Quando ponit oblata super altare, Memoria imperatoris et totius populi christiani, Memoria sacerdotis* and *Memoria defunctorum*. Rubric in *A*, however, was never provided, and the text of its third prayer has *rex*, not *imperator*. The series (which is short in comparison with the ones provided in the 'sacramentaries of Saint-Amand') concludes with a fifth prayer (no. 123), also standard, beginning *Ignosce domine quod dum rogare*, which is appointed in some books as a prayer to be said at the foot of the altar before the gifts are offered; but here, it may have been pronounced by the priest as he prepared for communion.[29] Following a further set of

---

[28] For a photograph of this page (fol. 11v), see F. Rose-Troup, 'The ancient monastery of St Mary and St Peter at Exeter 680–1050', *Transactions of the Devonshire Association* 61 (1931), 179–220, pl. V.

[29] The Amiens prayers are ed. Netzer, *L'Introduction*, pp. 230–1. On apologiae in general, see A. Nocent, 'Les apologies dans la célébration eucharistique', *Liturgie et rémission des péchés. Conférences Saint-Serge XXe semaine d'études liturgiques, Paris, 2–5 juillet*, ed. A. Pistoia, C. M. Triacca and A. M. Triacca, Biblioteca Ephemerides Liturgicae Subsidia 3ca (Rome, 1975), 179–96. On the formulae in the Saint-Amand sacramentaries, see *Le sacramentaire grégorien* III, 262–70, nos 4373–95, with J. Deshusses, 'Chronologie des grands sacramentaires de Saint-Amand', *RB* 87 (1977), 230–7. His chronology, however, is open to doubt.

later intrusions, we then come to the short benedictions, *Veni sanctificator*, and *Accipe sancte pater hostiam immaculatam* (nos 127–8), traditionally said over the paten and chalice after they had been set upon the altar. Finally there are two Mementos (nos 129–30), the second of which ends incomplete. Everything is in the right order and in its right position (despite Drage's doubts) and the only major disruption to the Ordinary as a whole, aside from the erasing of certain items, seems to be the loss of the outer bifolium of what was originally the second gathering of *A* (fols 13–16). This is presumably why the texts on fol. 12v and fol. 16v break off abruptly.

Thanks to Paul Tirot, it seems clear that *A*'s 'Ordinary', despite its lacunae and relatively cursory form, is for the most part 'normal' for northern Europe. But one prayer is unusual. This is the blessing *Accipe sancte pater hostiam immaculatam*, which only otherwise occurs in an early-eleventh-century sacramentary from the great north Italian abbey of Bobbio, now Milan, Biblioteca Ambrosiana, DSP 10/27 bis (formerly D. inf. 84).[30] All other surviving versions begin with the words *Suscipe sancte pater*, the opening given in the modern Roman Missal. Tirot drew two conclusions: first, that *Accipe* was probably the precursor of *Suscipe*; and second, that it might, in view of Bobbio, have originated in an Irish milieu. If he is right, *A*'s Ordinary could either have been 'insular' in form and later Gallicanized; or 'Gallican' in form but intruded upon by 'insular' elements. The latter is probably more likely, since the bidding prayers in the Ordinary and those preceding the litany have phrases typical of the prayers *post nomina* of Vat. Reg. lat. 317, the early to mid-eighth-century 'Missale Gothicum'. Notable parallels are: *Et offerentium ac pausantium quae recitata nomina; pro spiritibus carorum nostrorum qui nos in dominica pace praecesserunt ut eos dominus in requiem collocare et in parte primae resurrectionis resuscitet; Et nomina quae recitata sunt nostrorum carorum in caelesti pagina iubeas intimare; and qui in christo dormierunt refrigerium in regione uiuorum*, which occur regularly in different formulations.[31] A number of

---

[30] See P. Tirot, 'Histoire des prières d'offertorie dans la liturgie romaine du VIIe au XVe siecle', *EL* 98 (1984), 148–97, 323–91, esp. 336–9. On Ambrosiana DSP 10/27 bis, see Ebner, *Quellen*, pp. 80–2, with N. A. Orchard, 'St Willibrord, St Richarius, and Anglo-Saxon symptoms in three mass-books from northern France', *RB* 110 (2000), 261–83, at 274–81 CLLA, no. 1473.

[31] *Missale Gothicum*, ed. Mohlberg, nos 130, 248, 391 and 459. See also, *DACL* 4.i, cols 1069–72.

phrases can also be paralleled in the Carolingian *apologiae* printed by Deshusses, and in the Romano-Frankish prayers for the dead that found their way into 'Gelasian' sacramentaries and Benedict of Aniane's Supplement.

The 'alternative' Mementos with which *A*'s Ordinary now ends were doubtless included in the Ordinary, rather than the Canon, where the the standard forms are to be found (nos 333 and 339), simply for convenience's sake: at any rate, similar prayers figure in the Ordinary of Wolfenbüttel, Herzog August. – Bibliothek, Helmst 1151, the so-called 'Missal of Flaccus Illyricus' (actually an early-eleventh-century sacramentary from Minden); and, as additions, in the Ordinary of BNF lat. 9432, the Amiens book mentioned above.[32] *Signes de renvoies* in the latter helpfully note at which points in the Canon the formulae were to be said. In *A* the reader is simply referred (*ut supra*) to a version of the prayer that must have been erased in the mid tenth century. However, it is perfectly clear what the Mementos are for. The first is simply an expanded version of a standard Memento for the living, and the second a Memento for the dead.[33] When, and if, an analagous version comes to light it may be possible to say how this last continued. Other remembrances and concluding prayers are likely to have followed on the leaf now lost.

The Canon (nos 330–44)

In common with many early sacramentaries, especially those produced at Saint-Amand, the prayers *Vere dignum* and *Te igitur* of *A*'s Canon (fols 60v–61v) were lavishly decorated, as we have seen. From a textual standpoint, *A*'s Canon is for the most part perfectly normal too. However, there are two points of note. First, the closing portions of the *Te igitur* contain what appears to be a significant early variant, as the following comparison will show. On the left we have the relevant

---

[32] For the ordinary of the 'Missal of Flaccus Illyricus', see Martène, *AER*, Bk I, cap. iv, art. xi, ordo 4, and PL 138, cols 1305–36; for the book as a whole and related fragments, *CLLA*, no. 990.

[33] Both have been republished twice from Warren's edition. See A. Mocquereau, *Antiphonarium Ambrosianum du Musée Britannique (XII siècle), Codex Additional 34209*, Palaéographie Musicale 5 (Solesmes, 1896), p. 166; and *DACL*, 4.i, col. 1077.

passage in the *Hadrianum*, in the centre that of 'Gellone', and on the right *A*'s:[34]

Hadrianum.	Gellone.	A.
. . . una cum beatissimo famulo tuo papa nostro .ill.	. . . una cum beatissimo famulo tuo papa nostro .ill., et antestite nostro .ill., et omnibus ortodoxis adque apostolicę fidęi cultoribus.	. . . una cum beatissimo famulo tuo .ill., et antistite nostro .ill., et omnibus ortodoxis atque catholicae et apostolicae fidei cultoribus.

So far as one can tell, *A* is one of the earliest surviving books to introduce the word *catholicae* in a generally Hadrianic context, others being:

Paris, Bibliothèque nationale de France, lat. 1141: a sacramentary probably produced at Metz for the coronation of Charles the Bald in 869.[35]

Milan, Biblioteca del Capitolo metropolitano, D. 3–3: a late-ninth-century sacramentary from the convent of S. Simpliciano in Milan.[36]

Vatican, Biblioteca Apostolica Vaticana, Vat. Reg. lat. 567: a fragment of a tenth-century sacramentary from Sens.[37]

Milan, Biblioteca Ambrosiana, A. 24 bis. inf.: a mid-tenth-century sacramentary from Biasca.[38]

and the additions made in the mid tenth century to the original text of Padua, Biblioteca Capitolare, D. 47, a copy of an augmented pre-Hadrianic Gregorian sacramentary from Pavia (perhaps from the Imperial Chapel) produced at Aachen or Liège, presumably at

[34] Ed. respectively, *Le sacramentaire grégorien* I, 87, no. 5, and Dumas and Deshusses, *Liber Sacramentorum Gellonensis* I, 253, no. 1933.
[35] Ed. F. Muterich, *Sakramentar von Metz. Fragment MS Lat. 1141, Bibliothèque Nationale, Paris*, Codices selecti phototypice impressi (Graz, 1972), fol. 7r. *CLLA*, no. 771.
[36] Ed. J. Frei, *Das ambrosianische Sakramentar D. 3–3 aus dem mailändischen Metropolitankapitel*, Corpus Ambrosiano-Liturgicum 3, LQF 56 (Münster-im-Westfalen, 1974), p. 271, no. 661. *CLLA*, no. 510.
[37] Ed. A. Nocent, 'Un fragment de sacramentaire de Sens au Xe siècle', in *Miscellanea liturgica in onore di sua eminenza il Cardinale Giacomo Lercaro*, 2 vols (Rome, 1966–7) II, 649–794. See also, Delisle, 'Mémoire', 162–7. *CLLA*, no. 866.
[38] Ed. O. Heiming, *Das Ambrosianische Sakramentar von Biasca*, Corpus Ambrosiano-Liturgicum 2, LQF 51 (Münster-im-Westfalen, 1969), p. 105, no.762. *CLLA*, no. 515.

the request of Emperor Lothar. The book later found its way to Verona.[39]

Later examples, as Moeller has shown, are more numerous.[40] The second anomaly in *A*'s Canon lies in the way that the prayers *Simili modo posteaquam* and *Unde et memores* (nos 336–7) have been divided up. *Simili modo posteaquam,* unusually, ends short with the words *effundetur in remissionem peccatorum,* and its last sentence, beginning *Haec quotienscumque* is prefixed to, and capitalized as, the beginning of *Unde et memores.* So far as I have been able to establish the only other book in which such a division is made is Vatican City, Biblioteca Vaticana Apostolica, Chigi C. V. 134, a late-eleventh-century ritual and missal from a church near Sarsina in the diocese of Ravenna.[41] German, Italian and northern French books generally give the normal ('Roman') arrangement of the formulae concerned.

Temporal (nos 345–1295)

A's temporal, like its sanctoral (which we will come to in due course), looks fairly straightforward at first sight. We have nearly all the masses contained in the 'Hadrianic Gregorian' sacramentary and Benedict of Aniane's Supplement (with most of the prayers in their proper places), and a small number of 'Gelasians'. But appearances can be deceptive. For as has already been mentioned, *A* began life as some sort of 'Eighth-Century Gelasian'. Particularly telling in this respect are its masses for the Sundays after Pentecost. To take the example of the fourth Sunday (nos 1086–90). The incipits of *A*'s prayers are given on the left; and on the right the numbers assigned to the corresponding prayers in the most recent editions of the Supplement, and BNF lat. 12048, the so-called sacramentary of Gellone, the 'Eighth-Century Gelasian' sacramentary written for Hildoard of Cambrai:[42]

[39] Ed. A. Baumstark and K. Mohlberg, *Das älteste erreichbare Gestalt des Liber sacramentorum anni circuli der romischen Kirche,* Liturgiegeschichtliche Quellen und Forschungen 11–12 (Münster-im-Westfalen, 1927), p. 72, no. 876. *CLLA,* no. 880.
[40] *Corpus Orationum,* ed. Moeller, *et al.,* X, no. 6122. See also B. Capelle, T*ravaux liturgiques de doctrine et d'histoire,* 3 vols (Louvain, 1955–67) II, 258–67, esp. 258–61.
[41] Fol. 11v.
[42] Ed. *Le sacramentaire grégorien* I, 391–2; Dumas and Deshusses, *Liber Sacramentorum Gellonensis* I, 148.

A.	*Suppl.*	*Gellone.*
Collecta. Deprecationem . . .	1135	1116
Secreta. Munera domine . . .	1136	1118
Prefatio. Quoniam illa . . .	1626	1119
Ad complendum. Haec nos . . .	1137	1120
Ad populum. Tempora nostra . . .		1117

The second 'Eighth-Century Gelasian' collect is regularly turned into a prayer *ad populum* in the Sunday masses provided in *A*'s temporal. No other early book re-uses these formulae (which do not figure in the 'Gregorian' scheme) so rigorously.[43] That the 'Gelasian' model employed by *A*'s compiler was Italian seems clear from the *ad populum* provided for the twelfth Sunday, *Da quesumus domine populo tuo* (no. 1138), which is only otherwise to be found assigned to the day in the late-ninth-century sacramentary of S. Simpliciano mentioned above, and in a late-eleventh-century collectar from Trani.[44]

A also contains six complete mass-sets which are standard in 'Gelasian' books, occur frequently in later 'Gelasianized-Gregorians', but which do not figure in the *Hadrianum* or its Supplement. These are:

> Vigil of Epiphany (5 Jan.)
> Octave of Epiphany (13 Jan.)
> *Pascha annotina* (the day set aside for celebrating the baptisms of Holy Saturday the year before).
> Rogation Tuesday and Wednesday.
> Thursday after Pentecost Sunday.
> Octave of Pentecost.

All are provided with proper prefaces (but not the other prayers necessary for the performance of mass) in the Supplement.[45] The only

---

[43] Jean Deshusses, 'Sur quelques anciens livres liturgiques de Saint-Thierry: les etapes d'une transformation de la liturgie', in *Saint-Thierry, une abbaye du VIe au XXe siècle*, ed. M. Bur (Saint-Thierry, 1979), 122–45, at 142, remarks that the prayers affected for the Sundays after Pentecost in Reims Bibliothèque municipale, 214, a late-tenth-century sacramentary from Saint-Thierry, are similar to those in *A*. Closer inspection shows, however, that the two series are entirely unrelated. A fragment of a twelfth-century Italian book, ed. O. Heiming, 'Kleinere Beiträge zur Geschichte der ambrosianische Liturgie', *Archiv für Liturgiewissenshaft* 12 (1970), 130–47, at 141–5, is closer to *A*, but runs only to the tenth Sunday.

[44] Ed. Frei, *Das ambrosianische Sakramentar D. 3–3*, p. 252, no. 555; G. Batelli, 'L'orazionale di Trani', *Benedictina* 19 (1972), 271–87, at 275.

[45] See *Le sacramentaire grégorien* I, 495–575, 687–97; and III, 19–59, for the contents of the books in question.

unusual 'Gelasian' feast provided for in *A*'s temporal is the Saturday before Quadragesima Sunday.

A new collation of the 'Gregorian' parts of *A* with the texts of some twenty or thirty ninth and tenth-century sacramentaries bears out Hohler's view that a book similar to Cambrai BM 162–3 was used to turn the 'Eighth-Century Gelasian' underlying *A* into *A* as we have it today: similar, but not identical, for a number of variants, particularly in *A*'s votive masses, are found in the early books from Tours; and what is more, the three prayers given for the third Thursday in Lent (nos 635–9) seem only to appear together otherwise in Paris, Bibliothèque nationale de France, lat. 10504, a thirteenth-century missal from the cathedral of St Maurice (later re-dedicated to St Gaetian).[46] The most obvious connexion between Tours and Saint-Vaast is Alcuin, who acted as abbot of St Martin from 796 until his death in 804, and worked for the monks of Arras in the late 790s. That *A* should have the variants of books from both houses should therefore not be surprising, though it would be difficult to say on the one hand how the reviser went about his work, and on the other precisely what sort of book he used for his revisions. But the story is not simply one of an 'old' text ruthlessly being brought up to date. For as we shall see, two unexceptional masses have exceedingly rare, that is to say, non-Hadrianic prefaces, which suggests that the formulae concerned were deliberately left in place and not 'revised out'; and here and there, we have readings that are by ninth and tenth-century standards patently archaic.

Yet the general picture seems clear enough: a book similar to Cambrai BM 162–3 was employed in the making of *A*'s temporal and sanctoral. *A*'s benedictions, however, were clearly taken from an un-adulterated copy of Benedict of Aniane's Supplement, and not from the expanded set of blessings employed at Arras and Tours, as Prescott has noted.[47] *A* is therefore hybrid, having the variants of Arras but not its benedictions. Worth noting too are:

(i) the position of the standard Gregorian masses for the feasts of the Purification and Annunciation of the Virgin (2 Feb. and 25 Mar., respectively). These (nos 451–7 and 458–66) have not been separated out into

---

[46] For a brief description of this book, see Leroquais, *Les sacramentaires* II, 42–3.
[47] Hohler, 'Books', p. 79; Prescott, 'The text of the benedictional of St Aethelwold', pp. 125 and 135. If surviving books are anything to go by, the expanded set of benedictions seems to have been compiled in north-eastern France in the first half of the ninth century. We first encounter them in BNF lat. 12051.

the sanctoral with the other feasts of fixed date, but appear side by side between the groups of masses for the Sundays after Epiphany and the Sundays leading up to Lent. It is hard to say why precisely they were positioned in this way. But there must have been some governing reason for locating, or perhaps at least, keeping them in the temporal, for Alcuin's mass *in uigiliis festiuitatum sanctae mariae* (nos 448–50), which also occurs in the sacramentaries of Echternach and Tours, two communities with which he was closely associated, is attached. This arrangement presumably met with approval, since *A*'s scribe could easily have transferred the texts of all three masses into the sanctoral had he been asked. We must return to this point in due course.[48]

(ii) the penitential order for Ash Wednesday (nos 485–93). The introductory rubric and the four prayers that ensue are common enough, so too the series of five psalms *Domine ne in furore tuo .ii.* (37); *Benedic anima mea* usque *renouabitur aquilae iuuentus tua* (102); *Miserere mei* usque *dele iniquitates meas* (50); *Deus in nomine tuo* (53); and *Quid gloriaris* (51), which, from the time of Halitgar, bishop of Cambrai (817–31), were sometimes attached to particular prayers. But what sets *A* apart is that the texts of its psalms are Roman rather than Gallican. Most penitential orders draw from the latter.[49] The series of ten preces beginning *Ego dixi* is also without parallel, though a Reims book published in 1736 by Martène is close.[50] Most houses, aside from those that took over the prescriptions of the Romano-German Pontifical wholesale, made their own selection; and while further searches may of course eventually turn up sets similar to *A*'s, it seems unlikely that any other book will follow exactly. Immediately after the preces, we have the prayer *Deus cuius indulgentia nemo* (no. 491), which occurs in Halitgar's penitential; Paris, Bibliothèque de l'Arsenal, 227, the so-called 'Pontifical of Poitiers', a pontifical written in the mid ninth century for Vulfadus, bishop of Bourges; a late-ninth-century sacramentary from the abbey of St Martin at Tours, but in none of the other sacramentaries used by Deshusses; and in various later northern European service

---

[48] See below, pp. 46–56.
[49] Numerous *ordines* are ed. Martène, *AER*, Bk I, cap. vi, art. vii, and H. J. Schmitz, *Die Bussbücher und die Bussdisciplin der Kirche*, 2 vols (Mainz, 1883–98), though their conclusions concerning the origin and authorship of the texts they print are now somewhat dated.
[50] Martène, *AER*, Bk I, cap. vi, art. vii, ordo 9.

books and penitentials.[51] Then, after a short rubric, we have the prayer of absolution (based on Matthew *x*. 32*): Omnipotens deus qui dixit qui me confessus* (no. 492). This is highly unusual. It figures again in *A*'s order for the visitation of the sick, and in a number of other non-standard sources:

> Rome, Biblioteca nazionale, 2081 (Sessorianus 95): a late-ninth-century ritual-cum-prayerbook from the abbey of Nonantola, in northern Italy. The prayer appears in the book's order for the visitation of the sick.[52]

> Lerida, Archivo Capitulare, 16: a pontifical from the cathedral of Roda in northern Spain, written sometime close to the year 1000.[53]

> Vienna, Österreichische Nationalbibliothek, lat. 1888: the late-tenth-century sacramentary-cum-ritual from Mainz published in part by Martin Gerbert, abbot of the monastery of Saint-Blaise in the Black Forest.[54]

> Göttingen Universitätsbibliothek, theol. 231: the late-tenth-century sacramentary from the great Anglo-Saxon foundation at Fulda published by Richter and Schönfelder.[55] As in the book from Mainz, the prayer appears, in company with a confession in Old High German, in the order of confession of a sick man or woman.

> Vatican City, Biblioteca Apostolica Vaticana, lat. 4772: a copy of a sacramentary from a house in the diocese of Mainz produced at

[51] Schmitz, *Die Bussbücher* II, 292; *Le sacramentaire grégorien* III, 117, no. 3969; A. Martini, *Il cosidetto Pontificale di Poitiers*, Rerum ecclesiasticarum Documenta, Series maior, Fontes maior 14 (Rome, 1979), 178, no. 299; *PRG* II, 20 (cap. xcix, no. 66). As its editor notes, the 'Poitiers' book has a certain amount of pentiential material in common with Cologne, Bibliothek des Metropolitankapitels, 106, a *libellus precum* from Tours, ed. A. Wilmart, *Precum Libelli Quattuor Aevi Karolini* (Rome, 1940).
[52] Ed. J. Morinus, *Commentarius historicus de disciplina in adminstratione sacramenti penitentiae* (Antwerp, 1682), pp. 18 and 22. For a description of the book, see G. Gulotta and J. Ruysschaert, *Gli antichi cataloghi e i codici della abbazia di Nonantola*, 2 vols, Studi et Testi 182a–b (Vatican City, 1955) I, 304–23, and further, pp. 119–20, below.
[53] Ed. J. R. B. Planas, *El sacramentari, ritual i pontifical de Roda* (Barcelona, 1975), p. 377 (cap. xxxvi, no. 50). *CLLA*, no. 1575.
[54] Gerbert, *Monumenta* II, 31, with *OR* I, 404–19 for a description of the book as a whole. On the confession and its relation to Old High German in general, see J. N. Bostock, *A Handbook of Old High German Literature* (Oxford, 1955), pp. 135–6. On the surviving confessional formulae in Old English, see M. Förster, 'Zum Liturgik der angelsächsischen Kirche', *Anglia* 66 (1942), 1–51, esp. 1–42.
[55] Ed. G. Richter and G. Schönfelder, *Sacramentarium Fuldense saeculi X*, repr. HBS 101 (London, 1977), p. 283, no. 2378.

Arezzo in the mid-eleventh-century. In Arezzo, an extensive penitential containing the prayer *Omnipotens deus qui dixit qui me confessus*
(in the form of a benediction) was worked in.[56] Volterra, Biblioteca
Guarnacciana, XLVIII. 2. 3, an early-twelfth-century missal-cum-
ritual from a house in central Italy, later owned by Ugo, bishop of
Volterra (1173–84), contains a related order.[57]

Oxford, Magdalen College, 226: a mid-twelfth-century pontifical
from Christ Church, Canterbury, and in a number of later, related
books.[58]

London, British Library, Cotton Vespasian, D. xv, fols 1–67: a
booklet of pontifical services written at Canterbury in the late twelfth
century, but at Exeter soon after.[59] The prayer figures on fol. 35v.

Oxford, Bodleian Library, Barlow 7: an early-fourteenth-century
manual from Evesham Abbey.[60]

London, British Library, Harley 5289: a late-fourteenth-century
missal from Durham Cathedral.[61]

and in the manual printed for the chapter of Lincoping Cathedral,
southern Sweden, in 1525.[62]

Jungmann thought *Omnipotens deus qui dixit* a tenth century composition, but it is clearly older, and doubtless Italian in origin, presumably
having found its way to the diocese of Mainz (in which Fulda lies) in
one of the books introduced by Boniface or one of his pupils.[63] Finally
we have a short rubric which, so far as I have been able to establish, only
otherwise occurs complete in the 'Irish penitential' that Warren said he

---

[56] For a description of the book, see Ebner, *Quellen*, pp. 224–7. The penitential is ed.
Schmitz, *Die Bussbücher* II, 403–7.

[57] Ed. M. Bocci, 'Il messaletto votivo e rituale di Ugo', *De sancti Hugonis actis liturgicis*,
Documenti della Chiesa Volterrana 1 (Florence, 1984), p. 299. See *CLLA* Suppl., p. 111,
for further literature.

[58] Ed. H. A. Wilson, *The Pontifical of Magdalen College*, HBS 39 (London, 1910), pp.
153 and 284–5.

[59] The book's contents are briefly described by J. Brückmann, 'Latin manuscript pontificals and benedictionals in England and Wales', *Traditio* 29 (1973), 391–458, at 436–7.

[60] Ed. H. A. Wilson, *Officium ecclesiasticarum abbatum secundum usum Eveshamensis
monasterii*, HBS 6 (London, 1893), col. 79.

[61] Ed. J. T. Fowler, *The Rites of Durham*, Surtees Society 107 (Durham, 1903), p. 177.

[62] Ed. J. Freisen, *Manuale Lincopense, Breviarium Scarense, Manuale Åboense.
Katholische Ritualbücher Schwedens und Finlands im Mittelalter* (Paderborn, 1904), p. 80.

[63] J. A. Jungmann, *Die lateinischen Bussriten in ihrer geschichtlichen Entwicklung*,
Forschungen zur Geschichte des Innerkirchlichen Liebens 3–4 (Innsbruck, 1932), p. 210.

had found at St Gall.[64] In fact the book is not a pentential at all, but a fragmentary mid-ninth-century miscellany from Fulda, now Basel Universitätsbibliothek F. iii. 15e, as Dom Louis Gougaud had probably deduced in 1910. The *ordo* (fols 10v–11v) is a marginal addition of the early tenth century (according to Bischoff), possibly intended to accompany the *Capitulare* of Theodulf of Orléans, which occupies the preceding section (fols 1r–9v) of the manuscript.[65] In the following comparison the text of *A* is given on the left, and that published by Warren on the right.

A.	*Fulda.*
Et si homo intellectus sit, da ei consilium ut ueniat ad te statuto tempore, aut ad alium sacerdotem in coena domini, ut reconcilietur ab eo, quia quod manens in corpore consecutus non fuerit, hoc est, reconciliationem, exutus carne consequi poterit.	Et si homo ingeniosus est, da ei consilium ut ueniat statuto tempore ad te aut ad alium sacerdotem in cena domini, et reconciliaretur sic in sacramentario continetur. Quicquid manens in corpore consecutus non fuerit, hoc est reconciliatio, exutus carne consequi non potuerit. Si uero minus intelligens fuerit, quod ipse non intelligit, in uno statu reconciliare potes eum . . .

Warren's Fulda rubric also has elements of the rubric of a fragmentary early-ninth-century sacramentary from Gellone, now Montpellier, Bibliothèque municipale, 12. Its text, which was published by Martène in the eighteenth century, reads: *Item si tempus habueris, sicut in sacramentario continetur. Si tibi non uacat, istae sufficiunt reconciliationi penitentis*, 'istae' being the two prayers that follow. Whoever inserted the rubric in *A* intelligently struck out the redundant phrase *sicut in sacramentario continetur*: *A* itself is the *sacramentarium* concerned.[66] The gist of the rubric was also known in northern Spain and England in the tenth century. Vich, Museo Episcopal, 66, an eleventh-century sacramentary from the abbey of Vich in northern Spain has, embedded in a set of more extensive directions, the words: *Et si homo intellectuosus est, dona ei consilium ut ueniat statuto tempore ad te*; and the short order attached to a copy of the penitential of Egbert, archbishop of York, preserved in Oxford, Bodleian Library, Bodley 718, which was written

---

[64] Warren, *The Liturgy and Ritual of the Celtic Church*, pp. 151–2.
[65] See *DACL* 2.ii, cols 2969–3032, at 2977, and Bischoff, *Katalog* I, nos 276–7.
[66] Martène, *AER*, Bk. I, cap. vi, art vi, ordo 6. See also G. Martimort, *La documentation*, p. 331, no. 605.

at Canterbury in the late tenth century, has on fol. 15v the instruction: *Post expletum paenitentiam, si homo intelligibilis ueniat ad sacerdotem et reconciliatur ab eo. Si uero simplex uel brutus fuerit, statim reconciliet eum.* Two prayers follow, as in Martène's sacramentary.[67] The relationship between these *ordines* is likely to be complex since the texts involved seem constantly to have been revised, taken out of context and reunited in varying formats at different houses and times. But given that the prayer *Omnipotens deus qui dixit,* which is certainly neither Frankish nor Carolingian, and *A*'s rubric were both known at Fulda, it seems reasonable to conclude first, that the underlying *ordo* is either north Italian (as its presence at Vich and Gellone tends to suggest) or insular in origin, and probably ancient; and second, that it was adopted early by the Anglo-Saxon church. It remains to say that *A*'s penitential order for Maundy Thursday (nos 766–70) is fairly normal: an expanded version appears later in Andrieu's *Ordo L* and in the Romano-German Pontifical.[68]

(iii) the provision of masses for the Tuesday and Wednesday before Ascension Day (always a Thursday). The formulae adopted for the Tuesday (nos 970–5) are essentially those adopted in a series of 'Eighth-Century Gelasian' masses *in letania uel quacumque tribulatione*; while those for Wednesday (nos 976–81) seem to be a stock set, since they also turn up in St Petersburg Q. v. I. 41, the late-ninth-century 'Saint-Amand' sacramentary produced for Tournai, and later, in Orléans, Bibliothèque municipale, 127 [105], a late-tenth-century sacramentary from the abbey of Winchcombe in Gloucestershire. The prayers normally affected for these days elsewhere are those of BNF lat. 12051.[69]

(iv) the text of the Exultet preface (no. 805). For the most part the text of this preface, which was normally read by the deacon after the Paschal Candle had been blessed, is fairly standard. However, in the third or possibly fourth decade of the tenth century nine lines towards the foot of on fol. 111v were erased and re-written in a somewhat cramped manner

---

[67] See *El sacramentario de Vich*, ed. A. Olivar, Monumenta Hispaniae sacra 4 (Barcelona, 1953), p. 285. *CLLA*, no. 960. On Bodley 718, see A. J. Frantzen, *The Literature of Penance in Anglo-Saxon England* (New Brunswick, New Jersey, 1983), pp. 169–72, with R. Gameson, 'The origin of the Exeter Book of Old English Poetry', *ASE* 25 (1996), 135–85, at 162–79.

[68] *OR* V, 192–202.

[69] See Dumas and Deshusses, *Liber Sacramentorum Gellonensis* I, 415–18, nos 2681–98; *Le sacramentaire grégorien* I, 696, nos 139*–44*; A. Davril, *The Winchcombe Sacramentary*, HBS 109 (London, 1995), pp. 104–6; and PL 78, cols 107–8.

by a scribe whose hand appears elsewhere in the manuscript.[70] Since the passage he supplied cannot possibly have been in the original – *A*'s scribe would have needed twice the number of lines to write it – it seems clear that his aim was to include something new rather than simply rewrite lines that had become worn or illegible. So the question is: how did the preface run at this point originally? Now, as Thomas Kelly has recently shown, the text of the Exultet preface attracted the attentions of revisers and abridgers at numerous houses throughout Europe; and one of the largest changes regularly to have been made was the suppression of the short section on Adam's sin and the long and rather affecting passages in praise of the bee: in other words from *O certe necessarium ade peccatum* to *in qua terrenis celestia iunguntur* in the versions given in Frankish 'Eighth-century Gelasian' sacramentaries. The earliest book to excise this material seems to have been the Romano-German Pontifical of *c.* 950.[71] But it is quite clear that the lines in praise of the bee had been dropped at least a half century before as they were not only omitted in *A*, but also in the late-ninth-century sacramentaries from Tours.[72] *A*'s text, at the relevant point, must have run:

> Qui licet diuisus in partes, mutuati luminis detrimenta non nouit. Alitur liquentibus cereis quam in substantiam pretiose huius lampades apis mater eduxit. O uere et beata nox que expoliauit egyptios ditauit hebreos nox in qua terrenis celestia iunguuntur. Oramus te domine ut cereus iste in honorem nominis tui consecratus ad noctis huius caliginem destruendam indeficiens perseueret.

That *A* and the Tours books should have a shortened text takes on an even greater significance when one realises, as Kelly indicated, that similarly short versions appear in a number of sources from central Italy, notably:[73]

> Vatican, Biblioteca Vaticana Apostolica, San Pietro, F. 12: an early-eleventh-century sacramentary not from Rome, as Ebner thought, but Florence.[74]

---

[70] Illustr. Nicholson, *Early Bodleian Music* III, pl. XXVII.
[71] T. F. Kelly, *The Exultet in Southern Italy* (Oxford, 1996), esp. 65–9, 272–89, and 289–302.
[72] See *Le sacramentaire grégorien* I, 362, no. 1022b.
[73] Kelly, *The Exultet*, p. 69, notes 100 and 102.
[74] Described *op. cit.*, pp. 185–6.

Rome, Biblioteca Vallicellana, B. 8: a late-eleventh-century sacramentary from the abbey of Sant'Eutizio at Norcia, near Spoleto. Judging by its decoration, copied from a much older book.[75]

Vatican, Biblioteca Vaticana Apostolica, San Pietro, F. 14: a mid-twelfth-century sacramentary from the church of S. Trifone in Rome.[76]

and Vatican, Biblioteca Vaticana Apostolica, San Pietro, B. 78: a fourteenth-century breviary from the abbey of Sant'Eutizio, Norcia.[77]

Any one of these could easily preserve an early form of central Italian text, that is to say, a type of text not known to the compilers of the Frankish Gelasians, but one perhaps later sought out by the man or men who compiled the Romano-German Pontifical. *A*'s Exultet preface may well be 'received' Italian too. We will come to the closing formula, *Precamur*, in due course.

To sum up, *A*'s temporal is by no means as straightforward as it might appear. For now and again, lying beneath the main, revised text, we can catch glimpses of the 'Eighth-Century Gelasian' from which *A* was copied. Sometimes, as in the case of the Pentecostal Sundays, the view is clear. As far as the comparatively extensive and patently 'insular' penitential *ordo* for Ash Wednesday is concerned, our question must be: how far does it go back? With Fulda and Mainz in view, the eighth century seems certain, but it could easily be much older, perhaps even as old as St Augustine's mission. It may be easier to tell when further early *ordines* for the day, especially those in Italian books, have found their way into print. But that is not to say that those from other parts of Europe should be passed over. Indeed, the one preserved in Paris, Bibliothèque nationale de France, lat. 13764, a late-ninth-century ritual written at Saint-Amand for Reims Cathedral looks to be an exceptionally interesting (and lengthy) hybrid.[78] A good deal of work remains. However, we must now direct our attention to *A*'s sanctoral.

---

[75] See P. Pirri, 'La scuola miniaturistica di S. Eutizio', *Scriptorium* 3 (1949), 3–10, Pls 4–6a.

[76] Described by Ebner, *Quellen*, pp. 187–8.

[77] See Garrison, 'Contributions', pp. 162–4, note 4.

[78] See E. Palazzo, 'Les deux rituels d'un *libellus* de Saint-Amand (Paris, Bibliothèque nationale, lat. 13764)', in *Rituels. Mélanges offerts à Pierre-Marie Gy, O. P.*, ed. P. de Clerck and E. Palazzo (Paris, 1990), pp. 423–36.

The Sanctoral (nos 1312–1856)

The first point to note about *A*'s sanctoral, its series of saints' masses in other words, is that it is separate. As Hohler, Yitzhak Hen and others have indicated, this is unusual. There are only five earlier (complete) books arranged in this way: Vat. Reg. lat. 316, the so-called 'Old Gelasian' sacramentary; Stockholm Holm A. 136, the late-ninth-century sacramentary written at Saint-Amand for Ansegis, bishop of Sens; Milan, Biblioteca del Capitolo metropolitano, D. 3–3, the late-ninth-century sacramentary from the convent of S. Simpliciano; and Paris, Bibliothèque nationale de France, lat. 9433, a late-ninth-century sacramentary from the abbey of Echternach.[79] Both Hohler and Hen have suggested that separate *sanctoralia* are an 'English symptom'; and they may well be right.[80] But we are then faced with the question of why these books were arranged this way in the first place. Hohler stated of the 'Old Gelasian' that:[81]

> The purpose of the separate sanctoral would then have been not to predetermine the liturgical calendar of any church but to check whether an Italian prayer was available for a saint who happened to figure in such a calendar. The process of forming a separate sanctoral, other than one logically assembling all immoveable feasts including Christmas implies a feeling that saint's days are secondary; and that this feeling is still alive is shown when Candlemas and Lady day, as feasts of our Lord join Christmas in the temporal.

Having like masses together would certainly make life easier: but only for someone interested in saints' days rather than the prayers provided in the temporal, which runs perfectly predictably from Sunday to Sunday. But an easier life for whom? The answer is probably the bishop or archbishop, since the sacramentary from which Vat. Reg. lat. 316 was

---

[79] Ed. respectively, Wilson, *The Gelasian Sacramentary*, and L. C. Mohlberg, *Liber Sacramentorum Romanae ecclesiae ordinis anni circuli*, Rerum ecclesiasticarum Documenta, Series maior, Fontes 4 (Rome, 1960); Frei, *Das ambrosianische Sakramentar D. 3–3* ; *Le sacramentaire grégorien* under the siglum T4 (see note 36 above); and Y. Hen, *The Sacramentary of Echternach*, HBS 110 (London, 1997). See also N. A. Orchard, 'Some notes on the Sacramentary of Echternach', *Archiv für Liturgiewissenschaft* (forthcoming).

[80] Hohler, 'Books', pp. 61–2; Hen, *The Sacramentary of Echternach*, pp. 33–4.

[81] Hohler, 'Books', p. 62.

copied; *A*; and the Stockholm manuscript were all made for or owned by such men. To be able to find with speed the mass for such-and-such a saint, without having to leaf through half the book to find it, would doubtless be a help to a busy prelate, especially one visiting and officiating at another church. Singers soldiered on for centuries with books that had both *propria* combined; and so did readers. But for the bishop and archbishop things were different, and we find, especially in England, that the *propria* of benedictionals were regularly separated out too, though the earliest benedictional with a separate sanctoral that has come down to us seems to be that of the sacramentary of Gellone, which was copied, as we have seen, for Hildoard, bishop of Cambrai.[82] Perhaps Hildoard simply had an English book to hand which he caused to be written out anew. That the monks of Echternach and the nuns of S. Simpliciano possessed sacramentaries with separate *propria* merely tends to illustrate the fact that from time to time episcopal or archiepiscopal books could find their way to other houses, where they were taken over more or less complete. The book underlying BNF lat. 9433 may have come from Trier, Tours or possibly even some English cathedral; and in this respect it is worth mentioning that England almost certainly supplied the model for BNF lat. 9432, the early-tenth-century sacramentary from Amiens, which not only has a separate sanctoral too, but additionally, and quite unexpectedly, a mass for St Nicander of Naples (17 June), whose feast is one of those found by the Old English Martyrologist in the 'old mass-book'.[83] The question of the origins of separate sanctoralia, however, requires further investigation.

Turning now to what *A* contains. We have benedictions and prefaces from the Supplement in their proper places throughout, as in the temporal. The saint's masses of the *Hadrianum* are all present, normally with their Hadrianic formulae, but there are exceptions, as Hohler indicated. St Michael Archangel (29 Sept.), for instance, has the normal 'Gelasian' *super populum* and a rare prayer for vespers, *Deus qui per*

---

[82] Ed. Dumas and Deshusses, *Liber Sacramentorum Gellonensis* I, 264–300, nos 1987–2100.

[83] On the book itself, see Delisle, 'Mémoire', at pp. 325–45; Leroquais, *Les sacramentaires* I, 38–43, with Orchard, 'St Willibrord, St Richarius, and Anglo-Saxon symptoms', pp. 263–70. *CLLA*, no. 910. On the 'old mass-book', see *Das ältenglische Martyrologium*, ed. G. Kotzor, Bayerische Akademie der Wissenschaften phil.-hist. Klasse, Abhandlungen ns 88, 2 vols (Munich, 1981) II, 122, and B. Bischoff and M. Lapidge, *Biblical Commentaries from the Canterbury School of Theodore and Hadrian* (Cambridge, 1995), pp. 155–72.

beatissimum archangelum tuum Michahelem (no. 1746), which appears in the following books:

Vatican City, Biblioteca Apostolica Vaticana, Ottob. lat. 145: a mid-eleventh-century collectar-cum-manual from Monte Cassino.[84]

London, British Library, Harley 2961: a collectar written at Exeter *c.* 1050–70 for Leofric.[85]

Rome, Biblioteca Vallicellana, E. 52: a late-eleventh-century collectar from the monastery of Sant' Eutizio near Spoleto. The prayer figures on fols 73v–4r.

Oxford, Bodleian Library, Canon. Lit. 320: an early-twelfth-century ritual-cum-breviary from Citta di Castello. *Deus qui per beatissimum* occurs on fol. 61r.

Oxford, Bodleian Library, Canon. Lit. 345: a mid-twelfth-century sacramentary from Pistoia. The prayer is adopted for the May and September feasts of the saint: fols 116v and 140r.

and the breviary printed in 1510 for the chapter of Agde in southern France.[86]

Deus qui per beatissimum is almost certainly central or northern Italian in origin, and presumably found its way from *A* into Leofric's collectar at Exeter. *A* after all was his book too. Other 'non-Gregorian' symptoms worth noting are the presence of the name of St Maximus, a 'Gelasian' saint, in the superscription of the otherwise 'Gregorian' mass in honour of SS Tiburtius and Valerian (14 Apr.); the adoption of 'Gelasian' rather than 'Gregorian' prayers for the feasts of SS Simplicius, Faustinus, Beatrix and Felix (28 July), and the Vigil of St Andrew (29 Nov.) (nos 1572–4 and 1835–9); and the extended superscription for the mass of the Four Crowned Martyrs (8 Nov.), which reads (no. 1795):

Quattuor coronatorum nomina haec sunt, seuerus, seuerianus, uictorinus, et carpophorus, quorum dies natalis per incuriam neglectus minime repperiri poterat, ideo statutum est ut in eorum

[84] Ed. K. Gamber and S. Rehle, *Manuale Casinense*, Textus patristici et liturgici 13 (Regensburg, 1977), p. 140, no. 436.

[85] Ed. E. S. Dewick and W. H. Frere, *The Leofric Collectar*, 2 vols, HBS 45 and 56 (London, 1914–21) I, col. 237.

[86] See J. Lemarie, 'Textes relatifs au culte de l'Archange et des Anges dans les bréviaires manuscrits du Mont-Saint-Michel', *Sacris Erudiri* 13 (1963), 113–52, at 151–2.

ecclesia horum quinque sanctorum qui in missa recitantur, illorum etiam natalis celebretur, ut cum istis eorum quoque memoria.

The five saints named in the prayers of mass are: Claudius, Nicostratus, Simphorianus, Castorius and Simplius, the standard 'Hadrianic' saints.[87] As Dom Quentin showed in 1908, the confusion over which set of martyrs were genuine seems to have stemmed first from the *Liber Pontificalis*, more particularly the writer who dealt with the activities of Pope Leo IV (847–55); and second, from Ado, the martyrologist. According to his biographer, Pope Leo, for some undisclosed reason, had the relics of what were thought to be the 'Martyrs' searched out, and once found, translated to high altar of the basilica on the Coelian Hill, where they were enshrined *cum Claudio, Nicostrato, Simphoriano atque Castori et Simplicio, necnon Seuero, Seueriano, Carpoforo et Victorino, iv fratribus, verumtamen, Marius, Audifax et Abbacuc, Felicissimo et Agapito.* Evidently, and rather disturbingly, the true names of the 'Martyrs' were generally not recognised in Rome, even though they appeared correctly in the copies of the *Hadrianum* used in St Peter's, the Vatican, and countless other churches and chapels throughout the city: and in his attempt to unravel the complexities of the matter, Ado, a decade or so later, simply made matters worse by introducing Severus, Severianus, Carpophorus and Victorinus as rightful claimants to the title.[88] Since no-one before Ado had made this claim, he, then, is likely to be the source from which the compiler of the superscription took his or her lead. This is important not only for *A*, that is to say for the Arras-Tours book used in its making, but also, and possibly more so, for BNF lat. 12051, the ninth-century sacramentary-cum-pontifical possibly written at Corbie for Beauvais, and for Reims, Bibliothèque municipale, 213, the ninth-century sacramentary of Noyon.[89] For Ado's martyr-ology, which is generally agreed to have been drawn up in 858, necessarily provides us with a *terminus ante quem non*. A reduced version of the superscription figures in BL Loans 36 (14), the mid

---

[87] Ed. *Le sacramentaire grégorien* I, 284, nos 739–41.

[88] See H. Quentin, *Les martyrologes historiques* (Paris, 1908), pp. 504–5; H. Delehaye, 'Le culte des Quatre Coronnés à Rome', *AB* 32 (1913), 63–71; and A. Amore, 'Il problema dei SS Quattro Coronati', in *Miscellanea Amato Pietro Frutaz*, ed. C. Egger (Rome, 1978), 123–46.

[89] Ed. PL 78, col. 147; *Le sacramentaire grégorien* I, 706, no. 295*. Also see PL 101, col. 1230.

to late-tenth-century sacramentary-cum-pontifical from Noyon.[90] No further versions have so far come to light.

In addition to its complement of masses for 'Gregorian' feasts and saints, *A* contains a number of pure 'Eighth-Century Gelasians'. They are:

SS Mary and Martha (19 Jan.).	St Vitus (15 June).
SS Emerentiana and Macharius (23 Jan.).	Translation of St Benedict (11 July).
Conversion of St Paul (25 Jan.).	St James (25 July).
St Iuliana (16 Feb).	Macchabees (1 Aug.).
Cathedra Petri (22 Feb.).	St Donatus (7 Aug.).
Invention of the Cross (3 May).	Octave of St Laurence (17 Aug.).
SS Nereus, Achilleus and Pancras (12 May).	St Bartholomew (24 Aug.).
	St Gorgonius (9 Sept.).
SS Primus and Felicianus (9 June).	Vigil of St Matthew (20 Sept.).
	St Matthew (21 Sept.).
SS Basilides, Cyrinus, Nabor and Nazarius (12 June).	St Luke (18 Oct.).
	Vigil of SS Simon and Jude

Although fifteen of these are provided with their standard 'Eighth-Century Gelasian' proper prefaces in the Supplement, it is clear that *A*'s scribe copied something other than the Supplement, for a number of its prefaces are not taken up. That should not come as too much of a surprise, though. No surviving book adopts all the masses it apparently prescribes, and anyone with a copy of the *Hadrianum* will, in any case, have had to find the collects, secrets and postcommunions to accompany the Supplement's prefaces for themselves. But as we have seen, *A* is essentially a modified copy of an 'Eighth-Century Gelasian' book, and assuming that this precursor was something like the sacramentary of Gellone, then the process at work should mainly be one of omission, not addition. However, two 'old' prefaces were probably left in place or adapted (nos 1702 and 1854): those for the feasts of the Exaltation of the Cross (3 May) and St Thomas (21 Dec.). Both are rare. The former is only otherwise found (as a cotidian) in Prague, Metropolitan Library, O. 83, a late-eighth-century sacramentary from Regensburg that later found its way to Prague:[91]

---

[90] BL Loans 36 (14), p. 263.
[91] Ed. A. Dold and L. Eizenhöfer, *Das Prager Sakramentar*, Texte und Arbeiten 38–42 (Beuron, 1944–9) II (text), 125*, no. 234, 2. *CLLA*, no. 630.

A.	*Prague.*
Qui crucem ascendit, sanguinem fudit, et omnem mundum a peccato redemit. Ipse est enim agnus dei, ipse qui abstulit peccata mundi. Qui numquam moritur immolatus, et semper uiuit occisus. Quem laudant.	Qui crucem ascendit, sanguinem fudit et omnem mundum a peccato redemit. Ipse est agnus dei, qui tollit peccata mundi, qui numquam moritur, sed semper uiuit occisus, ipsum <adorauit per> angeli et archangeli adorant.

and the latter, as Hohler indicated, is a version of a formula for SS Peter and Paul, in the late-sixth-century 'Leonine' sacramentary, now Verona, Biblioteca Comunale, 85:[92]

A.	*'Leonine'.*
Qui secundum promissionem tuam domine ineffabile constitutum apostoli tui thomę confessionis superna dispensatione largiris. Vt in ueritate tua fundamine soliditate, nulla mortifere falsitatis iura praeualeant. Per quem maiestatem.	Qui secundum promissionis tuae ineffabile constitutum apostolicae confessionis superna dispensatione largiris, ut in ueritatis tuae fundamine soliditate nulla mortiferae falsitatis iura praeualeant, et quantalibet exsistat errantium multitudo, illi sint redemptionis tuae filii et illis aeclesia tota numeretur, qui ab electorum tuorum principali traditione non dissonant. Per.

But the matter of whether *A*'s prayers for the feast of the Decollation of St John the Baptist (29 Aug.) were those of its model remains open to doubt, for the formulae stipulated for the day (nos 1671–6) are those of BNF lat. 12051 (and its relatives), not those of 'true' 'Eighth-Century Gelasian' sacramentaries. Safe to say no other book has the same selection of 'Gregorian' and 'Gelasian' feasts as *A*. The sacramentaries of Saint-Amand are close, and so too is that of Echternach, but they are larger, and the prayers chosen often different. Perhaps the best match is Cambrai BM 162–3; but it cannot have been the reviser's model by any means.

Last, we have seven feasts belonging neither to the Gregorian nor the 'Eighth-Century Gelasian' cursus. They are:

St Matthias (24 Feb.).
Depostion of St Benedict (20 Mar.).
St Maurice and companions (22 Sept.).
St Jerome (30 Sept.).

---

[92] Ed. L. C. Mohlberg, *Sacramentarium Veronense*, Rerum ecclesiasticarum Documenta, Series maior, Fontes 1 (Rome, 1956), p. 37, no. 282.

SS Denis, Rusticus and Eleutherius (9 Oct.).
Vigil of All Saints (31 Nov.).
All Saints (1 Oct.).

Generally speaking these are not uncommon in ninth and tenth-century books, nor, for the most part, are the prayers provided in *A*. There are two notable exceptions, however. The formulae adopted for St Maurice (nos 1730–34), which appear for the first time in Paris, Bibliothèque nationale de France, lat. 816, an 'Eighth-Century Gelasian' sacramentary possibly written for Siderammus, bishop of Angoulême (801–44), and half a century later, in a handful of books from northern France, were never particularly popular. Sets have come down to us from Tours, Noyon by way of Saint-Amand, Echternach and insofar as the ninth and early tenth centuries are concerned, that is that.[93] *A*'s mass has every chance, then, of being northern French; and given that it turns up at Tours, it seems fair to conclude that the formulae appear in *A* simply because they appeared in the Arras-Tours book used by *A*'s reviser. But *A*'s secret and postcommunion for St Denis and his companions (nos 1757–8), which are derived from the normal mass for the commons of many martyrs in 'Eighth-Century Gelasian' sacramentaries and their descendents, as the following comparison will show, is unlikely to have arrived by the same route:[94]

A.	*'Eighth-Century Gelasian'.*
Salutari sacrificio domine populus tuus semper exultet, quo et debitus honor sacris martyribus exhibetur, et sanctificationis tuae munus adquiritur. Per	Salutari sacrificio domine populus tuus semper exultet, quo et debitus honor sacris martyribus exhibetur, et sanctificationis tuae munus adquiritur. Per.
Haec domine quae sumpsimus uotiua mysteria, festa celebrantes sollemnia, quae pro beatorum martyrum tuorum, dionysii, rusticii et eleutherii, gloriosa passione peregimus, ipsorum nobis quesumus fiant intercessione salutaria, in quorum natalitiis sunt exultanter impleta. Per.	Celebrantes quae pro martyrum tuorum illorum beata passione peregimus . . . . . . ipsorum nobis quesumus fiant intercessione salutaria in quorum nataliciis sunt exultanter impleta. Per.

[93] See *Liber Sacramentorum Engolismensis*, ed. P. Saint-Roch, CCSL 159C (Turnhout, 1987), pp. 200–1, nos 1355–8; *Le sacramentaire grégorien* II, 322, nos 3598–3601 and 3702; and *The Sacramentary of Echternach*, ed. Hen, pp. 300–1, nos 1435, 1437, 1440 and 1441.

[94] See for instance, *Le sacramentaire grégorien* II, 270, nos 3260–1.

Normally, we should expect to find:[95]

> *Collecta.* Deus qui hodierna die beatum dionisium martyrem tuum
> uirtute . . . aduersa formidare. Per.
> *Secreta.* Hostia domine quesumus quam in sanctorum tuorum . . .
> dona conciliet. Per.
> *Praefatio.* Qui sanctorum martyrum tuorum pia certamina . . .
> munera capiamus. Per christum.
> *Ad complendum.* Quesumus omnipotens deus ut qui caelestia
> alimenta . . . aduersa muniamur. Per.

A only has the collect. That a French house should have been unable to
produce a standard set of propers for the saint if required would be
strange to say the least. So it may well be that Hohler was right in thinking that the man overseeing the making of *A,* finding that the feast was
not encompassed in the book he had acquired from Arras (there is certainly none in Cambrai BM 162–3), made up a mass on the spot in order
to bring *A* more into line with its marginal gradual. Cues for the feast are
found in books of chant as least as old as the ninth century, the best
known example being Monza, Biblioteca capitolare, fol. 1/101, the
beautiful but fragmentary gradual from a house, possibly Bergamo, in
northern Italy; and St Denis' name regularly occurs in the Canon of
books from all over Europe too.[96] Equally, it may be that *A*'s non-
standard non-French mass simply came into the underlying 'Eighth-
Century Gelasian' as an addition.

But far and away the most unusual feature of the sanctoral, aside from
its separateness, is the position of St Mark's day: the 18th of May, which
is his 'English' day. His feast is entered on this date in a fragment of a
mid-eighth-century calendar in Northumbrian script that later found its
way to the abbey of Illmunster and which is now Munich, Bayerisch
Hauptstaatsarchivs, Rariten-Selekt, 108; in all copies of the late-eighth-
century metrical martyrology composed at York; and in certain versions
of the so-called *Martyrologium Hieronymianum,* the earliest of which is

[95] See *Le sacramentaire gregorien* I, 704, nos 258*–61*, and II, nos 3636–9.
[96] *Antiphonale missarum sextuplex,* ed. A. Hesbert (Brussels, 1935), no. 158b. *CLLA*, no.
1336. The late-ninth-century Saint-Amand cues for the feast are ed. Netzer, *L'introduction,*
p. 341.

Berne, Burgerbibliothek, 289, late-eighth-century from Metz.[97] And it also figures in the calendars of the following:

Salisbury Cathedral Library, 150: a psalter written for a nunnery in the south of England in the period 969–87. Wilton and Shaftesbury, only twenty miles away from each other, are both possible.[98]

Bodley 579 (Leofric B): written at Christ Church, Canterbury in Dunstan's time.[99]

BL Add. 37517: the so-called 'Bosworth Psalter'; an addition written at and for St Augustine's, Canterbury c. 1000.[100]

Paris, Bibliothèque nationale de France, lat. 819: a sacramentary copied at Liège in the mid eleventh century from an English model. The book was later at the abbey of Saint-Bertin.[101]

and London, British Library, Cotton Vitellius A. xii: a partial copy of a calendar similar to the ones embodied in Leofric B and the 'Bosworth Psalter' written at Salisbury in the late eleventh century.[102]

There is nothing from France after c. 780, and the sole book from the Low Countries derives from an English model. Indeed, the only other place in Europe that seems to have venerated the evangelist on the 18th of May is northern Italy, as a skeletal early-tenth-century ordinal from a

[97] K. Gamber, *Das Bonifatius-Sakramentar*, Textus Patristici et Liturgici 12 (Regensburg, 1972), 51; A. Wilmart, 'Un témoin anglo-saxon du calendrier métrique d'York', *RB* 46 (1934), 41–6, at 57 and 66, with M. Lapidge, 'A tenth-century metrical calendar from Ramsey', *RB* 94 (1984), 326–70, esp. 327–42; and *Martyrologium Hieronymianum*, ed. G. B. de Rossi and L. Duchesne, *Acta Sanctorum Novembris* II.i (Brussels, 1894), 1–156, at 62. On the Berne manuscript, see J. P. Kirsch, 'Die Berner Handschrift des Martyrologium Hieronymianum', *Romische Quartalschrift für christliche Altertumskunde und für Kirchengeschichte* 31 (1923), 113–24.
[98] *EK*, p. 20. See D. Stroud, 'The provenance of the Salisbury Psalter', *The Library*, 6th series, 1 (1979), 225–35.
[99] *EK*, p. 48. On the calendar as a whole, see below p. 158.
[100] *Op. cit.*, p. 62. See below, pp. 158, 178–9.
[101] See the synopsis in *Catalogus codicum hagiographicorum latinorum qui asservantur in Biblioteca Nationali Parisiensi*, {ed. Bollandists}, 3 vols (Brussels, 1889–93) III, 581–733, at 589 and 648.
[102] *EK*, p. 90, where the calendar is probably wrongly ascribed to Exeter. On Vitellius A. xii's Salisbury scribes, see T. Webber, *Scribes and Scholars at Salisbury Cathedral, c. 1075–c. 1125* (Oxford, 1992), pp. 14, 23, 144–5 and 159. Note that the calendar of Cambridge University Library, Kk. 5. 32, an early-eleventh-century psalter from some house in the west country, has an entry for some undisclosed feast of St Luke on 18 May. In London, British Library, Cotton Vitellius A. xviii, the sacramentary of Giso of Wells, the evangelist becomes pope. *Op. cit.*, pp. 76 and 104.

house near or in Bologna and the calendar of Canon Lit. 345, a twelfth-century sacramentary from Pistoia, indicate, though it must be said that the prayers provided for mass in the Pistoia book were to be said on the saint's 'normal' day in April.[103] A search through the two hundred or so Italian calendars transcribed by Edward Garrison has failed to turn up further examples. We are therefore faced with two questions. On what authority, if any, was the feast moved to May, and why did England persist in celebrating the saint as it did when Europe as a whole had settled on the 25th of April? The answer to the first lies in the apocryphal acts of St Mark.

The marble calendar of Naples, which was drawn up in the mid eighth century, has two entries for the evangelist: one on the 25th of April entitled *Passio sancti Marci evangelistae*, and another on the 17th of May entitled *Natale sancti Marci evangelistae*.[104] The date on which this second entry occurs is significant. In his anaylsis of the apocryphal writings surrounding the life of St Mark, Richard Lipsius dealt at some length with the matter of which churches kept the evangelist's feast on which days. The Armenians, for instance, favoured the 24th of March; but the Copts, Arabs, the Latin West, and the majority of Greek houses adopted the 25th of April, which was chosen, as Lipsius showed, because the most common version of the saint's acts related that his *passio* took place on the day after the Ethiopic feast of Sarapis (24 April).[105] What is important for our purposes though, is the fact that almost all surviving versions of these acts end with a dating clause. In the Greek, St Mark is said to have died on the seventeenth day of the Hebrew month of Nisan in the reign of Emperor Gaius. In one Latin translation, however, the day is given as the eighteenth of Nisan, and the year the fourteenth of Nero's reign. It seems possible, therefore, that the compiler of the marble calendar had before him, or knew the text of the Greek acts and chose to render 17 Nisan as the 17th of May, and that whoever first fixed St Mark's day on the 18th knew the Latin. Bede gives the 25th of April, and this date is accepted by the numerous martryologists who drew from his work. But the tradition of keeping the 18th of May, which may be Italian, is likely to be older than Bede since it survives 'uncorrected' in the face of all authoritative martyrologies

---

[103] For the ordinal, see G. Morin, 'Une list de fêtes chomées à Bologne à l'époque Carolingienne', *RB* 19 (1902), 353–6.

[104] H. Delehaye, 'Hagiographie Napolitaine', *AB* 57 (1939), 5–64, at 18 and 22.

[105] R. A. Lipsius, *Die apokryphalen Apostelgeschichten und Apostellegenden*, 2 vols in 3 (Brunswick, 1883–90), II.2, 321–54.

some way into the eleventh century: and we ought not lose sight of the fact that the Illmunster calendar, which is the earliest surviving witness to the celebration of St Mark's feast on this day, was written within twenty-five or so years of Bede's death. It remains to say that the *A*'s prayers for St Mark were apparently taken over from a book akin to Cambrai BM 162–3. But in company with all the books that have come down to us from Arras in particular and northern France in general, St Mark's day is given as the 25th of April. *A*'s reviser presumably 'moved' the formulae as he went about his transcribing: an unthinkable thing had *A* not been intended for use in England; and it is well to note in this connexion that a mass was still said for the saint in May at Canterbury a hundred years after *A* had been written, as we shall see.

Summarizing then, we can say with confidence, I think, that the picture presented by *A*'s sanctoral is analogous to the one presented by its temporal. On the 'surface', we have a number of texts and textual variants that appear to be typical of Arras, so far as we can tell from the one early book that survives from the house; but below these, we have material that is central and northern Italian, Anglo-Saxon and southern German in character, but never French. Had the book been copied for use in France, this would without a shadow of a doubt have been suppressed: and it is all the more significant therefore that they were not. For the reviser, whoever he was, carefully and scrupulously left *in situ* a body of material that either never appeared, or never appeared in the same form, in copies of the *Hadrianum* and its Supplement on the one hand, and Frankish, rather than Italian 'Eighth-Century Gelasians' on the other. That the revising of the underlying 'Eighth-Century Gelasian' took place when *A* as we have it today was written, and not at some earlier time, is indicated not only by the presence of a series of votive masses composed by Alcuin, which we will come to in a moment; but also by the appearance of a late-ninth-century 'martyrological' superscription for the mass for the Four Crowned Martyrs. We shall encounter yet greater concentrations of eccentric formulae, almost all of which are again Italian and Anglo-Saxon, in *A*'s pontifical and ritual. But now for the commons.

The Commons (nos 1857–1913)

'Commons', so-called, are the masses provided in sacramentaries and missals for use on the feasts of saints of various classes (martyrs, confessors, virgins and so on) for whom no propers were available. *A* encompasses all the relevant formulae set out in the Supplement, benedictions and prefaces included, but a number of extra prayers *ad populum*. Two 'Eighth-Century Gelasian' masses also appear more or less complete. The extras are interesting. We have an 'Eighth-Century Gelasian' prayer for St Andrew in the mass in honour of an apostle (no. 1862); an *ad populum* for many apostles which turns up in Trent, Museo Provinciale d'Arte (Castel del Buonconsiglio), 1590, a late-ninth-century copy of a pre-*Hadrianic* Gregorian sacramentary from Salzburg (no. 1867); two Tours propers in the masses for 'a martyr' and 'virgins' (nos 1877 and 1906); and the normal *ad populum* of Alcuin's mass for St Vedastus, *Deus qui nos sanctorum tuorum temporali tribuis*, in the mass for the feast of a confessor (no. 1893). Tours is therefore in view again; and given that this prayer began life as a prayer for confessors in the so-called 'Missale Gothicum', it seems possible that *A* preserves the form of mass used by Alcuin when he came to draw up propers for the monks of Arras. *Deus qui nos tuorum santorum*, moreover, appears in the standard Anglo-Saxon mass for St Cuthbert's day (20 Mar.), and there is some reason to believe that Alcuin was responsible for shaping his propers too.[106]

The Votives (nos 1920–2196)

'Votives' are essentially masses for special intentions, such as the safe passage of travellers, against lightning, or for particular people, notably priests, kings or the congregation present. Many different sets have come down to us, and these often vary considerably from book to book and place to place. Fulda, for instance, had a huge collection, drawn from a vast range of sources. Other communities seem to have been content with some standard set, such as the one provided in Benedict of Aniane's Supplement to the *Hadrianum*; but that said, even the briefest

---

[106] See N. A. Orchard. 'A note on the masses in honour of St Cuthbert', *RB* 105 (1995), 79–98.

of glances through Dom Deshusses's edition of the Gregorian Sacramentary shows that the Supplement was rarely taken over without some change or other having been made. *A*'s votive masses can be sorted out into three broad groups: those contained in 'Gelasian' books; those taken over from the Supplement; and those composed by Alcuin. It will be best to deal with these groups in reverse order.

Alcuin's votives

Of the 21 votive masses attributed to Alcuin by Dom Deshusses, *A* has 14. These are his masses for the Holy Trinity, Wisdom, Charity, the Cross, the Virgin, Angelic intercession, and All Saints; for the Grace of the Holy Spirit, Purity of Heart, a Living Friend, Living Friends, the Living and Dead, Sins, and for the Relics of Saints, which are, in Deshusses's discreet edition, nos 1–7, 10–15 and 22.[107] Unfortunately it is difficult at present to form a detailed picture of how Alcuin's masses circulated. A number were sent to friends and communities who in turn sent them further afield; others must simply have been copied from one book to another fairly randomly; but the task of determining which sets of prayers became particularly authoritative in different parts of Europe has yet to be attempted, and since the early books seldom agree, the evidence of later books will be critical. The sacramentary of Warmund of Ivrea, for instance, has a number of ninth-century Milanese variants, unsurprisingly perhaps, for Ivrea is only seventy or so miles away, and the famous tenth-century sacramentary of Fulda published by Richter and Schönfelder has a number of readings peculiar to the ninth-century sacramentaries of Saint-Amand, which is probably to be explained by the fact that the two types of book are related in other respects, as Hohler indicated in 1954.[108] But the closest agreement I have come across so far is between the sacramentaries of Tours and the late-ninth-century sacramentary of Echternach. The link is presumably Alcuin himself: for Beornræd, abbot of the latter (775–97) and a blood relative, not only commissioned a life of Echternach's patron, St Willibrord (7 Nov.), from him, but probably also proper masses for the vigil and day of the saint's feast. On a less microscopic level, however, quite what that means for the sacramentaries in view is hard to gauge. For, despite the claims of Deshusses and others, we still do not know how great a

---

107 J. Deshusses, 'Les messes d'Alcuin', *Archiv für Liturgiewissenshaft* 14.i (1972), 7–41.
108 Hohler, 'The type of sacramentary used by St Boniface', pp. 89–93.

part, if any, Alcuin might have played, or have been able to play, in the arranging of their principal, sometimes pre-Hadrianic, texts.[109] A good deal of work remains, and when that is undertaken, *A* should not be left out of account as it preserves among its Alcuinian votives, most of which are, from a textual standpoint, unexceptional, the rare preface for 'Charity', *Per quem discipulis spiritus sanctus* (no. 1914). We encounter this at much the same date at Echternach and in Paris, Bibliothèque nationale de France, lat. 2812, a late-ninth-century sacramentary from Arles; then, later, in Heidelburg, Universitäts-Bibliothek, Sal. IXb, a tenth-century sacramentary from the abbey of Reichenau on Lake Constance; in Cambridge, Corpus Christi College, 270, a late-eleventh-century sacramentary from St Augustine's Abbey, Canterbury, and insofar as published sources are concerned, nowhere else, so it was evidently of extremely limited and eccentric circulation.[110] Echternach, *A*, and Canterbury, might point to Alcuin: the mass otherwise has no preface of any sort. But until further examples have been brought to light, one must be cautious.

Supplement

The 36 masses taken over from the Supplement (including two of Alcuin's that had already found their way in) are, in spite of a few unusual readings, absolutely standard, and there is little to suggest that larger Gelasian masses were brought up to date by *A*'s reviser. A number of prefaces, also taken from the Supplement, appear in their proper places, as is normal in other books of the same date.

Gelasians

The 'Gelasians' are far more revealing. We have five distinctive sets of formulae known at Tours:

the mass for a priest (nos 1988–92); the second set of prayers in the

---

[109] See H. Barré and J. Deshusses, 'A la recherche du missel d'Alcuin', *EL* 82 (1968), 3–44; J. Deshusses, 'Le sacramentaire grégorien pré-Hadrianique', *RB* 80 (1970), 213–37; and *idem*, 'Les anciens sacramentaires de Tours'.

[110] See M. McCormick, 'A new ninth-century witness to the Carolingian mass against the pagans: Paris BN lat. 2812', *RB* 97 (1987), 68–96, at 86; Gerbert, *Monumenta* I, 262–3; and *The Missal of St Augustine's Abbey, Canterbury*, ed. M. Rule (Cambridge, 1896), p. 133. On the Reichenau book in general, see C. R. Dodwell and D. H. Turner, *Reichenau Reconsidered*, Warburg Institute Surveys 2 (London, 1965), pp. 38–51.

second mass for troubles (nos 2015 and 2019); the mass *pro salute uiuorum* (nos 2118–22); the first set of prayers in the mass *contra paganos* (2041, 2043–4 and 2046), with two 'alternatives' (nos 2042 and 2045) which appear first in the 'Eighth-Century Gelasian' sacramentary of Angoulême, and sporadically in later books; and the mass for someone close to death (2140–3).

Four masses have no exact parallels in the books edited by Deshusses:

against temptations of the flesh (nos 1993–5); for monks (nos 2051–3); in times of death (2054–60); and for a living friend (2087–91).

and another three generally have the prayers of BNF lat. 2290, the mid-ninth-century sacramentary produced at the abbey of Saint-Amand for Paris, but now and again, the readings (and corrections) embodied in other books, Cambrai BM 162–3 included. The formulae in question are:

the first set of prayers in the second mass for troubles (nos 2014, 2016 and 2018); the third *missa generalis pro salute uiuorum uel requie defuntorum* (nos 2126–8) and the mass for a dead woman (nos 2165–7).

A's 'Gelasian' formulae are therefore best described as 'Tours or Arras with changes'.

Perhaps the most striking feature of *A*'s votives, though, is the presence of the preface *Cui non pereunt moriendo corpora nostra* in the mass *pro defuncto in ipso die* (no. 2157). In his study of over ninety medieval orders for the dying and dead Dom Damien Sicard only came across this prayer in four other books:[111]

Albi, Bibliothèque Rochegude, 20 (formerly Bibliothèque municipale, 34): a tenth-century pontifical from a cathedral in southern France, possibly Albi itself.[112]

Vich 66: the eleventh-century sacramentary from Vich, which we have already encountered in connexion with *A*'s pentitential order for Ash Wednesday.[113]

---

[111] D. Sicard, *La liturgie de la mort dans l'église latine dès origines a la reforme Carolingienne*, LQF 63 (Münster-im-Westfalen, 1978), pp. 88–91, 97, 189.

[112] For a general description of this book, see Leroquais, *Les pontificaux* I, 8–15, and Rasmussen, *Les pontificaux*, pp. 39–88.

[113] Ed. Olivar, *El sacramentario de Vich*, p. 246, no. 1548.

Rouen, Bibliothèque municipale, 274: the so-called 'Missal of Robert of Jumièges': a splendidly decorated early-eleventh-century copy of an sacramentary from Ely or Peterborough later owned by Robert of Jumièges, bishop of London (1044–51). In favour of 'Ely' we have, principally, the presence of the name of St Aetheltryth (23 June), patron of the house, in the *Nobis quoque* of the Canon of the Mass; a proper mass for her feast-day and that of St Eormenhild (13 Feb.) in the sanctoral of the book; and invocations of both saints, together with those for SS Sexburh (5 July) and Wihtburh (17 Mar.), whose relics were also possessed by the community, in the litany for the visitation of the sick. Furthermore, as Tolhurst noted, the highly distinctive collect of the mass *De sanctis uirginibus*, which reads *Fragilitatem nostram quesumus domine perpetuo sustenta munimine et per gloriosa sanctarum uirginum merita quarum corpora in praesenti requiescunt* . . . turns up in Cambridge University Library, Ii. iv. 20, a thirteenth-century breviary from the house.[114] But these 'Ely' symptoms are plainly second-hand. For among other things, we have an entry in gold for St Tibba (29 Dec.) in the sacramentary's calendar, albeit on the wrong day, but obviously intended to be read as Tibba, not Tybi the Egyptian month, as Tolhurst claimed; and invocations grouped together in the litany of all the other major saints of which Peterborough had relics, namely: SS Florentius (27 Sept.), and Cyneburh and Cyneswiht (6 Mar.). Peterborough looks certain; and as Heslop has noted, we probably have the name of the man who wrote the book too: Ervenius (OE Earnwig), who was Wulfstan of Worcester's tutor in the 1020s, and later abbot of the house (1041–52).[115] But for whom was the sacramentary written? A monastic community pretty evidently, as a votive mass for St Benedict follows the mass for the virgins mentioned above, and the abbot addressed in the collect of the mass for the abbot and congregation is *abbatem nostrum*. Given, therefore, that the calendar is likely to be of tenth-century Peterborough, as Hohler indicated, the answer must be Peterborough under Ervenius' predecessor, Aelfsige (*c.* 1006–41). The preface figures on fol. 215v.[116]

---

[114] See *The Missal of Robert of Jumièges*, ed. H. A. Wilson, HBS 11 (London, 1896), pp. 47, 163, 181–2, 247–8 and 289, and J. B. L. Tolhurst, 'Le missel de Robert de Jumièges, sacramentaire d'Ely', *Jumièges. Congrès scientifique du XIIIe centenaire. Rouen, 10–12 Juin, 1954*, 2 vols (Rouen, 1955) I, 287–92. The litany is also ed. Lapidge, *Anglo-Saxon Litanies of the Saints*, pp. 270–2.

[115] See C. Hohler, 'Les saintes insulaires dans le missel de l'archévêque Robert', *Jumièges. Congrès scientifique* I, 293–303, and T. A. Heslop, 'De luxe manuscripts and the patronage of King Cnut and Queen Emma', *ASE* 19 (1990), 151–95, esp. 159–62, 176–7 and 181.

[116] Ed. Wilson, *The Missal of Robert of Jumièges*, p. 299.

and Chigi C. V. 134: the late-eleventh-century votive missal and ritual from a house near Sarsina, in the diocese of Ravenna.[117]

It also occurs in:

Lerida, Archivo Capitular, 16: the late-tenth or early-eleventh-century pontifical of the cathedral of Roda in northern Spain.[118]

Vich, Museo Episcopal, 67: a mid-eleventh-century sacramentary from the abbey of Ripoll, also in northern Spain.[119]

The preface is therefore clearly at home in southern Europe and in England. But it is difficult to say why this formula was of such limited circulation. Sicard pointed out that its opening clause derives from a formula widely used in services for the dead in the middle ages, *Deus apud quem omnia vivunt*. Another was simply borrowed from the preface *Per quem nos ad imaginem*, which occurs first in 'Eighth-Century Gelasian' books. In the following comparison the text of *A*'s preface is given on the left and the relevant portions of the collect and 'Eighth-Century Gelasian' preface on the right:[120]

A.	*Gellone.*
Cui non pereunt moriendo corpora nostra sed mutantur in melius, et timoris tui obseruatione, defunctis locus perpetuus adquiritur. Quapropter tibi piissime pater supplices fundimus preces, et maiestatem tuam deuotis mentibus exoramus, ut anima famuli tui .ill. peccatorum uinculis absoluta, transitum mereatur habere ad uitam. Per Christum dominum nostrum.	. . . cui non pereunt moriendo corpora nostra sed mutantur in melius . . . . . . tibi igitur clementissime pater precis supplicis fundimus et maiestatem tuam deuotis mentibus exoramus pro anima famuli tui illius . . .

The presence of 'Eighth-Century Gelasian' material in this prayer may suggest that the person who composed it was active at some point in the period *c.* 700–900; and in this case, Alcuin would certainly be a possibility since the five prayers that normally accompany *Cui non pereunt mortem* ('Robert' and 'Ripoll' are exceptions) were known at Tours. But one would then have to explain first, why the mass as a whole, with

[117] Fol. 164r.
[118] Ed. Planas, *El sacramentari, ritual i pontifical de Roda*, p. 671 (cap. xcviii, no. 5).
[119] Ed. A. Olivar, *Sacramentarium Rivipullense*, Monumenta Hispaniae Sacra, Serie liturgica 7 (Barcelona, 1964), p. 232, no. 1735. *CLLA*, no. 963.
[120] Ed. Dumas and Deshusses, *Liber Sacramentorum Gellonensis* I, 461, no. 2895, and 469, no. 2927.

the preface in place, seems so settled in Spain, and second, why it appears in the Sarsina missal when northern Italian books normally have a distinctively northern Italian set of formulae. The answer is probably that the mass is neither Frankish nor Carolingian, but that its formulae are of some antiquity, surviving only in those places where the influence exerted by Carolingian books was weak.

Services for the Dead (nos 2197–2241)

Our starting point must once again be Dom Sicard. Sicard demonstrated that *A*'s order for the dying consists of two distinct sets of rubric and chant: a shortened version of the Roman order generally known as *Ordo XLIX*; and the rubric and chant of a longer 'Gallican' order which survives in a number of ninth and tenth-century sacramentaries, the oldest of which is BNF lat. 2290 (his *Den*), now conveniently printed in full by Deshusses. As far as the 'Roman' portions of *A*'s rubric are concerned, he was able to show that in company with a ninth-century sacramentary from Lorsch and a tenth-century order from Cologne, *A* gives the verse *Requiem aeternam* instead of the more usual *Suscipiat te christus* after the response *Subuenite sancti* (no. 2199). But he went on to concede that this was not altogether unusual, since the eleventh-century sacramentary from Vich mentioned above also makes this change (if it is indeed a change) and what is more, re-uses, in common with *A*, *Subuenite* and *Requiem* as the chant for absolution, which is far more revealing.[121] No other book re-sets the pieces in this way. But Sicard's primary concern was with the particular, rather than the general, and he therefore said little about the actual structure of the various orders he analysed.

A's order was in fact arrived at by the simple expedient of adding to the prayers (and rubric) of an *ordo* similar to the one preserved in Berlin, Deutsche Staatsbibliothek, Phillipps 1667, the so-called 'Phillipps' sacramentary, an 'Eighth-Century Gelasian' from a church in eastern France, prayers from Benedict of Aniane's Supplement and other sources, sometimes in their 'proper' places, sometimes not, but always with a view to fleshing out certain 'Gallican' directions.[122] This is clear-

---

[121] Sicard, *La liturgie de la mort*, pp. 1–63.
[122] The *ordo* is ed. O. Heiming, *Liber Sacramentorum Augustodunensis*, CCSL 159B (Turnhout, 1984), pp. 242–6, nos 1914–38. *CLLA*, no. 853; Bischoff, *Katalog*, no. 405.

est in the prayers that *A* provides for recitation after the body of the dead man or woman has been washed. Since none were attached to the associated rubric in the 'Gallican' order he had before him, *A*'s compiler (or whoever compiled its *ordo*) was forced to improvise. He therefore chose one Gregorian formula and one Gelasian to be said as the cortège approached the church, and placed the 'Eighth-Century Gelasian' prayers normally said *in basilica* under the rubric: *Post missam autem stat sacerdos iuxta feretrum ubi corpus est et dicat orationem hanc. A*'s chant, mostly in its 'Gallican' form, was then assigned to the redistributed prayers. Unfortunately, as has already been said, Sicard did not say how the orders he discussed were arranged; one cannot tell, therefore, whether on the one hand, *A* repeats a tried and tested formula, or whether on the other, it stands alone.

But despite the obvious 'Gallicanization', *A*'s *ordo* has features that are clearly Italian in character. The combination of the antiphon *Ingrediar* with the psalm *Sicut ceruus* (no. 2223), for instance, is only otherwise found in seven Italian books and the late-tenth-century sacramentary of Fulda published by Richter and Schönfelder; and several of *A*'s apparently standard 'Eighth-Century Gelasian' prayers, *Diri vulneris nouitate* (no. 2224) in particular, have significant north Italian variants.[123] That the other 'Eighth-Century Gelasians' do not may simply be due to some accident of transmission; but the possibility that the underlying *ordo* was revised stage by stage as it travelled north from Rome remains an attractive one, and if *A* was produced for use in England the implications of the combination *Ingrediar-Sicut ceruus* are obvious. Anglo-Saxon missionaries exported the custom to Fulda.

Orationes in Commemorationibus Sanctorum (nos 2242–4)

Following the order for the dead and dying we have three collects, all written by the original scribe of *A*, under the superscription *orationes in commemorationibus sanctorum*. Since there is no good reason to suppose that they are connected in any way with the *ordo* that precedes them, it seems likely that they were simply added as an afterthought, perhaps at the prompting of the man for whom the book was written. Indeed, the rather careless nature of the script tends to bear this out.

The collects themselves are peculiar. The first is a version of a 'west

---

[123] Sicard, *La liturgie de la mort*, pp. 133 and 213–14.

country' secret for St Patrick (17 Mar.), as the following comparison will show. On the left we have the text of *A* and on the right that of BL Cotton Vitellius A. xviii, the sacramentary-cum-pontifical of Giso of Wells:[124]

A.	*Giso.*
Deus qui sanctorum nobis intercessione succurris, da quesumus ut eorum exultemus meritis, et patrocinio protegamur. Per.	Domine deus omnipotens qui nobis sanctorum intercessione succurris da quesumus ut sancti Patrici confessoris tui atque pontificis et exultemus meritis et patrocinio gaudeamus. Per.

The prayer does not survive in any book earlier than *A*. Furthermore, when it does occur, it is only ever employed for St Patrick.[125] The second collect is the normal Milanese collect for the feasts of SS Nabor and Felix (12 July) and St John the Baptist's decollation (29 Aug.); and the third is normal for St Mennas (11 Nov.) in northern Europe.[126] As we shall see, *A* embodies a number of Milanese and north Italian features in its pontifical, particularly in its order for the dedication of a church and the blessings provided for Holy Week; and north Italian characteristics are traceable too in the calendar (part of *B*) added in the late tenth century.

From a purely formal standpoint, the presence of a version of a rare prayer for St Patrick is yet another connexion with England, but not Glastonbury, however, as Hohler thought. For *A*, as has already been said, is a bishop or archbishop's book; if it was used by anyone in the west country it will have been the bishop of Wells. But *A*, as will become clear, is more likely to have been made for Archbishop Plegmund shortly after he had officiated at the consecration of the new cathedral. The collect *in commemorationibus sanctorum* has every chance of being the prayer on which the Wells (and later Sherborne) secret for St Patrick was based.

---

[124] Ed. *LM*, p. 303. See also, A. Correa, 'A mass for St Patrick in an Anglo-Saxon sacramentary', *St Patrick*, ed. Dumville, pp. 245–52, at 252, though some of her statements regarding BL Cotton Vitellius A. xviii require modification. See below, pp. 94–5.

[125] It remains to be seen whether this is the collect for the day in Milan, Biblioteca Ambrosiana, DSP 10/27, the early-eleventh-century missal from Bobbio. See Orchard, 'St Willibrord, St Richarius, and Anglo-Saxon symptoms', pp. 274–81.

[126] Ed. respectively A. Paredi, *Sacramentarium Bergomense*, Monumenta Bergomensiana 6 (Bergamo, 1962), p. 280, no. 1090; Heiming, *Das Ambrosianische Sakramentar von Biasca*, p. 135, no. 931; PL 78, col. 148. On the book from Bergamo, see *CLLA*, no. 505 and Bischoff, *Katalog*, no. 335.

The Litany (no. 2300)

In most early sacramentaries and pontificals (there are exceptions) the litany of saints is written out in full once in one of four places: (i) at the beginning of the book, generally before the Canon, for recitation by the celebrant before mass; (ii) in the order for the visitation of the sick; (iii) in the order for those dying; (iv) or in the baptismal *ordo*. *A*'s litany, while apparently independent and standing conveniently between the office for those dying and the pontifical, is probably to be 'connected' with the order for the dedication of a church, as we shall see.[127] The four prefatory bidding prayers (nos 2277–80), all of which have special intentions, are not to be found in other sacramentaries and are possibly either 'Gallican' or 'insular' in origin, as has already been mentioned.[128] As for the series of invocations of saints, that of St Vedastus, patron of the abbey of Saint-Vaast at Arras, is written in coloured capitals, so a text from Arras evidently underlies *A*'s, as has long been recognised. We also have an invocation of St Ragnulf, likewise of Arras, and invocations of a good number of important north-eastern French (Lotharingian) and eastern Frankish saints, notably: SS Firminus and Salvius of Amiens, SS Boniface and Albinus of Mainz (the former wrongly classed as a confessor), SS Maximinus, Paulinus and Modestus of Trier, SS Germanus and Ursus of Auxerre, St Lucianus (and companions) of Beauvais, St Bavo of Ghent, St Eusebia of Hamage, St Rictrudis of Marchiennes, St Aldegundis of Mauberge, SS Denis (and companions) and Genovefa of Paris, St Remigius of Reims, St Audoenus of Rouen, St Bertinus of Saint-Bertin, St Audomarus of Saint-Omer, St Richarius of Saint-Riquier, St Lupus of Sens, SS Crispinus and Crispinianus of Soissons, and St Quentin of Saint-Quentin-en-Vermandois. Most are common to the litanies of books of all dates from the region, including those of the so-called 'Saint-Amand' sacramentaries.[129] But as has been said, SS Gaugericus and Aubertus, the two

---

[127] *A*'s litany is also ed. M. Lapidge, *Anglo-Saxon Litanies of the Saints*, HBS 106 (London, 1991), pp. 226–30, with brief remarks, pp. 76–7.

[128] Above, p. 33. *A*'s bidding prayers are printed and discussed briefly by J. B. Molin, 'L'oratio communis fidelium du Xe au XIVe siècle', *Miscellanea liturgica in onore di sua eminenza Cardinale Giacomo Lercaro* II, 313–468.

[129] The 'Saint-Amand' litanies are ed. *Le sacramentaire grégorien* III, 136–40, 165–8, and 288–91.

principal saints of Cambrai, are not invoked.[130] Unlike the Saint-Amand litanies, however, and indeed those of all other continental sacramentaries, *A* contains a discrete group of invocations of English saints. We have: Patrick, Cuthbert, and Guthlac among the confessors, preceded by the invocations of SS Boniface and Alban (also Englishmen) already mentioned, and Brigid among the virgins. This leaves us with the question of who the St Paulinus who follows this group of confessors might be. St Paulinus of Trier, as we have seen, is invoked with his fellow archbishops, and St Paulinus of Nola usually appears in the company of other doctors of the church. So they can be ruled out: which leaves us with St Paulinus of Rochester, later archbishop of York (10 Oct.), and the principal saint of Pol-de-Leon in Brittany (12 May). That the Breton saint, who is normally called 'St Paule' in early French calendars and litanies, may have been venerated early on at Saint-Pol, a town twenty miles to the north of Arras, probably has no bearing on the matter, since he is only called 'St Paulinus' in the late eleventh and early twelfth centuries when the feast of his 'translation' (presumably from Leon) became popular. But some confusion must have arisen.[131] For the day set aside for the celebration of this translation, the 10th of October, is, as noted above, the day on which the feast of St Paulinus of Rochester and York was celebrated in England: and the cult of the latter is the older by far. Therefore, in view of the fact that the saint invoked in *A*'s litany appears with those of five other Englishmen, the man concerned is likely to be Paulinus of England, as Hohler thought, and no doubt of Rochester rather than York, since *A* is a southern English book.

Hohler also stated that St Guthlac is unknown in continental litanies. A fresh search through the material available in print and in numerous manuscripts bears him out, for the saint seems only to have been known on the continent after the Conquest when two copies of Felix's *uita*, both written in England in the tenth century, arrived, probably independ-

---

[130] Coens, *Recueil d'études Bollandiennes*, pp. 280–1.

[131] See F. Duine, *Inventaire liturgique de l'hagiographie bretonne*, La Bretagne et les payes celtiques 16 (Paris, 1922), pp. 25, 34, 37–8, 43, 47, 51, 58, 70, 75, 213–14 and 217, with *idem*, *Bréviaires et missels des églises et abbayes bretonnes de France* (Rennes, 1906), pp. 22, 26 and 149. St Paul de Leon is also called 'Paule' in the neighbourhood of Fleury, which possessed relics by the mid tenth century; and his invocation is distinguishable from that of St Paul the hermit by the company he keeps: the latter is always to be found with SS Anthony and other hermit desert fathers.

ently, at the abbeys of Saint-Vaast and Saint-Bertin.[132] It therefore looks
as though the litany of *A* was drawn up by someone with England in
mind. We do not, of course, anywhere have an invocation of St Augustine of Canterbury; but strange to say, that is perfectly in order. The
earliest English litany to encompass his name is that of Paris,
Bibliothèque nationale de France, lat. 10575, a pontifical (generally
known as the 'Egbert' pontifical) written in southern England in the last
quarter of the tenth century. Invocations of St Augustine of Hippo, on
the other hand, are common enough; and these are readily distinguishable since they normally occur with those of fellow church fathers SS
Jerome and Ambrose.[133] *A*'s scribe, in the main, seems to have been
content to follow the model that he had before him.

In terms of the litany's more general arrangement three further points
deserve mention. First, the invocations *Omnes sancti apostoli*, *Omnes
sancti martyres*, *Omnes sancti confessores*, and *Omnes sancti virgines*
which often serve to divide one class of saint from another have been
omitted. Had they been included, they would have appeared respectively
below the invocations of St Barnabas, St Iustus, St Arnulf and St
Oportuna, but instead, the name of the name of the first apostle, martyr,
confessor and virgin encompassed is written in red. *A* does not stand
alone however. General invocations are also lacking in the litanies of
comparable length and date preserved in:

Paris, Bibliothèque de l'Arsenal, 227: the so-called 'Pontifical of
Poitiers'.[134] Probably written at the abbey of St Peter at Rebais for
Vulfadus, bishop of Bourges (d. 876).

Cologne, Dombibliothek, 106: an early-ninth-century miscellany
from Werden.[135]

Zurich, Zentralbibliothek, Car. C. 161: a late-ninth-century Gallican
psalter from Corbie.[136]

[132] B. Colgrave, *Felix's Life of Saint Guthlac* (Cambridge, 1956), pp. 34–7, for the two
manuscripts: Arras, Bibliothèque municipale, 812 (1029), and Boulogne, Bibliothèque
municipale, 637 (106).
[133] The litany of BNF lat. 10575 is ed. Lapidge, *Anglo-Saxon Litanies*, pp. 254–8, and
H. M. J. Banting, *Two Anglo-Saxon Pontificals*, HBS 104 (London, 1989), pp. 32–5. For
the Anglo-Saxon masses in honour of St Augustine of Canterbury, see below p. 175.
[134] Ed. Martini, *Il cosidetto Pontificale di Poitiers*, pp. 221–3, 233–4, and 242.
[135] Ed. Coens, *Recueil d'études Bollandiennes*, pp. 139–44.
[136] Ed. Coens, *Recueil d'études Bollandiennes*, pp. 314–17. For another Corbie book, now
lost, see PL 78, col. 386.

Brussels, Bibliothèque royale, 7524–55: a single gathering from a psalter (?) from Lobbes.[137]

and Vatican City, Biblioteca Apostolica Vaticana, Ottob. lat. 313: a mid-ninth-century Gregorian sacramentary probably written at Lyons that had found its way to Paris at an early date, possibly *c.* 849–51. The litany, which is of Notre-Dame, was added in the early tenth century.[138]

The practice is therefore not unusual, and further examples could probably be turned up. The litany of the Corbie psalter at Zurich is perhaps the closest in general form since the name of the first saint of the various classes encompassed is written in capitals, but there is no familial resemblance otherwise.

Second, *A* lacks the general invocations of the archangels, angels, patriarchs, prophets and St John the Baptist which normally follow the invocation of the Archangel Raphael. These are absent in two of the litanies mentioned above, and again, were probably liable to be omitted or included according to taste. Third, and perhaps most important, *A* begins with a threefold invocation *Christe audi nos*: not with *Kyrie eleison*, and so on, as is more common. A number of well-known manuscripts also contain litanies (of varying lengths) beginning in this way. In approximate date order, they are:

London, British Library, Royal 2. A. xx: a prayerbook probably written at Worcester in the late eighth century. Litany for general purposes.[139]

Montpellier, Bibliothèque universitaire, 409: a psalter written at Mondsee in the late eighth century, later at Soissons. For general purposes.[140]

London, British Library, Cotton Galba A. xviii: the so-called 'Æthelstan Psalter', a psalter written in Lotharingia in the last third of the ninth century. Soon after in England. However, the litany in question, which is in Greek with a Latin transliteration, was evidently

[137] Ed. *Recueil d'études Bollandiennes*, pp. 251–5.
[138] Ed. H. A. Wilson, *The Gregorian Sacramentary under Charles the Great*, HBS 49 (London, 1915), pp. xxxi–xxxiv. The sacramentary is also ed. *Le sacramentaire grégorien* under the siglum P. *CLLA*, no. 740. See further, Robertson, *Saint-Denis*, pp. 420–1.
[139] Ed. Lapidge, *Anglo-Saxon Litanies*, pp. 212–13; *CLLA*, no. 170.
[140] Ed. F. Unterkircher, *Die Glossen des Psalters von Mondsee*, Spicilegium Friburgense 20 (Fribourg, 1974), pp. 508–11; *CLLA*, no. 1611.

added (along with other material) in the second quarter of the tenth. For general purposes.[141]

Berlin, Deutsche Staatsbibliothek, Phillipps 1731: an early-tenth-century lectionary from some (northern?) German house. Of unspecified purpose.[142]

Paris, Bibliothèque nationale de France, lat. 943: the pontifical written for St Dunstan (d. 988) at Christ Church, Canterbury, possibly shortly after 973. For the dedication of a church.[143]

Rouen, Bibliothèque muncipale, 369: the 'Benedictional of Archbishop Robert', so-called on the basis of an inscription on fol. 1r in a seventeenth century hand: 'Benedictionarius Archiepiscopi Roberti'. The Robert in question must either be Robert of Jumièges, archbishop of Canterbury (1051–2), or Robert, archbishop of Rouen (990–1037). Properly speaking, however, Rouen BM 369 is a pontifical. Its origin and ownership has at times been hotly debated. Henry Wilson, who edited the book for the Henry Bradshaw Society in 1902, followed John Gage, another eminent Victorian, in supposing, principally on liturgical grounds, that the manuscript had originally been produced for Aethelgar, bishop of Selsey (980–8), a view endorsed by Simon Keynes. David Dumville, on the other hand, has prefered, on palaeographical grounds, a date somewhere in the 'second quarter of the eleventh century'; and Richard Gameson, drawing back slightly, has, most recently, placed the book squarely in the first quarter of the century.[144] So we have all in all a possible span of forty, perhaps even fifty years. Now whatever one might say about the script and decoration, neither of which is securely dateable, three principal points, all raised by Wilson and Michael Lapidge, seem in danger of being lost sight of. First, Rouen BM 369 contains

[141] Ed. Lapidge, *Anglo-Saxon Litanies*, pp. 172–3.
[142] Ed. *DACL* 2.i, 812–13.
[143] Ed. Lapidge, *Anglo-Saxon Litanies*, pp. 247–8, and 249, for the second, shorter litany. On the book as a whole, see Leroquais, *Les pontificaux* II, 6–10; Rasmussen, *Les pontificaux*, pp. 258–317; and J. Rosenthal, 'The Pontifical of St Dunstan', *St Dunstan: His Life, Times and Cult*, ed. N. Ramsay, M. Sparks and T. Tatton-Brown (Woodbridge, 1992), pp. 143–65. An Exeter origin for BNF lat. 943 has been suggested by Conner, *Anglo-Saxon Exeter*, pp. 33–47 and 86–94. However, R. Gameson, 'The origin of the Exeter Book', pp. 172–5, provides the necessary corrective and re-states the indisputable palaeographical case for Canterbury. W. G. Henderson's transcripts of select parts of the pontifical are now Oxford, Bodleian Library, Lat. Lit. b. 10.
[144] *The Benedictional of Archbishop Robert*, ed. H. A. Wilson, HBS 24 (London, 1903), pp. xi–xii; *The Liber Vitae of the New Minster and Hyde Abbey, Winchester*, ed. S. Keynes, EEMF 27 (Copenhagen, 1996), p. 31; Dumville, *Liturgy*, p. 87; and R. G. Gameson, *The Role of Art in the Late Anglo-Saxon Church* (Oxford, 1995), p. 205, n. 89.

benedictions for SS Iudoc, Swithun and Grimbald, saints intimately connected with the New Minster, Winchester. Second, a double invocation of St Benedict appears in the two litanies provided for the ceremony of the consecration of a church; and third, again in both, St Iudoc's name precedes that of St Swithun. But a pontifical can scarcely have been prepared for a community of monks, as Gage and Wilson saw. Indeed, no-one has ever claimed that it was. Nor, for that matter, has anyone claimed that such a book could ever have been prepared for the bishop of Winchester's use at New Minster: Ælfheah II (984–1006), Cenwulf (1006), or Æthelwold II (1005 × 1006 – 1012 × 1013) could hardly have needed a service for the consecration of a church there. Yet it is quite clear that Rouen BM 369 cannot have been used by the bishop of Winchester in his cathedral either: for one thing, too many important Old Minster feasts are missing from the sanctoral of its benedictional. Perhaps sensing that, Gage and Wilson suggested, as I have indicated, that the book had been made at the New Minster for Æthelgar, the former abbot of the house who became bishop of Selsey (980 – *c.* 988). That, *pace* Dumville, looks likely. Æthelgar will presumably have been free to impose the New Minster liturgy on his new house.

Rome, Biblioteca Vallicellana, C. 32: an early-eleventh-century ritual from a house in central or southern-central Italy. For the dedication of the font on Holy Saturday.[145]

Vatican Ottob. lat. 145: the early-eleventh-century manual from Monte Cassino. Five ferial litanies beginning and ending with the invocation *Christe audi nos.*[146]

Vatican City, Biblioteca Apostolica Vaticana, Vat. lat. 4770: an important mid-eleventh-century sacramentary from a house in Abruzzo (central Italy), possibly Terano. Three litanies: for Good Friday, the dedication of the font, and Holy Saturday.[147]

Oxford, Bodleian Library, Canon. Lit. 321: a late-eleventh-century breviary from Ravenna. Several litanies (fols 16v–18r) to be said over a dying man or woman.

and Rome, Biblioteca Vallicellana, F. 88, an early-twelfth-century liturgical miscellany from the monastery of Sant' Eutizio in Spoleto. In general structure, though not in the saints invoked, its litanies (fols 1r–5r) are related to those of Canon. Lit. 321 and Chigi C. V. 134.

In general structure, though not in the saints invoked, its litanies (fols 1r–5r) are related to those of Canon. Lit. 321 and Chigi C. V. 134.

There are many others, mostly Italian; their relationship remains to be explored.[148] But the point to note here is that the litanies of the two English books listed above accompany an order for the dedication of a church. Since *A*'s litany also precedes a dedicatory *ordo*, it seems reasonable to think that the one was supposed to be used with the other.

The Pontifical (nos 2303–2469)

A's pontifical is one of the largest and most complete to have come down to us in a sacramentary. We have:

(i) a series of prayers and masses for the ordination of the seven grades of officer in the ecclesiastical hierarchy, from the Ostiarius to the Bishop.

(ii) a skeletal ordo for the dedication of a new church with a series of prayers for the consecration of its altar and the altar vessels and cloths.

(iii) prayers for the blessing of the chrism, the exorcism of the holy oil and consecration of the new fire on Maundy Thursday.

(iv) a series of benedictions of, and prayers over things, such as bread, new fruit, a well and a house.

(v) forms for the making of a cleric, deaconess, abbot and abbess, and the blessing of a virgin.

(vi) a nuptial mass.

(vii) prayers to be said for sterile women, the reconciliation of a heretic, those who have eaten poisoned food, and for the reconciliation of an altar.

(viii) three formulae to be said for temporal rulers; one for their army; and an order for a newly-elected king.

(ix) three prayers to be said over an archbishop as he receives his pallium.

[148] Lapidge, *Anglo-Saxon Litanies*, pp. 33–4, cites the sacramentary of Gellone as an example. Its *Kyrie*, however, is stipulated in the rubric immediately preceding the litany.

(x) a prayer to be said over a man penitent when sick, and suites of prayers for those troubled by demons.

Pontificals of this size were normally, at all dates, separate books, but a pontifical-cum-sacramentary will always have been useful to a bishop or archbishop who was obliged to officiate at other houses, sometimes, as the presence of proper prefaces in the two masses in honour of St Bene-dict in *A*'s sanctoral tends to suggest, monasteries.[149]

In common with most other separate pontificals of a similar date or earlier, *A* contains a relatively high proportion of the formulae adopted on the one hand by whoever compiled the 'Eighth Century Gelasian' sacramentary, and on the other, by Benedict of Aniane for his Supple-ment to the *Hadrianum*. *A*'s debt to the Supplement is perhaps clearest in the series of benedictions to be said over ancient vases and a well (nos 2413 and 2414; respectively items CXXI and CXXII in the Supple-ment); the prayer against lightning (no. 2419; item CXX), which also occurs in 'Eighth Century Gelasians', but without the accompanying rubric; and in the forms for the making of a cleric (nos 2424–7; item LVI). Others are seemingly more 'Gelasian' in character, notably the benediction of wine (no. 2408); the two benedictions over a font (nos 2415–16); and the prayers to be said for temporal rulers (nos 2454–6). Whether these belonged to the 'Eighth-Century Gelasian' from which *A* was copied must for the moment remain an open question. Far more interesting, however, is the matter of the formulae that found their way into *A* from a more distant and archaic source. When analogous versions of these prayers occur in 'mainstream' collections, pontificals included, their texts are normally quite different. As we shall see, *A*'s pontifical is almost certainly English.

Ordinations (nos 2303–56)

A contains eight sets of formulae: one each for the ordination of the Ostiary, Acolyte, Exorcist, Subdeacon, Deacon, Priest and Bishop, and a special mass for the ordination of a Deacon or Priest. In the main, the prayers adopted (and the rubric) are fairly standard, being common either to the 'Eighth-Century Gelasian' books and their allies, or to early Frankish pontificals and copies of the 'Hadrianic Gregorian' sacra-

---

[149] For a list of early pontificals without sacramentaries, see Leroquais, *Les pontificaux* I, xviii.

mentary. However, as has long been recognised, certain prayers are highly unusual. Two are unknown elsewhere (nos 2327–8); and the basic structure of the masses for the ordinations of a deacon (or priest) and a bishop can only be paralleled in the late-sixth-century 'Leonine' sacramentary from northern Italy, and in the 'Missale Francorum', a combined pontifical and votive sacramentary generally thought to have been written in northern France in the mid eighth century, but copied in part from an English model.[150] Perhaps the most unusual of all though is the second consecratory blessing for the bishop, *Pater sancte* (no. 2351), which Hohler could not find 'in genuinely French books', though he did not say which these were.[151] Bruno Kleinheyer took a slightly different view. He suggested first, that the blessing might once have accompanied a series of 'Late Antique' formulae in the 'Missale Francorum', and second, that the ordination formulae contained in *A* were those used by the early Anglo-Saxon and Breton church.[152] Brittany seemed possible for him, one suspects, because he found *Pater sancte* in a twelfth-century pontifical from Avranches. But as Hohler had no doubt seen, this is a copy of an English book. In approximate date order, the list of manuscripts and printed sources in which *Pater sancte* appears, *A* aside, is as follows. Those not cited by Kleinheyer are marked with an asterisk.

BNF lat. 943: the so-called 'Pontifical of St Dunstan'.[153]

BNF lat. 12052: the sacramentary written to the order of Ratoldus, abbot of Corbie (d. 986).[154] As has already been mentioned, the book contains an English pontifical of *c*. 960.

---

[150] Verona, Biblioteca capitolare, 85, the 'Leonine' sacramentary, is ed. L. C. Mohlberg, *Sacramentarium Veronense*, Rerum ecclesiasticarum Documenta, Series maior, Fontes 1 (Rome, 1960); and Vatican City, Biblioteca Vaticana Apostolica, Reg. lat. 257, the 'Missale Francorum', is ed. L. C. Mohlberg, *Missale Francorum*, Rerum ecclesiasticarum Documenta, Series maior, Fontes 2 (Rome, 1957). See also *CLLA*, nos 601 and 410.
[151] Hohler, 'Books', 79.
[152] B. Kleinheyer, 'Studien zur nichtrömisch-westlichen Ordinationsliturgie, Folge 1: Die Ordinationsliturgie gemäss dem Leofric-Missale', *Archiv für Liturgiewissenschaft* 22 (1980), 93–107; *idem*, 'Folge 2: Ein spätantik-altgallische Ordinationsformula', *ibid.* 23 (1981), 313–66. See also, H. B. Porter, *Ordination Prayers of the Ancient Western Churches*, Alcuin Club Collections 49 (London, 1967), pp. 72–5. Porter's study is exceptionally useful.
[153] Ed. Martène, *AER*, Bk I, cap. viii, art. 11, ordo 3. See also Martimort, *La documentation*, p. 99, no. 236.
[154] Ed. J. Morinus, *Commentarius de sacris ecclesiae ordinationibus*, 2nd ed. (Antwerp, 1695), p. 251. See also PL 78, col. 503D. On the book as a whole, see above, p. 27.

Rouen BM 369: the so-called 'Benedictional of Archbishop Robert'.[155]

*Cambridge, Corpus Christi College, 146: an early-eleventh-century English pontifical and benedictional.[156] With its benedictions for the feasts of SS Ælfheah I, Swithun, Æthelwold (two), the translation of St Æthelwold, St Birinus, and *quinta feria de sanctis in ecclesia Wentana ueteris coenobii quiescentibus*, CCCC 146 was clearly intended for use at Winchester, and not Canterbury as David Dumville and Laura Sole have recently proposed, though the earliest parts of the book may well have been copied from a Christ Church model by a scribe and musical notator who had been trained there.[157] Indeed, as Felix Liebermann discovered, CCCC 146 contains material only otherwise found in Cambridge, Corpus Christi College, 422, a sacramentary-cum-ritual copied at Winchester in the mid 1060s for a house in the diocese of Sherborne.[158] For CCCC 146, four possible owners are in view: Bishop Ælfeah II (984–1006); Cenwulf (1006); Æthelwold II (1006 × 1007 – 1012 × 1013); and Ælfsige II (1012 × 1013 – 1032). As Mildred Budny has noted, the pontifical, like a number of other Winchester books, later found its way to Worcester, where substantial additions were made in Sampson, bishop of Worcester's time (1096–1112). *Pater sancte* appears in the earlier sections of the volume on pages 132–3.

*London, British Library, Add. 57337: the so-called 'Anderson Pontifical'. An early-eleventh-century English pontifical-cum-benedictional once owned by Hugh Anderson, minister of the parish of Brainie, near Elgin.[159] Claimed by palaeographers and art-historians,

---

[155] Ed. Wilson, *The Benedictional of Archbishop Robert*, p. 127.

[156] For a description of the manuscript, see M. R. James, *A Descriptive Catalogue of the Manuscripts in the Library of Corpus Christi College, Cambridge*, 2 vols (Cambridge, 1912) I, 332–5, with Budny, *Insular, Anglo-Saxon and Early Anglo-Norman Manuscript Art*, I, 495–9.

[157] Dumville, *Liturgy*, p. 72, with L. M. Sole, 'Some Anglo-Saxon Cuthbert *liturgica*: the manuscript evidence', *RB* 108 (1998), 104–44, at 132. Dumville seems to find a Winchester provenance unthinkable on palaeographical grounds.

[158] F. Liebermann, *Gesetze der Angelsachsen*, 3 vols (Halle, 1903–16) I, pp. xxi and 435–6.

[159] Bought by the British Museum at Sotheby's, London on 12 July, 1971. Described and illustr. (in colour) in the catalogue of the sale. *Anderson* cannot be attributed to Durham, however, on the basis of the wording of its blessing for St Cuthbert's day (20 Mar.), as the catalogue suggests. The blessing is simply the normal blessing for St Vedastus (6 Febr.) re-used. See Prescott, 'The stucture of English pre-Conquest benedictionals', *British Library Journal* 13 (1987), 118–58, at 135. The contents of the manuscript as a whole are listed by Rasmussen, *Les pontificaux*, pp. 167–257.

probably correctly, for Christ Church, Canterbury.[160] Presumably made for an archbishop. Ælfheah (1005–12), Lyfing (1013–20) and perhaps even Æthelnoth (1020–38) are all possible. *Pater sancte* figures on fol. 48.

Rouen, Bibliothèque municipale, 368: the early-eleventh-century 'Lanalet Pontifical', so-called because an order of excommunication issued in the name of the monastery of 'Lanalet' (St German's in Cornwall) appears as an early addition on fol. 183r.[161] As Jane Toswell has demonstrated, the book was almost certainly written after *c.* 1020, as St Martial of Limoges is classed as an 'apostle' in the litany of the visitation of the sick. The inscription in Old English on fol. 196r recording that the volume was once owned by a certain Bishop Lyfing is therefore likely to mean the Bishop Lyfing who ruled Crediton between 1027 and 1046, and not Lyfing, bishop of Wells (*c.* 999–1013), as has been suggested. Rouen BM 368 was probably originally made, however, for one of Lyfing of Crediton's predecessors: either Bishop Eadnoth of Crediton itself (*c.* 1011–1027), or Bishop Burhwold of Cornwall (*c.* 1011–27). The two sees were united in 1027. Only later did the book find its way to Wells, where, among other things, blessings in honour of St Andrew, patron of the cathedral were added.[162] *Pater sancte* appears on fol. 84v.[163]

*Cambridge, Corpus Christi College, 44: a splendid and massive pontifical written in the third quarter of the eleventh century, probably at St Augustine's Abbey, Canterbury, for use at Christ Church.[164]

---

[160] See D. Dumville, *English Caroline Script and Monastic History. Studies in Benedictinism A.D. 950–1030* (Woodbridge, 1993), pp. 106–7. T. A. Heslop, 'The production of *de luxe* manuscripts and the patronage of King Cnut and Queen Emma', *Anglo-Saxon England* 19 (1990), 151–91, at 169–70, has suggested that the presence of an invocation of St Bartholomew in *Anderson*'s short litany can be connected with the reputed arrival of relics of the saint at Christ Church in 1022 or 1023. However, invocations of St Bartholomew also occur in the short litanies of London, British Library, Add. 28188, and London, British Library, Cotton Vitellius A. vii, books that have no immediate connexion with Canterbury or any other house known to have possessed relics of the saint, significant or otherwise. But it is possible that both manuscripts (a benedictional and pontifical) descend indirectly from Canterbury models. See below, p. 207. For their litanies, see Lapidge, *Anglo-Saxon Litanies of the Saints*, pp. 136–7 and 191–2.

[161] Ed. G. H. Doble, *Pontificale Lanaletense*, HBS 74 (London, 1937), pp. 130–8.

[162] See M. J. Toswell, 'St Martial and the dating of late Anglo-Saxon manuscripts', *Scriptorium* 51 (1997), 3–14. Dumville, *Liturgy*, p. 87, mistakenly takes Lyfing of Wells to be a possible owner. The added blessings in honour of St Andrew are ed. Doble, *Pontificale Lanaletense*, p. 143.

[163] Noted by Doble, *Pontificale Lanaletense*, p. 58.

[164] For a description, see M. Budny, *Insular, Anglo-Saxon and Early Anglo-Norman Manuscript Art at Corpus Christi College, Cambridge*, 2 vols (Kalamazoo, 1997) I, 675–85.

Its text, for the most part, runs in parallel with that of London, British Library, Cotton Vitellius A. vii, a copy of mid-eleventh-century pontifical (the so-called 'Ramsey Pontifical') from the cathedral of North Elmham made for Leofric at Exeter.[165] Both descend from a pontifical drawn up for Archbishop Stigand (1052–70). Unlikely to have been made for Lanfranc, as has recently been allowed. The litany adopted at Christ Church by Lanfranc is essentially that of Bec, his former house. CCCC 44's litany is distinctively Anglo-Saxon in arrangement.[166] *Pater sancte* figures on pp. 252–4.

Oxford, Magdalen College, 226: a mid-twelfth-century pontifical written at and probably for Christ Church, Canterbury. Three other pontificals, both containing *Pater sancte*, are closely related. The first is: *Dublin, Trinity College, 98, early-twelfth-century, again from Canterbury; the second: *Cambridge, Trinity College, 249, written at Canterbury in the mid twelfth century, but soon after at Ely; and the third: *Cambridge University Library, Ll. ii. 10 a twelfth-century copy of the Trinity book, but fully adjusted for Ely.[167]

Douai, Bibliothèque municipale, 67: the so-called 'Pontifical of Thomas à Becket', a mid-twelfth-century pontifical from Christ Church, Canterbury, later at the abbey of Marchiennes.[168]

Paris, Bibliothèque nationale de France, lat. 14832: a mid-twelfth-century pontifical from Avranches Cathedral copied from a book from Christ Church, Canterbury. As Dom Combaluzier has demon-

---

[165] On Cotton Vitellius A. vii, see below, pp. 140–1.

[166] M. Budny, *Insular, Anglo-Saxon and Early Anglo-Norman Manuscript Art at Corpus Christi College, Cambridge*, 2 vols (Kalamazoo, 1997) I, 675–85 says much in favour of Lanfranc, but in the end prefers Stigand. On the Bec/Canterbury litanies, see T. A. Heslop, 'The Canterbury calendars and the Norman Conquest', in *Canterbury and the Norman Conquest*, ed. Eales and Sharpe, pp. 53–85, and on the Old English material, T. Graham, 'The Old English prefatory texts in the Corpus Canterbury Pontifical', *Anglia* 113 (1995), 1–15.

[167] Ed. Wilson, *Pontifical of Magdalen College*, pp. 75–6. For a description of the other three books: *ibid.*, pp. xiii–xxiii; M. R. James, *A Descriptive Catalogue of theWestern Manuscripts in the Library of Trinity College, Cambridge*, 4 vols (Cambridge, 1900–4) I, 348–50; *A Catalogue of the Manuscripts Preserved in the Library of the University of Cambridge*, 6 vols (Cambridge, 1856–67) IV, 25–6; and M. L. Colker, *Trinity College Library, Dublin. Descriptive Catalogue of the Medieval and Renaissance Latin Manuscripts*, 2 vols (Dublin, 1991) I, 195–8.

[168] For a description, see Leroquais, *Les pontificaux* I, 148–55, and Wilson, *The Benedictional of Archbishop Robert*, p. 190. W. G. Henderson's calendar of the book's contents (incipits mostly) is now Oxford, Bodleian Library, Latin liturgy d. 21.

strated, its text is closely related to that of Magdalen College 226 (above).[169]

Two pontificals once at the abbey of Bec in Normandy, now lost. Based on English models. Judging by the arrangement of their ordination services as a whole, the book or books from which these pontificals descended must have been similar to *Robert* (above), as Dom Snijders saw.[170]

Toulouse, Bibliothèque municipale, 119: a mid-fourteenth-century pontifical from Lisieux.[171] *Pater sancte* presumably reached the cathedral either in a book introduced by Bishop Foucher (1101–2), brother of Ranulph Flambard, bishop of Durham (1099–1128); or by Ranulph himself, on behalf of his son Thomas, who served as bishop from 1102 to 1107.[172]

Downside Abbey, 26536: a late-fourteenth-century pontifical from Lyons encompassing elements from a pontifical of Bayeux.[173] Contains a substantial number of *ordines* drawn from a copy of the pontifical of Guillelmus Durandus (d. 1296). But the book also has elements stemming from a pontifical of Bayeux, and at least one other source.[174] Bayeux, it will be remembered had four eminent English bishops: Richard II (1108–34), brother of Thomas, bishop of Hereford, and son of Sampson, bishop of Worcester, the man to whom CCCC 146 at one time belonged; Richard of Gloucester (1135–42); Phillipe de Harcourt (1142–1163), Chancellor of England, and holder for a time at least of the bishopric of Salisbury; and Henry II (1164–1205).[175] *Pater sancte* is likely to have found its way into

---

[169] Ed. Morinus, *Commentarius de sacris ecclesiae ordinationibus*, pp. 275–6. See Leroquais, *Les pontificaux* II, 185–93, and F. Combulazier, 'Un pontifical du Mont Saint-Michel', *Millénaire monastique du Mont Saint-Michel*, ed. J. Laporte, R. Foreville, M. Baudot and M. Nortier, 4 vols (Paris, 1966–7) I, 383–93.

[170] Ed. Martène, *AER*, Bk I, cap. viii, art 11, ordo 11, with Martimort, *La documentation*, p. 62, nos 46–7; A. Snijders, '*Acolytus cum ordinatur*. Eine historische Studie', *Sacris Erudiri* 9 (1957), 163–98, at 173–5.

[171] See Leroquais, *Les pontificaux* II, 344–9.

[172] See F. Barlow, *The English Church 1066–1154* (London, 1979), pp. 72–4, with M. Dosdat, 'Les évêques normands de 985 à 1150', in *Les évêques normands du XIe siècle. Colloque de Cerisy-la-Salle, 30 sept. – 3 oct. 1993*, ed. P. Bouet and F. Neveux (Caen, 1995), 19–35, at 32.

[173] Martène, *AER*, Bk I, cap. viii, art 11, ordo 18.

[174] See N. R. Ker, *Medieval Manuscripts in British Libraries*, 4 vols (Oxford, 1969–92) II, 435–40, with Martimort, *La documentation*, pp. 139–40, no. 171, and R. Amiet, *Les manuscrits liturgiques du diocèse de Lyon* (Paris, 1998), pp. 1567, no. 210.

[175] See Barlow, *The English Church*, pp. 58, 64 and 83, with Dosdat, 'Les évêques', pp. 25–6.

the order *De examinatione, ordinacione et consecracione episcopi*, which is otherwise perfectly standard for its date, from a book introduced at Bayeux by one of these Englishmen.

and, to cite only one later English example, *London, British Library, Lansdowne 451: the early-fifteenth-century pontifical of Guy de Mohun, bishop of St David's (1397–1407), later owned by Richard Clifford, bishop of London (1407–21).[176]

As can be seen from this list, the blessing appears in only one tenth-century continental book: the sacramentary of Ratoldus, abbot of Corbie. As Hohler, Prescott and Gerald Ellard have demonstrated, Ratoldus's sacramentary is English, embodying, among other things, the earliest surviving version of the so-called 'Second English Coronation Order' and the Wells benediction for St Andrew.[177] *Pater sancte* is therefore at home in England at an early date and only appears in books from or connected with houses in Normandy after the Conquest, as do so many other English liturgical formulae.[178] If it had been used in north-eastern France or Brittany in the tenth century as Kleinheyer claimed, then one might naturally expect to find at least some trace of it in the numerous sacramentaries and pontificals that have come down to us from Breton and Flemish houses. But there is none. In 1976 Antonio Santantonio suggested that the blessing was Spanish in origin, principally on the grounds that a number of phrases have faint echos in the ordination formulae preserved in the eleventh-century 'Mozarabic' *Liber Ordinum*.[179] Unfortunately his comparisons are not telling. England, or perhaps even northern Italy seems much more likely, and it may well be, as Hohler suggested, that *Pater sancte* originally found its

[176] Fol. 52. For a short description of the book see W. H. Frere, *Pontifical Services*, 2 vols, Alcuin Club Collections 3–4 (Oxford, 1901) I, 87–9, and K. L. Scott, *Later Gothic Manuscripts 1390–1490*, 2 vols, A Survey of Manuscripts Illuminated in the British Isles 6, ed. J. J. G. Alexander (London, 1996) I, 211–13, no. 71.
[177] Hohler, 'Books', 64–7; Prescott, 'The text of the benedictional of St Aethelwold', 135–43, and G. Ellard, *Ordination Anointings in the Western Church before 1000 AD* (Cambridge, Mass., 1933), p. 82.
[178] See for instance, A. Hughes, *The Bec Missal*, HBS 94 (London, 1963), pp. 148, 150, 172 and 215, and London, British Library, Add. 26685, an early thirteenth-century missal probably from Evreux cathedral positively abrim with English prayers re-assigned to local saints.
[179] A. Santantonio, *L'ordinazione episcopale. Storia e teologia dei riti dell'ordinazione nelle antiche liturgie dell'occidente*, Studia Anselmiana 69, Analecta Liturgica 2 (Rome, 1976), pp. 98–106, 256–7.

INTRODUCTION

way to England in a book introduced by St Augustine in the late sixth or
early seventh century.[180]

Last, it is worth noting that plural forms, interlined by the original
scribe, occur throughout *A*'s ordination formulae. One can well imagine
that it might have been convenient to ordain a number of deacons, or for
that matter acolytes, at the same time, but a number of bishops? Only
under exceptional circumstances would an archbishop have had more
than one bishop to install. Yet such circumstances do in fact seem to
have arisen. For Plegmund is said by several reliable sources, including
William of Malmesbury, to have ordained seven bishops at one go in
909: four to the newly-created sees of Crediton, Ramsbury, Wells and
Sherborne; and three to the existing sees of Winchester, Dorchester and
Selsey, the men concerned being, in order: Eadwulf, Æthelstan, Athelm,
Æthelweard, Frithestan, Cenwulf and Beornheah.[181] If Plegmund did
not actually have *A* to hand as he went about consecrating his new
bishops, the formulae contained in it are likely to be copies of the formulae he knew. Only books connectable with Canterbury make provision for multiple ordinations.[182]

Order for the dedication of a church (nos 2357–73)

Compared with the *ordines* published by Deshusses from five
ninth-century manuscripts, and those of a number of early pontificals,
A's order is still relatively undeveloped, especially in view of the fact
that its prayers for the consecration of the instruments of the altar have
not been incorporated in the service proper, as is also the case, for
instance, in the mid-eighth-century 'Missale Francorum'.[183] We will
come to these consecratory formulae in due course. But it will be best to
begin with the mass.

[180] Hohler, 'Books', pp. 79–80. See also, N. A. Orchard, 'Pater sancte: an ordination
prayer used by the Anglo-Saxon church', *RB* (forthcoming).
[181] William of Malmesbury's *Gesta Regum*, ed. R. A. B. Mynors, R. M. Thomson and M.
Winterbottom, 2 vols (Oxford, 1998–9) I (text), 205. William presumably knew a charter
similar to the one now London, British Library, Additional 7138, which was written at
Canterbury in the mid to late tenth century. For a reproduction and description, see *Facsimiles of Anglo-Saxon Charters*, ed. S. Keynes, Anglo-Saxon Charters, Supplementary
Volume 1 (London, 1991), p. 5, no. 9, and Plates 9a–b. See also, Brooks, *The Early History
of the Church of Canterbury*, pp. 210–13. Note that a copy of the charter is preserved in
Bodley 579, part *C* (no. 8).
[182] Noted as peculiar by Rasmussen, *Les pontificaux*, p. 266.
[183] See *Le sacramentaire grégorien* III, 195–208, and Mohlberg, *Missale Francorum*, pp.
17–19, nos. 56–68.

The two collects are Roman and perfectly standard in books from all over Europe, but the first secret *Deus virtutum* (no. 2365) is not, being based on a prayer peculiar to books from Milan, as the following comparison will demonstrate. *A*'s text is given in the left column; that of the ninth-century Milanese (Ambrosian) sacramentary from Bergamo, now Bergamo, Biblioteca di San Alessandro in Colona, s. n., in the middle; and the earliest surviving short version from a late ninth-century sacramentary from Mainz, now Mainz, Seminarbibliothek, 1, in the right:[184]

A.	*Bergamo.*	*Mainz.*
Deus uirtutum caelestium, qui in omni loco dominationis tuae totus assistis, et totus operaris, accepta sacrificium nomini tuo benignus oblatum, et huius domus cuius es fundator, esto protector. Nulla hic fidelium nobis nequitia contrariae potestatis obsistat, ut uirtute sancti spiritus fiat hic semper seruientium tibi deuota libertas. Per.	Omnipotens sempiterne deus qui in omni loco dominationis tuae totus assistis et totus operaris adesto supplicationibus nostris et huius domus cuius es fundator esto protector nulla hic nequitia contrariae potestatis obsistat sed uirtute spiritus sancti operante fiat hic tibi semper purum seruitium et deuota libertas. Per.	Deus qui in omni loco dominationis tuae dedicator assistis, exaudi nos quesumus ut inuiolabilis huius loci permaneat consecratio, ac beneficio tui muneris uniuersitas quae supplicat mereatur. Per.

The Milanese and Mainz forms of this prayer were later taken up in the Romano-German Pontifical (compiled at Mainz *c.* 950), but not for mass.[185]

Moving on, *A*'s second secret, *Altare tuum* (no. 2366), is also Italian, only otherwise appearing in a mass for the dedication of a church in an early-eleventh-century Beneventan missal from Canosa, now Baltimore, Walters Art Gallery, W. 6.[186] Canosa is about 20 miles inland from Trani. So Italy is in view again. *A*'s alternative secret *Apostolicae* (no. 2367) and the preface *Obsecrantes* (no. 2369), on the other hand, are 'propers' for St Andrew, the one taken from the mass in his honour in the 'Old Gelasian' sacramentary, and the other unique to *A*. It therefore looks as though the complier of *A* incorporated a 'spare' set of formulae

---

[184] Ed. Paredi, *Sacramentarium Bergomense*, p. 305, no. 1232. For the Mainz book, *Le sacramentaire grégorien* III, 194, no. 4144.

[185] *PRG* I, 170 (cap. xl, no. 134).

[186] Ed. K. Gamber and S. Rehle, *Missale Beneventanum von Canosa*, Textus Liturgici et Patristici 9 (Regensburg, 1972), p. 167, no. 795; *CLLA*, no. 445.

for a church that either had been, or was to be, dedicated to St Andrew. This, presumably, was a major foundation since it seems highly unlikely that anyone would have gone to the trouble of composing new prayers for the dedication of a parish church. Indeed, throughout the middle ages, the same sets of formulae (there are several) were drawn on time and time again, and only those books that took their lead from the 'Old Gelasian' sacramentary, including the Romano-German Pontifical and countless later sacramentaries, have prayers expressly inviting the celebrant to name the patron of the house concerned, and then, as a rule, only in connexion with the honouring of a gift or the church's founder.[187]

If *Apostolicae* and *Obsecrantes* are, like *Deus virtutum*, Italian survivals, it is possible that the mass was devised for the cathedral at Brescia (originally dedicated to St Andrew, but after a move 774 × 838, to the Virgin), in the archdiocese of Milan.[188] That the mid-ninth-century votive-sacramentary from the church of St Salvator, now Brescia, Biblioteca Queriniana, G. VI. 7, contains none of these formulae should give no cause for concern, for they will have been peculiar to the book used by the officiant. The nuns of St Salvator, in any case, were Benedictines.[189] But the question then arising is why the dedication of the cathedral at Brescia should have been of interest to the person who caused *A* to be copied. Given that *A*'s pontifical contains features that are undoubtedly English, it seems much better to suppose that the church in question was English rather than Italian. Two are especially relevant here: Rochester, the second episcopal seat (Christ Church being the first) established by St Augustine, who had formerly been been prior of the church of St Andrew on the Coelian Hill in Rome; and Wells, which was created *c*. 908–9. Rochester's case is, I think, the weaker. For while *A*'s prayers might be those of the original dedicatory mass – which would be remarkable though not impossible – or perhaps those adopted at some later ceremony of re-dedication, there is little else to tie the book positively to the cathedral. That an invocation of St Paulinus,

---

[187] *PRG* I, 178–9 (caps xlv and xlvi). Purpose-made dedicatory masses do, however, figure in Drogo's sacramentary and Paris, Bibliothèque nationale de France, lat. 2292, a late-ninth-century sacramentary from Nonantola. The Nonantola mass, however, is an eleventh-century addition. See Unterkircher, *Zur Iconographie und Liturgie des Drogo-Sakramentar*, pp. 58–61, nos 447–81, and M. S. Gros, 'L'ordo pour la dédicace des églises dans la sacramentaire de Nonantola', *RB* 79 (1969), 368–74.

[188] See A. K. Porter, *Lombard Architecture*, 3 vols (New Haven, 1917) II, 199.

[189] The book is ed. A. Valentini, *Codice necrologico-liturgico de monasterio di San Salvator o S. Giulia in Brescia* (Brescia, 1887). *CLLA*, no. 820; Bischoff, *Katalog* I, no. 685.

who is almost certainly the bishop and principal saint of the house, should figure in *A*'s litany is not decisive either way.

Wells on the other hand looks much more promising, not least because we have a version of the (rare) west country collect for St Patrick's day as a sort of votive.[190] Yet *A,* in my view, is unlikely to have been made for Athelm as bishop of Wells (909–23). For its pontifical, as Hohler noted, is an archbishop's pontifical. Athelm, of course, went on to become archbishop (923–6) and it is just possible – I put it no more strongly than that – that the book was made for him then. But a date in the 920s, even with the best will, looks too late on palaeographical and art-historical grounds. That leaves the question of how a mass drawn up for the dedication of Wells could have found its way to Canterbury. The answer is straightforward enough. Plegmund, who will have officiated at the ceremony, simply had his scribe work into the book a copy of the *ordo* drawn up for the day; and that *A*'s *ordo* is a copy seems certain. For the rubric *Et oratione super oblata facta per Amen, dicitur alta voce: Oremus,* and the long prayer that follows, *Deus sanctificationum* (no. 2363), have wrongly been entered before the secret (*super oblata*), not after as indicated. The order as we have it is therefore a sort of shorthand. The matter of whether *A*'s mass is to be associated with the Wells blessing *Deus qui beatum andream apostolum per passionem crucis,* in which St Andrew is termed *patronus peculiaris,* remains to be explored.[191]

Consecrations of altar goods (nos 2374–91)

Three forms are provided for the consecration of an altar. The first two are perfectly normal, but in the 'wrong' order and with peculiar textual variants, the one beginning as the version of the prayer preserved in a mid-ninth-century sacramentary from Paris, the other more as less as 'Gellone'; but the third, which is not to be found elsewhere, is a peculiar conflation of two prayers normally pronounced when the bishop or archbishop first enters the church:

---

[190] See below, p. 176.
[191] The earliest version occurs in the sacramentary of Ratoldus. For others (in print), see *Corpus Benedictionum Pontificalium,* ed. Moeller, I, nos 817 and 819; II, no. 1695; and for the text at Wells in the third quarter of the eleventh century and at Durham in the mid twelfth: BL Cotton Vitellius A. xviii, fols 216v–217r; and London, British Library, Cotton Tiberius B. iii, fol. 121r. The blessing survived well into the fifteenth century.

A.	*'Old Gelasian'.*
Deus sanctificationum, omnipotens dominator, cuius pietas sine fine sentitur,	Deus sanctificationum omnipotens dominator, cuius pietas sine fine sentitur, deus qui caelestia . . .
effunde super hoc altare gratiam tuae benedictionis, ut ab omnibus hic inuocantibus te, auxilium tuae misericordiae sentiatur. Per dominum.	Deus qui loca nomini tuo dicanda sanctificas, effunde super hanc orationis domum gratiam tuam, ut ab omnibus inuocantibus te auxilium tuae misericordiae sentiatur. Per dominum.

Pontificals, both early and late, normally adopt the two 'Old Gelasian' formulae in their entirety.

Immediately after *Deus sanctificationum* we have: the prayer for the consecration of a *tabula* (no. 2377), which is rare outside books from Mainz, and which here has an opening clause that re-appears in BNF lat. 10575, the 'Egbert' pontifical; two forms each for the paten and chalice, all standard (nos 2378–81); and two for the paten and chalice together (nos 2382–3), both unique.[192] Following these we come to the two consecratory prayers for the corporal (nos 2384–5). The first, which is not found in books written before the mid ninth century, is in most respects perfectly normal, except for the fact that its opening clause has been brought into line with the prayer that follows; the second, however, is a modified version of a prayer for the consecration of an altar that appears in almost all surviving *ordines* for the consecration of a church (including *A*'s), as the following comparison with the text given in the sacramentary of Gellone will make clear.[193]

A.	*Gellone.*
Domine sancte pater omnipotens aeterne deus misericordiam tuam supplices deprecamur, ut hoc linteamen super altare tuum impositum in spiritale consecrandum officium, presenti benedictione sanctifices, et in eo, seu super illud, oblationem famulorum tuorum studio purificationis impositam benedicere digneris, et	Dei patris omnipotentis misericordiam dilectissimi fratres deprecemur, ut hoc altare sacrificiis spiritalibus consecrandum, uocis nostrae exoratus officio praesenti benedictione sanctificet. Vt in eo semper oblationes famulorum suorum, studio suae deuotionis impositas, benedicere et sanctificare

---

[192] See *Le sacramentaire grégorien* III, 194, no. 4145; *PRG* I (cap. xl, no. 66); and Banting, *Two Anglo-Saxon Pontificals*, p. 51.
[193] The text is conveniently ed. *Le sacramentaire grégorien* III, 179, no. 4092.

spiritali placatus incenso precantis
familiae tuae promptus exauditor
existas. Per.

dignetur, et spiritali placatus incenso,
precanti familiae suae promptus
exauditor assistat. Per.

Last, so far as this group of prayers is concerned, we have the consecration of the altar and its goods en bloc: the *consecratio altaris et calicis et
patenae et corporalis* (no. 2386). As Wilson showed in his edition of the
'Gelasian Sacramentary', this has peculiar variants, the most spectacular
of all being the transmutation of *aeneis uelis* into *ansulis, uelis*.[194] The
word *ansulus* is not known in any other early version.

The series of prayers as a whole closes with a formula for the laying-
on of hands (no 2387); two short formulae to accompany the laying-on
(nos 2388–9); and two standard prayers for the consecration of the
vessel in which the chrism was stored (nos 2390–1). The laying-on of
hands, presumably on whoever had prepared the chrism or handed it to
the bishop (assuming the formula is in the 'right' place), does not occur
in any other medieval *ordo*, so far as I have been able to establish. The
prayer is not a new composition, however, but a version of a common
post-baptismal prayer, more 'Eighth-Century Gelasian' than 'Hadrianic'
in character, though it starts as the *Hadrianum*. The sacramentary of
Gellone's text will serve well enough for comparative purposes.[195]

A.

Omnipotens sempiterne deus qui
regenerare dignatus es hunc famulum
tuum ex aqua et spiritu sancto, quique
dedisti ei remissionem omnium
peccatorum, tu domine inmitte in eum
septiformem spiritum tuum sanctum
paraclitum de caelis, da ei spiritum
sapientiae et intellectus, spiritum
consilii et fortitudinis, spiritum
scientiae et pietatis, adimple eum
spiritu timoris dei et domini nostri iesu
christi, et consigna eum signo sanctae
crucis tuae propitiatus in uitam
aeternam. Per eundem dominum
nostrum ihesum christum filium tuum,
cum quo uiuis et regnas deus. Per
omnia secula seculorum. Amen.

Gellone.

Domine omnipotens, pater domini
nostri iesu christi, qui regenerasti
famolum tuum ex aqua et spiritu
sancto, quique dedisti ei
remissionem omnium peccatorum,
tu domine inmitte in eum spiritum
sanctum paraclitum
et da ei spiritum sapientiae et
intellictum, spiritum consilii et
fortitudinis, spiritum scientiae et
pietatis, adimple aeum spiritum
timoris <dei et> domini nostri iesu
christi, et iube eum consignare
signum crucis in uitam aeternam.
Per eundem dominum nostrum
iesum christum cum quo uiues et
regnas deus per omnia secula
saeculorum.

---

[194] Wilson, *The Gelasian Sacramentary*, pp. 133–7.
[195] Dumas and Deshusses, *Liber Sacramentorum Gellonensis* I, 336–7, no. 2326.

'Hadrianic' books always read: *remissionem omnium peccatorum, emitte in eos septiformem spiritum tuum sanctum paraclitum de caelis, spiritum sapientiae et intellectus*, and so forth. *A*'s version of this prayer may therefore simply be a hybrid; but one cannot rule out the possibility that *A* preserves an older Italian form of text.

Prayers for Maundy Thursday and Holy Saturday (nos 2392–2400)

In the main, *A* largely follows the Supplement. However, as Andrew MacGregor has shown, there are departures in the formulae provided for the consecration of the new fire on Holy Saturday. The first and second of *A*'s five prayers (nos 2395–6) are fairly common, occurring in a number of books from all over Europe. But the third, which begins *Domine sancte pater omnipotens aeterne deus exaudi nos lumen indeficiens* (no. 2397) is not. Now interpolations aside, it is clear that the variant forms of prayers for Holy Saturday beginning in this way (classified by MacGregor as B1–10) fall into two distinct groups.[196] On the one hand we have those that read *exaudi nos lumen indeficiens* and *qui illuminasti omnem mundum*, and on the other those that read *lumen indeficiens . . . exaudi nos famulum tuum* and *omnem hominem uenientem in mundum*, as the following comparison will show. On the left we have the text of the sacramentary of Gellone, and on the right the version used at Salisbury and at numerous other houses in England in the thirteenth century:[197]

Gellone (B2a).	*Salisbury* (B4).
Domine deus noster, pater omnipotens, exaudi nos lumen indeficiens, tu es sancte conditor omnium luminum, benedic domine hoc lumen quod a te sanctificatum atque benedictum est. Tu inluminasti omnem mundum, ut ab eo lumine accendamur et inluminemur igne claritatis tuae, sicut igne inluminasti moysen, ita inluminatis sensibus et cordibus nostris ut ad uitam aeternam peruenire mereamur. Per.	Dominus deus pater omnipotens lumen indeficiens, qui es conditor omnium luminum, benedic hoc lumen quod a te sanctificatum atque benedictum est, ut ab eo lumine accendamur, atque illuminemur igne claritatis tuae, et sicut illuminasti moysen exeuntem de aegypto, ita illumines corda, et sensus nostras, ut ad uitam et lucem aeternam peruenire mereamus. Per.

[196] For the texts, see A. J. MacGregor, *Fire and Light in the Western Triduum. Their Use at Tenebrae and at the Paschal Vigil*, Alcuin Club Collections 71 (Minnesota, 1992), pp. 457–67, and for the books in which they figure, pp. 157–70.

[197] Ed. *Le sacramentaire grégorien* III, 258, no. 4358. The Salisbury text is ed. J. W. Legg, *The Sarum Missal* (Oxford, 1916), pp. 115–16.

The differences are clear; and it should be clear too that A's prayer, which is printed below, is based on a prayer similar to that of Gellone (the standard 'Eighth-Century Gelasian' form), not the one used at Salisbury. This is important as Gellone's prayer, in company with MacGregor's B1, B2b–e, B3 and B6, which are all related, seems to be Italian in origin, deriving along with its fellows from a series of variable but related Italian originals. So whoever drew up A's text seems simply to have interpolated one of these with clauses beginning with the word *Tu* in praise of what the Lord is, or has done, possibly with a view to giving the man who had to light the candles the time to light them while the prayer was pronounced. In other words, the ceremonial itself demanded the insertions.[198] MacGregor did not list any other book with a text of *Domine sancte pater* corresponding to A's. But A is by no means unique as Lilli Gjerløw saw.[199] The same extended version also figures in:

London, British Library, Cotton Claudius A. iii, fols 31–8, 106–36, 39–86, 137–50: a pontifical (normally called 'Claudius I') written in England in the first quarter of the eleventh century. Owned and annotated by Wulfstan I, bishop of Worcester (1002–16) and archbishop of York (1002–23).[200] Probably written for him at Worcester.

CCCC 146: the early-eleventh-century Winchester pontifical later owned by Sampson, bishop of Worcester. The blessing occurs on page 199.

and London, British Library, Harley 2892: a mid-eleventh-century benedictional and select pontifical from Christ Church, Canterbury.[201]

'Dunstan' makes no provision for the Holy Saturday ceremonies, and the formulae added to 'Anderson' in the course of the eleventh century and those original to BNF lat. 10575, the 'Egbert' pontifical, are quite different, so the lengthened form of *Domine sancte pater* was evidently of limited circulation in the tenth and eleventh centuries, and may even have been out of date by then. Since a search through a good number of

---

[198] For B1, B2, B3 and B6, see MacGregor, *Fire and Light*, pp. 158–64 and 458–60.

[199] L. Gjerløw, *Adoratio Crucis* (Oslo, 1961), pp. 41 and 58.

[200] Ed. D. H. Turner, *The Claudius Pontificals*, HBS 97 (London, 1971), pp. 67–8. For further analyses and descriptions of the book, see Ker, *Catalogue of Manuscripts containing Anglo-Saxon*, pp. 177–8, no. 141; Prescott, 'The structure', pp. 139–41; Lapidge, *Anglo-Saxon Litanies*, p. 69; and Wormald, *The Making of English Law* I, 191–5.

[201] Ed. R. M. Woolley, *The Canterbury Benedictional*, HBS 51 (London, 1917), pp. 44–5.

German, French and central and northern Italian books not consulted by MacGregor has failed to turn up any further versions, it seems likely that *A*'s prayer was drawn up in England. A faint 'echo' does occur, however, in a manual printed for the chapter of Lübeck Cathedral in 1485, and I give its text here alongside *A*'s:[202]

A.

Domine sancte pater, omnipotens aeterne deus, exaudi nos lumen indeficiens. Tu es enim domine deus noster conditor omnium luminum. Benedic domine et hoc lumen et hanc caeram quod a te incensum sanctificatumque ac benedictum est. Tu qui inluminasti omnem mundum, ab eo lumine accendamur, et illuminemur igne claritatis tuae, tu es ignis, qui famulo tuo moysi in rubo apparuisti, tu es columna ignis, qui populum israel in nocte defendebas et inluminabas, tu enim tres pueros de fornaci ignis liberasti domine cum filio tuo ihesu christo et spiritu sancto tuo, qui in igne super apostolos singulos, die pentacosten, et post tempus super cornelium cum omni domo sua tibi primum ex gentibus credentem de celo descendisti, ut sicut eos omnes conseruasti et inluminasti, ita sensus nostros cordaque et animas nostras in hac paschali sollempnitate, et omni uitae nostrae tempore inluminare igne spiritus sancti digneris, ut ad uitam aeternam peruenire mereamur in caelis. Per eundem dominum.

Lübeck.

Domine sancte pater omnipotens deus exaudi nos lumen indeficiens, tu es enim deus noster conditor omnium luminum, qui omnem illuminasti mundum, benedic hoc lumen sanctificato igne incendendum,

et da ut igne tuae caritatis accendamur et illumiamur. Tu es enim uerus ignis qui moysi famulo tuo in rubo apparuisti. Tu es enim columna ignis qui populum israeliticum in nocte defendisti et illuminasti. Tu es domine qui cum filio tuo ihesu christo

ita sensus nostras cordaque nostra et animas nostras in hac paschali solennitate et in omni uitae nostrae tempore igne sancti spiritus illuminare digneris in terris ut ad uitam aeternam peruenire mereamur in celis. Per eundem dominum eiusdem.

The decisive phrases are *Tu es enim uerus ignis qui moysi famulo tuo in rubo apparuisti*, and *Tu es enim columna ignis qui populum israeliticum in nocte defendisti et illuminasti*, neither of which occurs in any of the versions (other than *A*'s) printed by MacGregor. *A*'s fourth prayer (no. 2399), as MacGregor saw, is simply the last paragraph of the *Exultet* made independent, and the fifth (no. 2400) the standard Roman prayer of the 'Old Gelasian' sacramentary.

---

[202] *Manuale Lubicense* (1495).

Blessings of things (nos 2401–21)

As has already been mentioned, *A*'s blessings of things seem for the most part to have been taken over from the Supplement and a version of the 'Eighth-Century Gelasian' sacramentary, or an existing book, perhaps a pontifical, embodying material adopted from both. We have the blessing for the striking of lightning with the rubric provided in the Supplement ('Eighth-Century Gelasians' have the blessing alone), and a number of prayers preserved in the sacramentary of Gellone and related sacramentaries. These were presumably taken over from the book from which *A* was copied. Four forms, however, are less common.

The blessing of the 'font', milk and honey (no. 2401), which first occurs in the late-sixth-century 'Leonine' sacramentary, is rare in early books. It figures as an addition of *c.* 800 to Vatican City, Biblioteca Apostolica Vaticana, Barberini, Gr. 636, a collection of prayers in Greek; in the original portions of Florence, Biblioteca Medicea Laurenziana, Edili 121, a late-ninth-century sacramentary from a house in northern Italy; in the Romano-German Pontifical of *c.* 950 and its descendents; and in various English and Italian books of the late tenth and early eleventh century. Thanks to André Wilmart and Pierre-Gy, three main traditions of this prayer are identifiable.[203]

(i) the 'Leonine' sacramentary; the Florence sacramentary; *A*; the so-called 'Egbert' pontifical; Vatican City, Biblioteca Apostolica Vaticana, Barberini Lat. 560, a late-tenth-century sacramentary from a house in central Italy; Vat. lat. 4770; and Oxford, Bodleian Library, Canon. Lit. 350, an early-twelfth-century sacramentary from a house somewhere in the Veneto (to take a relatively late example) have the best and oldest form of text. They begin *Benedic domine (et) has creaturas fontis, lactis et mellis*, and have other distinctive variants such as *enutri eos de hac (hoc) melle et lacte*, instead of *lacte et melle*, or *mellis et lactis*.[204] *A* agrees closely with Barberini Lat. 560. A more distant version of this type of text is to be found as a late-tenth-century

[203] A. Wilmart, 'La bénédiction romaine du lait de et du miel dans l'eucologe Barberini', *RB* 45 (1933), 10–19; P.-M. Gy, 'Die Segnung von Milch und Honig in der Osternacht', in *Paschatis Sollemnia*, ed. D. Fischer and J. Wagner (Fribourg, 1959), pp. 206–12. See also Franz, *KB* I, 598–601. The version of the prayer preserved in Rome BN 1565, the late-ninth and early-tenth-century miscellany from Nonantola, remains to be collated. Its existence is signalled by Gulotta and Ruyschaert, *Gli antichi catalogi* I, 60.
[204] See Mohlberg, *Sacramentarium Veronense*, p. 26, no. 205; *Le sacramentaire grégorien* III, 257, no. 4355; Banting, *Two Anglo-Saxon Pontificals*, p. 137; Vat. lat. 4770, fols 113v–114r; and Canon. Lit. 350, fol. 99r.

addition in the Durham Collectar, but the scribe, as Hohler noted, unfortunately managed to work in part of the Romano-German blessing of a cross. London, British Library, Stowe 944, the so-called 'Liber Vitae' of the New Minster, Winchester, written in 1031 by the scribe Ælfsige, also has a text similar to that of *A* and its relatives, but seems to have been 'corrected' from a book of recension (ii).[205]

(ii) Rouen BM 274, the early eleventh-century sacramentary of Robert of Jumièges; 'Claudius I'; CCCC 146 (early-eleventh-century Winchester portions); and BL Harley 2892, the mid-eleventh-century benedictional from Christ Church, Canterbury, name only the milk and honey, not the *fons*, and omit the phrase *qui est spiritus ueritatis*. The version in the 'Canterbury Benedictional', however, has been extensively rewritten. 'Lanalet' has a text like Robert's, but adopts a number of readings peculiar to the Romano-German Pontifical.[206]

(iii) the Romano-German Pontifical and its many followers also name only the milk and honey, but introduce after *Coniunge domine famulos tuos* the words *spiritu caritatis et pacis*. This form of text is found in the sacramentary of Ratoldus as a continental addition (along with a number of other extracts from the Romano-German Pontifical), but in no other English book, though the 'Lanalet' pontifical has been collated with it at some point, as has been mentioned.[207]

Three manuscripts stand apart from these main traditions: the Greek Euchologium published by Wilmart; the portiforium of Wulfstan II, bishop of Worcester; and London, British Library, Cotton Vitellius A. vii, a copy of a pontifical from North Elmham written at Exeter for Leofric *c.* 1050. Both Wulfstan's text and that of the Vitellius manuscript have been been heavily tampered with.[208]

In view of the abundance of English examples, it seems likely that the

[205] For the Durham Collectar, *Rituale ecclesiae Dunelmensis*, ed. Lindelöf, pp. 129–30, with *The Durham Ritual*, ed. Brown, fols 62v–63v, and Hohler, 'Books', p. 72; for the 'Liber Vitae', *The Liber Vitae of the New Minster and Hyde Abbey, Winchester*, ed. Keynes, fol. 50v.
[206] Wilson, *The Missal of Robert of Jumièges*, p. 280; Turner, *The Claudius Pontificals*, p. 63; CCCC 146, p. 196; Woolley, *The Canterbury Benedictional*, p. 42; and Doble, *Pontificale Lanaletense*, p. 81.
[207] *PRG* I, 116 (cap. xcix, no. 410). See also, M. Pizarak, 'Les bénédictions de la table paschale', *EL* 93 (1979), 202–26, at 217–18, no. 31.
[208] A. Hughes, *The Portiforium of Saint Wulfstan*, 2 vols, HBS 89–90 (London, 1959–60) I, 46, no. 723; BL Cotton Vitellius A. vii, fol. 69r. For more on 'Vitellius', see below, pp. 140–1.

prayer came to England from Italy at an early date, and that changes were made to its text as it circulated. Italian versions, by contrast, seem relatively fixed in form. All French and German versions stem from the recension adopted by the compiler of the Romano-German Pontifical. Since the latter text has been reworked it is not possible to be certain whether the model available at Mainz came north from Italy or south from England at the hands of an English missionary. Archbishops Boniface and Lull were of course Englishmen, and Hrabanus Maurus had been Alcuin's pupil, but their presence at Mainz does not constitute proof absolute.

The three other sets of unusual formulae in *A* can be dealt with more briefly. The first blessing for bread (no. 2402), which is couched in the first person, occurs in three English books: Rouen BM 274, the original portions of CCCC 146, and BNF lat. 10575, the 'Egbert' pontifical; and in one from the continent: Vatican City, Biblioteca Apostolica Vaticana, Vat. Pal. lat. 485, a late-ninth-century sacramentary-cum-ritual from the great Saxon abbey of Lorsch. Adolf Franz could not otherwise find the prayer in Germany or Austria; nor does it figure in ninth or tenth-century French sacramentaries and pontificals, though I have not searched systematically through later French manuscripts.[209] The weight of the published evidence, at least, is therefore English. The second blessing is equally arresting since it has an extra clause which is apparently not to be found elsewhere, as the following comparison will show. On the left we have *A*'s text, in the middle the 'Eighth-Century Gelasian' version as it appears in the sacramentary of Gellone, and on the right, the rarer short version preserved in the 'Pontifical of Poitiers':[210]

A.	*Gellone.*	*Poitiers.*
Benedic domine hanc creaturam nouam panis, sicut benedixisti quinque panes in deserto, quinque milibus hominum saturatis, ut sit dominis eiusdem abundans in annum alimentum,	Benedic domine creaturam istam panis, sicut benedixisti quinque panes in diserto, ut sit dominus eiusdem habundans in annum	Benedic domine creaturam istam panis, sicut benedixisti quinque panes in deserto,

[209] Wilson, *The Missal of Robert of Jumièges*, p. 281; CCCC 146, p. 296; Banting, *Two Anglo-Saxon Pontificals*, p. 124; and Franz, *KB* I, 260. See also Pisarzak, 'Les bénédictions de la table paschale', p. 219, no. 42.
[210] Ed. Dumas and Deshusses, *Liber Sacramentorum Gellonensis* I, 448, no. 2841, and Martini, *Il cosidetto Pontificale di Poitiers*, p. 334, no. 764.

gustantesque ex eo, accipiant tam corporis quam anime sanitatem. Qui uiuis et regnas cum deo patre.

alimentum, gustantesque ex eo accipiant tam corporis, quam animae sanitatem. Per.

ut omnes gustantesque ex eo accipiant tam corporis, quam animae sanitatem. Per dominum.

Numerous books follow 'Gellone', and a few follow 'Poitiers', but as I have said, none follow *A*.

A's blessing for apples and nuts (no. 2406) resembles the standard 'Eighth-Century Gelasian' blessing for apples alone:

A.
Santifica domine poma et nuces nucleosque, et omnes fructus tam arborum quam herbarum, qui tuo imperio usum omnibus animantibus prebent, per te ihesu christe qui uiuis et regnas in saecula saeculorum.

Gellone.
Benedic domine hunc fructum nouarum <arborum>, ut hii qui utuntur ex eo sint sanctificati. Per.

It is hard to say which is the older. Since 'all creatures' (*omnes animantes*) are expressly mentioned in *A*'s text, rather than simply 'those who' (presumably man alone) partake of the apples in 'Gellone's', it may be that the latter was simply slimmed-down at some point from the former and given over to a more obvious use. So far as I have been able to establish, however, only two other versions of *A*'s prayer exist. The one in the Durham collectar (an addition of *c*. 970), which is the closest from a textual standpoint, and the other in ÖNB lat. 1888, the late-tenth-century sacramentary-cum-ritual from Mainz published by Gerbert, which is more distant.[211] There is no sign of the prayer in any of these forms in surviving manuscripts of the Romano-German Pontifical. But later, particularly in England, the 'Eighth-Century Gelasian' prayer seems to have revised from a prayer akin to the one preserved in *A*. So, for example, in London, British Library, Harley 585, an early-eleventh-century collection of charms and recipes mostly in Old English written at a house in southern England, we have:[212]

Sanctifica domine hunc fructum arborum ut qui ex eo uiuimus simus sanctificati. Per.

---

[211] *Rituale ecclesiae Dunelmensis*, ed. Lindelöf, p. 130 with *The Durham Ritual*, ed. Brown, fol. 63v; Gerbert, *Monumenta* II, 92. See also, Franz, *KB* I, 379.
[212] Ed. G. Storms, *Anglo-Saxon Magic* (The Hague, 1948), no. 19, pp. 240–1. For the manuscript as a whole, see Ker, *Catalogue of Manuscripts containing Anglo-Saxon*, no. 231, pp. 305–6.

and in Bodleian Barlow 7, the early-fourteenth-century manual from Evesham:[213]

BENEDICTIO NOVORVM POMORVM PIRORVM
Sanctifica domine hunc novum fructum arborum, ut qui eo ututuntur sint semper in tuo sancto nomine sanctificati. Per.

There are many other English examples all beginning *Sanctifica* but continuing with the short 'Gelasian' text.

Two of *A*'s three prayers for the cross are worth noting too. The second (no. 2410) is a truncated version of the normal 'Eighth-Century Gelasian' formula with a subsidiary clause interposed, as the following comparison will show:[214]

A.	*Gellone.*
Benedic domine hanc crucem tuam per quam eripuisti mundum a potestate daemonum, et superasti passione tua suggestorem peccati, qui gaudebat praeuaricatione primi hominis, tristis enim dimisit per lignum crucis tuae quos seductos habuit per lignum uetitum. Per.	Benedic domine hanc crucem tuam per quam eripuisti mundum a potestate daemonum et superasti passionem tuam subiessorem peccati, qui gaudebat in praeuarigatione primi hominis per lignum uetitum. Sanctifica domine istut signaculum passionis tuae, ut sit inimicis tuis obstaculum, et credentibus in te perpetuum perfice uexillum. Per.

A number of books follow *A*:

Göttingen 231: the late-tenth-century sacramentary of Fulda published by Gregor Richter and Albert Schönfelder, though its interpolation runs *in reparatione secundi tristis efficiebatur et amisit per lignum crucis tuae, quos seductos habuit per lignum uetitum.*[215]

BNF lat. 943: the 'Pontifical of St Dunstan'.[216]

Rouen BM 369: the 'Benedictional of Archbishop Robert'.[217]

Rouen BM 368: the 'Lanalet' pontifical. The phrase *tristis tamen*

[213] Ed. Wilson, *Officium ecclesiasticum abbatum secundum usum Eveshamensis monasterii*, col. 51.
[214] Dumas and Deshusses, *Liber Sacramentorum Gellonensis* I, 370, no. 2447; *Le sacramentaire grégorien* III, 250, no. 4326.
[215] Richter and Schönfelder, *Sacramentarium Fuldense*, p. 355, no. 2727.
[216] See Rasmussen, *Les pontificaux*, pp. 274–5, with Henderson's transcript, Bodleian Lat. Lit. b. 10, fol. 30r.
[217] Ed. Wilson, *The Benedictional of Archbishop Robert*, pp. 106–7.

dimisit per lignum crucis tue quos antea seductor habuit is supplied interlinearly.[218]

BL Add. 57337: the early-eleventh-century 'Anderson' pontifical, from Christ Church, Canterbury. The blessing figures on fol. 66r.[219]

BL Harley 2892: the mid-eleventh-century benedictional of Christ Church, Canterbury.[220]

Rouen, Bibliothèque municipale, 272: a sacramentary written *c.* 1033–53 at the abbey of Saint-Wandrille in Normandy. The book embodies a copy of an extensive English abbatial benedictional. As Dom Lohier indicated in 1914, the scribe, whose name was William, imitated the script of his English model.[221] The blessing occurs on fol. 220r.

CCCC 44: the mid-eleventh-century pontifical from Christ Church, Canterbury. The blessing figures on pages 126–7.

BL Cotton Vitellius A. xviii: the 'Sacramentary of Giso of Wells'. In recent years several writers have tried to 'steal' this book away from both Giso and Wells. Their efforts unfortunately have not been successful. In the first place the sacramentary is a pontifical sacramentary. We have a set of episcopal benedictions on fols 199r–222v; an extensive order for Holy Thursday on fols 222v–232v; and a second *missa pro congregatione* on fol. 162 expressly naming the bishop as the head of the house at which the book was used. The collect, which normally forms a part of a mass entitled *pro abbate et congregatione*, as we have already seen, reads: *Omnipotens sempiterne deus qui facis mirabilia magna solus pretende super famulum tuum pontificem nostrum*. Then we have the sanctoral of the book, which, like the calendar, makes extensive provision for saints of Lotharingia, and encompasses, among the many masses for English saints, one each for SS Aidan and Patrick, whose relics were preserved at Glastonbury; and finally, we have the collect of the first

---

[218] Ed. Doble, *Pontificale Lanaletense*, p. 18.

[219] See Rasmussen, *Les pontificaux*, p. 206.

[220] Ed. Woolley, *The Canterbury Benedictional*, p. 130.

[221] On the book's script, see F. Lohier, 'Notes sur un ancien sacramentaire de l'abbaye de Saint-Wandrille', in *Mélanges d'histoire offerts à Charles Moeller*, ed. A. Cauchie, 2 vols (Louvain, 1914) I, 407–18, and Samaran and Marichal, *Catalogue des manucrits en écriture latine* VII, 277 and pl. XIVa. On the sacramentary as a whole, see Leroquais, *Les sacramentaires* I, 135–6, with E. M. C. van Houts, 'Historiography and hagiography at Saint-Wandrille: the *inventio et miracula sancti Vulfrani*', *Proceedings of the Battle Conference on Anglo-Norman Studies* 12, 1989, ed. M. Chibnall (Woodbridge, 1990), pp. 233–51, esp. 235–6.

missa pro congregatione on fol. 162r, which reads: *Familiam huius sacri cenobii quesumus domine intercendete beato Andrea.* Which other English bishop, originally from Lotharingia, and ruling over a cathedral dedicated to St Andrew close to Glastonbury, could possibly be in question? And as Wickham Legg showed in the 1890s, the underlying basis of the sacramentary is intimately related to that of the late-fourteenth-century missal from Sherborne.[222] Neither of these two books has any particular relationship with Canterbury, indirect or otherwise. Giso's prayers to the cross figure on fols 237v–238r.

We also encounter the English version of *Benedic domine hanc crucem* in numerous post-Conquest books.[223] Italian, French and German books follow the 'Eighth-Century Gelasians'. That *A*'s text is peculiarly English is made all the more certain by the presence of the prayer that follows: *Omnipotens sempiterne deus qui per lignum perdito mundo* (no. 2412). This appears in 'Dunstan', 'Robert', 'Lanalet', 'Anderson', 'Giso', and one book not mentioned above:[224]

> CCCC 146: the early-eleventh-century Winchester pontifical later owned by Sampson of Worcester. The prayer is to be found on page 106.

Of these, only CCCC 146 and 'Giso' have an 'unreformed' version which runs as *A*'s; the others follow 'Dunstan' in substituting *uexillum* for *lignum* and adding the clause *et crismate in christi nomine perunctum*:

A.	*Dunstan.*
Omnipotens sempiterne deus, qui per lignum perdito mundo, lignum redemptionis, tuam crucem praedestinasti, quesumus ut benedicere digneris hoc lignum similitudine crucis	Omnipotens sempiterne deus qui per lignum perdito mundo, lignum redemptionis tuae crucis praedestinasti quesumus ut benedicere digneris hoc uexillum

[222] See Hohler, 'Books', pp. 70–1, 76–7; *LM*, pp. 303–7; and *Missale ad usum ecclesiae Westmonasteriensis*, ed. Legg, III, 1447–1628, for a partial synopsis of the book's contents.
[223] See for example, Paris, Bibliothèque nationale de France, lat. 1218: the pontifical of David de Bernham, bishop of St Andrews (1239–53), which is in essence a copy of a Canterbury pontifical, ed. C. Wordsworth, *Pontificale ecclesiae sancti Andreae. The Pontifical Offices used by David de Bernham, bishop of St Andrews* (Edinburgh, 1885), pp. 43–4.
[224] BNF lat. 943, fol. 77r, with Rasmussen, *Les pontificaux*, p. 275, and Henderson's transcript in Oxford, Bodleian Library, Lat. lit. b. 10, fol. 30r; *The Benedictional of Archbishop Robert*, ed. Wilson, p. 107; *Pontificale Lanaletense*, ed. Doble, p. 18; BL Add. 57337, fol. 66v, with Rasmussen, *Les pontificaux*, p. 206; BL Cotton Vitellius A. xviii, fol. 238r.

tuae signatum,

et prepara in eo tuis fidelibus uirtutem, inimicis autem obstaculum, et augendum nomini tuo credentium chorum uirtute caelesti. Per.

similitudine crucis tuae signatum, et crismate in christi nomine perunctum et praepara in ea tuis fidelibus uirtutem, inimicis autem obstaculum ad augendum nomini tuo credentium chorum uirtute caelesti. Per.

Whoever composed the formula seems deliberately to have lifted the phrase *inimicis autem obstaculum* from the last lines of the 'Eighth-Century Gelasian' version of *Benedic domine hanc crucem*, lines which, as has already been said, do not appear in *A*. Nor, for that matter, do they figure in 'Robert', 'Fulda' and the Romano-German Pontifical, though its text of *Benedic domine hanc crucem* is unrelated. So we are faced with the question of when the revising was done. Two possibilities confront us: first, that *A*'s prayers were revised away from an 'Eighth-Century Gelasian' form of *Benedic* at some point during the course of the eighth or ninth centuries; and second, that *Benedic* and *Sanctifica* were originally separate and brought together for the first time when the 'Eighth-Century Gelasian' books or their models were drawn up. If this last is correct, then the prayers as we have them in *A* may well be seventh or perhaps even sixth-century compositions. Indeed, there are signs that this is so, for *Benedic* and *Sanctifica* appear separately in a number of books, not least the Romano-German Pontifical and the late-eighth-century 'Prague' sacramentary. It is striking too that *Sanctifica* should occur alone in the two ninth-century Ambrosian pontificals published by Magistretti.[225] But further versions will have to be hunted out in the many Italian missals, sacramentaries and office books that remain unpublished before the matter can be advanced. Significantly though, 'Robert', 'Anderson' and 'Lanalet' have *A*'s three prayers for the cross in order, followed closely by *Omnipotens sempiterne deus*, which was, as its rubric notes, to be said after the cross had been anointed with holy oil. The group seems to be peculiarly English.[226]

---

[225] *PRG* I, 157 (cap. xl, nos 97 and 103); Dold and Eizenhöfer, *Das Prager Sakramentar* II, 151*, no. 273.1; and M. Magistretti, *Pontificale in usum ecclesiae Mediolanensis necnon ordines Ambrosiani ex codicibus saec. ix–xv*, Monumenta veteris liturgicae Ambrosianae 1 (Milan, 1897), p. 21.

[226] See *PRG* I, 157–60 (cap. xl, nos 96–104); Franz, *KB* II, 13, 283–4, 306–7 and 477; and for the formulae used on Good Friday, Gjerløw, *Adoratio Crucis*.

Consecrations of people (nos 2422–57)

For the most part *A* follows the *Hadrianum*, Benedict of Aniane's Supplement and 'Eighth-Century Gelasian' books. However, it diverges in two noticeable respects. The second consecratory prayer for a virgin, *Deus castorum corporum benignus habitator* (no. 2434), was first shown to be strange by Wilson, who recorded its variants in the notes to his edition of the Gelasian Sacramentary. Wilson, however, did nothing more. That fell to Odelia Harrison, a nun of Stanbrook Abbey in Worcestershire.[227] She demonstrated that *A*'s prayer is hybrid, starting more or less in accordance with the normal 'Gelasian' form, but continuing after the second sentence as the shortened form in the Supplement. No other book has a comparable version. But in its general arrangement, especially the juxtaposition of the prayers *Respice domine* and *Te inuocamus* (nos 2431 and 2433), which are normally separated by some other formula, on occasion the blessing *Accipe puella pallium*, *A* agrees with Cambrai BM 162–3, the late-ninth-century sacramentary from Arras; and it is worth noting too that the same order is repeated in the original, early-tenth-century portions of the 'Durham Collectar'.[228]

Second, the alternative consecratory prayer for an abbot or abbess, *Deus institutor* (no. 2438), does not seem to have been at all popular early on. Indeed, it only appears initially in the Gellone and Phillips 'Eighth-Century Gelasians', and in books from northern Italy and southern Germany:

ÖNB Vindob. ser. nov. 2762: the pontifical and collectar of Baturich, bishop of Regensburg (817–48).[229]

Padua, Biblioteca Capitolare, D. 47: the mid-ninth-century copy of a pre-Gregorian Hadrianic sacramentary, probably written at Liège. The last of the three formulae for the ordination of an abbot or abbess is entitled: *Item benedictio*. All were therefore viewed as blessings rather than collects.[230]

---

[227] Wilson, *The Gelasian Sacramentary*, pp. 156–7; O. G. Harrison, 'The formulas *ad virgines sacras*. A study of the sources', *EL* 66 (1952), 252–74, and 353–7. Her study is much to be prefered to that of J. Magne, 'La prière de consecration des vierges *Deus castorum corporum*', *EL* 72 (1958), 245–67.

[228] See *Le sacramentaire grégorien* III, 226, *ordo* 480.

[229] Ed. Unterkircher, *Das Kollektar-Pontificale des Bischofs Baturich*, pp. 110–11, no. 496.

[230] Ed. *Le sacramentaire grégorien* III, 221, no. 4239.

Freiburg Univ. 363: a mid-ninth-century pontifical and collectar from Basel.[231]

The 'Donaueschingen' pontifical: a mid-ninth-century pontifical produced at Saint-Gall for the use of Salomon I, bishop of Constance (838–71). The book was sold at Sotheby's in 1982 and again in 1990. Its present whereabouts are unknown.[232]

and Milan, Biblioteca del Capitolo Metropolitano, 14: the late-ninth-century pontifical from Milan.[233]

With further work, the number could probably be added to; but the point to note here is that *A*'s text is quite unlike any of the others, as the following comparison will demonstrate. *A*'s major divergences have been italicised.

A.	*Baturich.*
Deus institutor cunctorum, qui per moysen famulum tuum, ad gubernandas ecclesias prepositos instituisti, tibi preces supplices fundimus, teque deuotis mentibus exoramus, ut hunc famulum illum uel illam quem hodie electio famulorum tuorum, abbatem uel abbatissam ouium tuarum esse instituit *clementer respicias, pietatis tuae misericordia inlustres*, sicque regat subditos, quasi commendatos *non proprios*, quatinus te opitulante, apostolicis iugiter doctrinis fultos, *simul cum ipsis laetus* portas paradysi introeat, atque *te donante*, mereatur audire, euge bone serue et fidelis, quia super pauca fuisti fidelis, supra multa te constituam, intra in gaudium domini tui. Quod ipse prestare digneris, qui cum patre uiuit.	Cunctorum institutor deus qui per moysen famulum tuum ad gubernandas ecclesias praepositos insituisti, tibi supplices fundimus preces, teque deuotis mentibus exoramus, ut hunc famulum tuum ill. quem conuenientia et electio famulorum tuorum hodie abbatem ouium tuarum esse instituit, sicque regat subditos commendatos, ut cum illis omnibus regna caelorum adeptus, quatenus te opitulante domine apostolicis iugiter fultus doctrinis, centesimo cum fructu laetus introeat portas paradisi, atque te domine conlaudantem audire mereatur, euge serue bone et fidelis, quia super pauca fuisti fidelis, super multa te constituam, intra in gaudium domini tui. Quod ipse praestare digneris.

Aside from 'Dunstan', which does not have the prayer at all, later

---

[231] Ed. Metzger, *Zwei karolingische Pontifikalien*, p. 44*, no. 145.

[232] Ed. *ibid.*, p. 44*, no. 145. *CLLA*, no. 1552. See also, W. Berschin, 'Das Benedictionale Salomons III für Adalbero von Augsburg (Cambridge, Fitzwilliam Museum, MS 27)', in *Churrätisches und St. Gallisches Mittelalter. Feschrift für Otto P. Clavadetscher zu seinem fünfundsechzigsten Geburstag*, ed. H. Maurer (Sigmaringen, 1984), 227–36, at 227–8.

[233] Ed. Magistretti, *Pontificale in usum ecclesiae Mediolanesis*, p. 91.

English pontificals also have a text akin to Baturich's. *A* therefore stands alone.

Last of the 'peculiars' are *A*'s prayers for the reconciliation of a heretic (no. 2449). The main prayer corresponds more or less to the one provided in 'Gellone' and other 'Eighth-Century Gelasians' for the same purpose, which is based in turn on the standard 'Hadrianic' post-baptismal confirmatory prayer; but in *A* the notion of confirmation is further extended by the conclusion: *Signat te dominus signo crucis in uitam aeternam in consignatione fidei. Pax tecum. Et cum spiritu tuo* (no. 2450).[234] Concluding formulae of this sort figure in many early ceremonies of confirmation.

The royal order (nos 2458–66)

A's royal *ordo* has, for better or for worse, probably attracted more attention than any other part of the book, and the literature surrounding it is therefore immense. For Henry Wilson, Armitage Robinson and Percy Schramm, the order was English, though they might have disagreed about its date, purpose and 'shape'. But in 1958, Cornelius Bouman took a different line, claiming that it was actually an obsolete Frankish *ordo* that had somehow found its way to England, whereupon it had been taken up, and copied, but not directly from *A*, into two English pontificals: 'Egbert' and 'Lanalet'. He did not say whether it seemed strange that *A*, which he took to be Lotharingian and mid-tenth-century, should, independently of 'Egbert' and 'Lanalet', possess the remnants of an *ordo* that was later to become popular in England. Judging by the letters kept by the Bodleian, the impossibility of Bouman's position seems to have been apparent to Hohler in the early 1960s. His view, which first found expression in print in 1975, was that *A*'s *ordo* is English, which is what one might have expected him to say; but following his lead, Nelson has now shown convincingly that, in company with Wilson and Robinson, he was right.[235]

[234] Compare the version in 'Gellone', ed. Dumas and Deshusses, *Liber Sacramentorum Gellonensis* I, 350–1, no. 2396, with that of the *Hadrianum*, ed. *Le sacramentaire grégorien* I, no. 376.
[235] See H. A. Wilson, 'The English Coronation Order', *JTS* 2 (1901), 481–504, at 482–6; J. A. Robinson, 'The Coronation Order in the tenth century', *JTS* 19 (1917), 56–72, at 62–8; P. E. Schramm, *Die Krönung bei den Westfranken und Angelsachsen von 878 bis um 1000*, Zeitschrift für Rechtsgeschichte 55, Abt 23 (1934), 212–20; Bouman, *Sacring and Crowning*, pp. 10–15; Hohler, 'Books', 78; and J. L. Nelson, 'The earliest royal *ordo*: some liturgical and historical aspects', in her *Politics and*

There are four principal points to stress. First, as has already been said, the order as a whole is only otherwise found in two English books: the so-called 'Egbert' pontifical; and the early-eleventh-century 'Lanalet' pontifical', both of which have already been mentioned in different connexions. Extensive searches by specialists in the field have shown that it never appears in a sacramentary or pontifical written at, or for use at, a French, German, Spanish or Lotharingian house. Second, the so-called 'additions' in the two early-eleventh-century English books, notably the mass and more elaborate ceremonial directions, are not additions at all, but ancient parts of the underlying *ordo* that, for whatever reason, came to be left out of *A*. The king, for instance, is crowned with a *galea* (helmet) rather than a crown, which is fully in accord with the prayers (the word occurs twice); and *principes*, that is to say, laymen participate in the ceremony. Third, the two prayers borrowed from the order by Hincmar, archbishop of Reims, for the marriage of Judith, daughter of Charles the Bald, to Aethelwulf, King of the West Saxons in 856 did not circulate further in Francia, either in their original form or in Hincmar's adaptation.[236] And last, the general structure of the *ordo* and its constituent prayers only became known on the continent with the arrival of the so-called 'Second English Coronation Order' in the early tenth century possibly in the baggage of Louis IV d'Outremer, who returned to France from exile at Aethelstan's court in Wessex in 936. Hohler and Turner suggested that the order had actually been drawn up for Aethelstan, and that remains a compelling possibility. But reasons have also been advanced for thinking that it might have been drawn up for Alfred (871–99).[237]

A's *ordo* is therefore English and ancient. Blind assertions to the contrary simply will not wash.[238] But *A*'s order, as has long been noted, is not wholly 'new'. For example, the blessing *Benedic domine hunc presulem* (no. 2461), said while the bishops and *principes* consigned the

Ritual in Early Medieval Europe (London, 1986), pp. 341–60, with further references.
[236] Judith's *ordo* is ed. Jackson, *Ordines coronationis Franciae* I, 73–9.
[237] Turner, *The Claudius Pontificals*, pp. xxx–xxxiii; Hohler, 'Books', pp. 67–9. Nelson, 'The second English *ordo*', in her *Politics and Ritual*, pp. 361–74, prefers Alfred. The version of the 'Second Order' in the sacramentary of Ratoldus is ed. Netzer, *L'introduction*, pp. 266–76, and Jackson, *Ordines* I, 168–200.
[238] Attempting to dismiss Nelson's excellent analysis at a sweep, Dumville, *Liturgy*, pp. 42–3, seems to regard surviving coronation *ordines* as a sort of amorphous lump, and England little more than a passive conduit. For the borrowings made from the 'Second English Order' in the *ordines* of Sens, Stavelot and a number of other houses, see Jackson, *Ordines* I, 80–167.

sceptre to the king, seems to have been adapted from existing 'royal' material, namely the two benedictions for a king that have come down to us in the 'Eighth-Century Gelasian' sacramentary of Angoulême, an early-ninth-century benedictional from Freising in Bavaria, and a number of later books.[239] As the following comparison will show, continental tradition remained stable over the centuries: with trifling modifications the first benediction was still used at Reims around the year 1000. In the left hand column we have the complete text of the first benediction in the sacramentary of Angoulême with relevant passages from the second benediction interposed in italics; the complete text of *A* in the middle (staggered for ease of comparison); and that of Reims, Bibliothèque municipale, 214, the late-tenth-century sacramentary from the abbey of Saint-Thierry at Reims, also staggered in the right.[240]

Angoulême.	*A.*	*Reims.*
Benedic domine hos presules principes qui regna regum omnium a saeculo moderaris, et tali eos benedictione glorifica, ut dauiticum teneant. Sublimitatis sceptrum et sanctificati protenus reperiantur in merito.	Benedic domine hunc presulem principem, qui regna regum omnium a saeculo moderaris. Amen. Et tali eum benedictione glorifica, ut dauitica teneat sublimitate sceptrum salutis, et sanctificatus protinus reperiatur merito. Amen.	Benedic domine hunc principem qui regna regum omnium a seculo moderaris, et tali eum benedictione glorifica, ut dauidicum teneat sublimitatis sceptrum et sanctificatus repperiatur in mente.
Da eis tuo spiramine cum mansuetudine ita regere populum, sicuti Salomonem fecisti regnum obtenere pacificum, tibi semper cum timore sint subditi, tibique militent cum quiete, sint tuo clipeo protecti cum proceribus et ubique	Da ei a tuo spiramine cum mansuetudine ita regere populum, sicut salamonem fecisti regnum obtinere pacificum. Amen. Tibi semper cum timore sit subditus, tibique militet cum quiete, sit tuo clypeo protectus cum proceribus, et	Da ei tuo spiramine cum moderatione regere populum, sicuti salamonem fecisti regnum obtinere pacificum. Sit semper cum timore tibi subditus, tibique militet cum quiete. Sit tuo clippeo protectus cum omnibus suis

[239] Ed. Saint-Roch, *Liber Sacramentorum Engolismensis*, pp. 360–1, nos 2317–18; and R. Amiet, *The Benedictionals of Freising*, HBS 88 (London, 1974), pp. 101–2, nos 458–71. The sacramentary of Gellone has the blessing in full but recasts the first. See Dumas and Deshusses, *Liber Sacramentorum Gellonensis* I, 197–8, nos 2092 and 2094.
[240] Ed. Jackson, *Ordines Coronationis Franciae* I, 127.

maneant sine pugna
uictores.

*Sis eis contra acies
inmicorum lorica, in
aduersis galea, in
prosperis pacientia, in
protectione clypeum
sempiternum . . .*
Honorifica eos prae
cunctis regibus terrae,
felices populos
dominenter et feliciter
eos nationes adorent,
uiuant inter gentium
cateruas magnanimes, sit
in iudiciis aequitas
singularis locupletet eos
tua praeditos dextera,
frugalem constituant
patriam et eorum
liberaris tribuant
profutura.

Praesta eis prolixitatem
uitae per tempora et in
diebus eorum semper
oriatur iustitia. A te
robustum teneant
regiminis solium ut cum
iocunditate et iustitia
aeterno glorientur in
regno. Per.
*Et presta ut gentes illi
teneant fidem proceres
sui habeant pacem,
diligant caritatem . . .*

---

ubique maneat sine fine
uictor. Amen.

Sis ei contra facies
inimicorum lurica, in
aduersis galea, in
prosperis pacientia, in
protectione clypeum
sempiternum. Amen.

Viuat inter gentium
cateruas magnanimus,
sit in iudiciis aequitas
singularis. Amen.
Locupletet eum tua
predita dextera,
frugalem contineat
patriam, et suis liberis
tribuat profutura. Amen.

Da ei prolixitatem uitae
per tempora, et in diebus
eius oriatur iustitia.
Amen.
A te robustum teneant
regiminis solium, ut
cum iucunditate et
iustitia, aeterno glorietur
in regno. Amen.
Et praesta ut gentes illi
teneant fidem, proceres
sui habeant pacem,
diligant caritatem.
Amen.
Tu eius menti benignus
inlabere, ut amore te
timeat et timore diligat.
Amen.

---

proceribus et ubique
maneant sine pugna
uictores.

Honorifica eum pre
cunctis regibus terrae, ut
felicibus dominetur
populis et feliciter eum
omnes nationes adorent,
uiuat inter gentium
cateruas magnanimus, sit
ei in iudiciis aequitas
singularis, sit locuples et
subditos locupletes
reddat, ut tua fultus
dextera contineant
fortiter patriam
populumque sibi
commissum, liberis
ipsius tua pietate
prospera ac profutura
cuncta tribue, presta eis
per tempora
prolixitatem uitae et in
diebus eorum semper
oriatur iustitia, ut cum
iocunditate et iustitia post
labilem uitam aeterno
glorientur in regno.

Tu ei honor sis tu
gaudium, tu gaudium, tu
uoluntas, tu in merore
solatium, in ambiguitate
consilium, in itinere
consolator. Amen.
Tu in iniuriis defensor,
in tribulatione pacientia,
in egritudine medicina.
Amen.
In te habeat omne
consilium, per tuam
discat commissa
sapientiam regni
gubernaculua moderari,
ut semper felix semper a
te gaudens, de tuis
mereatur beneficiis
gratulari, et aeternis
ualeat commerciis
copulari. Amen.
Vt quem tu nobis hodie
tua misericordia
iocundum presentare
dignatus es, tua facias
multorum annorum
curriculis, protectione
securum. Amen.

Et ita populus iste   Et ita populus iste
pullulet coalitus   pululet coalitus
benedictione aeternitatis,   benedictione aeternitatis,
ut semper maneant   ut semper maneant
tripudiantes in pace   tripudiantes in pace
uictores.   uictores.
Quod ipse praestare
digneris, qui cum
aeterno patre, simul cum
spiritu sancto, uiuis et
regnas deus, per omnia
secula seculorum.
Amen.

The relationship is clear, as Robinson and Nelson indicated. Robinson
left the matter of the relative dates of the compositions open. Nelson,
however, suggested that the 'Eighth-Century Gelasian' blessings were
the earlier, copies having been extracted, probably in the seventh or
perhaps eighth century, from some Merovingian source by the English

compiler of *A*'s order. Clearly she is right: Anglo-Saxon missionaries are unlikely to have returned from the continent empty handed. Long versions of *Benedic domine hunc presulem principem*, moreover, only appear in French and German books as part of the 'Second English Order'. An English origin therefore seems assured, a feeling intensified by the fact that sections of its text were excerpted and reworked by the man who composed the standard English blessing for the consecration of an abbot, *Deus qui sub tuae maiestatis arbitrio omnium regnorum.*[241] I give the version preserved in the 'Benedictional of Archbishop Robert'.[242] The most important borrowings have been italicized:

Deus qui sub tuae maiestatis arbitrio omnium regnorum contines potestates, tibi supplices fundimus preces humiliter exorantes, ut hunc famulum tuum N. a nobis indignis in gradum abbatis electum tuae supernae summaeque sanctificationis gratia benedicere digneris, ut *in diebus eius* deuotio renascatur disciplinae, et ut te adiuuante suis subditis tibi placita prebere possit exempla, *tibique cum timore subditus* ac militans mansuetus, tuae maiestatis mereatur *ubique clypeo pacifice protegi. Dextera tuae diuinitatis eum digneris locupletare, ut opem frugalem fratribus inferre*, et omnibus undique aduenientibus pie possit profutura exhibere. *Tu illi esto honor, tu gaudium* in domo, *in itinere socius, in merore solatium, in ambiguitate consilium, in egritudine medicina*, in laboribus adiutor, *in aduersis defensor, in tribulatione patientia*, ponat in te prouidentiam mentis, *per te discat consilio commissi sibi gregis gubernacula sapienter moderari, ut semper felix semperque exultans de tuae bonitatis ditatus beneficiis mereatur gaudere, et prolixitatem praesentis uitae per tempora bona* benigne suscipere ac supernis ciuibus, *angelorumque choris per aeterna commercia copulari*. Per dominum nostrum.

As Turner pointed out in the introduction to his edition of the 'Claudius Pontificals', the formula figures in five other pre-Conquest books: 'Dunstan', 'Egbert', 'Lanalet', CCCC 146 (original portions), and CCCC 44.[243] It also occurs in the 'Anderson' pontifical; Rouen BM 272,

[241] The opening words *Deus qui sub tuae maiestatis arbitrio omnium regnorum* are borrowed from a 'Gelasian' prayer in honour of temporal rulers, ed. Mohlberg, *Liber Sacramentorum Romanae ecclesiae*, p. 216, no. 1490.
[242] Ed. Wilson, *The Benedictional of Archbishop Robert*, pp. 130–1.
[243] See Turner, *The Claudius Pontificals*, pp. xxxvi–vii and 104; BNF lat. 943, fol. 80, with Rasmussen, *Les pontificaux*, p. 277; BL Add. 57337, fols 85v–86r; *Two Anglo-Saxon Pontificals*, ed. Banting, p. 114; CCCC 146, pp. 123–4; and CCCC 44, pp. 331–3.

the mid-eleventh-century sacramentary of Saint-Wandrille; and a mid-twelfth-century manuscript from Monte Cassino containing Peter the Deacon's commentary on the Rule of St Benedict and related material.[244] The two continental versions were doubtless picked up from an English source. In view of 'Dunstan', it seems reasonable to think that *Deus qui sub tuae maiestatis arbitrio omnium regnorum* was composed in England in the mid to late tenth century by some monastic reformer who had before him the text of an English royal *ordo*.

It remains to say that Bouman took too pessimistic a view of the question of *A*'s 'usability'. Its order is perfectly usable: the chant and readings will have been in the archbishop's gradual and lectionary, further rubric in his 'ordinal', assuming of course that he needed it. That the formulae for mass would have to be searched for elsewhere (perhaps they were on a separate sheet) might have been a minor inconvenience, but that is all. *A* contains all the blessings required. Indeed, *A* could perfectly easily embody the substance of the *ordo* used by Plegmund at the coronation of Edward the Elder in 900 – which is not to rule completely out of account the possibility that the 'Second Coronation Order' had not yet come into being. For the conception of 'new' and 'old' in the middle ages was patently not the same as our own. That is clear enough from the forms of episcopal profession deposited at Canterbury throughout the eighth and ninth centuries. The 'form' used by Æthelnoth, bishop elect of Worcester 805 × 811 was, for instance, later adopted for Eadwulf, bishop elect of Elmham 942 × 956; and the ones used by Wigthegn, bishop elect of Winchester 805 × 814, and Heahbeorht of Worcester, were employed sporadically and according to no discernable plan throughout the course of the ninth century.[245] The scribes seem to have copied whatever came to hand: and the archbishops, evidently, did not baulk at that. Plegmund might, for whatever reason, have preferred an older coronation *ordo* for Edward.

---

[244] BL Add. 57337, fols 85v–86r, with Rasmussen, *Les pontificaux*, p. 217; Rouen BM 272, fol. 231; and Monte Cassino, Biblioteca dell'Abbazia, 257, ed. Martène, *AER*, Bk II, cap. ii, art. i, ordo 1. The Monte Cassino text is heavily interpolated. For a description of the manuscript see Martimort, *La documentation*, pp. 363 and 574, nos 708 and 1190.

[245] See Richter, *Canterbury Professions*, nos 7 and 30; nos 11, 14, 15 and 29; and nos 8, 20, 22 and 26.

Prayers for the consigning of the pallium (nos 2467–9)

A contains the earliest surviving texts of the three prayers that were said on the occasion of an archbishop receiving his pallium, that is to say, the long band of white wool that invested the metropolitan with certain spiritual and temporal powers, not least the right to consecrate suffragan bishops. The first two formulae are preliminary to the actual act of tradition: *Orationes quae dicendae sunt super archiepiscopo antequam pallium accipiat*, though there is seldom any rubric in later manuscripts to indicate exactly when these were to be pronounced; and the third subsequent: *Hic detur pallium. Oratio postea.* Versions of these formulae occur in a number of later sacramentaries and pontificals, most of which we have come across already:

BNF lat. 943: the late-tenth-century 'Pontifical of St Dunstan'.[246]

BNF lat. 12052: the late-tenth-century sacramentary of Ratoldus of Corbie.[247]

Certain eleventh-century copies of the Romano-German pontifical, the earliest of which is Monte Cassino, Biblioteca della Abbazia, 451, written *c*. 1022. As Vogel has shown, this in all probability descends from a pontifical drawn up, either in Rome, or less likely, Mainz, shortly after the year 1000.[248]

BL Add. 57737: the early-eleventh-century 'Anderson' Pontifical. The prayers figure on fols 50r–51v.

CCCC 146: the pontifical once owned by Sampson, bishop of Worcester. The formulae figure, however, in the original, early-eleventh-century Winchester part of the book. The prayers are on pp. 136–8.

CCCC 44: the mid-eleventh-century pontifical of Christ Church, Canterbury. The prayers appear in an extensive order for the installation and enthronement of an archbishop on pp. 261–78.

and Douai BM 67: the mid-twelfth-century Canterbury pontifical normally known as the 'Pontifical of Thomas à Becket'.[249]

---

[246] Ed. Martène, *AER*, Bk I, cap. viii, art. xi, ordo 3.

[247] Ed. Morinus, *Commentarius de sacris ecclesiae ordinationibus*, p. 252; PL 78, cols 507–8.

[248] The prayers are ed. *PRG* I, 229–30 (cap. lxiv, nos 1–3). On the book as a whole, see *PRG* II, 138–40 and III, 16–18; and *OR* I, 176–211.

[249] See Leroquais, *Les pontificaux* I, 154–5.

Collation shows that there are two early recensions of the prayers concerned: one English, as in *A* and 'Ratoldus', the other continental, as in the eleventh-century copies of the Romano-German Pontifical. The differences are perhaps most visible at the end of the third prayer, where *A*, 'Ratoldus' and indeed all later English books, have *ad destinata sanctis premia peruentens*, and copies of the Romano-German Pontifical *ad destinata sanctus per omnia*.[250] 'German' books, moreover, always mention the Pope in their superscriptions: *Orationes istae dicendae sunt a domno papa super archiepiscopum ante pallium*, or *Ordo quando pallium datur archiepiscopo. Istae orationes a domno papa super archiepiscopum dicendę sunt ante pallium*. English ones, however, rarely do, presumably because Englishmen always had in mind the privilege granted by Pope Honorius (625–38) to their church. The terms of this privilege were quite simple. In the event of the death of the archbishop of Canterbury, the archbishop of York could confer the pallium on his successor, and vice versa. There was no need to make a fatiguing journey to Rome to collect the pallium in person. That the details of this ancient custom were well known is assured: the text of Honorius's letter is given in Bede's *Historia ecclesiastica gentis Anglorum* and the attendant historical circumstances described at some length.[251] Indeed, at some point during the course of the tenth century, a 'note' referring to the *Historia* was worked into the Canterbury pontifical. The burden of this note, which first appears in 'Dunstan', is clear:

> Hoc additamentum sit, si archiepiscopus aecclesiae Christi uel aecclesiae sancti Petri archiepiscopum hinc uel inde secundum decretum Honorii papae ad Honorium archiepiscopum ordinare uoluerit, ut legitur in .xviii. capitulo libri .ii. historiarum Anglorum.

> Let this be the addition if the archbishop of Christ Church or of York should wish to ordain the other according to the decree of Pope Honorius to Archbishop Honorius, as we read in the eighteenth chapter of Book 2 of the History of the English.

The three prayers are marked out for the sole use of the consecrating archbishop. Since Dunstan apparently went to Rome for his own pallium quite happily, these prefatory lines, which concern not going, must therefore have been attached to the prayers by one of his predeces-

[250] I have a discrete edition of all accessible texts of the prayers in hand.
[251] Bede, *HE*, pp. 196–9 (II.18).

sors.[252] Archbishop Oda (941–58) seems most likely, for he succeeded Wulfhelm (927–41), the first archbishop of Canterbury in centuries to have collected the pall in person from the Pope.[253] It was presumably Oda too who took the opportunity to interpolate the third prayer in his typically wordy style. 'Dunstan', 'Anderson', CCCC 146 and CCCC 44 all have the same form of text. CCCC 44 represents a later stage of development though, since its prayers have been set in an *ordo*, and further formulae, all newly composed, worked in. The versions of the pallium prayers given in *A,* on the other hand, are likely to be ancient, and probably Roman in origin, even if the form of words with which the third of the three opens does have a somewhat 'Gallican' ring.[254] Whether they found their way into the Canterbury pontifical of the seventh century remains to be seen.[255]

[252] According to the confirmatory letter granted by Pope John XII, a copy of which survives in BNF lat. 943, Dunstan took his pallium from the altar of St Peter, rather than the Pope's hand: *Sed pallium a suis manibus non accepit sed eo iubente ab altare sancti Petri apostoli.* The text of the letter is ed. D. Whitelock, M. Brett and C. N. L. Brooke, *Councils and Synods with other Documents relating to the English Church, A. D. 871–1204,* 2 vols (Oxford, 1981) I, 226–9, no. 41, and H. Zimmermann, *Papsturkunden 896–1046,* 2 vols, Österreichische Akademie der Wissenschaften, Phil.-hist. Klasse, Denkschriften 174 and 177 (Vienna, 1984–5) I, 271–4, no. 149. The cleric B., *Vita sancti Dunstani,* ed. W. Stubbs, *Memorials of St Dunstan,* RS 63 (London, 1874), 3–52, at 38–40, relates the story of Dunstan's journey to Rome. Michael Lapidge has a new edition of the *uita* in hand.
[253] See the 'E' text of the Anglo-Saxon Chronicle, ed. C. Plummer, *Two of the Saxon Chronicles Parallel,* 2 vols (Oxford, 1892–99) I, 107, and II, 136, and W. Levison, *England and the Continent in the Eighth Century* (Oxford, 1946), pp. 18–22, 233–48. The surviving papal letters confirming the rights of numerous archbishops and listing the days on which their respective pallia were to be worn are analysed by C. B. von Hacke, *Die Palliumverleihungen bis 1143* (Marburg, 1898).
[254] See for example, the *benediccio ad omnia in usum basilice* of the 'Old Gelasian' sacramentary, ed Mohlberg, *Liber Sacramentorum Romanae ecclesiae,* pp. 109–10, no. 700; the preface of the first dominical mass of Paris, Bibliothèque nationale de France, lat. 13258, the so-called 'Bobbio Missal', a mid-eighth-century combined sacramentary and mass lectionary from a house in northern Italy, ed. E. A. Lowe, J. W. Legg, A. Wilmart and H. A. Wilson, *The Bobbio Missal, a Gallican Mass-Book,* 3 vols, HBS 53, 58 and 61 (London, 1917–24) II, 135, no. 453; and the blessing of the candles on the feast of the Purification of the Virgin (2 Feb.) in a number of early pontificals: *Domine omnipotens creator caeli et terrae, rex regum et dominus dominantium, exaudi nos famulos tuos clamantes.* None of these prayers, nor any of the many others that begin in this way, can be shown to be Roman.
[255] See the remarks of Hohler, 'Books', 79–80.

Exorcisms (nos 2470–9)

A's formulae, as their superscriptions indicate, were mostly either to be
pronounced over a candidate preparing for baptism (*A*'s baptismal *ordo*
follows) or for one already baptised. Generally speaking they are standard. However, a few brief remarks are called for. The first prayer is an
expanded version of a prayer later embodied in the Romano-German
Pontifical:[256]

A.	*Romano-German Pontifical.*
Omnipotens sempiterne deus, pater domini nostri ihesu christi te supplices exoramus, impera diabolo, qui hunc famulum tuum .ill. detinet, ut ab eo recedat, et extinguatur per impositionem manuum nostrarum, quas nos ponimus carnales per inuocationem tui nominis, et pro meritis beatorum angelorum tuorum, et patriarcharum, et prophetarum, et apostolorum, et martyrum, et confessorum, et uirginum, atque omnium sanctorum tuorum.	Omnipotens sempiterne deus pater domini nostri, te suppliciter deprecamur, impera diabolo qui hunc famulum tuum N. detinet, ut ab eo recedat,
Libera eum qui credit in uerum liberatorem dominum nostrum ihesum christum, ut expurgatus ab omni labe iniquitatis, maiestati tuae pura mente deseruiat, consecutus gratiam spiritus sancti, qui cum patre et filio uiuit et regnat per omnia secula saeculorum. Amen.	et libera eum ut credidit in uerum liberatorem dominum nostrum ihesum christum, ut expurgatus ab omni labe iniquitatis, maiestati tuae pura mente deseruiat, consecutus gratiam spiritus sancti. Qui cum patre uiuit et eodem filio tuo.

Andrieu could find no parallel for this prayer when he edited the Pontifical. However, it may well be Italian, since a version appears in in the
late-ninth-century Ambrosian sacramentary from Bergamo. The
Ambrosian variant seems never found to have found its way north of
southern Germany.[257]

    A's second prayer is a conflation of four well-known Roman baptis-
mal formulae:[258]

[256] *PRG* II, 202 (cap. cxiv, no. 35).
[257] Paredi, *Sacramentarium Bergomense*, p. 339, no. 1457.
[258] See *Le sacramentaire grégorien* I, 335, no. 980; 377, no. 1080; 371, no. 1065; and 454, no. 1390.

A.

Medelam tuam deprecor domine sancte pater omnipotens aeterne deus, qui subuenis in periculis, qui temperas flagella dum uerberas, te ergo domine supplices deprecamur, ut hunc famulum tuum ill. eruas ab hac uexatione diaboli, ut non praeualeat inimicus usque ad animae temptationum, sicut in iob terminum ei pone, ne inimicus de anima istius sine remedio tuae saluationis incipiat triumphare. Defende domine exitum mortis, et spacium uitae extende, et releua ab hostiis maligni temptationibus et figuris phantasmatum, famulum tuum, quem creasti ad imaginem tuam, et redemisti pretio magno sancti sanguinis filii tui. In cuius uirtute precipio tibi quicumque es, inmunde spiritus, ut exeas et recedas ab hoc famulo dei. Disrumpe domine per maiestatis tuae imperium, omnes laqueos satane quibus est conligatus, et auxilii tui ostende uirtutem et opus misericordiae tuae, ut fugatis infirmitatibus, sana mente, et uiribus sensibusque renouatis, nomen sanctum tuum, instaurata sanitate, protinus benedicat. Per.

Hadrianum.

Medellam tuam deprecor domine sancte pater omnipotens aeternae deus, qui subuenis in periculis, qui temperas flagella dum uerberas, te ergo domine supplices deprecamur, ut hunc famulum tuum eruas ab hac ualitudine ut non praeualeat inimicus usque ad animae temptationem, sicut in iob terminum ei pone, ne inimicus de anima ista sine redemptione baptismatis incipiat triumphare, defer domine exitum mortis, et spatium uitae extende reuela quem perducas ad gratiam baptismi tui.

. . . in cuius uirtute praecipio tibi quicumque es spiritus inmunde, ut exeas et recedas ab hoc famulo tuo . . . Disrumpe omnes laquaeos satanae quibus fuerat conligatus . . .

. . . ut fugatis infirmitatibus et uiribus receptis, nomen sanctum tuum instaurata protinus sanitate benedicat.

So far as I have been able to determine, *A* stands alone.

A's third prayer, *Vnguo te de oleo sanctificato*, a formula for unction (no. 2473) similar to those accompanying the unction of a sick man or woman, figures in ÖNB lat. 1888, the late-tenth-century sacramentary-cum-ritual from Mainz, and apparently nowhere else.[259] Versions of its last prayer, however, *Domine sancte pater* (no. 2479), are relatively common, thanks no doubt to the influence exerted by the Romano-German Pontifical:[260]

---

[259] Gerbert, *Monumenta* II, 133–4.
[260] *PRG* II, 190 (cap. cxiv, no. 7).

A.
Domine sancte pater omnipotens
aeterne deus, per impositionem
scripture huius et gustum aquae,
expelle diabolum ab homine isto. De
capite, de capillis, de uertice, de cerebro,
de fronte, de oculis, de auribus, de
naribus, de ore, de lingua, de sublingua,
de gutture, de collo, de corpore toto, de
omnibus membris, de compaginibus
membrorum suorum intus et foris, de
ossibus, de uenis, de neruis, de
sanguine, de sensu, de cogitationibus,
de omni conuersatione, et operetur in te
uirtus christi in eo qui pro te passus est,
ut uitam aeternam merearis. Per.

Romano-German Pontifical.
Domine sancte pater omnipotens
aeterne deus,
expelle diabolum de homine isto, de
capite, de capillis, de uertice, de
cerebro, de fronte, de oculis, de ore,
de auribus, de naribus, de lingua, de
sublingua, de gutture, de collo, de
corpore toto, de omnibus membris
tuis, de compaginibus membrorum
suorum, de intus, de foris, de uenis,
de neruis, de omnibus operibus malis,
de uirtute, de omni conuersatione, et
in futuro operetur in te uirtus christi.
Per.

But the prayer, in its original form, whatever precisely that may have been, is clearly much older than Pontifical, since it figures in Dublin, Royal Academy, D. II. 3, the so-called 'Stowe Missal', which is generally agreed to have been written for use in Ireland in the late eighth century; and in Munich, Staatsbibliothek, Clm 17027, an early to mid-tenth-century collectar from the abbey of Shäftlarn in Bavaria.[261]

From a textual standpoint, the Schäftlarn collectar agrees with the Romano-German Pontifical, while *A* and the Mainz sacramentary, in which it also occurs, generally agree with the 'Stowe'. But *A* has an interpolation, *per impositionem scripturae huius et gustum aquae,* not to be found in the other books just mentioned. This, so far as I can make out, only otherwise appears in two related prayers embedded in the OE service for the remedying of 'elf-sickness' or 'elf-disease' (OE aelfadle or aelfsogopan) printed in 1948 by Godfrid Storms from London, British Library, Royal 12. D. xvii, a collection of charms and remedies probably written at Winchester in the mid tenth century; and in the

---

[261] Ed. respectively G. F. Warner, *The Stowe Missal,* 2 vols, HBS 31–2 (London, 1906–15) II (text), 24, and Franz, *KB* II, 601–2. See also the useful remarks of F. E. Warren, *The Antiphonary of Bangor: an Early Irish Manuscript in the Ambrosian Library at Milan,* 2 vols, HBS 4 and 10 (London, 1893–5) II, 71–2. On the 'Stowe Missal' in general, see *CLLA,* no. 101, and M. Lapidge and R. Sharpe, *A Bibliography of Celtic-Latin Literature 400–1200,* Royal Academy Dictionary of Medieval Latin from Celtic Sources, Ancillary Publications 1 (Dublin, 1985), pp. 140–1, no. 537.

sacramentary of Ratoldus.[262] The text of the relevant part of the 'order', with Storms' translation, is as follows:

Writ þis gewrit (Write this writing): *Scriptum est rex regum* . . .

Sing þis ofer þam drence and þam gewrite (Sing this over the drink and the writing): *Deus omnipotens, pater domini nostri iesu christi, per impositionem huius scripturae expelle* . . . (a version of the prayer printed above).

Wyrc þonne drenc: fontwaeter, rudan, salvian, cassuc, draconzan, þa smeþan wegbraedan niþewearde, feferfugian, diles crop, garleaces .iii. clufe, finul, wermod, lufestice, elehtre, ealra empfela. Writ .iii. crucem mid oleum infirmorum und cweð (Then make a drink: baptismal water, rue, sage, hassock, dragonwort, the lower part of the smooth waybread, feverfew, a head of dill, three cloves of garlic, fennel, wormwood, lovage, lupine, equal quantities of each. Write three crosses with the oil of extreme unction and say): *Pax tibi.*

Nim þonne þaet gewrit, writ crucem ofer þam drince, and sing þis þaer ofer (Then take the writing, describe a cross with it over the drink, and sing this over it): *Deus omnipotens, pater domini nostri, iesu christi, per impositionem huius scripturae et per gustum huius, expelle* . . . (a further version of the prayer).

And *Credo* and *Pater Noster.*

Waet þaet gewrit on þam drence and writ crucem mid him on aelcum lime und cweð (Wet the writing in the drink and write a cross with it on each limb and say): *Signum crucis conserua te in uitam aeternam. Amen.*

Since no mention of writing or the giving of a draught of water is made in any continental manuscript, it seems reasonable to conclude that both *A* and 'Ratoldus' preserve an Anglo-Saxon form of text. Indeed, the prayer as a whole may be Anglo-Saxon in origin, and the German versions later reworkings.

---

[262] Ed. Storms, *Anglo-Saxon Magic*, pp. 222–9, no. 17; BNF lat. 12052, fol. 263v. On the Royal manuscript, see further, K. L. Jolly, *Popular Religion in Late Saxon England: Elf Charms in Context* (Chapel Hill, 1996), pp. 162–4, and Ker, *Catalogue of Manuscripts containing Anglo-Saxon*, no. 264, pp. 332–3.

The Baptismal Order (nos 2480–2506)

A's *ordo*, as one might expect, is like no other. Not only are its component parts apparently in the 'wrong' order, but we also have at least two archaic Italian prayers in the second ritual for the preparation of a catechumen. It will be best to outline briefly what the *ordo* as a whole contains.

First we have the standard prayers of the Supplement for the preparation of a catechumen for baptism (nos 2480–5), but not the accompanying series of exorcisms; instead, the standard Roman prayers for the blessing of the font follow, concluding with a version of the 'Eighth-Century Gelasian' rubric for the mixing and asperging of the chrism:[263]

A.	*Gellone.*
Post haec accipies chrisma cum uasculo et fundens in cruce super aquam dicens . . .	Inde uero accipiens chrisma cum uasculo fundens eam in crucem super ipsam aquam, et miscitas ipsa chrisma cum ipsa aqua. Adspargis tam super fontem quam super circumadstantes.
Et aspargis super adstantes, qui uoluerit accipiat de ipsa aqua et asparget ubicumque necesse fuerit.	Et qui uoluerint accipiat de ipsa aqua in uasis suis, ad spargendum ubi uoluerint.

This 'Eighth-Century Gelasian' rubric, sometimes adulterated, also survives in the books consulted by Deshusses. But *A*, unexpectedly, then gives further forms for the preparation of a catechumen, completely out of place: the prospective candidate for baptism gives his name; he is asked whether he renounces the devil and all his works; and he is then blown upon by the priest and signed with the cross on his forehead and chest (nos 2491–2). Two prayers follow, salt is administered, and a final prayer, preceded by a bidding for all to pray, pronounced. The closest corollaries for these forms are to be found not in Frankish or Carolingian books, but in Irish, southern German and central and northern Italian. Indeed, the best match for the general structure of this part of *A*'s *ordo* seems to be that of the original portions of the late-eighth-century 'Stowe Missal'.[264] After four preliminary exorcisms and consecrations, the catechumen is asked whether he renounces the devil and believes in

---

[263] Ed. Dumas and Deshusses, *Liber Sacramentorum Gellonensis* I, 100, no. 705.
[264] Ed. Warner, *The Stowe Missal* II, 24–6.

113

the Trinity. The priest then blows upon his face and makes the sign of the cross, but with oil, rather than with his finger. The catechumen renounces the devil once again, and the priest pronounces three prayers. There are two important points to note: first, that the interrogations *Abrenuntias satane, Et omnibus operibus eius, Et omnibus pompis eius*, in *A* and Stowe are detached from the short explanatory line *Epheta, quod est aperire*, which is usually pronounced immediately after the prayer *Nec te latet*; and second, that the first of *A*'s prayers after the making of the sign of the cross (no. 2493) agrees with 'Stowe', not the *Hadrianum* or 'Eighth-Century Gelasian' books, as the following comparison will show. On the left we have the first of the two versions given in the *Hadrianum*, in the middle that of 'Stowe' and on the right *A*'s:[265]

Hadrianum.	*Stowe.*	*A.*
Omnipotens sempiterne deus, respicere dignare super hunc famulum tuum	Rogamus te domine sancte pater omnipotens aeterne deus, miserere famulo tuo N.	Rogamus te domine sancte pater omnipotens aeterne deus, miserere famulo tuo uel famule tuae, quem uel quam
quem ad rudimenta fidei uocare dignatus es, caecitatem cordis ab eo expelle, disrumpe omnes laqueos satane quibus fuerat conligatus, aperi ei ianuam misericordiae tuae, et signo sapientiae indutus omnium cupiditatum faetoribus careat, atque ad suauem odorem preceptorum tuorum, laetus tibi in ecclesia tua deseruiat et proficiat de die in diem signatus promissae gratiae tuae.	quem uocare ad rudimenta fidei dignatus es caecitatem cordis omnem ab eo expellens disrumpe omnes laqueos satane quibus fuerat colligatus aperi ei ianuam ueritatis tuae + ut signo sapientiae tuae indutus omnibus cupiditatem fetoribus careat atque suaui odore preceptorum tuorum laetus tibi in aeclesia deseruiat et proficiat de die in diem ut idoneus efficiatur promisae gratiae tuae in nomine patris et filii et spiritus sancti in saecula saeculorum.	uocare ad rudimenta fidei dignatus es, omnem cecitatem cordis ab eo uel ab ea expelle, disrumpe omnes laqueos satane quibus fuerat conligatus. Aperi ei domine ianuam ueritatis tuae, ut signo sapientiae tue imbutus, uel induta, omnium cupiditatum foetoribus careant, atque suaui odore preceptorum tuorum laetus tibi in ecclesia tua deseruiat, et proficiat de die in diem, ut idoneus efficiatur promissae gratiae tuae, in nomine patris, et filii, et spiritus sancti in saecula saeculorum. Amen.

Trent, Museo Provinciale d'Arte, 1590, the late-ninth-century copy of a pre-'Hadrianic' Gregorian sacramentary from Salzburg, has 'Stowe's

---

[265] Ed. Warner, *The Stowe Missal* I, 24 and *Le sacramentaire grégorien* I, 180–1, no. 357.

ending but otherwise conforms to the *Hadrianum*.[266] It seems likely that *A* and 'Stowe' preserve the prayer in its archaic form. Also likely to be archaic are the two short exhortations in *A*, both beginning with the word *Accipe*, accompanying the blowing and crossing (nos 2491–2). These only otherwise occur together in the mid-eighth-century Bobbio Missal, which is now generally agreed to be a 'Gallican' rather than 'Irish' book, though the distinction largely depends on one's view of where and how the compilers of such 'Gallican' books obtained their material.[267]

A's prayer *Domine sancte pater* (no. 2494), on the other hand, seems not to have found its way from Italy into any other surviving book. Indeed, in Italy itself it is exceptionally rare, only occuring otherwise, so far as I have been able to determine, in Vallicellana C. 32, the early-eleventh-century ritual in Beneventan script published by Dom Ambros Odermatt.[268] In the following comparison, *A*'s text is given on the left and that of the ritual on the right:

A.	*Benevento.*
Domine sancte pater omnipotens aeterne deus, pater domini nostri ihesu christi, cuius antiquitas sine initio, aeternitas sine fine est. Deus omnium rerum creator, et ipse non genitus, deus inuisibilis et omnia uidens, deus incomprehensibilis et omnia comprehendens. Inuoco nomen sanctum tuum super opera manuum tuarum, ut hoc plasma quod in conspectu diuinae maiestatis tuae ad spem inmortalitatis aspirare dignatus es, per uirtutem sacramentorum caelestium, omnibus inimici loetalibus insidiis exuatur. Tu enim hominem ad imaginem tuam facere dignatus es, in cuius faciem insufflasti spiritum uitae, *suffla,* et factus est homo in animam uiuentem, sic itaque hunc famulum tuum ill.	Omnipotens sempiterne deus cuius antiquitas sine fine est, deus omnium creator et ipse non genitus, deus inuisibilis et omnia uidens, deus incomprehensibilis et omnia comprehendens, inuoco sanctum nomen tuum super opera manuum tuarum, quae in conspectu maiestatis tuae aspirat quibus inimicus letales insidias extendit, ut per uirtutem sacramentorum tuorum omnium molimina eius dissipentur. Tu enim domine hominem ad imaginem tuam facere dignatus es, in cuius faciem exsufflasti spiritum uitae et factus est homo in animam uiuentem, sic itaque et hunc famulum tuum

---

[266] See *Le sacramentaire grégorien* I, 181, apparatus for no. 357; *CLLA*, no. 724.

[267] Ed. E. A. Lowe, with J. W. Legg, A. Wilmart and H. A. Wilson, *The Bobbio Missal, a Gallican Mass-Book*, 3 vols, HBS 53, 58 and 61 (London, 1917–24) II (text), 71–2, nos 232–3. See also *CLLA*, no. 220, and Lapidge and Sharpe, *A Bibliography of Celtic-Latin Literature*, pp. 337–8, no. 1276.

[268] Odermatt, *Ein Rituale in Beneventanischer Schrift*, pp. 254–5, no. 41. *CLLA*, no. 1593.

uel famulam tuam, quesumus domine constituas in spiritu uiuificante, ut cognoscat te deum uiuum, te deum uerum, et unigenitum filium tuum ihesum christum quem misisti et spiritum sanctum. Signum quoque salutare quod in eum uel eam nunc conferre dignatus es custodias usque in finem, ut integer uel integra, et purus uel pura, perducatur ad lauacrum aquae regenerationis, data ei remission omnium peccatorum. Per.

constituas in loco uiuificationis, ut cognoscat te deum uerum et unigenitum filium tuum, quem misisti ad redemptionem populi tui, signum quoque in eo conferre dignatus, et custodias usque in finem.

A systematic search through the many central Italian books not yet in print may well turn up further versions; and such a search may also turn up a related version of *A*'s last preparatory prayer *Spes omnium finium terrae* (no. 2496), which either incorporates or inspired the latter portions of a common 'Gelasian' prayer (in the 'Supplement' too) also to be said over a catechumen:[269]

A.

Old Gelasian.

Spes omnium finium terrae et in mari longe qui sanctos montes tuos preparasti in uirtute tua, et accingeris potentia qua in te sperantes defensare digneris, deprecationem nostram clementer exaudi, et hunc catecuminum tuum, crucis dominicae cuius inpressione signatus est uirtute custodi, ut agnitionis tuae rudimenta seruans, per custodiam mandatorum tuorum ad regenerationis gloriam peruenire mereatur seruaturus per te quicquid te largiente percepit. Per.

... clementer exaudi, et hos electos tuos crucis dominicae cuius inpraessione signamur uirtute custodi ut magnitudinis gloriae rudimenta seruantes per custodiam mandatorum ad regenerationis peruenire gloriam mereatur. Per.

The opening words of the prayer as we have it in *A* may have been borrowed from the collect normally assigned to Psalm 64 in the so-called 'Romana' series.[270]

The third section of *A*'s order, the ceremonial surrounding the actual act of baptism, begins with the traditional prayer *Nec te latet satane* (no. 2497) and ends with the consignatory prayer *Omnipotens sempiterne deus qui regenerasti* (no. 2506). Most of the material is from the Supplement, but slightly rearranged. As we have seen, the three short questions

---

[269] Ed. Mohlberg, *Liber Sacramentorum Romanae ecclesiae*, p. 43, no. 286.
[270] Ed. L. Brou and A. Wilmart, *The Psalter Collects*, HBS 83 (London, 1949), p. 149.

beginning with the word *Abrenuntias* have been suppressed since they had already been asked elsewhere in the order. The standard short exorcism of late-ninth-century books *Exi inmunde spiritus, da locum spiritui sancto*, which was said during the anointing of the baptismal candidate, has been split in two to accompany the touching of his or her chest and shoulders by the officiant (nos 2499 and 2500); and since the ceremonial for the blessing of the font (which always follows the anointing in the numerous *ordines* that are arranged as proper 'orders of service') stands at the beginning of *A*'s *ordo*, we jump straight to the forms of examination, *Credis in deum patrem unigenitum*, and so forth, preliminary to the immersion. The only other detail to note is the presence of the question *Vis baptizari?* and the response *Volo*. Both figure in two northern French books used by Deshusses, but not in any of the so-called *Ordines romani* published by Andrieu, nor for that matter in the 'Eighth-Century Gelasian' sacramentaries.[271]

So, to recapitulate, *A*'s order is composed of four distinct sections: a short series of formulae to be said over the catechumens; the 'standard' ritual for the blessing of the font on Holy Saturday; a second set of prayers to be said over a male catechumen; and last, the remainder of the baptismal order proper. So the question is: why does *A* appear to be such a jumble? Possibly the scribe had never been present at a baptism, and when presented with two or perhaps even three different sets of source material to amalgamate, he either amalgamated them as they came to hand or followed now one then another, according to no set pattern. The resulting *ordo* is not, from a practical point of view, impossible to use, but life would not be easy for the man who had to baptize regularly. There may, of course, be good reason for its apparently quirky arrangement: but that will take some finding. The point to press home, however, is a general one. *Ordines* seem rarely to have been copied without modification: rubric, prayers, and chant could and often did travel separately, and it therefore becomes enormously difficult to establish not only where the various elements came from, but at what date and in which place or places they were first gathered together. As far as *A* is concerned, parts are certainly northern and central Italian, and probably ancient, while others appear to be 'insular', and possibly no earlier in date than the seventh century. But until someone traces the manuscript history of these *ordines* in greater detail, it will be impossible to

---

[271] *Le sacramentaire grégorien* III, 102 and 107.

say how unusual 'Stowe's' rudimentary order really is. For the habit of placing the three questions beginning *Abrenuntias* at the head of the service and suppressing them later on, for example, is also typical of books from the diocese of Trent.[272]

The Order for the Visitation of the Sick (nos 2507–44)

At first sight, *A*'s order looks up to date, for it embodies a well-known series of discrete formulae, all beginning *Vnguo*, to be pronounced as the different parts of the sick man or woman's body were anointed. As Harry Porter suggested in the late 1950s, unction was probably not regularly administered to the sick in Carolingian domains until Louis the Pious (814–40) came to the throne; and when rubric to the effect does occur in the earliest surviving manuscripts, a single invariable formulae normally suffices for the anointing of the neck, throat, shoulders, chest, and so forth, stipulated by the rubric.[273] That is certainly the case in the mid to late-ninth-century sacramentaries published by Deshusses, and also in those published by Dom Martène in the eighteenth century and Dom Carlo de Clercq in 1930.[274] Besides *A*, other early books containing formulae proper to the anointing of the different parts of the body are:

BNF lat. 9433: the late-ninth-century sacramentary from the abbey of Echternach.[275] The formulae begin alternately *Vnguo* and *In nomine*, an arrangement that can be paralleled in the tenth-century sacramentaries of Fulda and Mainz (below).

Düsseldorf, Universitäts- und Landesbibliothek, D. 2: an early-tenth-century sacramentary from Essen. The order for the visitation of the sick figures on fols 193r–194v.[276]

[272] See for instance, Vienna, Österreichische Nationalbibliothek, the sacramentary of Adalpert II, bishop of Trent (1156–72), ed. F. dell'Oro and H. Rogger, *Monumenta Liturgica Ecclesiae Tridentinae saeculo XIII antiquiora*, 3 vols in 4 (Trent, 1983–8) II.ii, 1039–1237, at 1092, nos 64–6.

[273] H. B. Porter, 'The origin of the medieval rite for anointing the sick or dying', *JTS* ns 8 (1956), 211–25, and *idem*, 'The rites for the dying in the early middle ages I: St Theodulf of Orleans', *JTS* ns 10 (1959), 43–62.

[274] *Le sacramentaire grégorien* III, 127–54; Martène, Bk I, cap. vii; and C. de Clercque, 'Ordines unctionis infirmi saeculi ix–x', *EL* 44 (1930), 99–123.

[275] Ed. Hen, *The Sacramentary of Echternach*, pp. 431–4, nos 2240–8.

[276] The manuscript is on loan from the City of Düsseldorf. For a brief account of the sacramentary and the literature surrounding it, see J. Semmler, 'Von Sakramentar zum Missale. Bemerkungen zu drei liturgische Handschriften der Universitäts- und Landes-

BNF lat. 9432: the early-tenth-century sacramentary from Amiens. The order figures on fols 144v–152r.

Albi, Bibliothèque Rochegude, 20: the tenth-century pontifical from some southern French cathedral.[277]

A tenth-century (?) sacramentary from Reims published by Ménard in the sixteenth century but now lost.[278]

The Romano-German Pontifical and related books, such as the tenth-century pontifical now at Lerida.[279]

ÖNB lat. 1888: the late-tenth-century sacramentary-cum-ritual from Mainz.[280]

and Göttingen 231: the late-tenth-century sacramentary from Fulda.[281]

Since the series of pieces reappears time and time again, though not always in the same order, it seems reasonable to conclude that the formulae issued from some important centre in northern Europe, presumably embedded in an *ordo,* from which revisers extracted. It is well to say too that these formulae were sometimes translated into the vernacular. A set in Old English are given in parallel with the Latin in the early-eleventh-century 'Missal of Robert of Jumièges'.[282]

When one looks at *A*'s order in more detail, however, it soon becomes clear that at least three separate *ordines* have been run together: one containing the formulae just mentioned; a second, along the lines of those published by Deshusses, containing prayers and a certain amount of guiding rubric; and a third, archaic and highly distinctive order, taken over from some north Italian book. Despite the assertions of Ruggero

bibliothek, Düsseldorf', in *Bucher für die Wissenschaft: Bibliotheken zwischen Tradition und Fortschrift. Festschrift für Günter Gattermann zum 65. Geburstag*, ed. G. Kaiser, H. Finger and E. Niggermann (Munich, 1994), 201–12, at 202–3; *CLLA* Suppl., no. 915.

[277] Ed. Rasmussen, *Les pontificaux*, pp. 66–7.

[278] Ed. PL 78, cols 529–38. On the character of the book, see H. B. Porter, 'The rites for the dying in the early middle ages II: the legendary sacramentary of Rheims', *JTS* ns 10 (1959), 299–307.

[279] *PRG* II, 258–70 (cap. cxliii).

[280] Ed. Gerbert, *Monumenta* II, 29–36.

[281] Ed. Richter and Schönfelder, *Sacramentarium Fuldense*, pp. 284–300, nos 2394–2457.

[282] See *The Missal of Robert of Jumièges*, ed. Wilson, pp. lxxi–lxxii, 290–4, with M.-M. Dubois, 'Les rubriques en vieil anglais du missel de Robert de Jumièges', *Rouen. Congrès scientifique* I, 305–8.

dalla Mutta, *A*'s order is neither that of Arras (the Artois, as he puts it) or indeed of any other northern French house.[283] We have:

(i) the ancient Italian/Anglo-Saxon penitential prayer for Ash Wednesday *Omnipotens deus qui dixit qui me confessus* (no. 2507), with its brief directions for the officiant, *episcopus aut presbiter*, who was to pronounce the suite of prayers that follow.

(ii) a passage of rubric beginning *Si autem episcopus adfuerit, imponat capiti manum* (no. 2510), followed, after preces and prayers, by the rare formula *Omnipotens deus qui in nomine unigeniti misit spiritum* (no. 2515). The two are only otherwise found together in Rome, BN 2081, the late-ninth-century ritual-cum-prayerbook from Nonantola; Paris, Bibliothèque nationale de France, lat. 818, a mid-eleventh-century sacramentary from Troyes; and St Florian, Bibliothek des Chorrenstiftes, XI. 467, a mid-twelfth-century ritual written at the great abbey of St Florian, eight miles to the south east of Linz in modern-day Austria.[284] In all three, the accompanying rubric indicates that the prayer was to be said during the laying-on of hands, and this therefore must have been its original use. *A*'s compiler, however, obviously thought it well to separate one from the other.[285] Since the penitential prayer *Omnipotens deus qui dixit* is also to be found in Rome BN 2081, as we have seen, the book to which he had access is likely to have been north Italian. Indeed, the only other place in Europe that seems to have had a special formula for laying-on at an early date was Milan.[286]

---

[283] R. dalla Mutta, 'Un rituel de l'onction des malades du IXe siècle en Flandre chaînon important entre le rituel *Carolingien* et les rituels des Xe–XIe', *Mens concordet voci (Mélanges offerts à Mgr A. G. Martimort)*, ed. C. Dagens (Tournai, 1983), pp. 608–18; *Le sacramentaire grégorien* III, 148–9, *ordo* 437, for Saint-Amand, and III, 145–6, *ordo* 433, for Corbie.

[284] Gulotta and Ruysschaert, *Gli antichi cataloghi* I, 309; Martène, *AER*, Bk I, cap. vii, art. iv, ordo 3, and A. Franz, *Das Rituale von St Florian aus dem zwölften Jahrhundert* (Freiburg-im-Breisgau, 1904), p. 77. On the Paris manuscript, see Leroquais, *Les sacramentaires* I, 151–4.

[285] Ed. Franz, *Das Rituale von St Florian*, p. 77.

[286] Ed. K. Gamber, *Das Sakramentar von Monza*, Texte und Arbeiten 3 (Beuron, 1957), p. 91*, no. 1041. See also the version in Milan, Biblioteca Ambrosiana, T. 27. Sup., a mid-eleventh-century collection of *ordines* from a house near Milan, ed. C. Lambot, *North Italian Services of the Eleventh Century*, HBS 67 (London, 1931), pp. 43–4. The Ambrosian *ordo* is discussed by A. M. Triacca, 'Le rite de l'impositio manuum super infirmum', *La maladie et la mort du chrétien dans la liturgie. Conferences Saint-Serge 21e semaine d'études liturgiques, Paris, 1974*, ed. A. Pistoia, C. M. Triacca and A. M. Triacca, Biblioteca Ephemerides Liturgicae Subsidia (Rome, 1975), pp. 354–60.

(iii) the prayer *Omnipotens deus qui per os* (no. 2519). This is perhaps more common, occurring in a number of books that we have come across already: the late-ninth-century sacramentary of Echternach; the pontifical of Roda; Gerbert's late-tenth-century sacramentary-cum-ritual from Mainz; the late-tenth-century sacramentary of Fulda in the University Library at Göttingen; and the twelfth-century ritual of St Florian. It also figures in the manual printed for the chapter of Constance Cathedral in 1510.[287] Echternach, St Florian and *A* are in general agreement against the other four:

A.	*Echternach.*	*Fulda.*
Omnipotens deus qui per os beati apostoli tui iacobi hunc ministerium infirmis hominibus facere precepisti, conserua famulo tuo ill. tuarum dona uirtutum, et concede ut medelam tuam non solum in corpore sed etiam in anima sentiat. Per.	Omnipotens deus qui per os beati iacobi apostoli tui hunc ministerium infirmis omnibus facere precepisti, conserua famulo tuo N. tuarum dona uirtutum, et concede ut medelam tuam non solum in corpore sed etiam in anima sentiat. Per.	Omnipotens deus qui per os beati iacobi apostoli tui hoc ministerium infirmis hominibus precepisti facere, conserua famulo tuo illo tuarum dona uirtutum, et concede ut medelam tuam non solum in corpore sed etiam percipiat in mente. Per.

Note that both 'Echternach' and *A* end with the words *anima sentiat*. So far as I have been able to establish, the prayer does not occur in Italian or northern French orders. It may therefore have found its way into *A* from the order containing the series of formulae for unction.

(iv) the prayer *Per istam unctionem* (no. 2523). Although this prayer is not to be found in any of the numerous *ordines* published by Doms Deshusses and Martène, versions have come down to us in a number of non-standard books, the oldest of which is Rome BN 2081.[288] Others are:

> Albi, Bibliothèque Rochegude, 20: the tenth-century pontifical from southern France.[289]

---

[287] Ed. respectively, Hen, *The Sacramentary of Echternach*, pp. 433–4, no. 2251; Planas, *El sacramentari, ritual i pontifical de Roda*, p. 642 (cap. xcii, no. 66); Gerbert, *Monumenta* II, 33; Richter and Schönfelder, *Sacramentarium Fuldense*, p. 295, no. 2435; Franz, *Das Rituale von St Florian*, p. 80; and *Manuale Constansiense* (1510), sig. C.iii^r. See also A. Dold, *Die Konstanzer Ritualientexte in ihrer Entwicklung von 1482–1721*, Liturgiegeschichte Quellen 5–6 (Münster-im-Westfalen, 1923), p. 79.

[288] Gulotta and Ruysschaert, *Gli antichi cataloghi* I, 309.

[289] See Rasmussen, *Les pontificaux*, p. 67.

The tenth-century (?) sacramentary of Reims published by Ménard.[290]

Rouen BM 368: The 'Lanalet' pontifical.[291]

Munich, Staatsbibliothek, Clm 3903: a mid-eleventh-century ritual from Augsburg.[292]

CCCC 422: a mid-eleventh-century votive sacramentary-cum-ritual compiled in part from a Winchester book for a church in the diocese of Sherborne. Probably later owned by the priest serving the church of St Helen's in Darley, Derbyshire, in the late twelfth century.[293]

Oxford, Bodleian Library, Laud Misc. 482: a mid-eleventh-century ritual in Old English and Latin, containing a penitential, confessional, and service for the visitation of the sick. The order for the visitation is in Latin.[294]

St Florian XI. 467 and XI. 434: the twelfth-century and fourteenth-century rituals of St Florian.[295]

and Macerata, Biblioteca Comunale, 'Mozzi-Borgetti', 378: a mid-twelfth-century pontifical from Benevento.[296]

The formula also found its way to Norway and Sweden, and it survived, surprisingly, well into the sixteenth century in Spain.[297] Further examples will probably come to light. *Per istam unctionem* and the rubric that follows (no. 2524) presumably came into *A*'s order from the north

---

[290] PL 78, col. 536.

[291] Ed. Doble, *Pontificale Lanaletense*, p. 138.

[292] Ed. F. A. Hoeynck, *Geschichte der kirchlichen Liturgie des Bistums Augsburg* (Augsburg, 1889), p. 421.

[293] Noticed by B. Fehr, 'Altenglische Ritualtexte für Krankenbesuch, heilige Ölung und Begräbnis', *Texte und Forschungen zur englischen Kulturgeschichte. Festgabe für Felix Liebermann zum 20 Juli 1921*, ed. M. Förster and K. Wildhagen (Halle, 1921), pp. 20–67, at 61. For a general description of this manuscript, see Ker, *Catalogue of Manuscripts containing Anglo-Saxon*, no. 70, pp. 119–21, and C. Hohler, 'The Red Book of Darley', *Nordiskt Kollokvium i Latinsk Liturgiforskning* 2 (Oslo, 1972), 39–47.

[294] Noticed by Fehr, 'Altenglische Ritualtexte', 61. For a general description of this book, see Ker, *Catalogue of Manuscripts containing Anglo-Saxon*, no. 343, pp. 419–22.

[295] Ed. Franz, *Das Rituale von St Florian*, p. 80.

[296] See R. F. Gyng, 'A pontifical of Benevento (Macerata, Biblioteca Comunale, "Mozzi-Borgetti", 378)', *Medieval Studies* 51 (1989), 355–423, at 403.

[297] See *Manuale Norvegicum*, ed. H. Faehn, Libri Liturgici Provinciae Nidrosiensis Medii Aevi 1 (Oslo, 1962), p. 13; *Manuale Lincopense*, ed. Freisen, pp. 85–6; *Manuale Hispalense* (1494), fol. iii[v]; and *Manuale secundum consuetudinem almae ecclesiae Salamaticensis* (1532), xlvi[v].

Italian source that provided (i) and (ii), as all appear together at Nonantola.

As for the actual wording of the prayer, collation shows that *A* embodies a shortened form of text, as the following comparison will demonstrate. On the left I give Ménard's 'Reims' text and on the right *A*'s:

Ménard.	*A.*
Per istam unctionem dei, et per ministerium nostrum, et dei benedictionem, mundentur et sanctificentur ab omni sorde et contagione peccati caput tuum, et sensus tui, uisus, auditus, odoratus, gustus et tactus, ut quicquid in humeris, uel in manibus aut pedibus, siue toto corpore, contagione, locutione et opere peccasti, misericordia saluatoris nostri expietur, ut idoneus efficiaris ad inuocandum dominum et benedicendum atque sanctificandum et sacrificandum in nomine eiusdem domini nostri iesu christi, reddatque tibi laetitiam salutaris sui, et spiritu principali confirmet te, et spiritum sanctum innouet in uisceribus tuis, et ne auferat illum a te, sed benedictio patris, et filii, et spiritus sancti, descendat super te, quae copiose super caput tuum defluat, et in extrema totius corporis tui descendat, interius et exteriusque repleat, atque circumdet, et sit semper tecum. Amen.	Per istam unctionem et domini benedictionem, mundentur ab omni sorde et contagione peccati ac sanctificentur, manus et os, cor quoque tactus, uidelicet sensus, uisus, auditus et gustus, totumque corpus et anima tua, ut idoneus efficiaris ad uocandum in nomine eiusdem domini dei nostri, reddat tibi dominus laetitiam salutaris sui, et spiritu principali te confirmet, sanctum quoque spiritum innouet in uisceribus tuis, et ne auferat illum a te. Sed benedictio dei patris, et filii, et spiritus sancti descendat super te quae copiose super te defluat, et in extrema corporis tui descendat. Interius exteriusque te repleat atque circumdet, ac sit semper tecum, nunc et in secula seculorum. Amen.

The 'Lanalet' pontifical, the two English rituals, the Beneventan pontifical, and the Norwegian manual follow Ménard; so too, with distinctive variants, the Augsburg ritual. St Florian, Seville and Salamanca on the other hand agree with *A*. Although I have not seen Rome BN 2081, it seems likely that the shorter version of the prayer form is the older, principally on the grounds that its text is plainer: fewer unctions are presupposed. The list of bodily parts to be anointed in Ménard's agrees closely with the later, more sophisticated, practice of pronouncing individual formulae as the different parts of the bod and the *loci* of the senses were blessed. Presumably, therefore, *Per istam unctionem* was at some point detached from its original surroundings, reworked, and circulated afresh. Only *A* and the Nonantola book have the rubric and short blessing that must originally have followed.

(v) the formula *Deus miserator omnium in te credentium* (no. 2544), which seems to be unique to *A*.

To sum up, *A*'s order for the visitation of the sick, like its baptismal *ordo*, embodies a mixture of the new and the old, the 'new' being the Carolingian rubric for the anointing of the various parts of the body and the accompanying series of formulae beginning *Vnguo,* the 'old' being *Omnipotens deus qui in nomine misit,* for the laying-on of hands, and *Per istam unctionem* for the anointing. This is not tacitly to reject what Porter said about sick unction not being given to the sick in the Empire until the reign of Louis the Pious, merely to suggest that *Per istam unctionem,* which clearly presupposes unction in some form or other, might easily have been the formula used in certain parts of Europe, perhaps even the Empire itself, before the Carolingian manuscripts examined by Porter had been written. That prayers and rubric often had separate lives is clear from the *ordines* published by Deshusses.

Daily Prayers and Benedictions (nos 2545–2691)

A's series of prayers for daily use in the main follows that of the *Hadrianum.* However, even the briefest of glances will show, that there are an unusually large number of omissions and inversions throughout. Some of these omissions can be paralleled in two books published by Dom Deshusses, namely Zurich, Zentralbibliothek, Rheinau 43, a late-ninth-century sacramentary probably from Rheinau, and Reims, BM 213, the sacramentary written at Saint-Amand for Noyon, but there are nowhere near as many; and in any case the order of prayers given in both these books is not that of *A*.[298] Unfortunately no thorough study of the sets of prayers involved exists, so it is difficult to say at present why *A*'s series seems so disorderly. From a textual standpoint too, we are on uncertain ground. Two formulae have variants known at Tours, whilst two more agree with the late-ninth-century sacramentary of Trent, which, as has been said, probably embodies the text of a pre-'Hadrianic'

---

[298] See *Le sacramentaire grégorien* I, 311–34, nos 840–979. On secondary uses of cotidian formulae, see A. Chavasse, 'Les oraisons pour les dimanches ordinaires', *RB* 93 (1983), 31–70 and 177–244, esp. 32–52.

Gregorian. Quite what this means is hard to determine: but it is by no means impossible that *A*'s daily prayers are simply those of its underlying (Italian) model. That Italian book may well have been ancient.

Chant

As has already been mentioned, the incipits of the sung parts of numerous masses were written in *A*'s margins by the original scribe, presumably with a view to helping the celebrant follow what the choir were doing, or at least what they were supposed to be doing, at given times. The pieces concerned are introduced by letters and abbreviations: *A* stands for *antiphona*, the introit (*introitus*) of later books; *Ps* or *Pl* for *psalmus*; *R* for *responsio gradualis* or gradual; *V* for *uersus*; *Al* for *alleluia*; *Tr* for *tractus*; *Of* for *offertorium* or offertory; and *Co* for *communio* or communion. These sets of incipits were later added to and sometimes changed at Exeter in the mid eleventh century, and the cues for the readings at mass added beneath. But for the moment only the original sets concern us here.

A is by no means the only book to have been provided with such cues. Others are:

Reims BM 213: the sacramentary of Ragenelmus, bishop of Noyon. Later at Reims.[299]

The so-called 'second sacramentary of Tours', written for the cathedral of St Maurice at Tours in the late ninth century. The remains of this book are now preserved in two manuscripts: Tours, Bibliothèque municipale, 184, and Paris, Bibliothèque nationale de France, lat. 9430.[300]

Paris, Bibliothèque nationale de France, nouv. acq. lat. 1589: another late-ninth-century sacramentary from the cathedral of St Maurice, Tours.[301]

[299] See n. 18, above, and the plate in M. de Lemps and R. Laslier, *Trésors de la Bibliothèque Municipale de Reims* (Reims, 1978), no. 10. *CLLA*, no. 1385.
[300] Partially ed. *Le sacramentaire grégorien* under the siglum Tu2. *CLLA*, no. 1385b. See also Deshusses, 'Les anciens sacramentaires de Tours', pp. 281–302, and Rand, *Studies in the Script of Tours* II, pl. CLXXI. 3.
[301] See Deshusses, 'Les anciens sacramentaires de Tours', and Leroquais, *Les sacramentaires* I, 53–5.

Reims BM 214: a sacramentary written at the abbey of Saint-Thierry, Reims, in the third quarter of the tenth century.[302]

Vat. Ottob. lat. 313: a mid-ninth-century sacramentary probably produced at Lyon that had found its way to the cathedral of Notre-Dame in Paris c. 849–51. The marginal cues were added in the late ninth and early tenth centuries.[303]

Düsseldorf, Landes- und Stadtbibliothek, D. 1: a mid-ninth-century copy of the *Hadrianum* augmented with several strata of additions, one clearly deriving from a book from a house in Burgundy. The manuscript was later at Essen, where marginal cues, with 'palaeofrankish' neums, were added in the tenth century.[304]

Angers, Bibliothèque municipale, 91: a late-tenth-century sacramentary from Angers Cathedral, with noted gradual parts before each mass (rather than in the margins).[305]

Note that all but Reims BM 214 are bishops' books. Another method of incorporating chant was to have the gradual separate at the front of the book, as is the case in:

Paris, Bibliothèque nationale de France, lat. 12050: a sacramentary written c. 853 by the priest Hrodradus for use at Corbie. The gradual was added in the late ninth century.[306]

Paris, Bibliothèque Sainte-Geneviève, 111: a sacramentary-cum-gradual written at Saint-Denis c. 877–82 for the use at Senlis.[307]

and BNF lat. 2291: the sacramentary-cum-gradual produced at Saint-Amand, probably for Gozlinus, bishop of Paris.[308]

Although these lists are by no means exhaustive, one thing seems certain: that the provision of marginal cues for the celebrant was essen-

[302] See Leroquais, *Les sacramentaires* I, 91–4.
[303] See n. 69 above.
[304] See *Le sacramentaire grégorien* III, 48–50, for a brief description of the book's contents; *CLLA*, no. 915. The formulae provided for the feasts of St Denis and his companions, which have attracted a good deal of inaccurate comment in the existing literature, are only otherwise to be found in sacramentaries from Nevers.
[305] See Leroquais, *Les sacramentaires* I, 48–51; *CLLA*, no. 1390.
[306] The gradual is ed. Hesbert as *Corbiensis*; and the sacramentary, *Le sacramentaire grégorien* under the siglum Q. *CLLA*, no. 742.
[307] The gradual is ed. Hesbert as *Silvanectensis*; and the sacramentary, *Le sacramentaire grégorien* under the siglum X. *CLLA*, no. 745. Also see Robertson, *Saint-Denis*, pp. 414–16.
[308] See above n. 24.

tially a northern European habit. It is well to say too, that so far as *A* is concerned, cues were not added to the pontifical sections of the book. For the most part, the chant is already embedded, where relevant, in the *ordines* as they stand.

Like its *ordo* for the visitation of the sick, *A*'s gradual, such as it is, is very much up to date. Perhaps the clearest indication of this lies in the fact that the proper chant provided for the second Sunday in Lent (*Sperent-Iustus-Domine deus-Custodi*), a feast not encompassed in the late-ninth-century graduals that have come down to us, also figures in Chartres, Bibliothèque municipale, 47, an early-tenth-century gradual probably from Redon in southern Brittany, and in numerous late missals from Brittany and Normandy, as Dom Anselm Hughes indicated in 1963.[309] But *A* is otherwise unrelated to these books, and we must look elsewhere in order to find closer relations. As has long been recognised, the psalm verses attached to the Alleluias in the Sundays of Pentecost are often decisive. Hughes expresses the position as follows:

> The choice of Alleluia verses for the Sundays after Pentecost in medieval manuscripts of the *antiphonarium missae* is known to be an important guide to the mutual relations of those manuscripts. The series of verses used on these Sundays may either correspond to the numerical order of the psalms from which they are drawn, or it may disregard this order. Again, the numerical series of Alleluya verses can be divided into three groups, according to the verse with which they begin.

The verses in question are: *Deus iudex iustus* (Ps. 7); *In te domine speraui* (Ps. 30); and *Dominus regnavit* (Ps. 92). *A*'s series begins *Deus iudex iustus*. A search through Victor Leroquais's notebooks, now preserved in the Bibliothèque nationale, reveals that five distinct sets of books are close to *A*. In order to simplify matters, these groups will be assigned sigla:

StV: Arras, Bibliothèque municipale, 339, 601, and 606: fourteenth-century missals from the abbey of Saint-Vaast, Arras.[310]

Dou: Lille, Bibliothèque municipale, 23: a mid-thirteenth-century Augustinian missal from Douai.[311]

---

[309] Hughes, *The Bec Missal*, pp. ix–x. Chartres BM 47 is ed. A. Mocquereau, *Antiphonale missarum sancti Gregorii Xe siècle: Codex 47 de la Bibliothèque de Chartres*, Palaéographie Musicale, ser. 1, vol. 11 (Solesmes, 1910); *CLLA*, no. 1350.

[310] Leroquais, *Notes*, fol. 27; *idem*, *Les sacramentaires* II, 232, 292 and 333–4.

[311] Leroquais, *Notes*, fol. 30; *idem*, *Les sacramentaires* II, 148–9.

Arr: Arras, Bibliothèque municipale, 271, 297, 309 and 391: early-thirteenth to late-fifteenth-century missals from Arras Cathedral.[312]

Re: Reims, Bibliothèque municipale, 225, 226 and 229: late-twelfth-century missals from the abbeys of Saint-Remi at Reims; and Reims, Bibliothèque municipale, 231 and 232: early-thirteenth-century missals from the abbey of St Thierry.[313]

Anc. and Mar, a conflate group, centring on books from Anchin and Douai: Douai, Bibliothèque municipale, 91: an early-seventeenth-century missal from Anchin; and Paris, Bibliothèque nationale de France, lat. 874: a fourteenth-century Cluniac missal from a house in northern France; Paris, Bibliothèque nationale de France, lat. 1095 and Arras, Bibliothèque municipale, 448: an early-twelfth and an early-fourteenth-century missal from Marchiennes; Paris, Bibliothèque nationale de France, lat. 843: a mid-twelfth-century missal from Saint-Amand; and Le Mans, Bibliothèque municipale, 23: a mid-eleventh-century missal from Saint-Denis de Nogent-le-Rotrou.[314] The series may be Cluniac in origin since the abbeys of Saint-Denis and Saint-Amand were important members of the order. Cluniac customs and liturgical practices were especially influential at non-Cluniac houses in northern France in the twelfth century.

PSALM VERSES

7b.	Deus iudex iustus.	108.	Confitebor domino.
17.	Diligam te.	110.	Redemptionem.
20.	Domine in uirtute.	113.	Qui timent.
30.	In te domine speraui.	116a.	Laudate.
46.	Omnes gentes.	116b.	Quoniam confirmata.
64.	Te decet ymnus.	117.	Dextera domine.
77.	Attendite.	121.	Laetatus sum.
80.	Exultate.	124.	Qui confidunt.
87.	Domine deus salutis.	129.	De profundis.
89.	Domine refugium.	137.	Confitebor.
94a.	Venite exultemus.	145.	Lauda anima.
94b.	Quoniam deus.	146.	Qui sanat.
104.	Confitemini.	147a.	Lauda hierusalem.
107.	Paratum cor.	147b.	Qui posuit.

[312] Leroquais, *Notes*, fol. 6; *idem*, *Les sacramentaires* II, 150, 333; and III, 109, 220.

[313] Leroquais, *Notes*, fol. 24; *idem*, *Les sacramentaires* I, 281–2, 360–1; and II, 6–7, 80.

[314] Leroquais, *Notes*, fol. 28; *idem*, *Les sacramentaires* I, 178–80, 221, 258–60; II, 170, 350–3; and III, 269–70.

COMPARATIVE TABLE

Sunday	A.	StV.	Dou.	Arr.	Re.	Anc. & Mar.
I	7b	7b	7b	7b	7b	7b
II	17	17	17	17	17	17
III	20	20	20	20	20	20
IV	30	30	30	30	30	30
V	46	46	46	58	46	46
VI	64	64	64	64	64	64
VII	77	77	77	77	77	77
VIII	80	80	80	80	80	80
IX	87	87	87	87	87	87
X	89	89	89	89	89	89
XI	94a	94a	94a	94a	94a	94a
XII	94b	94b	94b	94b	94b	94b
XIII	104	104	104	104	104	104
XIV	107	107	107	107	107	107
XV	113	113	113	113	108	110
XVI	116a	116a	116a	116a	113	113
XVIII	117	116b	116b	116b	116a	116a
XIX	124	121	121	121	129	129
XX	129	129	129	129	137	137
XXI	145	145	145	145	145	145
XXII	146	146	146	146	146	146
XXIII	147a	147a	147a	147a	147a	147a
XXIV	147b	147b	147b	147b	147b	147b

As can be seen, the books from Saint-Vaast and Douai are the closest. The late printed missals from Arras Cathedral have one minor difference, and the books from Reims, Anchin, Marchiennes and the Cluniacs of northern France, three or four. Given that *A*'s sacramentary was brought into line with a sacramentary from Saint-Vaast, it should perhaps come as no surprise that a gradual from the house was adopted too, allowing of course for later modifications and adjustment; and

Walter Frere's extensive comparison of over thirty books, including *A*, gives no cause to think otherwise.[315]

But *A* is unlikely simply to contain a straight copy of any book from Saint-Vaast since by late-ninth and early-tenth-century standards its gradual is massive and eccentric. Chant, for instance, is provided for the feasts of:

Emerentiana and Macharius (23 Jan.).	Vitus (15 June).
Conversion of Paul (25 Jan.).	Translation of Benedict (11 July).
Iuliana (16 Feb.).	James (25 July).
Cathedra Petri (22 Feb.).	Donatus (7 Aug.).
Matthias (24 Feb.).	Vigil of the Assumption (14 Aug.).
Benedict (21 Mar).	Bartholomew (25 Aug.).
John before the Latin Gate (6 May).	Jerome (30 Sept.).
Mark (18 May).	Luke (18 Oct.).
Nichomedis (1 June).	Thomas (21 Dec.).

None of these are encompassed in the graduals published by Hesbert and Netzer; nor are they encompassed in many later books. But *A*'s reviser seems not to have done what most revisers would have done and fitted these 'new' feasts out with chant from his gradual's commons. Instead, he seems to have taken a relatively free view of the book he had before him – occasionally with unusual results. St Vitus, for instance, has chant normally reserved for a pair of saints. The reviser, whoever he was, must therefore have been in the habit of celebrating the joint feast of SS Vitus and Modestus on 15 June, not that of St Vitus alone, and added the cues accordingly. Furthermore, few of the other feasts just listed have what became the standard sets of chant of later centuries.[316]

A, however, lacks chant for a number of important and ancient feasts, all of which are provided with proper prayers in the sacramentary:

SS Alexander, Eventius and Theodolus (3 May).
Vigil of St John the Baptist (23 June).
Vigil of St Peter (28 June).
SS Felix and Agapitus (6 Aug.).
St Eusebius (14 Aug.).
St Sabina (29 Aug.).
Cornelius and Cyprian (14 Sept).
Caesarius (1 Nov.).

---

[315] See W. H. Frere, *Graduale Sarisburiense*, Plainsong and Medieval Music Society 1 (London, 1894), pp. li–cii. *A* has no unusual Italian or Spanish variants.
[316] See for instance, *Missale ad usum ecclesiae Westmonasteriensis* III, ed. Legg, 1447–1628.

One might be forgiven for thinking that the forms for these feasts were simply borrowed from other saints' days, for *A*'s commons were not annotated. But *A*'s cues are simply that: cues. They give us only a tantalising glimpse of the sort of full, completely noted gradual, that must have accompanied *A*. *A*, unfortunately, cannot therefore give us the definitive use of Canterbury or Saint-Vaast, even though, as has already been said, the cues were probably excerpted in the main from a book from the latter house. Last, it remains to say that three feasts normal in graduals of all periods were left out: St Potentiana (19 May); St Praxedis (21 July) and St Apollinaris (23 July), the explanation for their absence being simply that *A* provides no proper prayers for their respective days.

Conclusions

As Hohler saw, *A* is an English book. It contains an English *ordo* for Ash Wednesday; numerous formulae that never figure in the numerous French and Lotharingian sacramentaries that have come down to us, but which appear regularly in service books written in England, and now and again, in those of northern Spain, northern Italy and the diocese of Mainz: it has an English pontifical and Coronation Order; part of an English service of exorcism and baptism; and it places St Mark's day on the 18th of May. It can only be English. That an invocation of St Vedastus should occur prominently in its litany is simply a consequence of the fact that a book from Arras, probably one akin to Cambrai BM 162–3, was used to turn the archaic Italian 'Eighth-Century Gelasian' sacramentary underlying *A* into *A* as we have it today. For reasons I hope already to have made plain, *A* cannot possibly have been written for the bishop of Cambrai-Arras. Its 'Artesian' symptoms are purely superficial. Indeed, in my view, *A* was Plegmund's sacramentary. Everything points to Canterbury; and since the archaic features of *A*'s Italian model, which could so easily have been suppressed, seem steadfastly to have been preserved, it may not be too fanciful to wonder, as Hohler did, whether *A* embodies material brought to England by St Augustine. But we must leave *A* now, and turn to *B*.

LEOFRIC B

General Introduction

Viewed as a whole, the material added to *A* in the earlier part of the the tenth century is pontifical in character. We have a number of episcopal benedictions to be said at mass; a series of blessings of things; new prayers and a particularly full set of chant for the ceremonies accompanying the ordination and consecration of a new prelate and a deacon; and, as Henry Bannister pointed out, the words *archiepiscopo nostro et rege nostro* as an insertion (probably of the second half of the tenth century) over an erasure of one and a half lines in the closing passage of the Exultet preface of Holy Saturday, that is to say the passage beginning *Precamur ergo te domine* (no. 805).[1] When an ecclesiastic is named in this way, he or she is almost certainly the head of the house at which the book was used. Since York is impossible, *A* must therefore have remained at Canterbury, passing from archbishop to archbishop after Plegmund's death in 923, its successive owners being: Athelm (*c.* 923–6); Wulfhelm (*c.* 926–41), during whose time the book was probably first added to; Oda (941–58), who caused more extensive changes to be made; Ælfsige (958–9), Byrhthelm (959) and finally Dunstan (959–88), who had the book unbound and massively augmented by the addition of new gatherings.[2] It may even be that some of the new material was written by the archbishops themselves.

From a palaeographical standpoint the additions made at Canterbury fall naturally into three groups. First, we have those which seem to have been written in the second quarter of the tenth century; second, those loosely datable to the third quarter; and third, those accompanying the writing and binding in of the calendar and computus on fols 38r–58v, an event which took place sometime between 979 and 987, as has already been mentioned. In the main the earlier additions were either written over erasures in *A*, or on spaces originally left blank. The material

---

[1] The page in question is illustr. E. W. B. Nicholson, *Early Bodleian Music* III, pl. XXVII. The addition is noted but not discussed by Warren, *LM*, p. 97. For more on this insertion, see below, pp. 153–4.

[2] For the careers of these men, see Brooks, *The Early History of the Church of Canterbury*, pp. 209–43.

contemporary with and (possibly) later than the calendar is nearly always on gatherings newly supplied. It will be best to deal with the three groups separately.

I. Formulae Added in the Second Quarter and Middle of the Tenth Century

Ten English scribes (A–J), writing in various forms of Square Minuscule, made additions to *A* in the second quarter and middle of the tenth century. They worked as follows:

Scribe A. Fol. 9r: blessing of a bell *Omnipotens dominator christe* (no. 50) on a page originally left blank.

Scribe B. Fol. 12r–v: prayers at the altar probably (nos 110–12). Possibly written on space that had been left blank, more likely over passages of *A*'s text that had been damped out.

Scribe C. Fol. 154v: exorcism and blessings of incense (nos 1295–8).

Scribe A. Fols 210v–211r: mass for troubles and remembrances of the dead (nos 1915–17).

Scribe D. Fol. 215v: an alternative collect for *A*'s mass for relics added in the margin (no. 1955*).

Scribe A. Fol. 253v: collect for Ember Saturday (no. 2245).

Scribe E. Fol. 267v, lines 12–17: general blessing *super populum* (no. 2301).

Scribe F. Fol. 267v, lines 18–27: chant in honour of the Virgin (no. 2302). Fully neumed.

Scribe B. Fol. 274r–v: at the beginning of gathering 36 (newly supplied), the rest of the text of the consecratory blessing of a priest and a prayer for the consecration of the priest's hands (nos 2331–32). Originally, that is to say in *A*, the blessing ran on to fol. 278. But the parts of the text written on this leaf were erased when the new quaternion was introduced and rewritten on fol. 274.

Scribe G. Fol. 275r–v, line 19: new prayers for the ordination of a deacon, ending half way through the formula for the consigning of the stole (nos 2333–6).

Scribe H. Fol. 275v, line 20 – 276r, line 5: the remainder of formula for the consigning of the stole (no. 2336).

Scribe I. Fols 276v–277r, line 18: new forms for the election and consecration of a bishop (nos 2337–41).

Scribe J. Fol. 277r, line 19 – 278v, line 9: chant and readings for the ordination of a bishop (nos 2342–7). The existing text on fol. 278, the beginning of gathering 38, was erased to make way for the new material.

Probably contemporary too are the marginal entries on fols 165r and 280r. The first, which is entered against the mass for St Agatha, notes, ungrammatically, the place of the feast of the Purification: *Hic purificatio sancta maria*. As we have seen, the prayers for mass are given in *A*'s temporal. The second notes that the bishop's head is to be anointed as the words *Hoc domine copiosae* are prounced in the service of consecration: *Hic ponendum oleum super caput*. More will be said about this in due course.[3]

Now Dumville has suggested that the work of scribes B and C on fols 12 and 154v is datable on palaeographical grounds to the 920s: and that is certainly a possibility worth considering, though he might also have said with equal justification, the 910s, 930s or even 940s.[4] It seems unwise at present to be too hard and fast on the subject. What does seem clear though, is that scribe B's work in *A*'s Ordinary, that is to say on fol. 12, pre-dates that of the scribes who made additions on fols 15 and 16.[5] For the material that scribe B added is appropriate to its surroundings; the later scribes simply erased passages of *A*'s text to make way for episcopal benedictions, material completely unrelated to an archbishop's preparations for mass. So *A*'s Ordinary seems to have fallen into disuse by the third quarter of the mid tenth century.

Scribe B also makes, on fol. 274, the first of a series of additions and alterations to *A*'s service for the consecration and ordination of bishops. His work, this time, is followed by that of three others whose hands look to be more or less contemporary, which suggests that there was a clear need at Canterbury in the 930s or 940s for a newer, or at least, larger set of forms of consecration. But what prompted such radical changes to this section of the book? The answer, in my view, probably lies in the

---

3   See below, p. 150.
4   Dumville, *English Caroline Script*, p. 95.
5   See below, pp. 151–2.

relatively large number of bishops appointed in Wulfhelm's time: well over a dozen. Oda, his immediate successor, only presided over the appointment of five, or possibly six.[6] An archbishop busy with consecrations is more likely to have wanted to keep up to date than one busy with other matters; and that most of these consecrations took place in the 930s accords well with the palaeography of the new material. The hard work of identifying the work of scribes A–J in other English books, however, remains.

Last, it is worth pointing out briefly, *pace* Dumville, that the appearance of the name of Madalbertus, bishop of Bourges (d. 910) among the *nomina defunctorum* at the foot of fol. 9r has no bearing on the date of *B* or the supposed arrival of *A* in England, since the text of the *nomina* is appended to a passage of writing by an English scribe.[7]

Liturgical character of the additions

Blessing of a bell (no. 50). A perfectly standard formula found in countless medieval sacramentaries and pontificals.[8]

Prayers at the Altar (nos 110–12). On fol. 12, in the middle of *A*'s Ordinary of the Mass, we have three new prayers for the officiant's use at the altar. As Warren pointed out, the first appears in the so-called 'Missal of Flaccus Illyricus', Wolfenbüttel 1151, the early-eleventh-century sacramentary from Minden, under the superscription: *Haec sequens oratio dicatur ab episcopo interim donec hymnus angelicus finiatur.*[9]

B.	*Illyricus.*
Deus qui iuste corrigis et clementer ignoscis, et non uis inuenire quod damnes, sed potius quod corones, qui etiam peccantium non mortem sed uitam magis desideras me miserum fragilemque peccatorem, sordibus delictorum plenum a tua pietate non repellas, neque respicias ad peccata	Deus qui iuste irasceris et clementer ignoscis
	qui etiam non mortem peccatorum, sed uitam desideras, me miserum, fragilemque peccatorum delictorum, sordibus plenum a tua pietate non repellas, neque respicias ad peccata

[6] See for instance the lists conveniently assembled in *A Handbook of British Chronology*, 3rd ed., ed. E. B. Fryde, D. E. Greenway, S. Porter and I. Roy (London, 1986), pp. 209–24.
[7] Dumville, *Liturgy*, p. 42. For more on fol. 8, see below pp. 212–13.
[8] For instance, *Liber Sacramentorum Gellonensis*, ed. Dumas and Deshusses, I, 369, no. 2446; *Zwei karolingische Pontifikalien*, ed. Metzger, p. 41*, no. 131.
[9] *LM*, p. 8; PL 138, cols 1314–15.

et scelera, et inmunditias, turpesque cogitationes meas, quibus tuae misericordiae dulcedinem merito mihi in maritudinem conuerti peccatorum, sed ad inmensas misericordias tuas quibus gratuito subuenire consuesti, precorque humiliter ut immemor sis peccatorum meorum, et memor misericordiarum tuarum, uota precesque meas clementer suscipias, tibique placita mihi postulare concedas, collegioque sanctorum tuorum qui in hoc ministerio tibi placuerunt me ascisci digneris, atque per eorum exempla facias tibi semper placere, et ad te cum fideli grege tuo peruenire. Per.

mea, quae male uiuendo commisi,

sed ad immensas misericordias tuas, quibus gratuito munere peccantibus subuenire consueuisti; obsecro itaque domine, ut inmemor sis peccatorum meorum, et memor misericordiarum tuarum, uota precesque meas dignanter suscipias, et dissimulatis fragilitatis meae peccatis, labia mea aperia, et ad confessionem me tuae laudis placatus admittas, qui per incarnationem et humanitatem domini nostri iesu christi filii tui dedisti pacem hominibus, et caelestium collegium angelorum, da me et de tuae pacis ubertate repleri, et de angelicae societatis unitate letari, sicque me facis his temporalibus officiis interesse, ut ad tuas misericordias in aeternum cum illis decantandas perpetuis electorum tuorum choris aggregari praecipuis. Per.

The version in 'Illyricus' is obviously longer, and alludes clearly, insofar as its opening is concerned, to the Roman collect *pro peccatis* which begins: *Deus qui iuste irasceris et clementer ignoscis, afflicti populi.*[10] But as Warren saw there can be no doubt that *B*'s prayer and that of 'Illyricus' sprang from a common source. They are both, after all, designed for recitation by the bishop as he prepared for mass. Quite what their common source was remains to be determinded, for no other version of the prayer has so far come to light to date. Since Leroquais makes no mention of any related example, Germany seems the obvious place to look: one must therefore wonder whether the underlying model might have been Anglo-Saxon in origin.

The second prayer, *Domine ihesu christe propitius esto mihi peccatori*, is found in five other early books:

Vercelli, Biblioteca Capitolare, Cartella s. n: an early-tenth-century sacramentary from the church of St Vigilius at Trent.[11]

---

[10] Ed. *Le sacramentaire grégorien* I, 312, no. 843.
[11] Ed. dell'Oro and Roger, *Monumenta liturgica ecclesiae Tridentinae* IIA, 527–8, no. 584. *CLLA* Suppl., no. 942*.

Vich 66: the eleventh-century sacramentary from Vich.[12]

A tenth-century sacramentary, now lost, from the abbey of Sankt Blasien in the Black Forest.[13]

Rouen BM 274: the early-eleventh-century sacramentary later owned by Robert of Jumièges.[14]

and Wolfenbüttel Helmst 1151: the so-called 'Missal of Flaccus Illyricus'.[15]

In 'Trent', 'Vich' and 'Robert' the prayer is the collect of a votive mass to be said by a priest for his fellow priests, the secret invariably being *Suscipe clementissime pater* and the postcommunion either *Saciatus corpore et sanguine* (Trent) or *Domine deus noster uerax* (Robert and Vich). 'Robert', has a further prayer *super populum*: *Conserua quesumus omnipotens deus*; while 'Vich' has *Perfice domine deus noster*. In 'Illyricus', 'St Blasien' and *B*, however, the prayer belongs not to a mass per se, but to the Ordinary of the Mass. Collation nonetheless shows that *B* agrees in the main with 'Robert', even though 'Robert's' text has been adapted to incorporate what seems to be a reference to monks in priest's orders *fratribus nostris sacerdotibus* and an invocation of St Peter, as the following comparison will demonstrate:

B.	*Trent.*	*Robert.*
Domine ihesu christe propitius esto mihi peccatori, qui misericordia tua primus indigeo, et pro consacerdotibus nostris exorare presumo, quia tu es inmortalis et sine peccato solus domine deus noster, tu es benedictus qui benedicis omnia, tu es sanctus qui sanctificas omnia, indulge nobis indignis famulis tuis quia peccatores sumus et	Domine ihesu christe, propitius esto mihi peccatori, quia misericordiam primus indigeo, et pro consacerdotibus nostris exorare presumo, quia tu es inmortalis et sine peccato. Tu solus dominus deus noster, tu es benedictus qui benedicis omnia, indulge nobis indignis famulis tuis, quia peccatores sumus et indigi, quod presumimus	Domine ihesu christe propitius esto mihi peccatori, quia misericordia tua primus indigeo et pro fratribus nostris sacerdotibus exorare praesumo, quia tu es inmortalis et sine peccato, solus dominus deus noster, tu es benedictus qui benedicis omnia, tu es sanctus qui sanctificas omnia, indulge nobis famulis tuis quia peccatores sumus et indigni quod

[12] Ed. Olivar, *El sacramentario de Vich*, pp. 142–3, no. 945.
[13] Ed. Gerbert, *Monumenta* I, 350–1.
[14] Ed. Wilson, *The Missal of Robert of Jumièges*, pp. 313–14.
[15] Ed. PL 138, col. 1313.

indigni, qui presumimus ad sanctum altare tuum inuocare te, quia peccauimus coram te et coram angelis tuis, sed tribue nobis indulgentiam delictorum, et confirma sanctam ecclesiam tuam in fide orthodoxa, et doce nos facere uoluntatem tuam

ad sanctum altare inuocare te, quia peccauimus coram te et coram angelis tuis. Noli nos iudicare secundum peccata nostra, sed tribue nobis ueniam delictorum et confirma sanctam aecclesiam tuam in fide ortodoxa, et <doce> nos facere uoluntatem tuam

praesumimus ad sanctum altare tuum inuocare te, quia peccauimus coram te, et coram angelis tuis tribue nobis indulgentiam omnium delictorum nostrorum, per merita et intercessionem beatissimi apostoli tui petri et da nobis facere uoluntatem tuam, ut tuae inspiratione conpuncti, libera tibi mente famulemur,

omnibus diebus nostris. Per.

omnibus diebus nostris. Qui cum patre et spiritu sancto.

omnibus diebus uitae nostrae ut participes aeternae uitae effici mereamur. Per dominum.

Note that both *B* and 'Robert' have *Tu es sanctus qui sanctus omnia*, and that 'Trent', in company with 'Vich', has *Noli nos iudicare secundum peccatum*. 'Illyricus' and 'St Blasien' have been much shortened. Taking a slightly wider view, it is possible that the English version later found its way to France, for Leroquais records three examples in books from Brittany and Normandy:[16]

> Montpellier, Bibliothèque de la Faculté de Médecine, 314: a late-eleventh-century sacramentary from the abbey of St Stephen at Caen.

> Paris, Bibliothèque nationale de France, lat. 9439: an early-twelfth-century missal from the abbey at Saint-Melaine in Brittany.

> Nantes, Bibliothèque du Musée Dobrée, s. n.: an early-thirteenth-century missal from Angers.

In all of these the prayer appears independently in the Ordinary. But in order to gain a more accurate picture of how *Domine ihesu christe* circulated and in what precise textual form, the French books will need to be collated, and further versions searched out in books from Spain and Germany.

The third prayer, *Beatae semper uirginis mariae*, ends incomplete at the end of fol. 12v, which as has already been said, is the last side of what was originally the first gathering of *A*. Although no exact parallels have come to light for this prayer, it appears to be loosely related to a

---

[16] Respectively, Leroquais, *Les sacramentaires* I, 183, 243 and II, 1.

similar prayer preserved in two ninth-century sacramentaries from
Verona, now Verona, Biblioteca Comunale, 86 and 91; and one from
Modena, now Modena, Biblioteca Comunale, O. II. 7, all published by
Dom Deshusses.[17] As can be seen from the following comparison,
however, *B*'s text diverges substantially from its Italian counterpart:

B.	*Verona.*
Beate semper uirginis mariae,	Beatorum martyrum et confessorum
beatorumque apostolorum, ac	tuorum illorum
martyrum, et confessorum, uirginum, et	
omnium electorum tuorum, et quorum	uel quorum hodie natalicia
hodie natalicia per uniuersum mundum	
celebrantur intercessionibus quesumus	celebramus intercedentibus,
domine gratia tua nos protege, et	quesumus domine gratiae tuae nos
famulis ac famulabus tuis, qui in nostris	protege, et famulis uel famulabus tuis
se commendauerunt orationibus et suas	qui nobis elemosynas suas
nobis elemosinas donauerunt, necnon et	condonauerunt . . .
qui nobis de propriis peccatis et	
criminibus coram tua maiestate	
confessi fuerunt, seu omnibus	
benefactoribus nostris, et omnibus	
inimicis, necnon in tribulatione positis,	
et consanguineis, cunctisque . . . ends	
incomplete.	

Although an Ambrosian (Milanese) version of the formula begins in a
similar way: *Beatae dei genetricis mariae et beatorum angelorum,
patriarcharum, apostolorum, martyrum, confessorum, uirginum et
omnium sanctorum tuorum*, it is generally speaking less closely related
to *B* than the version preserved in the Modena and Verona books mentioned above.[18]

Deshusses suggested on undisclosed grounds in his notes to Dumas'
edition of the sacramentary of Gellone that the north Italian prayer and
the mass to which it belonged had originally been drawn up at, or at
least issued from, Reichenau; but this seems unlikely since the
Reichenau sacramentary published by Gerbert, now Heidelberg,
Universitäts-Bibliothek, Sal. IXb, contains a third and far more widespread version of the collect.[19] Northern Italy, rather than southern
Germany, is therefore in view. One still has to explain, however, why

---

[17] *Le sacramentaire grégorien* II, 233, no. 3074.
[18] Ed. Heiming, *Das Ambrosianische Sakramentar von Biasca*, p. 173, no. 1196.
[19] Ed. Gerbert, *Monumenta* I, 268. The book was later at Peterhausen. See Dodwell and
Turner, *Reichenau Reconsidered*, pp. 39–51.

someone went to the trouble of adapting the collect for use in the Ordinary of the Mass instead of using one of the many standard formulae in
circulation, and second, by what route *Beatae semper mariae uirginis*
arrived at Canterbury if it had not originally been composed there.

Exorcism and Blessings of the Incense (nos 1295–8). All that remains of
the original mid-tenth-century addition to *A* is fol. 154v, the last leaf of
gathering 21. We have the exorcism *Exorcizo te omnis inmundissime
spiritus* with a fine pen-drawn initial, and the first few words of the
blessing *Aeternam ac iustissimam* at the foot of the page, but the rest of
this prayer and the two subsequent formulae were written on a new
bifolium by a well-known Exeter scribe in the mid-eleventh-century.[20]
Possibly all he did was copy out anew the texts given on an older
bifolium, one that had, perhaps, become worn or loose. However, as we
shall see, it seems more likely that the prayers were renewed for other
reasons.

In a number of early English pontificals *Exorcizo*, which has the same
opening words as the mid-tenth-century Romano-German Pontifical's
prayer for the blessing of oil on Maundy Thursday, and *Aeternam*,
which has no obvious corollary, are regularly associated with the ceremony of the dedication of a church.[21] In approximate date order, the
books in question are:

Rouen BM 369: the pontifical of Archbishop Robert.[22]

BL Add. 57337: the so-called 'Anderson' pontifical, written in the
early eleventh century at Christ Church, Canterbury.[23] The formulae
appear on fols 15v–16v.

Rouen BM 368: the so-called 'Lanalet' pontifical.[24]

London, British Library, Cotton Vitellius A. vii: the so-called
'Ramsey' pontifical, a pontifical (badly damaged in the Cottonian
fire) written by two well-known Exeter scribes for Leofric, bishop of
Exeter sometime close to 1050. One of these scribes was probably

---

[20] See below, p. 223, for the Exeter scribe. The initial is illustr. Temple, *Anglo-Saxon Manuscripts*, pl. 53.
[21] See *PRG* II, 70 (cap. xcix, no. 260), and P. Maier, *Die Feier der Missa chrismatis* (Regensburg, 1990), pp. 128–9, who states that the 'German' Maundy Thursday prayer is not to be found in older sources.
[22] Ed. Wilson, *The Benedictional of Archbishop Robert*, pp. 94–5.
[23] See Rasmussen, *Les pontificaux*, pp. 180–1.
[24] Noted by Doble, *Pontificale Lanalentense*, p. 18.

Leofric himself.[25] A good deal of the material embodied in the book reappears in London, British Library, Add. 28188, a late-eleventh-century benedictional-cum-pontifical also from Exeter. It has long been recognised, however, that the model or models from which these manuscripts were copied seems to have issued from some house in the fenlands, for invocations for SS Æthelred and Æthelberht of Ramsey; Yvo of Huntingdon; Felix, bishop of East Anglia; Botulf; Guthlac, and other 'fenland' saints figure in their near-identical litanies.[26] Ramsey, as a community of monks, can be ruled out, *pace* Ker and Dumville.[27] Pontificals are bishops' books. In view of the fact that much of Vitellius A.vii's text descends in parallel with that of CCCC 44 from a pontifical drawn up by Stigand at Christ Church, Canterbury in the 1050s, North Elmham seems likeliest. Stigand's brother Æthelmar was bishop of the house from 1047 until his expulsion in 1070. Leofric presumably acquired the North Elmham model or models at Exeter, rather than Crediton. *Exorcizo* and *Aeternam* appear on fols 40r–41r.

and CCCC 44: the mid-eleventh-century pontifical of Christ Church, Canterbury. The prayers figure on pages 122–4.

After the Conquest the practice seems to have continued at Canterbury, for the two prayers appear together in the service for the dedication of a church in several twelfth and thirteenth-century books, either from Christ Church itself, or copied from books from the house: the twelfth-century pontifical now at Magdalen College, Oxford; the so-called pontifical of Thomas-à-Becket, now at Douai; Paris, Bibliothèque nationale de France, nouv. acq. lat. 306, a copy of an twelfth-century English pontifical made for, and probably at, Rouen; and the pontifical of David de Bernham, bishop of St Andrews.[28] According to Leroquais, the order for

---

[25] Bishop, *English Caroline Minuscule*, p. 24; Drage, *Leofric*, pp. 149–50; and Gameson, 'The origin of the Exeter Book', pp. 144–5.

[26] The litanies are ed. Lapidge, *Anglo-Saxon Litanies of the Saints*, pp. 132–7, 187–93, and 235–9. The invocations of St Olaf and St Sativola are distinctive of Exeter. See D. Rollason, 'Lists of saints' resting places in Anglo-Saxon England', *ASE* 7 (1978), 61–93, at 92 (Sativola); and Dewick and Frere, *The Leofric Collectar* I, 209–14. Note that the litany of Oxford, Bodleian Library, Douce 296, a late-eleventh-century psalter from Crowland in Lincolnshire, ed. Lapidge, *op. cit.*, pp. 235–9, is simply a shorter version of the one preserved in the two Exeter manuscripts.

[27] Ker, *Catalogue of Manuscripts containing Anglo-Saxon*, pp. 278–9; Dumville, *Liturgy*, p. 79.

[28] See Wilson, *The Pontifical of Magdalen College*, p. 139; Douai BM 67, fol. 45, Leroquais, *Les pontificaux* II, 220–6; and Wordsworth, *Pontificale Ecclesiae sancti Andreae*, pp. 28–30.

the dedication of a church in the Rouen book is almost exactly that of 'Robert'. The distinctively English *Benedictio generalis ad cultum ecclesiae* (no. 1303), which we will come to later, is also present.

From time to time, though, *Exorcizo* and *Aeternam* seem to have been used in England on Holy Saturday, as in:

CCCC 146: the early-eleventh-century Winchester pontifical later owned by Sampson, bishop of Worcester. The prayers figure on pages 122–4.

Rouen BM 272: the sacramentary copied at Saint-Wandrille *c.* 1033–53 from an English model. The prayers appear on fols 253v–254r in company with others relating to Holy Week, but have no superscription to indicate exactly when they were to be used.

and in thirteenth-century copies of the Sarum missal. All Sarum books down to the sixteenth century contain the formulae.[29]

A version of *Aeternam* alone also seems to have been said on Holy Saturday in northern Italy and Spain, as Franz and Cuthbert Atchely noted.[30] The books in which the prayer has so far come to light are:

Frontale, Chiesa parrochiale di S. Anna, s. n.: an eleventh-century missal from a church in Venice.[31]

Madrid, Academia de la Historia, 56: an eleventh-century ritual from the church of San Millán in northern Spain.[32]

Silos, Codex Silensis: a ritual written in 1039 from the abbey of Silos in northern Spain.[33]

and the missal printed for the chapter of Narbonne Cathedral in 1528.[34]

Aeternam may have been separated from *Exorcizo* at an early date, for the latter stands alone in the Ordinary of the Mass of pontifical from

---

[29] Ed. Legg, *The Sarum Missal*, pp. 116–17.

[30] Franz, *KB* I, 425–7; E. G. C. F. Atchley, *A History of the Use of Incense in Divine Worship*, Alcuin Club Collections 13 (London, 1909), pp. 138–9 and 399–400.

[31] Ed. PL 151, 845–6. *CLLA*, no. 938.

[32] Ed. M. Férotin, *Le liber ordinum en usage dans l'église wisigothique et mozarabe d'espagne*, Monumenta Ecclesiae liturgica 5, ed. F. Cabrol and H. Leclercq (Paris, 1904), cols. 176–7. *CLLA*, no. 391.

[33] Ed. Férotin, *Le liber ordinum*, cols. 176–7. *CLLA*, no. 392.

[34] See Martène, *AER*, Bk. IV, cap. xxiv, with Martimort, *La documentation*, p. 489, no. 1071.

Roda, now at Lerida.[35] There will doubtless be other examples of both prayers in unpublished books from the Veneto, northern Spain and southern France.

As the following comparison will show, however, the continental versions of *Aeternam* differ from the standard Anglo-Saxon version, here represented by the so-called 'Benedictional of Archbishop Robert':[36]

Robert.	*Venice.*	*Mozarabic.*
Aeternam ac iustissimam pietatem tuam deprecamur domine sanctissime pater omnipotens aeterne deus, ut benedicere digneris haec timiamata uel incensi speciem, ut sit incensum maiestati tuae in odorem suauitatis acceptum, sit a te haec species benedicta, sit per inuocationem sancti nominis tui sanctificata,	Aeternam ac iustissimam pietatem tuam deprecor, domine sancte pater omnipotens deus, ut benedicere hunc speciem thymiamatis, uel cuiuslibet speciei, ut sit incensum maiestatis tuae in odorem suauitatis acceptum et a te domine benedicatur,	Aeternam hac iustissimam pietatem tuam deprecamur domine sancte, pater omnipotens, eterne deus, ut benedicere digneris hanc speciem thimiamatis uel qualibet species, ut sit incensum maiestatis tuae in odorem suabitatis acceptum et a te, domine, benedictum,
ita ut ubicumque fumus eius peruenerit, exstricetur et effugetur omne genus demoniorum sicut incensu iecoris piscis quem raphael archangelus tobiam famulum tuum docuit cum ascendit ad sarae liberationem.	ita ubicumque odor peruenerit, extricetur et effugetur omne genus daemoniorum, sicut fumus iecoris piscis, quem raphael archangelus tuus tobiae famulo tuo docuit accendi ad sanctam liberationem.	ita ut ubicumque odor eius peruenerit, stricetur et effugetur omne genus demoniorum, sicut fumus gecoris piscis, quam rafael archangelus tuus tobie famulo tuo docuit occidi et sarre liberationem.
Descendat benedictio super hanc speciem incensi et timiamatis, sicut in illo de quo dauid propheta tuus cecinit, dicens.	Descendat super hanc speciem incensi plena benedictio, ut sit tibi acceptum, sicut ille, de quo dauid propheta tuus cecinit dicens.	Descendat super hanc speciem incensa plena benedictio tua, ut sit tibi acceptus, sicut ille de eo dauid propheta tuus cecinit, dicens.
Dirigatur oratio mea sicut incensum in conspectu tuo, sit nobis odor consolationis, suauitatis	Dirigatur oratio mea, sicut incensum in conspectu suo. Sit nobis odor consolationis ac	Dirigatur oratio mea sicut incensum in conspectu tuo. Sit nobis odor consolationis, suabitatis

---

[35] Ed. Planas, *El sacramentari, ritual i pontifical de roda*, pp. 312–13 (cap. xx, no. 3).
[36] Ed. Wilson, *The Benedictional of Archbishop Robert*, p. 95.

et gratiae, ut fumo isto
effugetur omne fantasma
mentis et corporis, ut
simus pauli apostoli
uoce bonus odor deo.
Effugiant a facie incensi
huius et timiamatis
omnes demonum
incursus, sicut puluis a
facie uenti, et sicut fumus
a facie ignis, presta hoc
piissime pater boni
odoris incensum ad opus
ecclesiae tuae ob causam
religionis iugiter
permanere, ut mystica
nobis significatione
spiritualium uirtutum
flagrans ostenderet odor
suauitatem. Tua ergo
quesumus omnipotens
deus inmense maiestatis
dextera hanc creaturam
benedicere ex diuersarum
rerum commixtione
infectam dignare, ut in
uirtute sancti nominis tui
omnes inmundorum
spirituum phantasmaticos
incursus effugare,
omnesque morbos reddita
sanitate expellere,
ubicumque fumus
aromatum eius afflauerit,
mirabiliter possit atque in
odore flagrantissimo tibi
domine, perpetua
suauitate redolere. Per
dominum.

suauitatis et gratiae, ut
fumus eius effuget
omnes phantasias mentis
et corporis, ut simus
apostoli tui uoce, boni
odoris deo, effugiat a
facie huius incensi
omnis daemonium
incursus, sicut puluis a
facie uenti, et sicut
fumus a facie ignis.
Praesta hoc, piissime
pater, per unigenitum
tuum, cum quo uiuis et
regnas cum spiritu
sancto, deus in saecula
saeculorum. Amen.

et gratie, ut fumus
effugiet omni fantasie
mentis et corporis, ut
simus pauli apostoli tui
uoce boni odoris deo.
Effugiet a facie incensus
omnis demonum
incursus, sicut puluis a
facie uenti et sicut fumus
a facie ignis.
Presta hoc, piissime
pater, per unigenitum
tuum, cum eo regnans,
cum sancto spiritu
infinita semper secula
seculorum. Amen.

The principal question confronting us is therefore: which form of the
prayer is the more ancient? On purely formal grounds the Mozarabic
and north Italian formulae are likely to be the oldest, since they are the
shortest. The standard Anglo-Saxon version of *Aeternam* has been
lengthened considerably. But the prayer as we have it in *B* belongs to a
later stage of development, for phrases proper to the dedication of a
church appear at certain points in the text. For instance, about a third of

the way through, after the word *effugetur*, we have *eo loco*; and further down, after *bonus odor deo*, we have *in omne loco*. These additions seem to have been brought in sometime close to the Conquest, since they appear in the pontifical now in Magdalen College, and in the pontifical of David de Bernham. Also characteristic of this later form is the presence of the words *super carbones ponere* after *famulum tobiam tuum*. The Sarum version, however, is of the 'old-fashioned' type. It seems possible therefore that *B* contained an older version of *Aeternam* later brought up to date by Leofric, and that both it and *Exorcizo* were originally intended for use on Holy Saturday. The bifolium containing the text could easily have been inserted closer to *A*'s *ordo* for the dedication of a church had it been felt that the one should be connected with the other.

The third and fourth blessings of the incense are, generally speaking, common enough. *Domine deus omnipotens* appears in the Romano-German Pontifical and consequently found its way all over Europe; *Veniat*, a consecratory prayer for Holy Saturday, is also widespread. *Veniat*, we can leave aside, for the version in *C* has no textual variations of any note. *C*'s version of *Domine deus omnipotens*, however, is distinctively English in character, as Franz noted. On the left I give *C*'s text, and on the right that of the Romano-German Pontifical:[37]

C.	*Romano-German Pontifical*
Domine deus omnipotens cui assistunt omnes exercitus angelorum cum tremore, quorum seruitus in uentum et ignem conuertitur, respice de caelo quesumus, et benedicere dignare propitius hanc creaturam incensi, ut uniuersi morborum languores, odorem ipsius sentientes, effugiant et separentur a plasmate tuo, et ab omnibus qui in te confidunt quos pretioso sanguine filii tui redemisti, et numquam laedantur a morsu antiqui serpentis. Per.	Domine deus omnipotens cui adstat exercitus angelorum, dignare respicere et benedicere hanc creaturam incensi, ut omnes languorum demonumque insidiae odorem ipsius sentientes fugiant, et separentur a plasmate tuo, quod filii tui pretioso sanguine redemisti, ut numquam ledantur a morsu serpentis antiqui. Per.

Further searches, perhaps among Italian books, may uncover versions related more to *C* than 'Mainz'.

---

[37] Ed. *PRG* I, 62 (cap. xl, no. 109). See Franz, *KB* I, 425–7.

Missa in tribulatione (nos 1915–17). This is not quite a full mass, since a proper collect is lacking. Dom Moeller, the editor of the *Corpus Prefationum*, thought the preface Carolingian on the grounds that it turns up in at least one of the famous sacramentaries of Fulda.[38] He may well be right. But the formula clearly does not belong with the prayers given there. It must have been composed initially to accompany an entirely different mass, the one in question being:[39]

> *Oratio.* Deus qui contritorum non despicias . . . in ecclesia tua sancta gratias refert. Per.

> *Secreta.* Deus qui tribulatos corde sanas . . . delectetur exultare iudiciis. Per.

> *Postcommunio.* Dimitte domine peccata nostra . . . largiens clementer exaudias. Per.

These prayers are found together all over Europe, but never with a preface. Yet in *B, Per quem te immense deus*, which is patently in the same style, is found with the secret alone, the collect for some reason having dropped out and the postcommunion having been replaced by a less fitting one. Fulda's preface, however, is significantly longer than *B*'s:

B.	*Fulda.*
Per quem te immense deus rogamus, ut supplicationes nostras propitiabili dignatione adtendens, ad hanc nostram orationem quam pro ereptione et releuatione nostra offerimus, benignus respicias.	Per quem te summe deus rogamus, ut preces nostras propitiabili dignatione attendas et hanc oblationem, quam pro ereptione et releuatione famulorum tuorum pro tui nominis amore persecutionem patentium offerimus, benignus respicias. Iam
Iam nos domine quesumus placabili uultu intende, et tua singulari misericordia a nobis amoue, quod seuitia malorum promittit, quod inimicorum prauitas infert quod prauorum consiliis alligatur, quod ex iudicio imminet, quod ex sententia pendet, quod conspiratione machinatur, quod accusatione configitur, quod nostrae merentur iniquitates.	eos domine placabili uultu intende et misericordia singulari ab eis amoue quod seuitia prauorum promittit, quod inimicorum prauitas infert, quod prauorum consiliis aduersitas alligat, quod ex iudicio imminet, quod ex sententia pendet, quod conspiratione machinatur, quod accusatione confingitur, quod eorum merentur

[38] *Corpus Prefationum*, ed. Moeller, no. 795; *Sacramentarium Fuldense*, ed. Richter and Schönfelder, p. 383, no. 2867.
[39] Ed. *Le sacramentaire grégorien* II, 149, nos 2449–51; and, for instance, Gerbert, *Monumenta* I, 274–5.

Non iusticiam tuam in nostris iniusticiis exerceas, domine, sed potius pietatem tuam in nostris iniquitatibus manifesta. Non nos in persecutione deicias, non in tribulatione relinquas,

sed exerce per pietatem, attolle ac rege per misericordiam, quo per te ab inimicorum iaculis tuti, ab omni tribulatione exempti, te deum unum in trinitate consona uoce laudemus. Cum angelis et archangelis, ita dicentes: Sanctus. Sanctus. Sanctus.

iniquitates, quod alienis finctionibus alligat, quod pressuris deicitur, quod cruciatibus premitur, quod angustiis angustiatur. Non iustitiam tuam domine in iniusticiis iniquorum exerceas, sed potius pietatem tuam in eorum iniquitatibus manifesta. Non illos in persecutione deicias, non per intolerantiam perdas, sed per tribulationem exerce, per pietatem attolle, per misericordiam rege. Quo per te ab inimicorum iaculis tuti, ab omni tribulatione exempti te deum unum in trinitate consona uoce collaudent cum angelis et archangelis, cum thronis et dominationibus.

Without another example, it is impossible to say with absolute certainty which book preserves the 'authentic' text. But since many standard formulae were lengthened at Fulda, possibly by Hrabanus Maurus (if Gamber is to be followed), it seems likely that *B*'s version is the closest to the original.

Remembrances of the Dead (nos 1918–19). As we have seen, remembrances of the living and dead were normally said during the Canon of the Mass. The first of *B*'s additions, which is for the priest himself, occurs in books from all over Europe, at various dates, and need not detain us here. The second, for the dead, has no exact parallels, but is related to a Memento preserved in Wolfenbüttel Helmst. 1151 (the 'Missal of Flaccus Illyricus') and a book from St Blasien, no longer identifiable, published by Gerbert.[40] Cognate passages have been italicised:

B.
Memento domine famulorum famularumque tuarum, et omnium qui in sublimitate sunt ut quietam et tranquillam in fide tua uitam agant, *et quicumque mihi consanguinitate, uel familiaritate iuncti sunt,* et quicunque mihi *aliquod caritatis uel pietatis officium inpenderunt, et qui mei memoriam in orationibus suis habent,*

Illyricus.
Memento domine famulorum famularumque tuarum, .N. et N. praecipue deprecor pro his qui *memoriam mei coram te in suis precibus faciunt, uel qui se meis indignis precibus commendauerunt,* quique etiam in tuo conspectu sua mihi delicta confessi sunt, et qui mihi, uel congregationi tuae *aliquid*

---

[40] Ed. PL 138, col. 1331; Gerbert, *Monumenta* I, 349.

et qui se indignis precibus meis commendauerunt, quibuscumque mihi aliquod obstaculo uel scandalo fui et quicumque mihi aliquid aduersitatis intulerunt, et omnium congregationum, monachorum et canonicorum, sanctimonialium quorum nomina et numerum tu solus, deus omnipotens, agnoscis et omnium circumadstantium *charitatis officio siue pietatis, uel largitatis suae studio impenderunt, quique etiam mihi propinquitatis uel consanguinitatis, seu tuae charitatis affectu coniuncti sunt*, mihi quoque indignissimo famulo tuo propitius esse digneris, et ab omnibus delictorum offensionibus me emundare. Per.

The resemblance may be purely superficial since most of the phrases common to the two are to be found in votive masses and other prayers belonging to the Ordinary. However, given that the version in the two German books is clearly the 'standard' form (there are only trifling differences in wording), *B*'s is likely to be derivative.

New collect for the mass for relics (no. 1955*). The prayer *Auxilium tuum*, which was added as an alternative beside the existing prayer *Concede quesumus omnipotens deus* of *A*'s relic mass, is relatively common, occurring as a second collect along 'Eighth-Century Gelasian' lines in three books published by Deshusses, and as a secret at Tours.[41]

Chant in honour of the Virgin (no. 2302). *B*'s chant, which is partially neumed and without superscription, was probably designed to accompany a votive mass *in commemoratione sanctae mariae* rather than a mass of the sanctoral, that is to say, the Purification, Annunciation, Nativity and Assumption.[42] The prayers to which this chant is usually attached are:

Collecta. Concede nos famulos tuos domine deus . . . et futura perfrui laetitia. Per.

Secreta. Tua domine propitiatione et beatae mariae . . . haec oblatio nobis proficiat prosperitatem. Per.

Postcomunio. Sumptis domine sacramentis nostrae subsidiis . . . haec tuae obtulimus maiestati. Per.

which are generally agreed to have been composed by Alcuin.[43] Of the three, only a version of the collect, later rewritten, figures in *A* (no.

[41] *Le sacramentaire grégorien* II, 51, no. 1875.
[42] See for instance, the chant sung at Bec in the thirteenth century, ed. Hughes, *The Bec Missal*, p. 249.
[43] Ed. *Le sacramentaire grégorien* II, 45, nos 1841–3.

1955), but the chant provided in *B* would nonetheless have been perfectly 'appropriate' for the mass regardless of the prayers employed. It may well have been lack of space in the relevant margins that drove the scribe to enter the pieces on fol. 267v.

Additional material for ordinations and consecrations (nos 2331–47). Most of the formulae added to *A* at various times in the tenth century can be paralleled in the Romano-German Pontifical and its descendants, and so need not detain us here. That leaves us with the idiosyncracies. The prayer *In nomine sanctae trinitatis*, said after the deacon's stole had been consigned, is relatively rare, as Leroquais and Kleinheyer have indicated.[44] Indeed, the earliest surviving examples generally seem to be English. Besides *B*, examples occur in:

BNF lat. 943: the so-called 'Pontifical of St Dunstan'.[45]

BNF lat. 12052: the sacramentary-cum-pontifical written for Ratoldus of Corbie (d. 986).[46]

Paris, Bibliothèque nationale de France, lat. 1217: a pontifical from Moissac now thought to have been written in the late tenth century.[47]

Angers, Bibliothèque municipale, 80: a late-tenth or early-eleventh-century pontifical from the cathedral at Angers.[48]

Dijon, Bibliothèque municipale, 122: an eleventh-century copy of a pontifical from Langres and Lyon. The inscription stating that the book originally belonged to the archdeacon Imbert de Vergny (1030–60), who gave it in 1036 to Halinard, archbishop of Lyon, belongs to the model, not to the manuscript that we now possess.[49]

The prayer is a fixture in all eleventh and twelfth-century English pontificals. Since Andrieu seems not to have come across the formula in any form in the hundred or so sacramentaries and pontificals he examined for his edition of the so-called *Ordines romani*, it seems possible that *In*

---

[44] Leroquais, *Les pontificaux* I, lxvii–lxviii; B. Kleinheyer, 'Studien zur nichtrömisch-westlichen Ordinationsliturgie. Folge 4: Zur Bewertung diverser Gewandüberreichungsriten im Licht ihrer Deuteworte', *Archiv für Liturgiewissenshaft* 33 (1991), 217–74.

[45] See above, n. 143.

[46] See above, n. 15.

[47] See Rasmussen, *Les pontificaux*, pp. 322–42. The ordination formulae are ed. Martène, *AER*, Bk I, cap. vii, art xi, ordo 7.

[48] See Rasmussen, *Les pontificaux*, pp. 318–22.

[49] *Ibid.* pp. 401–6.

nomine sanctae trinitatis was drawn up in England at much the same date as we have it in *B*, and that it passed to the continent quickly thereafter. Further work is needed, however.[50]

Just as striking is *B*'s chant for the mass accompanying the consecration of a bishop. Indeed, only the Romano-German Pontifical makes such extensive provision.[51] But as even the briefest of glances will show, *B* has proper forms and alternatives for four separate services whereas most copies of the *RGP* only have one, albeit with alternatives. *B*'s arrangement is presumably local, and (from a palaeographical standpoint) likely to be earlier than that of the *RGP* by at least a decade, suggesting that the two drew independently from a common model. If they are independent, then a further question follows: do both largely represent the use of Rome, but at different dates? To these, no certain answer is forthcoming at present. What can be stated with confidence, however, is that the consecrating of new bishops was clearly a matter of great importance at Canterbury in the tenth century; and that brings us neatly to the note *Hic ponendum oleum super caput* added beside the words *Hoc domine copiosae* in the main consecratory prayer *Deus honorum omnium* (no. 2352) on fol. 280r. As Leroquais pointed out, the practice of anointing the bishop at this point in the service does not seem to have been peculiarly English, for a similar direction figures in Troyes, Bibliothèque municipale, 2141, a late-tenth-century pontifical from Worms, and in BNF lat. 12051, the mid-ninth-century sacramentary-cum-pontifical possibly for Beauvais, which Leroquais did not spot.[52] In both, however, the oil is termed *crisma*. In tenth-century English books, on the other hand, it is always refered to as *oleum*. 'Dunstan' and 'Robert', for instance, have *Hic effundatur oleum super caput eius;* and 'Ratoldus', as Ménard indicated, has *Hic ponatur oleum super caput eius*.[53] *B* is therefore our earliest surviving witness to this form of words.

[50] That many later formulae were composed along the same lines tends to show that some version of this prayer was highly influential on the continent. See the index in Leroquais, *Les pontificaux* III, 86.
[51] *PRG* I, 200–26, 240–1 (caps lxiii and lxvii).
[52] Leroquais, *Les pontificaux* I, lxxxvii; PL 78, col. 224.
[53] Ed. Martene, *AER*, Bk I, cap. viii, art xi, ordo 3; Wilson, *The Benedictional of Archbishop Robert*, pp. 125–7; and PL 78, col. 502.

II. Material Added in the Third Quarter of the Tenth Century

Four principal scribes worked as follows:

Scribe a. Fols 13v–14r: benediction for a king, and over a king at the time of a synod (nos 117–18).

Scribe b. Fol. 15v: blessing *super unum hominem* (no. 124); and fol.16r: two blessing for travellers (nos 125–6).

?Scribe c: Fol. 112r, lines 8–9: additions to the closing passages of the Exultet preface (no. 805) made over an erasure of one and a half lines. Script imitative of *A*'s.

Scribe a: Fol. 245v: blessing in time of war (no. 2197).

Scribe d: Fol. 336v: four collects for the dedication of a church added on a page originally left blank in *A* (nos 2692–5).

None of these scribes has so far been identified in any of the (numerous) books attributed to Canterbury on palaeolographical or art-historical grounds.

Liturgical character of the additions

Benediction for a King (no. 117). As Dom Moeiler has shown, the occasional blessing of a king, *Benedic domine hunc clementissimum regem*, is distinctively English.[54] *B*, however, preserves a much longer form of text than the other books listed by him: BNF lat. 943, the 'Pontifical of St Dunstan'; Rouen BM 369: the 'Benedictional of Archbishop Robert'; BNF lat. 10575: the 'Egbert Pontifical'; and Rouen BM 368, the 'Lanalet Pontifical'. It is well to note too that the blessing also figures in CCCC 146, the early-eleventh-century Winchester pontifical later owned by Sampson, bishop of Worcester.[55] The following comparison will show first, how *B* deviates from the standard English text as given in 'Robert', and second, how the two English versions relate to the older continental blessing of a king preserved, to take the earliest surviving example, in the sacramentary of Gellone:[56]

[54] *Corpus Benedictionum Pontificalium*, ed. Moeller, no. 89.
[55] Page 282.
[56] *Liber Sacramentorum Gellonensis* ed. Dumas and Deshusses, I, 298, no. 2094. See also Jackson, *Ordines Coronationis Franciae* I, 54.

B.

Robert.

Gellone.
Christe deus oriens ex alto, rex regum, et dominus dominantium, corona credentium, benedictio sacerdotum, qui regis gentes, exaltas reges, respicis humilis, ditas pauperis, custodis ueracis.

Benedic domine hunc clementissimum regem cum uniuerso populo, sicut benedixisti abraham in milia, isaac in uictoria, iacob in pascua. Amen.
Da ei de rore caeli benedictione, et de pinguedine, terrae ubertatem, da ei de inimicis triumphum, de lumbis eius sobolem regnaturum. Amen.

Sit in regno illius indeficiens amor in populo, sit pax peregrinis in regno, sit aduenientibus uictoria in transitu. Amen.
Ut ille transiens in seculo, uictoriam inueniat in caelo, et cum patre clementissimo sine fine mereatur regnatur in throno. Quod ipse.

Benedic domine hunc clementissimum regem cum uniuerso populo suo, sicut benedixisti abraham in familia, isaac in uictima, iacob in pascua. Amen.
Da ei de rore celi benedictionem, de pinguedine terrae ubertatem, de inimicis triumphum, de lumbis suis sobolem regnaturum. Amen.
Sit indeficiens amor in populo, et pax peregrinis in regno. Amen.
Quod ipse prestare dignetur.

Benedic domine hunc clementissime regem illum cum uniuerso populo suo, sicut benedixisti habraam in milia, isaac in uictima, iacob in pascua. Da eis de rore caeli benedictionem de pinguidinem terre, ubertatem, de inimicis, triumphum de lumbis sobolem regnatorem. Vt dum regales non defecit de sterpe successio, sed indeficiens amor in populo. Pax perennis in regno quod ipse prestare digneris qui in celestia regna super cerubin sedens uniuersa, qui regna regnis et regnas in saecula saeculorum.

Note that *B* and Gellone have the word *milia* instead of *familia*.

Blessing for Travellers (no. 125). Composed, as Adolf Franz indicated in 1896, of two ancient collects, both of which figure regularly in 'Eighth-Century Gelasian' sacramentaries:[57]

---

[57] Franz, *KB* II, 264, n. 2. For the prayers in question, see *Liber Sacramentorum Gellonensis*, ed. Dumas and Deshusses, I, 437, nos 2798 and 2799.

B.

Exaudi domine preces nostras et iter famuli tui .ill. propitius comitare, atque misericordiam tuam, sicut ubique es, ita ei largire. Amen.

    Quatinus a cunctis aduersitatibus defensus, gratiarum tibi referens actionem, tua opitulatione sit securus. Amen.

    Angelum pacis omnipotens deus mittere digneris, qui in uiam rectam comitetur famulum tuum. Amen.

    Et cum omni fiducia ac sine ullo impedimento ad desideratum locum perducat, et exinde ad pristinum locum deducat. Amen.

    Quod ipse prestare dignetur.

Gellone.

Exaudi domine preces nostras et iter famuli tui illius propitius comitare, adque misericordiam tuam sicut ubique es, ita ubique largire, quatenus a cunctis aduersitatibus tua opitulatione defensus, gratiarum tibi referat actionem. Per.

. . . direge angelum pacis nobiscum

. . . qui nos ad loca destinata perducat, sit nobis comitatus . . .

B's conflation is apparently unique. The only parallel I can find for the use of individual phrases excerpted from these prayers occurs in a collect preserved in the longer of the two late-ninth-century benedictionals from Freising, now in Munich, Staatliche Bibliothek, Clm 6420:[58]

> Angelum tuum domine mittere dignare qui comitetur circa famulum tuum illum, ut in loco predestinato eum cum salute facias uenire, et ad propria habitacula remeare concede.

Revision of the closing formula of the Exultet preface (no. 805). Our first question must necessarily be: what form did the original text of the clause beginning *Precamur* take? The immediate answer is that it must have been longer than the version given in the Supplement to the *Hadrianum*, since that runs:

> Precamur ergo domine, ut nos famulos tuos omnem clerum et deuotissimum populum, una cum patre nostro papa .ill. quiete temporum concessa in his paschalibus gaudiis conseruare digneris.

A plainly had some further clause that had been 'slotted in', occupying one and a half lines of its scribe's writing: but of what sort? In his study of well over a hundred Exultet texts, Kelly came across nearly that

---

[58] Ed. Amiet, *The Benedictionals of Freising*, p. 100, no. 450.

number of variants in this short prayer.[59] Given the length of the erasure in *A*, however, only two really seem to be possible: *nostro papa et gloriosissimo rege* (or even *imperatore*, if a continental text had been followed) *nostro .ill. eiusque nobilissima prole*, or perhaps *nostro papa et gloriosissimo rege nostro .ill. nec non et antistite nostro .ill.*, both of which are relatively common. The second principal question then confronting is: how unusual is it for the archbishop to be named? The answer, again, can be given quickly: exceptionally. So far as I have been able to discover, the only other books to mention a metropolitan are:

Venice, Biblioteca Marciana, lat. III, CXXIV: an early-eleventh-century sacramentary from Salzburg Cathedral, later at the church of S. Michele, Murano. The relevant section of the clause runs: *una cum papa nostro .N. et gloriossisimo rege nostro .N. necnon et archiantistite nostro .N.*[60]

Cambridge, Trinity College, 249, the mid-twelfth-century pontifical from Canterbury that later found its way to Ely. A later twelfth-century Ely copy of this book survives as CUL Ll. ii. 10.[61]

and Salerno, Archivio Capitolare, 3: a missal copied in 1431 for the archbishop of Salerno.[62]

A further search, however, may add to their number.

Blessing in Time of Trouble (no. 2197). An extended version of a popular 'Eighth-Century Gelasian' formula:

B.	*Gellone.*
Populi tui quesumus domine propitiare peccatis, et totius hostilitatis a nobis errores auerte. Amen.	Populi tui quesumus omnipotens domine, propitiare peccatis et totius hostilitatis a nobis errores auerte. Amen.
Omnisque populi in tua deuotione semper exultet et in tuis laudibus perseueret, et tibi domino subdito famulatu deseruiat. Amen.	Vt romani sibi francorum nomen secura libertas in tua deuutione semper exultent, et sibi subditu famulatu deseruiant.
Tua potentia contere uirtutem inimicorum eius, et delicta nostra quorum nobis causa dominanter emunda. Amen	

---

[59] Kelly, *The Exultet in Southern Italy*, pp. 69–70, 271, 285–6, and 302.
[60] See Ebner, *Quellen*, p. 279.
[61] See Wilson, *The Pontifical of Magdalen College*, p. xv.
[62] See Kelly, *The Exultet in Southern Italy*, pp. 258 and 271.

Cum mentibus nostris infuderis
puritatem, et pacem ubique in patria
largiaris, elide omnium aduerariorum
nostrorum superbiam, et uirtute dexterae
tuae, prosterne hostium uirtutem. Amen.

Fidelem hunc populum potentiae
tuae muniat inuicta defensio, et ab
inferis liberetur inimicis, et in tua gratia
semper perseueret in omnibus bonis.
Amen.
Ille nos.

Elide omnium aduersariorum
nostrorum superbiam et uirtute
dextere tuae prosterne hostium
contumacium.

Fidelem hunc populum potentiae
tuae muneat inuicta defensio, ut pius
semper tibi deuotus affectu, et ab
infestis liberetur inimicis et in tua
iugiter gratia perseueret.
Quod.

No other English book has this long form. Those that follow 'Gellone' – 'Robert' for example – suppress the phrase beginning *Ut romani sibi francorum nomen*, which would have been all but meaningless in England.[63]

Occasional prayers (nos 2692–5). Four formulae, written by a single scribe, at the foot of fol. 336r and top of fol. 336v, both of which spaces had originally been left blank; all are proper to services for the dedication and re-dedication of a church. *Descendat quesumus domine deus noster* and *Deus qui inuisibiliter omnia contines* are standard Roman prayers. *Deus qui dixisti domus mea* and *Percipientes domine munera salutis* are comparatively uncommon, however, only occurring in a *missa in reconciliatione ecclesiae* in BNF nouv. acq. lat. 1589, the late-ninth-century sacramentary from the cathedral of St Maurice at Tours, among the books surveyed by Deshusses.[64]

III. Material Contemporary with and Later than the Calendar

If *A* had ever been rebound in the earlier part of the tenth century, it was certainly unbound again when a number of new gatherings containing a calendar, computus and further additional material were incorporated in the body of the book. This was something of a departure from past practice: as we have seen, the older additions had in the main either been

[63] *Corpus Benedictionum Pontificalium*, ed. Moeller, no. 1856.
[64] For these formulae, see *Le sacramentaire grégorien* I, 304, nos 816 and 817; and III, 212, nos 4179 and 4181.

made over erasures or on leaves originally left blank. The late-tenth-century material is as follows:

Scribe i. Fol. 8r: votive prayer *Propitiare misericors deus supplicationibus nostris* (no. 40).

Scribe ii. Fol. 17r: mass for rain (nos 131–40).

Scribe iii. Fol. 38r: passage on leap years beginning *Inquirendum* (no. 275).

Scribe iv. Fols 38r–58r: calendar, computistical matter (nos 275–96, and 298–320). A riot of colour. Initials, superscriptions and certain lines of text, especially in the computus, are in purple, red, green, russet and occasionally blue.

Scribe i. Fol. 53r: additions to the Easter Table (no. 298). The latest is for archbishop Sigeric (d. 994).[65]

Scribe v. Fol. 58v: verses to be said during vesting (no. 321).

Scribe i. Fol. 59v, lines 1–9: common preface, with 'Breton' neums.[66]

Scribe vi. Fol. 111v: a new passage supplied over an erasure in the text of the Exultet preface (no. 805).

Scribe iv. Fol. 210r: termination of the common preface (no. 1914).

Scribe i. Fol. 215v: alterations over an erasure in the text of the collect of *A*'s mass for relics (no. 1955).

Scribe iv. Fol. 227v: alternative collect for the mass in honour of monks added in *A*'s margins (no. 2051*), and St Benedict's name interlined in the existing prayer.

Scribe i. Fols 254r–258r, line 8: short *ordines* for Candlemas and Palm Sunday; and a litany, unrelated (nos 2246–62).

Scribe iv. Fol. 258r, line 9 – 260r: a series of masses and individual formulae for feasts and saints' days (nos 2263–70).

---

[65] The table is illustr. Nicholson, *Early Bodleian Music* III, pl. XXVIII.

[66] Illustr. *ibid.* pl. XXIX. For a list of books with such neums, see the exhibition catalogue, *Landevennec 485–1485: aux origines de la Bretagne. XVe centenaire de la fondation de l'abbaye de Landevennec*, ed. J.-P. Gestin and E. Le Bris du Rest (Daoulas, 1985), p. 57, with S. Rankin, 'Some reflections on liturgical music at late Anglo-Saxon Worcester', *St Oswald of Worcester: Life and Influence*, ed. N. Brooks and C. Cubitt (Leicester, 1996), pp. 325–48, esp. 345–8, and Sole, 'Some Anglo-Saxon Cuthbert *liturgica*'.

Scribe iii. Fols 260v–261r: a mass for St Denis and companions (nos 2271–5).

Scribe vii. Fol. 261v: preface for the Trinity (no. 2276).

Scribe viii. Fol. 264r: mass in honour of All Saints (nos 2281–3).

Scribe ix. Fol. 264v: mass in honour of the Invention of St Stephen (nos 2284–9).

Scribe x. Fol. 265: mass for sinners (nos 2290–9).

Scribe xi. Fol. 336r, lines 18–24: two prayers to be said over salt and water added at the foot of the page (nos 2692–3).

Scribe iv, it should be said, also renewed parts of the text of *A*'s blessing for the Vigil of Christmas (no. 349) on fol. 65v.

Again, the work of these scribes has so far not been identified in any of the numerous late-tenth-century manuscripts normally attributed to Canterbury on art-historical, palaeographical and historical grounds. A huge amount of work therefore remains to be done. But it may never be possible to be absolutely certain whether all were from Christ Church, for as has long been recognised, Christ Church scribes regularly worked in books apparently from St Augustine's, and vice versa. To add to the tangle, art-historians have often taken views contrary to those put forward by the palaeographers.[67]

As for the material itself, the question is: why is it there at all? The answer is not hard to find. First, the incorporation of a new calendar and practical computus, not to mention the supplement of saints' masses incorporated later on in the volume, suggest that *A* was still regarded as being a useful, working book; and second, that certain changes in liturgical practice had taken place at Canterbury by the the last quarter of the tenth century. One cannot help but think that these changes were largely introduced by Dunstan. Indeed, as we shall see, *B*'s calendar seems to have been based on a sacramentary brought by the new archbishop to Canterbury from Glastonbury, where he had formerly been abbot. It will be best to begin with the calendar.

---

[67] For instance, see T. A. M. Bishop, 'Notes on Cambridge manuscripts Part IV: Manuscripts connected with St Augustine's, Canterbury'; 'Part VI: Manuscripts connected with St Augustine's, continued'; and 'Part VII: The early minuscule of Christ Church, Canterbury', *Transactions of the Cambridge Bibiliographical Society* 2 (1954–8), 323–36; and 3 (1959–63), 412–13, 413–23; and Temple, *Anglo-Saxon Manuscripts*, pp. 46–7 and 55–8.

The Calendar (no. 277)

As has already been mentioned, the calendar has generally been assigned to Glastonbury on the grounds that entries are provided for the feasts of St Patrick (17 Mar.), St Aidan (31 Aug.) and St Ceolfrith (25 Sept.), saints intimately connected with the house.[68] But as Rock and Dumville have noted, this Glastonbury contigent must be 'second-hand', for Glastonbury itself is named. The entry for St Aidan's day, for instance, runs: *in glaestonia, sancti aidani.* The person who perhaps contributed most to our understanding of the calendar in wider terms, however, was Edmund Bishop. Although Bishop took the mention of Glastonbury at face value, and was therefore wrong about *B*'s provenance, he provided the answer to one of the calendar's more intriguing characteristics.

In 1908 Bishop published, in company with Aidan Gasquet, then abbot of the English Benedictine Congregation, a monograph on the so-called 'Bosworth Psalter', a mid to late-tenth-century English monastic psalter-cum-hymnal that had lain for centuries in Bosworth Hall in Leicestershire more or less unnoticed by the scholarly world. The manuscript, bought by the British Museum in 1908, is now London, British Library, Additional 37517. Among other things, Bishop was able to show first, that the psalter's calendar, which had been added to the book about sometime close to the year 1000, and *B*'s were intimately related; and second, that both revealed the sacramentary or rather sacramentaries for which they had initially been drawn up. He stated that:[69]

A feature common to G [*B*] and B [*Bosworth*] is peculiar to them among the extant calendars of the Anglo-Saxon period; it is the presence of the letter 'F' or 'S' prefixed to the names of certain saints. No time will be spent here in discussing, or guessing, the precise words which these letter are intended to represent; but it is of importance to recognize what it is they are meant to designate. As to this the explanation is simple and not open to doubt; they designate the contents of the Sanctorale – that is, the collection of proper masses of saints – of the mass-book for which the calendar

[68] Gasquet and Bishop, *The Bosworth Psalter*, pp. 15–27; *EK*, pp. 43–55; and Hohler, 'Books', pp. 69–70.
[69] Gasquet and Bishop, *The Bosworth Psalter*, p. 15.

was written. By 'proper mass' is meant a mass the prayers of which are special, and peculiar to a particular saint.

The letters in question are placed in the margin immediately to the left of the entries to which they refer.[70] Feasts of the highest grade, that is those of the Lord, the Virgin, the Apostles and a number of others are classed 'F'; those of the second grade 'S'. In the main the feasts marked out with one of these two letters belong to the Gregorian and Gelasian sacramentaries, but there are certain striking omissions. To take each 'strand' separately.

Gregorian feasts

The following masses of the *Hadrianum* are not specially distinguished in *B* and *Bosworth*:

B.	*Bosworth.*
St Leo (28 June).	St Felix (14 Jan.).
St Peter's Chains (1 Aug.).	St Vitalis (28 Apr.).
Vigil of the Assumption of the Virgin (14 Aug.).	Dedication of the Church of St Mary Martyr (15 May).
St Sabina (29 Aug.).	St Urban (25 May.).
St Caesarius (1 Nov.).	St Leo.
St Felicity (23 Nov.).	SS Processus and Martinian (2 July).
St Saturninus (29 Nov.).	St Peter's Chains.
	St Eufemia (16 Sept.).
	St Caesarius.
	St Felicity.
	St Chrisogonus (24 Nov.).

The entries for the Vigil of SS Peter and Paul (28 June) and the Vigil of St Andrew (29 Nov.), do not have a prefatory letter 'S' in *Bosworth*, but they are written in capitals, which is indication enough of their importance. The scribe of *B*, on the other hand, was careful to prefix the grading to all capitalized entries.

Evidently the sacramentary underlying the two calendars lacked

---

[70] See the photographs *ibid.*, pl. IV; T. A. M. Bishop, *Early Caroline Minuscule* (Oxford, 1971), pl. 2; and A. Watson, *Catalogue of Dated and Datable Manuscripts c. 700–1600 in the Department of Manuscripts, the British Library*, 2 vols (London, 1979) II, pl. 23. A small section of *B*'s computus is illustrated Watson, *Catalogue of Dated and Datable Manuscripts c. 435–1600 in Oxford Libraries*, 2 vols (Oxford, 1984) II, pl. 16.

masses for the feasts of Pope Leo I, the Vigil of the Assumption, St Peter's chains, and saints Cesarius and Felicity, all of which are common to the *Hadrianum* and its derivatives, including those books that embody a good deal of 'Gelasian' material. There are two ways of accounting for their absence.

(i) The feasts of St George, Pope Leo I, the Vigil of the Assumption and St Peter's Chains came to the Gregorian sacramentary relatively late. The first and last were introduced in the pontificate of Sergius (687–701), the other two under Pope Leo III (682–3). It is possible therefore that the book underlying *B* and *Bosworth* was based on a pre-'Hadrianic' Gregorian that had partially brought up to date: in other words, it will have been similar in its basic arrangement to the ancestor of the famous sacramentary of Trent, which 'escaped' from Rome *c.* 680.[71] If this interpretation is correct, then the feasts of saints Cesarius and Felicity are likely to have been 'squeezed out', the one by All Saints Day (1 Nov.), and the other by St Clement's (23 Nov.).

(ii) The five feasts were not catered for in early graduals, the books that contain the chant for mass.[72] A reviser may therefore have felt entitled to jettison the masses for these days. Further, the graduals provide chant in honour of SS Pudentiana (19 May), Praxedes (21 July) and Apollinaris (23 July), whose feasts are marked 'S' in both calendars, but do not figure in 'Hadrianic' books.

Occasionally lesser feasts are rejected in favour of more important ones. *B* abandons St Sabina's for that of the Decollation of St John the Baptist (a 'Gelasian'); and *Bosworth* abandons SS Processus and Martinian's for St Swithun's (2 July), and St Eufemia's for SS Lucy and Geminian's (16 Sept.). It is not clear why *Bosworth* rejects the others. Perhaps preference alone dictated which were to remain and which to go.

---

[71] Trent, Museo Provinciale d'Arte, 1590, ed. F. Dell'Oro, *Il sacramentario di Trento*, Monumenta liturgica ecclesiae Tridentinae saeculo XIII antiquiora 2A (Trent, 1985), 83–416.
[72] The earliest Frankish books are ed. Hesbert, *Antiphonale Missarum Sextuplex.* For more extensive bibliographies, see *CLLA*, nos 1310, 1320, 1322, 1325, 1330 and 1335.

Gelasian feasts

The feasts encompassed by the sacramentary underlying the two calendars are:

Octave of the Epiphany (13 Jan.).
Conversion of St Paul (25 Jan.).
Cathedra Petri (22 Feb.).
SS Nereus and Achilleus (12 May).
SS Primus and Felician (9 June).
SS Basilides etc. (12 June).
St James (25 July).
Octave of St Lawrence (17 Aug.).
St Bartholomew (24 Aug.).
St Augustine (28 Aug.).
Decollation of St John the Baptist
 (30 Aug.).

St Adrian (8 Sept.).
St Gorgonius (9 Sept.).
Vigil of St Matthew (20 Sept.).
St Matthew (21 Sept.).
St Luke (18 Oct.).
Vigil of SS Simon and Jude (27
 Oct.).
SS Simon and Jude (28 Oct.).
Octave of St Andrew (6 Dec.).
St Thomas (21 Dec.).

Bosworth gives no letter for the Vigil of St Matthew and the Vigil of SS Simon and Jude, but the entries are in capitals.

All in all, this is a relatively lean selection of 'Gelasian' feasts, most of which are proper to 'Eighth-Century Gelasian' sacramentaries. However, one would expect to find in books containing a similar amount of 'Eighth-Century Gelasian' material masses for at least two or three of the following saints:[73]

St Praiectus of Saint-Prix (25 Jan.).
St Juliana of Cumae (16 Feb.).
St Juvenal of Narni (3 May).
St Vitus of Lucania (15 June).

St Donatus of Arezzo (7 Aug.).
St Magnus of Anagni (19 Aug.).
St Rufus of Capua (27 Aug.).
SS Marcellus and Apuleius of
 Capua (7 Oct.).

That none are Roman may go some way towards explaining why these were passed over. Moreover, since the sacramentaries for which *B* and *Bosworth* were originally drawn up do not survive, we cannot be sure that the formulae adopted were in every case those of the *Hadrianum*, which is certainly Roman, or those of the 'Gelasians', which are Roman in part. Standard prayers could always be replaced, and numerous sacramentaries exist with different admixtures of 'Gregorian', 'Gelasian' and other forms. Indeed, some of these seem to have been at

---

[73] For books with smaller complements of 'Gelasian' feasts, see *Le sacramentaire grégorien* I, 687–718, and III, 19–59.

least as influential as the *Hadrianum* and copies of the 'Eighth-Century Gelasian'; but no surviving book resembles *B* or *Bosworth* in their 'Roman' parts, and nor, for that matter, does any book have quite the same run of 'later' masses. It is to these last that we must now turn.

Feasts belonging neither to the Gregorian nor Gelasian cursus

If we separate out for the moment the feasts of English saints, those that remain fall naturally into three groups: feasts common to *Bosworth* and *B*, and feasts peculiar to one or other. It will be best to deal first with those common to both; and since we are dealing in effect with a sacramentary (or sacramentaries), rather than calendar entries pure and simple, our primary concern must be with the question of whether *Bosworth* and *B*'s proper masses are unusual in any way.

Apostle Matthias (24 Feb.). The earliest surviving masses in his honour occur in ninth-century books from houses in north-eastern France: Reims BM 213 (Saint-Amand for Noyon), Cambrai BM 162–3 (Arras, Saint-Vaast, or Cambrai); and BNF lat. 2291 (Paris, Notre-Dame). The prayers are generally standard throughout the middle ages.[74]

St Benedict (21 Mar.). By the tenth century the mass originally composed by Alcuin was the one normally adopted for the feast throughout northern Europe.[75]

St Pudentiana (19 May). Patroness of the church in Rome at which the pope, from the seventh century, said mass on the Tuesday in the third week of Lent.[76] The earliest surviving masses for her day occur in two eleventh-century Italian sacramentaries: Vat. lat. 4770, from a house in the Abruzzo region; and Vatican City, Biblioteca Apostolica Vaticana, Vat. lat. 4772, from Arezzo Cathedral by way of Mainz. A proper reading for mass is provided in a copy of a Roman epistle-list written *c.* 700 by an Englishman and now preserved at Würzburg; as has already been mentioned, chant is given in a number of ninth-century graduals.[77]

---

[74] See Leroquais, *Les sacramentaires* I, 23, 37, 57. The mass is ed. *Le sacramentaire grégorien* I, 691, nos 68*–70*, and II, 92, nos 3449–54, from the Arras and Paris sacramentaries respectively.

[75] Ed. *Le sacramentaire grégorien* II, 301, nos 3463–7.

[76] *Ibid.* I, 149.

[77] See Ebner, *Quellen*, p. 220; Leroquais, *Les sacramentaires* I, 132; and G. Morin, 'Le plus ancien Comes ou lectionnaire de l'église romaine', *RB* 27 (1902), 41–74.

St Praxedes (21 July). Patroness of the church in Rome at which the pope said mass on the Monday after Palm Sunday.[78] The earliest surviving masses in her honour occur in BNF lat. 9430, part of a late-ninth-century sacramentary from the abbey of St Martin at Tours; and in Vat. lat. 4770.[79] Again, a proper reading is provided in the Wurzburg epistle-list and chant in the early graduals.

SS Vincent and Apollinaris (23 July). The feast of St Vincent, a Roman martyr about whom little is known, is only to be found on the 23rd of July in certain copies of the *Martyrologium Hieronymianum*.[80] Other martyrologies give the 24th. A church in honour of St Apollinaris, the first bishop of Ravenna, was founded in Rome by Pope Honorius (625–38). According to William of Malmesbury, Glastonbury possessed relics; and if his account is to be followed, King Edgar (959–75) provided a shrine to house them.[81] Presumably this is why the two saints are also commemorated on the 23rd, in company with St Primitivus, in the early-eleventh-century west country calendar of CUL Kk. 5. 32. There are apparently no surviving masses for the two saints together, but propers for St Apollinaris alone figure in several ninth-century sacramentaries, notably the early-ninth-century sacramentary from Bergamo, now Bergamo, Biblioteca de San Alessandro in Colonna, s. n. England, however, seems to have had access to a different Italian mass. The highly unusual *oratio post evangelium* in Vat. lat. 4770 (and a number of other northern and central Italian books) is the first prayer for St Apollinaris in the portiforium written *c.* 1065 for Wulfstan II, bishop of Worcester (1060–95).[82] A reading for mass is provided in the Wurzburg epistle-list and chant in the ninth-century graduals.

SS Denis, Rusticius and Eleutherius (9 Oct.). Relics preserved at Saint-Denis, and a standard mass widespread by the ninth century.[83]

[78] *Le sacramentaire grégorien* I, 168.

[79] Leroquais, *Les sacramentaires* I, 46, with Deshusses, 'Les anciens sacramentaires de Tours', 41–74; Ebner, *Quellen*, p. 220.

[80] *Martyrologium Hieronymianum*, ed. De Rossi and Duchesne, *Acta SS Nov.* II.i, 95.

[81] See William of Malmesbury, *De antiquitate Glastoniensis Ecclesiae*, ed. J. Scott, *The Early History of the Church of Glastonbury* (Woodbridge, 1981), p. 130, with the better translation of F. Lomax, *The Antiquities of Glastonbury* (repr. Llanerlech, 1992), p. 103; *EK*, p. 78; and S. E. Irvine, 'Bones of contention: the context of Ælfric's homily on St Vincent', *ASE* 19 (1990), 117–32.

[82] Ed. Paredi, *Sacramentarium Bergomense*, p. 261, nos 1004–9; Hughes, *The Portiforium of Saint Wulfstan* I, 134, no. 1856. See also, N. A. Orchard, 'The medieval masses in honour of St Apollinaris of Ravenna', *RB* 106 (1996), 172–84.

[83] Ed. *Le sacramentaire grégorien* I, 704, nos 258*–61*, and II, 328, nos 3626–9.

Note that the *B*'s scribe began to write the entry for St Denis and his companions on the line for the 8th of October, the day on which the feast is entered in the 'Old English Martyrology', but realising his mistake, erased what he had written and began afresh on the line below. Warren's contention that the erased entry was originally for the translation of the remains of SS Aidan and Ceolfrith to Glastonbury cannot be sustained.[84]

St Quentin (31 Oct.). Relics preserved at the church of Saint-Quentin-en-Vermandois and at the abbey of Saint-Riquier. Collects for his day are given in Reims, Bibliothèque municipale, 304, a collectar of *c.* 900 from the abbey of Saint-Thierry at Reims; Durham A. IV. 19, the so-called 'Durham Collectar'; and in the portiforium of Wulfstan of Worcester.[85] The earliest complete mass listed by Leroquais occurs in Paris, Bibliothèque nationale de France, lat. 2297, an early-eleventh-century sacramentary from a house in Brittany; the next in BNF lat. 10500, the sacramentary of Hughes de Salines, archbishop of Besançon. But proper chant for office is provided in an early antiphonar from Compiègne.[86]

Vigil of All Saints and All Saints Day (31 Oct. and 1 Nov.). The masses for these days were composed by Alcuin and therefore circulated widely in the middle ages.[87] There is no mention of the Vigil in *Bosworth*, but this must be an oversight on the part of the scribe since the day itself is graded 'F'.

So we have two strong elements: Roman, or Roman as transmitted in Frankish lands by lectionaries and graduals, in the shape of masses for SS Pudentiana, Praxedes and Apollinaris (with the proviso that St Apollinaris may be more directly connectable with Glastonbury than Italy); and northern French, in the shape of masses for St Quentin, and SS Denis and companions.

[84] Ed. Kotzor, *Das ältenglische Martyrologium* II, 227–8; LM, p. 32.
[85] Ed. A. Corrêa, *The Durham Collectar*, HBS 107 (London, 1992), 106–8 and 194, no. 453; Hughes, *The Portiforium of Saint Wulstan* I, 147, no. 1965.
[86] Leroquais, *Les sacramentaires* I, 109 and 141; J. Hesbert, *Corpus Antiphonalium Officii*, 6 vols, Rerum ecclesiasticarum Documenta, Series Maior, Fontes 7–12 (Rome, 1963–79) I, 2–419, with *CLLA*, no. 1330.
[87] See Deshusses, 'Les messes d'Alcuin', pp. 1–2 and 33–4, with Wilmart, 'Un témoin Anglo-Saxon du calendrier métrique d'York', pp. 51–7 and Lapidge, 'A tenth-century metrical calendar from Ramsey', pp. 326–70.

Masses peculiar to B:

St Geneviève (13 Jan.). Relics enshrined by Clovis I (d. 511) in the church of SS Peter and Paul in Paris, on the site of which the Pantheon now stands. The earliest surviving masses in her honour figure in the sacramentaries of Saint-Thierry and Tours.[88]

Forty Martyrs of Sebaste (9 Mar.). Sebaste (now Sivas) lies in eastern Turkey. Important relics were kept at Rome, Brescia and Jerusalem, and the feast is regularly entered in martyrologies and calendars, though occasionally on the 10th of March. Prayers are provided in eleventh and twelfth-century Roman books, notably Rome, Biblioteca Vallicellana, E. 15, an early-eleventh-century sacramentary from the church of S. Laurenzo in Damaso; Vatican S. Pietro F. 14, the late-eleventh or early-twelfth-century sacramentary from the church of S. Trifone; and S. Pietro F. 11, a late-twelfth-century book of unknown Roman provenance. But due to the complete disappearance of ninth and tenth-century sacramentaries from the city's suburbican churches, it is difficult to say when these formulae were first used.[89] That a mass was said in England for the martyrs in the late tenth century, and possibly before, is therefore of the greatest interest, not least because Wulfstan of Worcester knew and probably used one of its collects in the mid eleventh century.[90] The question of when the cult first became important in England requires further investigation.

SS Victor, Quartus and the Four Hundred and Four Martyrs (14 May). According to the *Martyrologium Hieronymianum* and the martyrology of Bede, St Victor, a soldier from Cilicia, was martyred with St Corona in Syria. It is rare to find one without the other. St Quartus was martyred with St Secundinus and a number of others in Africa; and the Four Hundred and Four Martyrs suffered with SS Cyricus and Iulitta of Tarsus, although all four hundred and six were sometimes venerated on the continent on the 16th of June, and SS Cyricus and Iulitta separately on the 15th of July. However, *B* is not alone, for SS Victor, Quartus and

---

[88] The Tours mass is ed. *Le sacramentaire grégorien* II, 297, nos 3445–8. See also R. Amiet, *Le culte liturgique de sainte Geneviève* (Paris, 1981), esp. pp. 77–99.
[89] See E. B. Garrison, 'Twelfth-Century initial styles of Central Italy: Indices for the Dating of MSS. Part II: Materials (contd)', in his *Studies in Early Italian Painting*, 4 vols (Florence, 1953–62) IV, 277–307, at 281. The contents of the *sanctoralia* of most of the surviving Roman sacramentaries are listed in the notes he bequeathed to the Courtauld Institute.
[90] Ed. Hughes, *The Portiforium of Saint Wulstan* I, 120, no. 1753.

the Four Hundred and Four Martyrs are also recorded on the 14th of May in *Bosworth* (but without a prefixed 'S'), and on the 13th of May in the calendar of CUL Kk. 5. 32. So it seems that the feast of these saints was kept only in England. It is worth noting too that an entry for St Victor, again without St Corona, but accompanied instead by St Boniface, appears in the calendar of Salisbury Cathedral Library, 150; and an entry for the Four Hundred and Four Martyrs with St Machutus (Malo), who should in fact have been St Maximianus, in the early-eleventh-century calendar, perhaps from St German's in Cornwall, and now London, British Library, Cotton Nero A. ii.[91]

Masses peculiar to Bosworth:

The masses added by *Bosworth* are, generally speaking, less unusual. We have:

St Scholastica (10 Feb.). St Benedict's sister; major relics at Monte Cassino and Le Mans. The earliest surviving mass in her honour is preserved in a fragement of a sacramentary from northern Italy, the next in the late-ninth-century sacramentary from Saint-Thierry.[92] Common therafter.

St Mark (18 May). As has already been noted, the evangelist's feast is only common on this date in England.[93]

Translation of St Benedict (11 July). Early sources, including 'Eighth-Century Gelasian' sacramentaries and their derivatives, make the 11th of July the day of St Benedict's *natale* or *depostio*. But the 11th later became the day on which his *translatio* was celebrated, the *natale* having been 'moved' to the 20th of March. *A* is one of the earliest books to provide masses with proper superscriptions for both feasts.[94]

---

[91] See Quentin, *Les martrologes historiques du moyen âge*, pp. 52, 154, 335, 430 and 482; *EK*, pp. 20 and 34. For the suggestion that BL Cotton Nero A. ii is from St German's, see M. Lapidge, 'Some Latin poems as evidence for the reign of Æthelstan', *ASE* 9 (1981), 61–98, at 85–6.

[92] Ed. K. Gamber, 'Ein oberitalienisches Plenarmissale des S-Typus', *Sacris Erudiri* 13 (1962), 353–9. The mass from the sacramentary of Saint-Thierry is ed. *Le sacramentaire grégorien* II, 297, nos 3449–54. See also R. Gregoire, 'Les prières liturgiques médiévaux en l'hônneur de saint Benoît, sainte Scholastique et saint Maur', *Studia Anselmiana* 54 (Rome, 1965), 1–86, esp. 28–86; and J. Hourlier, 'La translation de sainte Scholastique au Mans', *Studia Monastica* 21 (1979), 313–33.

[93] See above, pp. 53–6.

[94] Gregoire, 'Les prières liturgiques médiévaux', pp. 1–86; J. Deshusses and J. Hourlier, 'Saint Benoît dans les livres liturgiques', *Studia Monastica* 21 (1979), 143–204.

Invention of St Stephen Protomartyr (3 Aug.). St Stephen's relics were discovered at Jerusalem in 415. Masses for the invention occur in the ninth-century sacramentaries of Saint-Thierry and Tours, but are otherwise uncommon until the eleventh century. A proper office composed by Stephen, bishop of Liège (901–20) survives in two early books from the abbey of St Maur-des-Fosses, and in several later manuscripts from French and Belgian houses; and there are hymns, though not by Stephen, in Douai, Bibliothèque municipale, 170, an early-eleventh-century psalter from Marchiennes, and Modena, Bibliotheca Comunale, 102 (109), an early-eleventh-century hymnal from Mantua.[95] The hymns and office name St Stephen's companions: Gamaliel, Abibon and Nichomedis. New propers naming St Stephen alone, however, were added to *A* at Canterbury sometime in the last third of the tenth century, as we shall see, and a new proper benediction figures in BL Harley 2892, the mid-eleventh-century benedictional of Christ Church, Canterbury. Furthermore, a fragmentary (secular) office in the saint's honour is preserved in London, British Library, Harley 3271, a mid-eleventh-century miscellany, containing a copy of Ælfric's Grammar and select liturgical and computistical material.[96] The feast therefore seems to have attracted a considerable degree of interest in England, particularly at Canterbury.

Conception of St John the Baptist (24 Sept.). The Conception is often noted in calendars and martyrologies, but proper masses and offices are unusual. Two different sets of formulae were current in the west country (and apparently nowhere else in England) throughout the middles ages. One, consisting of newly composed prayers, figures among the additions made to Bodley 579 at Exeter in the mid eleventh century (part *C*: nos 2899–2908) and in the original portions of the magnificent late-fourteenth-century missal from the abbey of Sherborne, in Somerset; the other, comprising of older compositions re-used, in BL Cotton Vitellius A. xviii, the sacramentary written for Giso of Wells, and in part, in a

---

[95] Leroquais, *Les sacramentaires* I, 24 and 46. On the office, see A. Auda, *L'école musicale liègoise au Xe siècle: Étienne de Liège* (Brussels, 1923), pp. 42–66; and for the hymns, G. M. Dreves, C. Blume and H. M. Bannister *Analecta hymnica medii aevi*, 55 vols (Leipzig, 1886–1922) XI, 244, and XIX, 256.

[96] See below, p. 203. The blessing is ed. Woolley, *The Canterbury Benedictional*, pp. 103–4. BL Harley 3271 is described by Ker, *Catalogue of Manuscripts containing Anglo-Saxon*, no. 239, pp. 309–12. The office is essentially a reduced version of Stephen of Liège's.

fragmentary collectar now preserved in the *Liber ruber* of Wells Cathedral.[97] The sacramentary underlying *Bosworth* presumably contained one or other.

St Bricius (13 Nov.). Bishop of Tours (d. 444); buried in his cathedral. Although it is clear from Gregory of Tours (d. 594) that a mass was said in honour of the saint in the sixth and seventh centuries, no provision is made for his feast in the sacramentaries that survive from the abbey of St Martin and cathedral of St Maurice. The earliest masses that have come down to us are those in Angers BM 90, late-tenth-century additions to an early-tenth-century sacramentary from Angers; Paris, Bibliothèque nationale de France, lat. 817, an early-eleventh-century sacramentary from Cologne; and BNF lat. 2297. But antiphons for office are given in the antiphoner of Compiègne, which as we have already seen, also gives chant for St Quentin.[98] King Æthelred the Unready (978–1016) ordered the Danes living in England to be slaughtered on the feast of St Bricius, 1002. Thereafter, St Bricius' day will have acquired a special significance, and a mass may well have been drawn up in response. If so, we would then have a new *terminus post quem* for *Bosworth's* calendar.[99]

Feasts of English saints

A short table will give the clearest possible representation of how these feasts appear in the two calendars. Entries in capitals are in capitals in the manuscripts.

9 Jan.		F. St Hadrian, Abbot.
2 Feb.		S. St Lawrence, Archbishop.
17 Mar.		S. St Edward, King and Martyr.
20 Mar.	F. ST CUTHBERT.	F. ST CUTHBERT.
17 Apr.	S. ST GUTHLAC.	F. ST GUTHLAC.

[97] The Sherborne Missal, which belongs to the Duke of Northumberland, is for the time being London, British Library, Loans 82. It is described by J. W. Legg, 'Liturgical notes on the Sherborne Missal, a manuscript in the possession of the Duke of Northumberland at Alnwick Castle', *Transactions of the St Paul's Ecclesiological Society* 4 (1896), 1–31. For a brief description of the collectar, see A. Watkin, 'Fragment of a twelfth-century collectarium in the *Liber Albus* of Wells', *Downside Review* 69 (1950), 85–91.

[98] *Gregorii episcopi Turonensis historia Francorum*, ed. W. Arndt, MGH SS rer. Meroving. 1 (Hannover, 1885), 31–450, at 445; Leroquais, *Les sacramentaires* I, 98, 109; and Hesbert, *Corpus Antiphonalium Officii* I, 330–1.

[99] *Anglo-Saxon Chronicle* 1002: *Two of the Saxon Chronicles Parallel*, ed. Plummer, I, 135 (text).

24 Apr.	S. St Mellitus, Archbishop.	F. St Mellitus, Archbishop of the English.
19 May.		F. St Dunstan.
26 May.	F. ST AUGUSTINE, ARCHBISHOP.	F. ST AUGUSTINE, FIRST ARCHBISHOP OF THE ENGLISH.
15 June.		S. St Eadburh.
22 June.	S. St Æthelthryth.	S. St Æthelthryth.
2 July.		S. St Swithun.
13 July.		S. St Mildreth.
15 July.		S. Archbishop Deusdedit.
5 Aug.		S. St Oswald.
24 Aug.	S. St Patrick senior.	S. St Patrick senior, *in glaestonia*.
31 Aug.	S. *In glaestonia*, St Aidan.	S. St Aidan.
19 Sept.		S. St Theodore, Archbishop of the English.
25 Sept.	S. *In glaestonia*, St Ceolfrith	S. St Ceolfrith, *in glaestonia*.
30 Sept.		S. St Honorius, Archbishop of the English.
10 Nov.		S. St Justus, Archbishop of the English.

Taking the masses added by *Bosworth* to the common stock first, we have:

St Hadrian. Seventh abbot of St Augustine's, Canterbury (d. 709); buried, according to Goscelin of Saint-Bertin, precentor of the abbey in the last decade of the eleventh century, in the church of St Mary founded by King Eadbald (*c.* 616–40) to the east of the abbey. Hadrian's feast only otherwise occurs before the Conquest in the calendar of CUL Kk. 5. 32; a mass in his honour is provided in Cambridge, Corpus Christi College, 270, a late-eleventh-century sacramentary from St Augustine's.[100]

St Lawrence. Second archbishop of Canterbury (601 × 604 – 619); buried, according to Goscelin, in the north porticus of St Augustine's Abbey, where St Augustine had been buried before him. Archaelogical excavations undertaken earlier this century by William St John Hope have tended to bear out what Goscelin says of the resting places of the

---

[100] See Goscelin's *Historia translationis S. Augustini*, ed. D. Papebroch, *Acta Sanctorum Maii* VI, 408–21, at 431. Richard Sharpe has a new edition in hand. See also Sharpe's article, 'Goscelin's St Augustine and St Mildreth: hagiography and liturgy in context', *JTS* ns 41 (1990), 502–16; and on St Hadrian in general, Bischoff and Lapidge, *Biblical Commentaries*, pp. 82–132. For the calendars, *EK*, p. 71; and the mass, *The Missal of St Augustine's Abbey*, ed. Rule, p. 72.

Canterbury archbishops in the Anglo-Saxon abbey complex. Their relics were ceremonially translated to the new church in 1091. A mass for St Lawrence figures in CCCC 270.[101]

St Edward Martyr. King of England 975–8. His relics were translated from Corfe (where he was murdered) to Shaftesbury Abbey in 981. Two masses in his honour are provided in Rouen BM 274, the early-eleventh-century sacramentary later owned by Robert of Jumièges, and a proper benediction in BL Harley 2892, the 'Canterbury Benedictional'.[102]

St Dunstan. Archbishop of Canterbury (d. 988); buried in the cathedral. He is termed *patronus noster* in the mass given in Robert's sacramentary, which may mean that its prayers issued from Canterbury. However, two of these prayers were borrowed from an apparently much older mass originally composed in honour of St Hilary of Poitiers (14 Jan.).[103] Certainly of Christ Church origin are the five benedictions provided for St Dunstan's feast and its vigil in BL Harley 2892. The mass in CCCC 270 is not to be found elsewhere.[104]

St Eadburh. Daughter of King Edward the Elder (899–924) and first abbess of the Nunnaminster, Winchester (d. 960). A mass for her day figures in Le Havre, Bibliothèque municipale, 330, the mid-eleventh-century missal from the New Minster, Winchester.[105]

St Alban. Protomartyr of England (third century); relics preserved at the abbey of St Albans. His feast is entered in Bede's martyrology, and in numerous English and continental calendars (often on the continent as

---

[101] See Bede, *HE*, pp. 144–8, 152–6; Goscelin, *Historia translationis*, 412 (Bk i, ch. 2, 17E); W. St John Hope, 'Recent discoveries in the abbey church of St Austin at Canterbury', *Archaeologia Cantiana* 32 (1917), 1–26, fig. 7 for a plan of the arrangement of the tombs in the north porticus; and *The Missal of St Augustine's*, ed. Rule, p. 77.

[102] D. Rollason, 'Lists of saints' resting places', p. 92; S. Ridyard, *The Royal Saints of Anglo-Saxon England* (Cambridge, 1985), pp. 44–50; *The Missal of Robert of Jumièges*, ed. Wilson, pp. 3–5; and *The Canterbury Benedictional*, ed. Woolley, p. 88.

[103] On various aspects of Dunstan's career, see *St Dunstan: His Life, Times and Cult*, ed. Ramsay, Sparks and Tatton-Brown. On the masses for the day, see *The Missal of Robert of Jumièges*, ed. Wilson, pp. 175–6; *Le sacramentaire grégorien* II, 295, nos 3443–4; and *Missale ad usum ecclesiae Westmonasteriensis*, ed. Legg, III, 1549–50.

[104] *The Canterbury Benedictional*, ed. Woolley, pp. 93–5; *The Missal of St Augustine's*, ed. Rule, p. 89.

[105] Rollason, 'Lists of saints' resting places', p. 92; *idem, The Royal Saints of Anglo-Saxon England*, pp. 16–37, 103–21; Turner, *The Missal of the New Minster*, p. 104.

St Albinus). The most common mass for his day is the one given in the sacramentary of Robert of Jumièges.[106]

St Swithun. Bishop of Winchester (d. 863); buried at the Old Minster (cathedral). His relics were translated by Bishop Æthelwold on the 15th of July 971. The earliest surviving liturgical composition in his honour is the benediction in BL Add. 49598, the magnificent benedictional written *c.* 973 for Æthelwold. The mass in the mid-eleventh-century New Minster Missal was popular throughout the middle ages, though some houses used its prayers for his translation.[107] The formulae also found their way to the continent where, in the eleventh century and perhaps before, they were re-assigned to the feasts of local saints.

St Mildreth. Abbess of Minster-in-Thanet (d. *c.* 700). In 1030 her relics were removed to the church of St Mary near St Augustine's in Canterbury and enshrined in its western porticus. The episcopal benediction provided in BL Harley 2892, the benedictional of Christ Church, Canterbury, is probably the only liturgical composition in her honour to have survived from the Anglo-Saxon period.[108] Note also that missals from Utrecht provide a mass for her day.

St Deusdedit. Fifth archbishop of Canterbury (655–64); buried in the north porticus of St Augustine's Abbey. As far as surviving Anglo-Saxon calendars and martyrologies are concerned, his feast is only otherwise entered in the fragmentary calendar now preserved in Paris, Bibliothèque nationale, lat. 10062, fols 162r–163v, but on the 14th of July, not his 'St Augustine's day'. This calendar, which seems to have been copied from a model from Bourges (the name of Bishop Gundulf appears before that of St Botulf on the 17th of June) was probably at

[106] Bede, *HE*, pp. 28–34, 58; Rollason, 'Lists of saints' resting places', 87; *Édition practique des martyrologes de Bede, de l'Anonyme lyonnais et de Florus*, ed. J. Dubois and G. Renaud (Paris, 1976), p. 112; and *The Missal of Robert of Jumièges*, ed. Wilson, pp. 5–6, with Hohler, 'Les saintes insulaires', 303.
[107] *The Benedictional of St Aethelwold*, ed. Warner and Wilson, p. 39 and facs (fols 97r–98v), with Prescott, 'The text of the benedictional of St Aethelwold', 117–47; Turner, *The Missal of the New Minster*, p. 117, with T. Schmid, 'Om Sankt Swithunmassen i Sverige', *Nordisk Tidskrift for Bok- och Biblioteksvasen* 31 (1944), 25–34; *The Portiforium of St Wulstan*, ed. Hughes, I, 129, nos 1821–6; and *Missale ad usum ecclesiae Westmonasteriensis*, ed. Legg, III, 1562–3, 1565–6.
[108] R. Sharpe, 'The date of St Mildreth's translation from Minster-in-Thanet to Canterbury', *Medieval Studies* 53 (1991), 349–54; *The Canterbury Benedictional*, ed. Woolley, p. 102; and *The Missal of St Augustine's Abbey*, ed. Rule, pp. 87, 97, with Sharpe, 'Goscelin's St Augustine and St Mildreth', pp. 510–13.

Christ Church by 1023, for three entries relating to the arrival of the remains of St Ælfheah at the cathedral were added in a contemporary hand. A mass in honour of St Deusdedit figures in CCCC 270.[109] The calendar in BNF lat. 10062 has not been published.

St Oswald. King of Northumbria, slain in the battle of Oswestry in 642. In the Anglo-Saxon period his relics were exceptionally well-travelled. His head finally ended up at Durham in 995, having been translated initially to Lindisfarne *c.* 643; his arms were taken to Bamburgh, though one was later spirited away to Peterborough and then Ely; and his body was translated to Bardney *c.* 675 and then to Gloucester in 909. Other relics were taken to Germany, some by St Willibrord, whose calendar, like many others from German houses, has an entry for the day.[110] Two versions of the standard mass for St Oswald exist: one as in the New Minster Missal, the other as in Robert's sacramentary. The New Minster version was taken abroad at an early date.[111]

St Theodore. Sixth archbishop of Canterbury (668–90); buried in the main body of St Augustine's, the north porticus being full.[112] His feast is a late-eighth-century addition in St Willibrord's calendar, but appears as an original entry in the calendars of: Milan, Biblioteca Ambrosiana, M. 12 Sup., mid-ninth-century from Corvey; Bodley 579 (*B*); Solothurn Zentralbibliothek, U. 1, a late-tenth-century sacramentary from the abbey of Hornbach; Verona 87, the sacramentary of Wolfgang of Regensburg (972–94); and BL Cotton Nero A. ii. A mass in his honour is given in the St Augustine's sacramentary.[113]

---

[109] Bede, *HE*, p. 278; Goscelin, *Historia translationis*, *Acta SS Maii*, VI, 412; St John Hope, 'Recent discoveries', fig. 7; *The Missal of St Augustine's Abbey*, ed. Rule, p. 98.
[110] Bede, *HE*; Rollason, 'Lists of saints' resting places', p. 87; *Anglo-Saxon Chronicle* 909 (C): *Two of the Saxon Chronicles Parallel*, ed. Plummer, I, 94; *The Calendar of St Willibrord*, ed. H. A. Wilson, HBS 55 (London, 1918), p. 10, pl. viii. See also the essays in *Oswald: Northumbrian King to European Saint*, ed. C. Stancliffe and E. Cambridge (Stamford, 1995).
[111] *The Missal of Robert of Jumièges*, ed. Wilson, pp. 195–6; *The Missal of the New Minster*, ed. Turner, pp. 135–6; and N. A. Orchard, 'The English and German masses in honour of St Oswald of Northumbria', *Archiv für Liturgiewissenschaft* 37 (1995), 347–58, with *idem*, 'The English and German masses in honour of St Oswald of Northumbria: a postscript', *Archiv für Liturgiewissenschaft* 40 (1998), 49–57.
[112] Bede, *HE*, pp. 144, 330–4, 348–52, 474; Goscelin, *Historia translationis*, *Acta SS Maii* VI, 412; St John Hope, 'Recent discoveries', fig. 7. On St Theodore, see Bischoff and Lapidge, *Biblical Commentaries from the Canterbury School of Theodore and Hadrian*, pp. 5–81, and the essays in *Archbishop Theodore*, ed. Lapidge (Cambridge, 1995).
[113] *The Calendar of St Willibrord*, ed. Wilson, p. 11, pl. IX; B. Bischoff, 'Das karolingische Kalendar der Palimsesthandschrift Ambros. M. 12 Sup.', *Colligere*

St Honorius. Fourth archbishop of Canterbury (624 × 627 – 653); buried in the north porticus of St Augustine's Abbey. As far as Anglo-Saxon calendars are concerned, his feast only otherwise occurs in the fragmentary mid-eighth-century calendar taken to Regensburg by an English missionary. A mass for his day is provided in CCCC 270.[114]

St Justus. Third archbishop of Canterbury (624–627 × 631); buried in the north porticus of St Augustine's. His feast appears in the calendars of Salisbury 150 and BL Cotton Nero A. ii. A mass for his day is provided in CCCC 270.[115]

These saints fall naturally into three groups: SS Edward, Alban and Oswald were popular nationally; SS Swithun and Edburga specially venerated at houses reformed from Winchester, and more widely by *c.* 1000; and the remainder were only venerated together at St Augustine's, Canterbury. St Augustine's, Canterbury is therefore in view. Yet both Bishop and Michael Korhammer have argued that *Bosworth* cannot be a St Augustine's calendar because no entry is given on the 7th of May for St Liudhard, whose remains were interred at St Augustine's at an early date, and whose feast was provided with a proper mass in CCCC 270.[116] But there is a simple reason for this. Goscelin relates that Abbot Wulfric II (1047–59) removed the saint's relics from the south porticus, where they had lain for centuries alongside those of Queen Bertha (whose chaplain Liudhard had been) and King Æthelbert (560–616), her husband, and enshrined them somewhere in the main church.[117] There is nothing whatsoever to suggest that a cult had developed around his relics before this time. Indeed, the first firm evidence we have is the presence of a mass in the post-Conquest sacramentary. So there can be absolutely no doubt that Bosworth is from St Augustine's; the sugges-

---

Fragmenta. Festschrift Alban Dold zum 70 Geburtstag, ed. B. Fischer and V. Fiala, Texte und Arbeiten 2 (Beuron, 1962), 247–56, at 254; Gerbert, *Monumenta* I, 469–81, at 478; G. Swarzenski, *Das Regensburger Buchmalerei des X und XI Jahrhunderts* (Leipzig, 1901), pp. 196–218, at 203; *EK*, pp. 38, 52; and *The Missal of St Augustine's Abbey*, ed. Rule, p. 111.

[114] Bede, *HE*, pp. 190–6; Goscelin, *Historia translationis*, *Acta SS Maii* VI, 412; Gamber, *Das Bonifatius-Sakramentar*, p. 58; *The Missal of St Augustine's Abbey*, ed. Rule, p. 114.

[115] Bede, *HE*, pp. 104, 142, 152–8 and 196; Goscelin, *Historia translationis*, *Acta SS Maii* VI, 412; *EK*, pp. 26 and 40; and *The Missal of St Augustine's Abbey*, ed. Rule, p. 120.

[116] Gasquet and Bishop, *The Bosworth Psalter*, pp. 34–5; P. M. Korhammer, 'The origin of the Bosworth Psalter', *ASE* 2 (1973), 178–87.

[117] Goscelin, *Historia translationis*, *Acta Sanctorum Maii* VI, 435. On the saint in general, see M. Werner, 'The Liudhard medalet', *ASE* 20 (1991), 27–41.

tion that it is somehow a Christ Church calendar but without the feasts typical of Christ Church must be rejected.

The 'common stock'

These are the only masses provided for the feasts of English saints in the sacramentary underlying *B*:

St Cuthbert. Bishop of Lindisfarne (d. 687); one of the most popular of all English saints. His relics were evacuated to the mainland by the Lindisfarne community, probably *c*. 830, Danish raids having made the island unsafe. The community eventually settled at Chester-le-Street (883–995) and then permanently at Durham. Entries for the saint are common in English and continental martyrologies (starting with Bede), even though he was not martyred; and his feast regularly figures in early calendars. The 'standard' mass for his day, which is preserved in the sacramentary of Robert of Jumièges and the famous sacramentary of Fulda now at Göttingen, was probably known to, and may even have been compiled by, Alcuin.[118] The mass that figures in *B*, however, is a corrected version of this 'standard' type. As we shall see, there is every reason to believe that the corrections in question were made at Canterbury in the late tenth century.[119]

St Guthlac. Hermit of Crowland (d. 714); relics preserved there. His feast is common in Anglo-Saxon calendars. Two different masses have come down to us in eleventh-century books: one in Robert's sacramentary, which is based on a mass originally drawn up at Tours in honour of 'one confessor'; the other in the sacramentary of Giso of Wells.[120] Robert's prayers were known at Westminster, Hereford, Sherborne, Ely and one might therefore suspect at many other houses besides. But the oldest surviving prayer in Guthlac's honour is the one

---

[118] See *Two Lives of Saint Cuthbert*, ed. B. Colgrave (Cambridge, 1940); *The Missal of Robert of Jumièges*, ed. Wilson, pp. 166–7; and *Sacramentarium Fuldense*, ed. Richter and Schönfelder, p. 31. See also the essays in *St Cuthbert: His Cult and His Community to AD 1200*, ed. G. Bonner, D. Rollason and C. Stancliffe (Woodbridge, 1989); C. Hohler, 'The Durham services in honour of St Cuthbert', in *The Relics of St Cuthbert*, ed. C. F. Battiscombe (Oxford, 1956), pp. 155–91; Orchard, 'A note on the masses in honour of St Cuthbert', pp. 79–98; and D. A. Bullough, 'A neglected early-ninth-century manuscript of the Lindisfarne *Vita S. Cuthberti*', *ASE* 27 (1998), 105–37, esp. 122–8.
[119] See below, p. 199.
[120] *The Missal of Robert of Jumièges*, ed. Wilson, p. 3; *LM*, pp. 303–4; and *Le sacramentaire grégorien* II, 280–1, nos 3340–4.

appended to a late-tenth-century copy of Felix's life once owned by the monks of Saint-Bertin, but probably written at Bath.[121]

St Mellitus. Third archbishop of Canterbury (619–24); buried in the north porticus of St Augustine's. His feast figures in Bede's martyrology and subsequently found its way into a vast number of calendars, both English and continental. He was specially venerated in London, where he had been bishop; in the west country; and naturally at Canterbury. The mass in CCCC 270 was used throughout the diocese of London in the fourteenth century.[122]

St Augustine. Apostle of England, first archbishop of Canterbury (596–604); buried in the north porticus of St Augustine's. The observance of his feast was made obligatory in England by the Council of Cloveshoe (747) and is entered in all English calendars that are complete for the month of May, except St Willibrord's.[123] His feast also features in numerous continental calendars and martyrologies, probably thanks to Bede. No identifiably pre-Conquest Canterbury mass survives. Robert's is adapted from a mass originally composed by Alcuin in honour of St Vedastus; the New Minster's is made up of prayers borrowed from a variety of sources; and Giso's is part Winchester and part west country. Three proper benedictions are given in BL Harley 2892.[124]

St Æthelthryth. Foundress and first abbess of Ely (d. 679). Her feast is entered in Bede's martyrology, in a fragment of an eighth-century calendar written in Northumbrian majuscule that later found its way to the abbey of Illmunster in upper Bavaria, and in English calendars of most periods, though St Willibrord's again is an exception.[125] The earliest surviving liturgical composition in her honour is the abecedarian hymn composed by Bede. The benediction in BL Add. 49598 and the mass in

---

[121] See *Missale ad usum ecclesiae Westmonasteriensis*, ed. Legg, III, 1543; and *Felix's Life of St Guthlac*, ed. B. Colgrave (Cambridge, 1953), p. 171.

[122] Bede, *HE*, pp. 104, 106, 142, 146 and 152–8; Quentin, *Les martyrologes historiques*, p. 50; *Missale ad usum ecclesiae Westmonasteriensis*, ed. Legg, III, 1544, with, for instance, M. Rickert, *The Reconstructed Carmelite Missal* (London, 1952), pp. 30 and 43.

[123] A. W. Haddan and W. Stubbs, *Councils and Ecclesiastical Documents relating to Great Britain and Ireland*, 3 vols in 4 (Oxford, 1869–78) III, 361.

[124] *The Missal of Robert of Jumièges*, ed. Wilson, p. 177 with *Le sacramentaire grégorien* I, 690–1, nos 55*–63*; *The Missal of the New Minster*, ed. Turner, pp. 98–9; *Missale ad usum ecclesiae Westmonasteriensis*, ed. Legg, III, 1551; and *The Canterbury Benedictional*, ed. Woolley, pp. 95–6.

[125] Quentin, *Les martyrologes historiques*, p. 106; Gamber, *Das Bonifatius-Sakramentar*, p. 52.

Robert's sacramentary are likely to have been commissioned by St Æthelwold, who refounded Ely 964 × 970.[126]

St Patrick senior. Relics at Glastonbury by the early tenth century; described in one Irish calendar (now lost) as being 'of Armagh' and in two martyrologies as *episcopus Glosdoniensis* or *Golstoniensis*, which may be Glastonbury. A further two simply record that he was buried at the abbey. His feast is entered in an early-eleventh-century copy of Usuard's martyrology from Abingdon, now Cambridge, Corpus Christi College, 57, and in the calendars of CUL Kk. 5. 32 and Cambridge, Corpus Christi College, 9, which is late-eleventh-century, and from Worcester. No mass for the September feast survives. St Patrick *iunior*, however, was also important in the west country and known to be different from his namesake, for a mass was provided for his feast (17 Mar.) in Giso's sacramentary and the Sherborne Missal among others.[127] This is presumably the Irish mass that figures in Ambrosiana DSP 10/27 bis, an early-eleventh-century missal from Bobbio. What is more, Giso's collect, as we have seen, figures in *A*; and *A* almost certainly contains liturgical formulae used at the dedication of Wells *c.* 909.[128]

St Aidan. Bishop of Lindisfarne (d. 651).[129] According to William of Malmesbury his relics were translated to Glastonbury in the tenth century, which presumably explains why his feast occurs in a number of calendars from houses in the west country: Salisbury 150; BL Cotton Vitellius A. xii; BL Cotton Vitellius A. xviii; and CCCC 422. It also appears in the late-eleventh-century Worcester calendar preserved in Oxford, Bodleian Library, Hatton 113.[130] The west country mass, which may have issued from Glastonbury, survives in Giso's sacramentary and the Sherborne Missal. The collect alone is adopted in London, British

---

[126] Bede, *HE*, pp. 396–400; *The Benedictional of St Aethelwold*, ed. Warner and Wilson, p. 37 and facs. (fols 90v–92r); *The Missal of Robert of Jumièges*, ed. Wilson, pp. 181–2, with *The Missal of the New Minster*, ed. Turner, p. 108.

[127] See Rollason, 'Lists of saints' resting places', p. 92; L. Abrams, 'St Patrick and Glastonbury Abbey: *Nihil ex nihilo fit?*', and *idem*, 'St Patrick in an Anglo-Saxon Martyrology', in *Saint Patrick, A. D. 493–1993*, ed. D. N. Dumville (Woodbridge, 1993), pp. 233–44; *EK*, pp. 79 and 233; and *LM*, p. 303.

[128] See above, p. 65.

[129] Bede, *HE*, pp. 218–28 and 258–68.

[130] For the translation, see *Willelmi Malmesburiensis Monachi, De Gestis Pontificum Anglorum, Libri Quinque*, ed. N. E. S. A. Hamilton, RS 52 (London, 1870), p. 198, with Rollason, 'Lists of saints' resting places', p. 92. For the calendars, *EK*, pp. 23, 93, 191 and 205.

Library, Add. 43406, the second volume of a thirteenth-century breviary from Muchelney Abbey in Somerset. Both feasts of St Aidan (deposition and translation) are provided for in the fragmentary collectar at Wells.[131] The collect for the deposition is the normal Winchester collect for St Malo (15 Nov.); and the second for the translation (8 Oct.) is as follows:[132]

TRANSLATIO SANCTORVM AIDANI ET CEOLFRITHI
Deus qui per sanctos tuos confessores Aidanum atque Ceolfridum mirabilis predicaris intraris, concede nos eorum obtentu a mundanis liberari erroribus, quorum translationem piissimo ueneramur effectu. Per.

The feast of the translation is only otherwise entered in the calendar of Hatton 113 and as a *memoria reliquiarum* in that of a fifteenth-century psalter once owned by a monk of Glastonbury and now at Upholland College in Lancashire.[133]

St Ceolfrith. First abbot of the monastery of Monkwearmouth-Jarrow.[134] Buried at Langres; later translated to Jarrow, then to Glastonbury. No proper liturgical formulae in his honour survive, but his feast is recorded in several Anglo-Saxon calendars from southern England, presumably in response to the translation of his relics and those of St Aidan to Glastonbury.[135]

Now as has already been mentioned, *B* cannot be a Glastonbury calendar because Glastonbury itself is named. The monks would hardly have spelt out what would have been perfectly clear anyway. Moreover, if Glastonbury really were in view, then the feast of St Benedict's translation would have been graded 'S' at the very least, for the house was served by Benedictine monks, and the feasts of SS Aidan, Patrick and Ceolfrith graded 'F', like Abbot Hadrian's at St Augustine's. The only house from which *B*'s model might have come, other than Glastonbury,

---

[131] For the mass, *LM*, p. 306. The collectar is briefly described by Watkin, 'Fragment of a twelfth-century collectar', pp. 85–91.

[132] First endleaf (un-numbered).

[133] *EK*, p. 207, and F. Wormald, 'The liturgical calendar of Glastonbury Abbey', *Festschrift Bernard Bischoff zu seinem 65 Geburtstag*, ed. J. Autenrieth and F. Brunholz (Stuttgart, 1971), pp. 325–45.

[134] See the *Historia abbatum* of Bede and *uita* by an anonymous ninth-century writer, ed. C. Plummer, *Venerabilis Bedae Opera Historica*, 2 vols (Oxford, 1896) I, 364–7, and 388–404.

[135] See above, n. 130.

is Wells, that nursery of archbishops: Athelm (*c.* 923 × 925 – 926), Wulfhelm (926–41) and Byrhthelm (959), had all been abbots. But what shows that the calendar and sacramentary underlying *B* cannot have been that of Wells is the presence of an entry in both *B* and *Bosworth* for the Glastonbury feast of SS Vincent and Apollinaris. So what we actually have in *B* is a 'secular' calendar with strong Glastonbury symptoms. The implications seem obvious: *B* must be a copy of a sacramentary brought from Glastonbury to Canterbury by St Dunstan in the mid tenth century. No other agent of transmission is possible. Æthelgar (988–990), Dunstan's immediate successor, came from Selsey and Sigeric (990–4) and Ælfric (995–1005) from Ramsbury. We shall come to the question of whether *B*'s calendar was written in Dunstan's lifetime in due course.[136]

I argued in a recent article that the main body of the 'Bosworth Psalter', which is a good twenty or thirty years older than its calendar, was likely to have been made for, and probably at, St Augustine's.[137] The psalter's scribe, it is true, also wrote a charter in favour of Westminster, one of Dunstan's houses, but this is not a difficulty, since the scribes of one house often wrote charters and books for another or others. But the principal question concerning 'Bosworth's' calendar is: why was it added in the first place? It is, as we have seen, certainly a St Augustine's calendar, and the psalter may originally have been a St Augustine's psalter since its psalms and canticles are monastic in arrangement. As Nicholas Brooks has pointed out, there is every likelihood that the cathedral was not fully monastic until the early years of the eleventh century. Yet we cannot rule out the possibility that the community was mixed, in other words, that there were some monks at Christ Church, even though they may not have been in the majority.[138] Therefore, it seems to me now that the psalter may well have belonged to one of these men, perhaps even Dunstan himself. Dunstan of course had been a monk. With that in mind it is easy to understand why a new calendar might have been fitted: the psalter simply passed from Christ Church to St Augustine's, where naturally enough, the

---

[136] See below, pp. 193–4, 204.
[137] N. A. Orchard, 'The Bosworth Psalter and the St Augustine's Missal', *Canterbury and the Norman Conquest: Churches, Saints and Scholars*, ed. R. Eales and R. Sharpe (London, 1995), pp. 87–94. The reader is warned that this article contains some unusual textual corruptions.
[138] Brooks, *The Early History of the Church of Canterbury*, pp. 256–61. See also B. Langefeld, '*Regula canonicorum* or *Regula monasterialis uitae*? The Rule of Chrodegang and Archbishop Wulfred's reforms at Canterbury', *ASE* 25 (1996), 21–37.

existing calendar was replaced with one newly drawn up to accord with the abbey's liturgical use. If this version of events is right, we not only have a mid to late-tenth-century Canterbury sacramentary in the shape of *A* and *B*, but also a psalter.

Martyrological entries

The first thing to note is that majority of *B*'s ungraded feasts, that is to say, those not marked with a letter 'F' or 'S', were abstracted from some augmented copy of the so-called *Martyrologium Hieronymianum*, a compilation initially created sometime during the course of the fifth century.[139] However, the copy used by the compilers of *B* and *Bosworth* seems to have been substantially later, perhaps of the ninth century, though it is difficult to say for sure. What is striking too is that the two calendars encompass feasts not found elsewhere in England in the Anglo-Saxon period.[140] For example, on the 15th of November we have St Secundus, and on the 27th of October, St Gagus, both lifted from the numerous entries for these days in the *Hieronymianum*. The common martyrological stock in *B* and *Bosworth* is as follows:

JANUARY.

2.	St Isidorus.
5.	St Simeonis.
9.	St Fortunatus.
10.	St Paul the hermit.
12.	Deposition of St Benedict.
17.	Deposition of St Anthony.
24.	St Babilus and the three children.
29.	St Gildas the wise.

FEBRUARY.

1.	St Brigid.
12.	St Eulalia.
14.	SS Valentine and Vitalis.

MARCH.

2.	St Ceadde.
4.	SS DCCC Martyrs.
7.	SS Perpetua and Felicitas.
14.	St Leo.
16.	St Eugenia.
17.	St Patrick.
30.	Ordination of St Gregory.
31.	St Domninus.

APRIL.

3.	St Theodosia.
8.	SS Successus and Solutor.
13.	St Eufemia.
16.	SS Felix and Lucianus.
19.	SS Gagus and Rufus.
27.	St Germanus Antoninus.

[139] *Martyrologium Hieronymianum*, ed. De Rossi and Duchesne, *Acta SS Nov.* II.i. See also the volume of commentary, ed. H. Delehaye, P. Peeters and M. Coens, *Acta SS Nov.* II.ii (Brussels, 1931).
[140] See those collected in *EK*, with *The Missal of Robert of Jumièges*, ed. Wilson, pp. 9–20; *The Calendar of St Willibrord*, ed. Wilson; and Gamber, *Das Bonifatius-Sakramentar*, pp. 50–2, 54–9.

MAY.
8. St Victor.
28. St Germanus.
30. St Felix.
31. St Petronella.

JUNE.
3. St Erasmus.
5. St Bonifacius.
6. SS Amandus and Lucus.
8. Deposition of St Medard.

JULY.
3. Translation of St Martin.
5. The prophet Isaiah.
7. St Marina.
28. St Samson.
31. St German

AUGUST.
20. St Valentine.

SEPTEMBER.
1. St Priscus.
4. St Marcellinus.
5. St Berhtinus.

OCTOBER.
1. St Remigius.
2. SS Eleutherius and Quirilius.
12. St Wilfrid.
22. SS Philippus and Eusebius.
25. SS Crispin and Crispinianus.
27. St Gagus.
30. St Ianuarius.

NOVEMBER.
4. St Perpetua.
15. St Secundus.
16. St Augustine.
18. St Romanus.
21. St Gelasius.
26. SS Saturninus, Peter and Amator.

DECEMBER.
1. St Candida.
3. SS Claudius and Felix.
5. SS Delfinus and Trofimus.
16. SS Victor and Victoria.
23. SS Sixtus and Apollinaris.

A late copy of Usuard's martyrology probably provided the impetus for the inclusion of the feasts of St Felix (30 May) and St Bertin (5 Sept.).[141] The others not encompassed in the earliest manuscripts of the *Hieronymianum* will presumably have been drawn from sources current in England, very possibly some version of the 'Old English Martyrology'. Those in question are: St Paul the hermit (10 Feb.), St Benedict Biscop of Monkwearmouth/Jarrow (12 Feb.), St Ceadda of Lichfield (2 Mar.), the Ordination of St Gregory, as celebrated at Soissons (29 Mar.), the Prophet Isaiah (5 July), St Wilfrid of Ripon (12 Oct.), and most unusually St Delfinus (5 Dec.). Yet *B* and *Bosworth* are otherwise very different. *B*'s peculiars, which are the most numerous of the two, are:

---

[141] See *Le martyrologe d'Usuard*, ed. J. Dubois, Subsidia Hagiographica 40 (Brussels, 1965), pp. 237 and 297.

JANUARY.
1. St Macharius.
19. SS Maria and Martha.
26. Dormition of St Paula.
30. St Aldegundis.

FEBRUARY.
6. St Amand.
11. St Radegundis.
19. St Policronus.
23. St Policarp.
25. St Donatus.

MARCH.
1. St Donatus.
4. St Adrianus.
5. St Eusebius.
6. St Victor.
13. St Cyriacus.

APRIL.
1. St Quintinianus.
2. SS Urbanus and Nicetus.
3. St Pancras.
7. SS Timotheus, Diogenis and Victor.
8. St Maximus.
9. St Mary of Egypt.
16. St Faustinus.
17. SS Peter and Ermogenis.
21. St Fortunatus.
22. SS Gagus and Leo.
30. SS Crispinus, Quirinus and Sophia.

MAY.
2. SS Germanus, Saturninus and Celestinus.
7. SS Augustinus, Marcellinus and Placidus.
16. St Eracleus.
22. SS Basil, Venustus and Castus.
25. St Desiderius.
27. SS Aquilus, Iulius and Quintinus.

JUNE.
3. St Thomas.
13. SS Bartholomew and Felicula.

15. SS Vitus, Clement and Crisogonus.
25. St Luciana (25 June).

JULY.
1. SS Gagus and Iudas.
12. SS Nabor, Felix and Primitivus.
14. St Donatus.
15. SS Cyricus, Philippus and Florentius.
16. SS Theodosius and Macharius.
19. St Sisinnus.
20. St Sabina.
27. SS Felix and Simeon.

AUGUST.
5. St Cassianus.
26. St Habundus.
28. St Augustinus.

SEPTEMBER.
9. St Audomarus.
10. St Hilarius.
17. St Lambertus.

OCTOBER.
2. St Primus.
3. SS Felix and Leodegarius.
5. SS Cristina and Sabina.
11. St Aethelburh.
15. St Fortunatus.
16. St Alexandrinus.
19. SS Ianuarius and Proculus.
21. St Hilarion.
23. SS Severus and Longinus.
29. SS Quintus and Felicianus.

NOVEMBER.
5. SS Cesarius, Felix and Vitalis.
6. SS Donatus and Adrianus.
10. St Demetrius.
17. St Tecla.
22. Longinus.
28. St Eusebius.
30. St Ambrose.

DECEMBER.
5.   St Felix.
8.   SS Eusebius and Successus.
10. SS Victurus and Eulalia.
11. St Damasus.

13. SS Casta and Felix.
14. SS Zosimus and Lupicinus.
15. SS Faustus, Lucus and
     Maximus.
22. St Theodosia.

For the most part these entries either stand alone on their day, or are appended to entries which also stand in *Bosworth*. So, for example, on the 1st of January the name of St Macharius in *B* occurs after that of St Isidore, whose feast is noted in both calendars, whereas *B*'s entry for SS Maria and Martha on the 19th of January stands on a day left blank in *Bosworth*. There are exceptions, however. The entry for St Pancras, for instance, precedes that of St Theodosia on the 3rd of April, and that of St Maximus appears between those of SS Successus and Solutor on the 8th. The most noteworthy feasts not in early copies of the *Hieronymianum* are: St Cyriacus (13 Mar.), St Mary of Egypt (9 Apr.), St Basil (22 May), St Cyriacus (15 July), SS Christina and Sabina (5 Oct.), and St Æthelburh of Barking (11 Oct.). I have yet to find SS Christina and Sabina in any published martyrology. The feasts peculiar to *Bosworth* are:

JANUARY.
8.   SS Lucianus and Iulianus.
16. St Furseus.
30. St Batildis.

FEBRUARY.
3.   St Werburh.
10. St Maerryn.
13. St Eormenhild.
20. SS Didimus and Gagus.
23. St Mildburh.

APRIL.
1.   St Valericus.
20. SS Marcellinus and Peter.
22. St Leo.

MAY.
16. St Eugenia.
18. St Ælgifa.
25. St Aldhelmus.

JUNE.
8.   St Audomarus.
11. St Barnabas.
17. St Botulf.
26. St Salvius.
28. St Leo.

JULY.
2.   St Swithun.
3.   Translation of St Thomas.
7.   St Æthelburh.
8.   SS Grimbaldus and Wihtburga.
15. Translation of St Swithun.
16. St Berhtinus.
17. St Kenelm.
20. St Wulfmar.
22. St Wandregisilis.
27. The Seven Sleepers.

OCTOBER.
17. St Nothelm.

NOVEMBER.   DECEMBER.
2.   St Rumwald.   14.   St Spiridon.
18. Baralus.

Local English and French feasts aside, only St Eugenia's (16 May), which appears in Usuard's martyrology, and that of the Seven Sleepers (27 July) are not entered in versions of the *Hieronymianum*. The others are standard. As far as the French entries are concerned, we have: St Furseus of Peronne (16 Jan.), St Valericus of Saint-Valéry (1 Apr.), St Audomarus of Saint-Omer (8 June), St Salvius of Valenciennes (26 June), the translation of St Bertinus of Saint-Bertin (16 July), St Wulfmar of Samer (20 July), and St Wandregisilis of Saint-Wandrille (22 July). All are of north-eastern France, more particularly the Pas-de-Calais. Now Edmund Bishop argued in 1908 that the entry for St Salvius should be connected with the cult that grew up around a relic kept at Christ Church, Canterbury in the eleventh century, his proof being principally that BL Harley 2892 provides a proper benediction for the day.[142] As I have pointed out elsewhere, his suggestion, supported in recent years by Korhammer, cannot be sustained. First, the feast is a simple, ungraded, martyrological entry. Second, St Salvius is quite at home with the other saints from the Pas-de-Calais; and third, the liturgy of Christ Church changed radically after the Viking invasions of 1012. Bishop's view was that Winchester had influenced Canterbury; but material evidently 'flowed back'. Further work will probably resolve the question of whether all liturgical books associable with Canterbury, that is to say, not just the psalters and calendars, show signs of Winchester influence, or *vice versa*.

Turning now to the English saints proper to *Bosworth*, we have: St Werburh of Chester (3 Feb.), St Maerwynn of Romsey (10 Feb.), St Eormenhild of Ely (13 Feb.), St Mildburh of Much Wenlock (23 Feb.), St Ælgifa of Shaftesbury (18 May), St Aldhelm of Sherborne (25 May), St Botulf of Icanho (17 June), St Swithun of Winchester (2 July), St Grimbaldus of Winchester and St Wihtburh of Ely (15 July), St Nothelm of Canterbury (17 Oct.), and St Rumwold of Buckingham (2 Nov.). According to David Knowles, Maerwynn was abbess of Romsey between 967 and 975, so that is a firm *terminus post quem* for *Bosworth*.[143] The principal point to stress, however, is that the martyrological entries in *B* and *Bosworth* seem to have been drawn from

---

[142] Gasquet and Bishop, *The Bosworth Psalter*, pp. 36–7.
[143] D. Knowles, C. N. L. Brooke and V. C. M. London, *The Heads of Religious Houses: England and Wales, 940–1216* (Cambridge, 1972), p. 218.

two related copies of the *Hieronymianum*. The martyrological entries in *Bosworth* cannot have been modelled on *B*'s, nor can *B*'s have been reduced from an older version of *Bosworth*. Christ Church and St Augustine's therefore presumably adapted some convenient exemplar, much as they did after the Conquest. The matter of whether this exemplar was a Glastonbury book or one aquired from the abbey of Saint-Bertin, whose patron is represented twice in *Bosworth*, remains to be investigated. That will be a lengthy task, but all may not be in vain: the martyrology's origins may eventually be given away by the fact that many of its feasts are one day out.

Computus (nos 275–6 and 278–320)

As has long been recognised, the computus accompanying *B*'s calendar is highly sophisticated. In summary, it contains fourteen full-page tables for the calculation of various dates, days and phases not only in the church year but in the lunar and solar cycles; four full-page drawings to illustrate the prognostical material; and a suite of mnemonic verses and simple rules in prose to help the book's owner work out, if he could not remember, the terms (*termini* or date-limits) of Easter Sunday and other moveable feasts. As Heinrich Henel and Patrick McGurk have shown, *B*'s closest relative is London, British Library, Cotton Tiberius B. v, a volume of miscellaneous material probably written in the early to mid eleventh century at Christ Church, Canterbury.[144] What needs resolving, however, is the matter of whether the material common to both computi had initially been assembled at Glastonbury or Canterbury, the two houses with which *B*'s calendar is intimately associated, or at some third house, possibly Winchester. But it will not be possible to sort out the various strands involved until a representative body of continental computi have been brought into view.

Three recent works, however, have contributed to our understanding of how medieval computi were actually used. The first is Faith Wallis's splendid unpublished doctoral thesis on Oxford, St John's College, 17, an astronomical and computistical manuscript written at Thorney *c*.

---

[144] See H. Henel, *Studien zum ältenglischen Computus*, Beitrage zur englischen Philologie 26 (Leipzig, 1934); P. McGurk, 'The Computus', *An Eleventh-Century Anglo-Saxon Illustrated Miscellany: Cotton Tiberius B. v*, ed. P. McGurk, D. N. Dumville, M. R. Godden and Ann Knock, EEMF 21 (Copenhagen, 1983), pp. 51–4.

1110–11; the second, Beate Günzel's introduction to the computus in London, British Library, Cotton Titus D. xxvii and xxviii, the so-called prayerbook of Ælfwine, dean of the New Minster, Winchester (c. 1023–31); and the third, Peter Baker and Michael Lapidge's edition of, and commentary on, the *Enchiridion* of the monk Byrhtferth of Ramsey. All build on the painstaking groundwork published in the 1930s by Henel and Charles Jones.[145] In what follows, reference will be made, where possible and appropriate, to definitions and explanations of terms and principles already in print. There seems little point, for instance, in simply regurgitating what Günzel said in 1992. Some material, on the other hand, is only dealt with at all systematically in English by Wallis, whose study will not be easily accessible to most. Her commentary on the workings of certain tables will therefore be repeated as the need arises. References will also be given to the Tiberius manuscript, which is available in facsimile. So, turning to *B*, we have:

(1) An explanation of what a leap year is, beginning *Inquirendum est quare dicitur bisexus. Dicitur bisexus propter his kalendis* (no. 275). Apparently not found elsewhere.

(2) Table of solar regulars, concurrents, epacts and lunar regulars, for calculating the age of the moon, or weekday name of a certain day (no. 276). Roman regulars, which start on 1 March, are given in the main table, and Bede's, which start on 1 Jan., underneath.[146] Tiberius, fol. 2v.

(3) A note on the ides and nones of March, beginning *De singulis mensibus* (no. 276). Popular in medieval computi.[147]

(4) The calendar (no. 277). In the far left column we have the Golden Numbers; in the next, the repeating series of Lunar Letters A–O, corresponding to the Table below; then, the repeating series A–K, again corresponding to a Table below; in the fourth column from the left we have

[145] F. E. Wallis, 'MS Oxford St John's College 17: A Medieval Manuscript in its Context' (unpubl. Ph.D. thesis, Univ. of Toronto, 1984); *Ælfwine's Prayer-Book*, ed. B. Günzel, HBS 108 (London, 1992); *Byrhtferth's Enchiridion*, ed. P. Baker and M. Lapidge, Early English Text Society, supplementary series, 15 (Oxford, 1995); Henel, *Studien*; C. W. Jones, *Bedae Pseudepigrapha* (Ithaca, New York, 1939); and *Bedae Opera de Temporibus*, ed. C. W. Jones, Medieval Academy of America Publications 41 (Cambridge, Mass., 1943). Bede's treatise *De temporum ratione* was recently transl. F. E. Wallis, *Bede: The Reckoning of Time* (Liverpool, 1999).
[146] See *Ælfwine's Prayerbook*, ed. Günzel, pp. 20–21; Wallis, *St John's College 17*, pp. 281–3 (fol. 13v); and *Byrhtferth's Enchiridion*, ed. Baker and Lapidge, pp. 268–73, 381.
[147] *Byrhtferth's Enchiridion*, ed. Baker and Lapidge, pp. 261 and 280.

the repeating series of Lunar Letters A–V, A–V and A–T, corresponding to the two tables that follow; and finally the Dominical Letters A–G. The second set of letters A–V should, however, have been given dots (.A–.V), as should the set A–T (A.–T.). Tiberius, fols 3r–8v.

(5) Table for calculating age of the moon on any day in a lunar month (lunation) of 30 days. Based on the column A–V, A–V and A–T in the calendar (no. 278). On the left hand side of the table days i–xxx of the lunation are given; along the top, the Golden Numbers; and on the right the days of the lunation in the event of an *embolismus* (an 'extra' month, inserted solely for the purposes of calculation) or a *saltus lunae*, literally 'a leap of the moon'. The lunar month ending in November was shortened from 30 to 29 days in order to make the number of days in the lunar cycle of 235 months (6936 days) tally with the number in the solar cycle of nineteen years (228 months, or 6935 days). Tiberius, fol. 9r.

(6) Table for lunations of 29 days (no. 279). As Günzel has pointed out, the right hand side of the table, giving days xxix, i–xxviii, is redundant. Tiberius, fol. 9v.

(7) Table showing the age of the moon on the first day of a given month (no. 280). On the left we have the letters C and E, which serve to indicate whether a month is *communis*, that is to say, normal, or an *embolismus*, which is irregular; along the top the months; and to the right the Golden Numbers. At the foot of the table as a whole is the note *De ratione saltus lunae. Memento quod . . . computare debes.*[148] Tiberius, fol. 10r.

(8) Table showing the day of the week on the first day of a given month (no. 281). On the left are the Dominical Letters, which are paired for leap-years; along the top the months; to the right the years of the 28 year solar cycle; and within the table itself the numbers representing the weekdays. Sunday is i, Monday ii and so on. One simply finds the year in question and reads off the day.[149] Tiberius, fol. 10v.

(9) Table for calculating the age of the moon on a given day (no. 282). Based on the calendar's Lunar Letters AEIOV. One letter is given every

---

[148] On nos 4–7, see *Ælfwine's Prayerbook*, ed. Günzel, pp. 16–23, Wallis, *St John's College 17*, pp. 342–4 (fol. 22v), and *eadem, Bede: The Reckoning of Time*, p. 111, note 356.
[149] See F. Pickering, *The Calendar Pages of Medieval Service Books*, Reading Medieval Studies 1 (Reading, 1980), pp. 7–8, for Dominical Letters in leap-years.

three days. As Baker and Lapidge note, the table has been doubled-up. The lunations for a 30 day lunar month are given in two rows to save space, i–xv and xvi–xxx; along the top and bottom, we have the Golden Numbers, but not in numerical order; and on the left, the lunations for a 29 day month, again in two rows, ii–xvi and xvi–xxx. To use the table, first go to the calendar to establish which letter, if any, is assigned to the day of the month in question. When there is simply a space, note its relation to the letter that follows or precedes. For dates in January and February, find the row given in the table for the year of the decennovenal cycle in view, note where that letter or space occurs in that row, and read off the age of the moon in the column to the left or right. For dates in other months the process is the same, but one must look for the letter in the row to the right of the one used for the finding of dates in January and February.[150] Written in the form of a cross in Tiberius, fol. 13v.

(10) Table for calculating the moon's position in the zodiac on any day of the year. Based on the calendar's Lunar Letters A–O (no. 283). Sometimes called Bede's table, as the principles governing the calculations are set out in his *De Temporum Ratione*. In Carolingian books. On the left we have the names of the signs of the zodiac, along the top, the Golden Numbers, and to the right, the months. To use the table, find the letter or space corresponding to the day in question in the calendar, locate that letter or space in the column corresponding to the year of the decennovenal cycle in question, and read over to the zodiac sign on the left.[151] Tiberius, fol. 11v.

(11) Another table for calculating the moon's position in the zodiac, generally always found with the preceding table (no. 284). Also described by Bede. On the left we the relevant days of a 30 day lunation in numerical series, along the top the months, with the first letter of their name in Greek below; and to the right, the letter S twice on every second row. Within the table itself the names of the zodiacal signs are written diagonally, alternately bottom left to top right, and top left to bottom right. As Jones has noted, the letter S, which probably stands for *semi* (indicating that the moon is half in one sign, half in the next), should be

---

[150] Wallis, *St John's College 17*, pp. 351–3 (fol. 24v); and *Byrhtferth's Enchiridion*, ed. Baker and Lapidge, Bk III, ch. 2, ll. 140–67, and p. 418.

[151] Bede's *De Temporum Ratione*, ch. XIX, ed. Jones, and transl. Wallis, *Bede: The Reckoning of Time*, pp. 63–4. See also Wallis, *St John's College 17*, pp. 346–9 (fol. 23v), and *Ælfwine's Prayerbook*, ed. Günzel, p. 19, note 10.

on the left-hand side of the table to make the best sense. The divided moons of the lunar cycle are 3, 8, 13, 23 and 28.[152] Tiberius, fol. 12v.

(12) A table for calculating the age of the moon on a given day of the year (no. 285). Based on the Lunar Letters A–K in *B*'s calendar. On the left we have lunar increments; along the top, 30 day lunations; on the right, 30 day lunations; and along the bottom, Golden Numbers. To find the age of the moon, locate the letter or space corresponding to the date in question in the calendar. Find the column corresponding to the year of the decennovenal cycle, and read across from the letter or space to the sign of the zodicac on the left. However, for dates corresponding to the first space after a letter, one locates that space in the column eleven to the right of the decennovenal year in question, and for dates corresponding to the second space, one uses the column 22 spaces to the right. The table at the foot of fol. 48v is only otherwise to be found in Oxford, St John's College, 17. Easter falls within a range of seven days of the lunar month: *luna* xv–xxi. All feasts connected with Easter therefore also fall within a seven day span, as the table shows. St John's 17 omits *B*'s column for *Moysicum Paschae*.[153] Tiberius, fol. 13r.

(13) The so-called 'Paschal Hand' (no. 286). Described in Bede's *De Temporum Ratione*. Apparently first depicted in Anglo-Saxon books. The oldest version of the drawing to have come down to us is the one preserved in the computus added in the early-tenth-century to BL Cotton Galba A. xviii, the so-called 'Aethelstan' psalter. The dates of Easter Sunday throughout the nineteen year cycle are given on the hand's fingers and palm. A drawing related to *B*'s, but without a decorative border, figures in London, British Library, Cotton Tiberius C. vi, a mid-eleventh-century psalter from a southern English house. As Jones pointed out, *B*'s iconography is hybrid. A 'normal' Paschal Hand, that is to say, one without figures, seems to have been combined with elements commonly found in representations of the legend of Pachomius. The text normally accompanying such representations is given later in *B* (20).[154]

[152] See Bede's *De Temporum Ratione*, ch. XVIII, ed. Jones, and transl. Wallis, *Bede: The Reckoning of Time*, pp. 60–3; Wallis, S*t John's College 17*, pp. 349–50 (fol. 24r); and Jones, *Bedae Pseudepigraphia*, pp. 64–5.
[153] See Wallis, *St John's College 17*, pp. 258 and 359–60 (fol. 26v).
[154] For an illustration of *B*, see Temple, *Anglo-Saxon Manuscripts*, pl. 54; and for 'Tiberius', F. Wormald, 'An English eleventh-century psalter with pictures', *Walpole Society* 38 (London, 1962), 1–13, pls 1–30. On the iconography and underlying text see

(14) Line drawing of 'Vita', Christ as King of Life (no. 287). A prognostical diagram to establish whether a patient would live or die. One adds the numerical value of the patient's name to the age of moon and the number of the weekday on which the illness first became known, divides the total by thirty, and looks for the resulting number in the diamond-shaped panel on at the foot of 'Mors', on fol. 50r. If the number falls in the upper half, the patient will live, if below, he will die.[155] In Tiberius C. vi the figure of 'Vita' stands above the figure represented on fol. 50r in *B*. Wallis notes that similar representations are also to be found in London, British Library, Harley 3667, an early-twelfth-century manuscript from Peterborough containing a set of annals and computus, but in the guise of a triumphant and degenerate Adam or Christ-figure.[156]

(15) Line Drawing of 'Mors', Satan as Death (no. 288).[157]

(16) Dionysian *rotae* (no. 289). The upper roundel has a 'portrait' of Dionysius at its hub. Both *rotae* express the same point: that Easter Sunday should only be celebrated on lunations 15 to 21 of the Easter moon. The significance of the inner ring of numbers beginning *initium iii* (opposite Pascha xv) and ending *initium ix* (opposite Pascha xxi) are not clear.[158]

(17) A table of terms of Quadragesima (Lent), Easter, Rogations, Pentecost and Septuagesima (no. 290). The terms appear in this order in several Anglo-Saxon manuscripts and in St John's College 17.[159] Tiberius, fol. 14r.

(18) Fifteen short pieces on the terms and fall of Septuagesima, Quadragesima, Easter, Rogations and Pentecost. The first five begin with the word *Omnis* (no. 291); the second five *Post* (no. 292); and the

Bede, *De Temporum Ratione*, ch. LV, and transl. Wallis, *Bede: The Reckoning of Time*, pp. 137–9, 342–46; C. W. Jones, 'A legend of Pachomius', *Speculum* 18 (1943), 198–210, at 210; Wallis, *St John's College 17*, pp. 364–6 (fol. 28r); and *Byrhtferth's Enchiridion*, ed. Baker and Lapidge, p. 419.
[155] See L. E. Voigts, 'The Latin verse and Middle English prose texts on the Sphere of Life and Death in Harley 3719', *The Chaucer Review* 21 (1986), 291–305, esp. 395–8.
[156] Illustr. Temple, *Anglo-Saxon Manuscripts*, pl. 55. See Wallis, *St John's College 17*, pp. 459–60.
[157] Illustr. Temple, *Anglo-Saxon Manuscripts*, pl. 53.
[158] See Bede, *De Temporum Ratione*, ch. LIX, ed. Jones, and transl. Wallis, *Bede: The Reckoning of Time*, pp. 142–4; and Wallis, *St John's College 17*, pp. 216–18 (fol. 5v).
[159] See *Ælfwine's Prayerbook*, ed. Günzel, p. 198; and Wallis, *St John's College 17*, pp. 368–71 (fol. 28r).

third five *Vbicumque* (no. 293). These are not common in continental books, but Baker and Lapidge found the first five in an eleventh-century computistical manuscript from the abbey of Brauweiler, which lies about ten or so miles north of Cologne. The book in question is now Vatican City, Biblioteca Apostolica Vaticana, Vat. lat. 290.[160] Tiberius, fols 14v and 15r.

(19) Verses on the term of Easter: *Octone martis kalende quinque* (no. 294).[161] Tiberius, fol. 14v

(20) Three short sentences on the Pachomian legend starting *Epistola quomodo postulauit*, and continuing with the normal introduction *Legimus in epistolis grecorum* (no. 295).[162]

(21) The verse *Nonas Aprilis norunt quinos* flanked on each side by two columns (no. 296). The outer left and right columns, as Warren notes, were added later. The first phrase of each line gives the date of the Easter full moon in the nineteen year lunar cycle. The second gives the lunar regulars. By adding the lunar regular to the concurrent, one can then work out the day of the week on which the Easter moon falls.[163] Tiberius, fol. 14v.

(22) Calculation of feast limits, *Si quis per regulares XXVI uidelicet, terminum cuiusque anni inuenire cupit. . .*, added at the foot of fol. 52v by the Exeter scribe who wrote the outer columns beside the verse *Nonas Aprilis* above.

(23) Easter table with two cycles of 19 years: 969–87 and 988–1008 (no. 298). Tiberius, fol. 16r.

(24) Mnemonic verses (nos 299–302). *Linea christe tuos prima est quae continet annos* on the columns of the Easter table; *Prima dies phoebi sacrato numine fulget* on the names of the months; *Ianus et october*

---

[160] See *Byrhtferth's Enchiridion*, ed. Baker and Lapidge, pp. xlviii, lii–liii and 19–20; *Ælfwine's Prayerbook*, ed. Günzel, p. 108, no. 11; and Wallis, *St John's College 17*, pp. 345–6 (fol. 23r).

[161] *Ælfwine's Prayerbook*, ed. Günzel, p. 106, no. 7; Wallis, *St John's College 17*, pp. 365–6 (fol. 28r); and *Byrhtferth's Enchiridion*, ed. Baker and Lapidge, pp. xlvi–xlvii, 420. See also, D. Schaller and E. Könsgen, *Initia Carminum Latinorum saeculo undecimo Antiquiorum* (Göttingen, 1977), no. 11148.

[162] See Jones, 'A legend of Pachomius'; and Wallis, *St John's College 17*, pp. 367–8 (fol. 28r).

[163] See Jones, 'A legend of Pachomius', pp. 198–210; Wallis, *St John's College 17*, pp. 365–6 (fol. 28r); and Schaller and Köngsen, *Initia Carminum*, no. 10525.

binis regulantur habenis on ferial regulars; and *September semper quinis octimber habenis* on lunar regulars.[164] Tiberius, fol. 15v has *Ianus* and *September*.

(25) Two sets of verses ascribed to Bede (nos 303–4). *Bissena mensium uertigine uoluitur annus* and *Primus romanas ordiris iane kalendas.*[165] Tiberius, fol. 15v.

(26) A series of miscellaneous short notes on computistical matter relating to:

(a) Advent, beginning *Quicumque aduentum* (no. 305). In numerous books, English and continental.[166] Tiberius, fol. 15v.

(b) The fourteenth Paschal moon: *Si uis inuenire quotus terminus paschalis* (no. 306). Only otherwise in Tiberius, fol. 15v.

(c) Concurrents: *Si uis inuenire concurrentes* (no. 307). Only otherwise in Tiberius, fol. 15r.

(d) Epacts: *Et qualem lunam* (no. 308). A related version figures in Ælfwine's Prayerbook.[167]

(e) Concurrents, epacts, and cycles: *Muta concurrentes* (no. 309). Tiberius, fol. 18v. Also in 'Ælfwine'.[168]

(f) Lengths of lunar and solar years: *Annus communis habet dies CCCCLIIII* (no. 310). Tiberius, fols 15r and 18v. Also in 'Ælfwine'.[169]

(g) Gregory the Great's injunction to the English concerning Ember days: *Quattuor ieiunia sunt legitima* (no. 311). Tiberius, fol. 18v. A version figures in 'Ælfwine' and a number of English and continental books.[170]

(h) Terms of Easter: *Pascha namque celebratur* (no. 312). Tiberius, fol. 18r. Only the last section, beginning *Christianorum pascha*, occurs in 'Ælfwine'.[171]

---

[164] *Byrhtferth's Enchiridion*, ed. Baker and Lapidge, Bk I, ch. 3, and pp. xlvii, 384–6; Wallis, *St John's College 17*, pp. 291–4, 372–3 (fols 14 and 29r); and Schaller and Köngsen, *Initia Carminum*, nos 8931, 12491, 7613 and 14907.

[165] *Byrhtferth's Enchiridion*, ed. Baker and Lapidge, pp. xlvii and 383; Wallis, *St John's College 17*, pp. 291 and 312 (fols 14r and 15v); and Schaller and Köngsen, *Initia Carminum*, no. 12559.

[166] See *Ælfwine's Prayerbook*, ed. Günzel, p. 115, no. 31.

[167] *Ibid.*, p. 108, no. 12.

[168] *Ibid.*, p. 114, no. 29.

[169] *Ibid.*, pp. 114–15.

[170] *Ibid.*, pp. 108–9, no. 13. See also Wallis, *St John's College 17*, pp. 350–1 (fol. 24v).

[171] *Ibid.*, p. 114, no. 26.

(i) Moon's age on moveable feasts: *Luna initio quadragesimae* (no. 313).[172] Tiberius, fols 15r and 18r.

(j) The six ages of the world beginning *A principio Adae usque ad diluuium, anni mille sexcenti quadraginta sex* (no. 314). Tiberius, fol. 15r. Also in 'Ælfwine'. A piece of chiliastic superstition. As Wallis notes, the theory seems first to have been advanced in the *Laterculus Malalianus* of Archbishop Theodore. The lines cannot be used for dating *B*, as has recently been claimed.[173]

(k) Good and bad moons: *Luna prima bona est* (no. 315). Also in St John's 17.[174]

(l) When the moon rises: *Luna ianuarii accenditur* (no. 316). Tiberius, fol. 12v. Also in St John's 17.[175]

(m) How long the moon shall shine: *Luna prima quattuor punctos lucet* (no. 317).[176]

(27) Table showing in weeks and days the length of time between Christmas and Ash Wednesday year by year throughout the nineteen year cycle (no. 318). The first column gives the Dominical Letter, the second the date of Easter Sunday, and the third and fourth, the number of weeks and days. A similar table appears in St John's 17.[177]

(28) Table of tides (no. 319). The first column lists the lunations; the second gives the commentary; the third the letter L for *luna*; the fourth two repeating series of numbers, 1–7, and 1–8, for the days in two quarters of the moon; the fifth the letter A for *aqua*; and the last the letters L and M for *Ledon* and *Malina*, that is to say, the spring and neap tides. 'Ælfwine' has an Anglo-Saxon version of *B*'s commentary.[178]

---

[172] See Wallis, *St John's College 17*, pp. 388–9 (fol. 34r); and *Byrhtferth's Enchiridion*, ed. Baker and Lapidge, p. 423.

[173] See *Ælfwine's Prayerbook*, ed. Günzel, pp. 143–4, no. 54; Wallis, *Bede: The Reckoning of Time*, pp. xxx, 359–62; and H. L. C. Tristram, *Sex aetates mundi. Die Weltzeitalter bei den Angelsaschen und den Iren*, Untersuchungen und Texte, Anglistiche Forschungen 165 (Heidelburg, 1985), pp. 331, 37–42, 58–9 and 85. St John's 17 has a note on the four ages of the world. See Wallis, *St John's College 17*, pp. 122, 195–9 (fol. 3v).

[174] Wallis, *St John's College 17*, pp. 202–4 (fol. 4r).

[175] See Wallis, *St John's College 17*, p. 384 (fol. 33r), and *Byrhtferth's Enchiridion*, ed. Baker and Lapidge, p. 421.

[176] For a related calculation, see Wallis, *St John's 17*, pp. 397–8 (fol. 35v), and *Byrhtferth's Enchiridion*, ed. Baker and Lapidge, pp. 424–5.

[177] See Wallis, *St John's College 17*, p. 378 (fol. 31v).

[178] *Ælfwine's Prayerbook*, ed. Günzel, p. 122, no. 41. See also, Bede's *De Temporum Ratione*, ch. XXIX, ed. Jones, and transl. Wallis, *Bede: The Reckoning of Time*, pp. 82–5; and *Wallis, St John's College 17*, pp. 246–7 (fol. 8r).

(28) Horologium composed of six circles (no. 320). Also in 'Ælfwine'. Not uncommon. But St John's 17 has the full form, with a central *rota*.[179]

The two principal questions surrounding B's computus are first, where did it originate, and second, when was it written? It will be best to address the second first.

As has already been mentioned, B's Easter tables run from 969 to 1006, and its table of intervals between Christmas and Easter Sunday from 979 to 1001, so it has generally been supposed that both computus and calendar were copied sometime after 979. If we assume that the tables are at all relevant then the *terminus ante quem* for this part of B must be 987, the last year of the first decennovenal (Easter) cycle. But Patrick McGurk has expressed doubts about the significance of these tables for dating purposes, noting that they might have been the only ones available to B's scribe.[180] Indeed Henel noted in 1934 that two other English books have cycles for the years 969–1006: Salisbury Cathedral Library, 150, a psalter written somewhere in the south of English, possibly Wilton or Shaftesbury; and B's close relation, BL Cotton Tiberius B. v.[181] Since both script and decoration suggest that the Salisbury book was produced sometime in the late tenth century, it seems likely that its tables are up to date, a point stressed by Celia and Kenneth Sisam in 1959.[182] However, the Tiberius manuscript, as has already been mentioned, was copied in the second quarter of the eleventh century, in McGurk's view, closer to c. 1050 than c. 1020, so its tables were at least twenty years out of date when the scribe sat down to write. Consequently it would be dangerous to assume that B's computus can be dated by its tables alone; and the last line of the note on the six ages of the world, *A natiuitate domini usque ad aduentum antichristi anni DCCCCXCIX*, which appears to provide a *terminus ante quem* of 999, is not of much help either, as has already been indicated.[183] For this also appears in Ælfwine's prayerbook, which was written c. 1023–31, and in the Tiberius miscellany. Any date between c. 970–1010 would

---

[179] See *Ælfwine's Prayerbook*, ed. Günzel, pp. 107–8, no. 10, and p. 199, and Wallis, *St John's College 17*, pp. 400–3 (fol. 37r).

[180] P. McGurk, 'The Computus', p. 54, note 23.

[181] Henel, *Studien*, p. 22.

[182] See C. Sisam and K. Sisam, *The Salisbury Psalter edited from Salisbury Cathedral MS 150*, Early English Text Society 242 (Oxford, 1959), p. 11. Its calendar is ed. *EK*, pp. 16–27, and its litany, Lapidge, *Anglo-Saxon Litanies*, pp. 283–7, and discussed, pp. 83–4.

[183] Dumville, *Liturgy*, p. 44.

square with the palaeography in any case. Indeed the scribe's work is
close to that of the scribe of the Bosworth psalter's calendar: and that
has always been dated *c*. 1000. But on balance it seems reasonable to
suppose that *B*'s calendar and computus were inserted in *A* in Dunstan's
time for two principal reasons. First, *B*'s calendar is in effect his, that is
to say, it is based on the Glastonbury calendar with which he was familiar. Second, *A* is likely to have been his book. Nicholson may well have
been right in taking the presence of a mark after the entries for 972 to
mean that the Easter table and associated material had been prepared for
use in and after 973.[184] That leaves us with the question of where the
computus was originally compiled, which at present is not so easy to
answer. In my view, the strongest case to be made is for Canterbury,
with Glastonbury a close second. Winchester, a possibility raised by
Deshmann, for instance, I would rule out, as *B* and Tiberius share
certain elements never taken up, so far as one can tell, in Winchester
computi, or computi deriving from Winchester models. But further
work will be necessary to settle this matter conclusively.[185]

The other late-tenth-century additions

Remnants of a blessing ad mensam *and a votive prayer* (nos 39–40).
Identification of the former has so far proved impossible. It is perhaps
worth noting, however, that it is not to be found among those for similar
intentions collected together by Doms Cabrol and Leclercq.[186] The
prayer *Propitiare misericors deus supplicationibus nostris* derives from
a fairly standard formula for the first Sunday after Christmas.[187]

Mass for rain (131–40). Composed of standard forms.[188]

Verses to be said during vesting (no. 321). The verses beginning *Virtus
summa deus cunctorum rector opimus* were added on the last page of the
last gathering of the computus in a more or less contemporary hand, and
have been printed twice: once by Warren and again, from Warren, by

[184] Nicholson, *Early Bodleian Music* III, lviii.
[185] Deshmann, 'The Leofric Missal'. For a short synopsis of the contents of the most
important Winchester computi, see the notes provided by Günzel, *Ælfwine's Prayerbook*,
pp. 198–202, and Baker and Lapidge, *Byrhtferth's Enchiridion*, pp. xlviii–lii.
[186] *DACL* 2.ii, 713–15.
[187] See for instance, *Liber Sacramentorum Gellonensis*, ed. Dumas and Deshusses, I, 12,
no. 92.
[188] *Le sacramentaire grégorien* I, 343, no. 1000; 449, nos 1366–70.

Schaller and Köngsen. The only other manuscript to contain this series seems to be BNF lat. 12052, the sacramentary of Ratoldus, abbot of Corbie, which Schaller and Köngsen seem not to have known.[189] BNF lat. 12052, as has already been said, embodies in whole or in part, a tenth-century English pontifical. In view of what we know of *B*, it is likely that the verses were composed at Canterbury.

Modifications to the text of the Exultet preface (no. 805). As we have already seen, *A*'s text originally lacked the long passage relating to the activities of the bee, present in so many other versions. Faced with the task of remedying this deficiency, the English scribe seems to have taken the view that erasing and rewriting a short portion of the text was preferable to making additions in the margins or between the lines of the original. The short sentences actually inserted in this process were:

> Apes ceteris quae subiecta sunt homini animantibus antecellit. Quum sit minima corporis prauitate, uiribus imbecillis se fortis ingenio. O uere beata et mirabilis apes. O uere beata et mirabilis apes cuius nec sexum masculi uiolant, fetus non quassant nec filii destruunt castitatem. Sicut sancta concepit uirgo maria, uirgo peperit, et uirgo permansit.

These at least say something more of the creature that produced the wax for the Paschal Candle.

New passages in the collect of A*'s mass for relics* (no. 1955). *A*'s text seems to have been rewritten initially with a view to expanding the hierarchy of saints named, as the following comparison will show. On the left we have the text of the prayer as it appears in all the books surveyed by Deshusses and countless others, and on the right that of *B*, before *B* in turn was added to:[190]

Alcuin.	*B.*
Concede quesumus omnipotens deus,	Concede quesumus omnipotens deus
ut sancta dei genetrix sanctique tui	ut sancta dei genetrix perpetuo uirgo
apostoli, martyres, confessores,	maria sanctique tui omnes angeli
uirgines atque omnes sancti quorum in	archangeli, patriarchae, prophete,
ista continentur ecclesiae patrocinia nos	apostoli martyres, confessores,
ubique adiuuent, quatinus hic in	uirgines atque omnes sancti quorum

---

[189] Schaller and Köngsen, *Initia Carminum*, no. 17365. Ratoldus's verses are ed. PL 78, col. 240 and Netzer, *L'introduction*, p. 230.
[190] Ed. *Le sacramentaire grégorien* II, 50, no. 1870.

illorum praesenti suffragio tranquilla pace in tua laude laetemur. Per.

reliquię in ista sancta continentur aecclesia nos ubique adiuuent, quatinus hic et ubi quae in illorum presenti suffragio, tranquilla pace in tua laude letemur. Per dominum nostrum.

No other book I have come across follows *B* in this. However, at least one parallel exists in the alterations made to a similar prayer in northern France in the tenth century. On the left we have the 'standard' form of the text as it appears in the Supplement, and on the right that of Paris, Bibliothèque nationale de France, lat. 9429, a late-ninth-century sacramentary that later found its way to Beauvais cathedral.[191] The Beauvais interlineations have silently been incorporated.

Supplement.
Concede quesumus omnipotens deus ut intercessio nos sanctae dei genetris mariae, sanctorumque omnium apostolorum, martyrum, et confessorum, et omnium electorum tuorum ubique laetificet, ut dum eorum merita recolimus, patrocinia sentiamus. Per.

Beauvais.
Concede quesumus omnipotens deus ut intercessio nos sanctae dei genetricis mariae, sanctorumque omnium angelorum, archangelorum, patriarcharum, prophetarum, apostolorum, martyrum et confessorum, atque uirginum, et omnium electorum tuorum ubique laetificet, ut dum eorum merita recolimus, patrocinia sentiamus. Per.

In a late-eleventh-century book from St Augustine's, Canterbury, now Cambridge, Corpus Christi College, 270, these 'additions' form part of the main text, so it is clear that the practice of augmenting prayers of this sort was just as alive in England after the Conquest as it was before.[192] *B*'s text was later modified so that the mass as a whole could be said at any altar in a side chapel either within or without the cathedral walls: *uel in isto continentur oratorio.*

Order for the feast of the Purification of the Virgin (nos 2246–56). *B*'s short order for the procession before mass on the feast of the Purification appears in three other English books, all of which we have met with before: BNF lat. 943: the 'Pontifical of Dunstan'; BL Add. 57337: the 'Anderson' pontifical; and Rouen BM 368: the 'Lanalet' pontifical.[193]

---

[191] Ed. *op. cit.* I, 417, no. 1243 and notes. The prayer is said to be Aquileian in origin by G. Peressotti, 'Le messe votive nel messale Aquileiese', *EL* 113 (1999), 139–55.
[192] The prayer is ed. Rule, *The Missal of St Augustine's, Canterbury*, p. 140.
[193] See Rasmussen, *Les pontificaux*, pp. 284–5 (fols 104r–5v), and Lat. lit. b. 10, fol. 33r;

Most of the constituent prayers in the ordo are perfectly standard. However, insofar as older sources are concerned, *Quesumus omnipotens deus tua nos protectione*, which was pronounced at the station of the Virgin, wherever that happened to be, is not. Moeller noted five other sources in which it appears:[194]

A book from Cologne published by Jacob Pamelius in 1571. As has long been known, Pamelius made use of Cologne, Dombibliothek, 88 and 137, two ninth-century sacramentaries, and the prayer may have been added later to one of the two. It is certainly not original part of their main texts. Alternatively, he may have interpolated the prayer from some other manuscript.[195]

Göttingen 231: the late-tenth-century sacramentary of Fulda.[196]

Rouen BM 274: the early-eleventh-century sacramentary of Robert of Jumièges.[197]

Le Havre BM 330: the mid-eleventh-century missal of the New Minster, Winchester.[198]

and Oxford, Bodleian Library, Rawlinson Lit. g. 10: a late-fourteenth-century prayer-book from Westminster Abbey.[199]

It also figures in a book that Moeller did not know:

Cambridge, Corpus Christi College, 41: an early-eleventh-century copy of Bede's *Historia Ecclesiastica* in OE, with near-contemporary liturgical marginalia.[200]

Given this geographical distribution, it seems reasonable to conclude that the formula is Anglo-Saxon. Yet that said, the *ordo* as a whole has

Rasmussen, *Les pontificaux*, pp. 230–1 (fols 110v–111v); and Doble, *Pontificale Lanaletense*, pp. 89–90.

[194] *Corpus Orationum*, ed. Moeller, no. 4866.

[195] Ed. J. Pamelius, *Missale sanctorum Patrum Latinorum, sive Liturgicon Latinum*, 2 vols (Cologne, 1571) II, 206. On Pamelius' editorial work, see R. Amiet, 'Les sacramentaires 88 et 137 du chapitre de Cologne', *Scriptorium* 9 (1955), 76–84.

[196] Ed. Richter and Schönfelder, *Sacramentarium Fuldense*, p. 25, no. 201.

[197] Ed. Wilson, *The Missal of Robert of Jumièges*, p. 159.

[198] Ed. Turner, *The Missal of the New Minster*, p. 70.

[199] Ed. Legg, *Missale ad usum ecclesiae Westmonasteriensis* III, 1356.

[200] The additions are ed. in summary, R. Grant, *Cambridge, Corpus Christi College 41: the Loricas and the Missal* (Amsterdam, 1978), pp. 56–7, and the given in full by S. Keefer, 'Margin as archive: the liturgical marginalia of a manuscript of the Old English Bede', *Traditio* 51 (1996), 147–77. The best account of the liturgical material as a whole, however, remains Hohler's review of Grant's book in *Medium Aevum* 49 (1980), 275–8. The decoration is described by Budny, *Insular and Anglo-Saxon Manuscripts* I, 501–24.

little in common with the directions given in the *Regularis Concordia*, which must give pause for thought, for the two principal manuscripts of the rule both come from Canterbury.[201] Indeed, as Dom Symons indicated, its stipulations are only discernable to any visible degree in BL Harley 2892, the 'Christ Church Benedictional'. That CCCC 41 should have a paraphrase of the closing rubric, but nothing else, suggests that the Concordia was regarded in the west country, at least, as little more than a store of useful material to be plundered at will.[202]

Formulae for Ash Wednesday and Palm Sunday (nos 2257–60). All four prayers are perfectly standard, and were presumably intended as a supplement to the formulae adopted in *A*. What is not standard, by any means, is the litany.

The Litany (no. 2261). As Lapidge has pointed out, the litany has nothing to do with the Palm Sunday prayers preceding it and the formula that follows, which in other books is normally to be said *in lardario*. Although no distinctive invocations are encompassed, English or continental, its series of petitions corresponds with those of the litany of Oxford, Bodleian Library, Bodley 775, a late-tenth-century troper from Winchester (one of the two so-called 'Winchester Tropers'), and an early-twelfth-century missal written in Ireland, now Oxford, Corpus Christi College, 282, a point first made by Aubrey Gwynn in 1953.[203] Gwynn showed that this series is almost certainly Frankish in origin, citing the most important examples he had found, among which was Paris, Bibliothèque nationale de France, lat. 11522, a mid-eleventh-century breviary and missal from Corbie. In view of the fact that

---

[201] *Regularis Concordia Anglicae Nationis Monachorum Sanctimonialiumque*, ed. T. Symons (Edinburgh, 1953), pp. liii–lix, and 30–1. On the Concordia in general, see now L. Kornexl, 'The Regularis Concordia and its Old English Gloss', *ASE* 24 (1995), 95–130, and C. A. Jones, *Ælfric's Letter to the Monks of Eynsham* (Cambridge, 1998).

[202] The piece of rubric in question is: *Finita benedictione conspargantur aqua benedicta et purificentur et sic ab edituo singuli singulas, accipiant acceptas que accedant psallentes antiphonam. Ave gratia plena*, ed. Grant, *Cambridge, Corpus Christi College 41*, p. 57. The passage from which this derives is: *et conspergat aqua benedicta, accepto cereo ab aedituo, psallentibus cunctis, accipiant singuli singulas, acceptasque accendant*, ed. Symons, *Regularis Concordia*, p. 31.

[203] A. Gwynn, 'The Irish Missal of Corpus Christi College, Oxford', *Studies in Church History* 1 (London, 1964), 47–68, at 61–4. The litany of Bodley 775 is ed. Lapidge, *Anglo-Saxon Litanies*, pp. 233–4, and that of the 'Irish Missal' by F. E. Warren, *The Manuscript Irish Missal belonging to the President and Fellows of Corpus Christi College, Oxford* (Oxford, 1888), p. 133. See also F. Henry and G. Marsh-Micheli, 'A century of Irish illumination', *Proceedings of the Royal Irish Academy* 62 (Dublin, 1962), 101–65, at 137–40, with pls XVII–XXI.

Æthelwold brought monks from Corbie to Abingdon in 963 to teach the choir how to chant properly, it may well be that these petitions, possibly appended to a short litany similar to the one in the three English books just mentioned, found its way to England by this route.[204] This putative Corbie-Abingdon-Winchester type of litany will therefore still have been relatively new when the scribe copied it into *B*.

Supplementary saints' masses and prayers

These are best dealt with one by one.

Preface for SS Abdon and Sennen (no. 2263): the standard prayer of most early sacramentaries and missals. Doubtless added because no proper form had been given in *A*.[205]

Mass for St Cuthbert (nos 2264–9): *B* contains the earliest surviving example of a corrected version of an ancient mass possibly originally compiled, rather than composed anew, by Alcuin. The corrections can best be seen in the secret. On the left, we have *B*'s text, and on the right that of the sacramentary of Robert of Jumièges:[206]

B.	*Robert.*
Haec tibi quesumus domine beati cuthberhti pontificis tui intercessione nunc grata reddatur oblatio, et per eam gloriosam nostrum famulatum purifica. Per.	Haec tibi domine quesumus beati cuthberhti sacerdotis grata reddatur oblatio, et per eam nostram gloriosa famulatum purificet. Per dominum nostrum.

The sense in *B* is greatly improved. Other trifling alterations were made to the collect and postcommunion: the saint is called *pontifex* rather than *sacerdos* or *martyr* (as in the sacramentaries of Fulda); and the sense again made clearer. The next earliest example of this reformed mass is to be found in: BNF lat. 819, the mid-eleventh-century sacramentary possibly copied at Liège (certainly from an English model) which later found its way to the abbey of Saint-Bertin, though in this only the collect, secret and postcommunion are taken up.[207]

---

[204] On Abingdon, see A. Thacker, 'Æthelwold and Abingdon', *Bishop Æthelwold*, ed. B. Yorke (Woodbridge, 1988), pp. 43–64.

[205] See *Le sacramentaire grégorien* I, 541, no. 1641.

[206] Ed. Wilson, *The Missal of Robert of Jumièges*, p. 166. A corrupt text is also given in the sacramentaries of Fulda, ed. Richter and Schönfelder, *Sacramentarium Fuldense*, p. 31, no. 248.

[207] See Leroquais, *Les sacramentaires* I, 105–7.

B's first alternative postcommunion, which does not figure in any other English book, was also known on the continent, but separated from the rest of the mass, and reassigned to St Samson of Dol (28 July). It appears with this affectation in Rouen, Bibliothèque municipale, 273, a late-eleventh-century sacramentary from Saint-Evroult which descends from a book brought to the house either from Thorney or Crowland by Orderic Vitalis (whose hand has been identified in the manuscript), and in Rouen, Bibliothèque municipale, 298, a mid-twelfth-century sacramentary from Jumièges. I print the text from the former:[208]

B.	*Saint-Evroult.*
Conserua domine populum tuum sub umbra protectionis tuae per inuocationem nominis sancti et summi pontificis tui cuthberhti, ut illius adiuuemur exemplis, et nos esse participes regni mereamur caelestis. Per.	Conserua nos quesumus domine sub umbra protectionis tuae, per summi pontificis tui Sansonis merita, quoque et ipsius suffragiis fac nos esse participes regni celestis. Per.

Since the Saint-Evroult and Jumièges prayer is not known in Brittany, it may well be that the two Norman houses adopted an existing English formula, not the other way around, as I have suggested elsewhere.[209] After the Conquest *B*'s mass, or one like it, was further altered by Archbishop Lanfranc (1070–89) and circulated to numerous houses in southern England. There is every likelihood therefore that the mass as we have it in *B* originated at Canterbury, a point further borne out by the findings of Laura Sole in her excellent article on the manuscripts containing offices in honour of the saint.[210] The only point I would add is that the office (and mass) were probably extremely widely-known. The third antiphon for matins, *Dum iactantur puppes salo*, for instance, is quoted verbatim in Byrhtferth's life of St Oswald.[211]

---

[208] Ed. Duine, *Inventaire liturgique*, p. 68. See Leroquais, *Les sacramentaires* I, 176–8 and II, 11.

[209] See Orchard, 'A note on the masses in honour of St Cuthbert'. On the two standard Breton masses in honour of St Samson, see Duine, *Inventaire liturgique*, pp. 20–3 and 28–33.

[210] Sole, 'Some Anglo-Saxon Cuthbert *liturgica*'.

[211] See Hohler, 'The Durham services', 170, and Byrthferth's *Vita S. Oswaldi*, ed. J. Raine, *Historians of the Church of York and its Archbishops*, 3 vols, RS 71 (London, 1879–94) I, 399–475, at 446.

Preface for a votive mass in honour of the Cross (no. 2270): the 'Eighth-Century Gelasian' preface. Not uncommon.[212]

Mass for St Denis and his companions (nos 2271–5): a number of books have the second collect and secret, the earliest of which is Trent, Museo Diocesano, 43, a late-eleventh-century sacramentary probably from Freising. Others, on the other hand, have the secret and postcommunion, but neither of the two collects. Notable are BL Cotton Vitellius A. xviii, the sacramentary of Giso of Wells; BL Loans 82, the fourteenth-century Sherborne Missal; and Oxford, Bodleian Library, Canon Lit. 344, a late-fourteenth-century missal from Chartres Cathedral.[213] But the earliest version of the mass as a whole, that is to say, one employing the first collect, secret and postcommunion, is to be found in Florence, Biblioteca Nazionale, B. R. 231, an early-tenth-century sacramentary written at Reichenau for a house nearby. In this the formulae are assigned to St Januarius of Naples (19 Sept.), whose relics were claimed by Reichenau in the late ninth century.[214] So the question confronting us is: for which saint were the propers originally composed: Denis or Januarius? The answer seems to lie in the regularity of their usage, and that would naturally argue for St Denis. In other words, Reichenau took over an existing mass. But that leaves us with a further question to which no firm answer seems forthcoming at present: where were the prayers composed: in England or on the continent? They are certainly by no means a rival to the standard set at Saint-Denis:[215]

Collecta. Deus qui hodierna die beatum dionysium matryrem tuum uirtute . . . aduersa formidare. Per.

Secreta. Hostia domine quaesumus quam in sanctorum tuorum . . . misericordiae dona conciliet. Per.

Praefatio. Qui sanctorum martyrum tuorum pia certamina . . . munera capiamus. Per dominum.

Ad complendum. Quesumus omnipotens deus ut qui caelestia alimenta . . . contra aduersa muniamur. Per.

---

[212] Ed. Dumas and Deshusses, *Liber Sacramentorum Gellonensis* I, 127–8, no. 947.
[213] Ed. dell'Oro and Roger, *Monumenta liturgica ecclesiae Tridentinae* III, 75, nos 160* and 161*; CLLA, no. 921*. For English books, see *Missale ad usum ecclesiae Westmonasteriensis*, ed. Legg, III, 1599.
[214] See Dodwell and Turner, *Reichenau Reconsidered*, p. 72.
[215] Ed. *Le sacramentaire grégorien* II, 328, nos 3636–9.

Indeed, their circulation is extremely limited by comparion. But it may be no coincidence that by far the greater number of examples of *B*'s mass, in whole, or in part, stem from England. The first collect, secret and postcommunion also turn up, for instance, in Laon, Bibliothèque municipale, 238, a mid-twelfth-century missal from the abbey of Bury St Edmunds.[216]

Now if Goscelin of Saint-Bertin is to be believed, St Edith of Wilton (961–84) constructed an oratory in honour of St Denis close to her abbey sometime in the 980s. This was subsequently dedicated by St Dunstan, and that might go some way to explaining why a new mass was adopted at Canterbury in the late tenth century, a proposition supported by the fact that the preface of *B*'s mass is not to be found elsewhere.[217] What remains to be explained, however, is the matter of where the collects of the mass had originally been composed. Wilton and Canterbury in the late tenth century are impossible since, as we have seen, the collect, secret and postcommunion had already been brought together at Reichenau sixty or so years previously. But until some other reason can be found for the existence of this mass, all questions surrounding its origins must remain open.

Preface for a mass in honour of the dead (no. 2276): composed by Alcuin and widespread.[218]

Votive mass for All Saints (nos 2281–3): a more extensive version of this mass occurs in BNF lat. 2291, the sacramentary of Gozlinus, bishop of Paris; the eleventh-century sacramentary of Vich; and apparently nowhere else.[219]

Mass for the feast of the invention of St Stephen's body (nos 2284–9): mostly unique, so far as one can tell. The only prayer to figure in other books is the alternative postcommunion *Da quesumus domine hanc presenti familiae tuae gratiam*. The books in question are: Le Havre, BM, 330, the mid-eleventh-century missal from the New Minster, Winchester; CCCC 391: the portiforium of Wulfstan II, bishop of Worcester (1062–95), which derives, as Hohler pointed out, from a Winchester

---

[216] For a short description of this book, see Leroquais, *Les sacramentaires* I, 219–21.

[217] Goscelin's life of Edith is ed. A. Wilmart, 'La légende de Ste Edith en prose et vers par la moine Goscelin', *AB* 56 (1933), 5–101, 265–307.

[218] See *Le sacramentaire grégorien* II, 231, 338 and 342, nos 3058, 3687 and 3733.

[219] See *Le sacramentaire grégorien* II, 57–8, nos 1913, 1915 and 1918, and *El sacramentario de Vich*, ed. Olivar, pp. 161–2, nos 1055–61.

model; and Leofric *C* (no. 2724).[220] It is not clear why this prayer circulated alone, plucked from context. Perhaps things should be put the other way round: the prayer may just as well have been taken from some Winchester book and added to the new mass. Both the missal and portiforium have a perfectly standard set of prayers for the invention otherwise. As has already been mentioned, *B*'s mass is probably to be associated with the new benediction for the feast preserved in BL Harley 2892, the 'Canterbury Benedictional', and the office preserved in BL Harley 3271.[221]

Votive mass in honour of the Trinity (nos 2290–9): entitled *missa pro peccatoribus*. Essentially Alcuin's mass with a variant version of the secret beginning *Omnipotens sempiterne deus maiestas et una deitas*, instead of *Omnipotens sempiterne deus qui fide purificas corda*, and a preface not to be found elsewhere.[222]

Blessings of Salt and Water (nos 2692–3): two 'Gelasian' prayers to be said over salt and water respectively, added at the foot of fol. 336r.[223]

Conclusions

As we have seen, *A* was expanded massively in England during the course of the tenth century, often to no discernable plan. Benedictions occur sporadically and unexpectedly in the Ordinary, which seems, in part at least, to have become surplus to requirements by *c.* 960; and we have stray prayers, normally without superscription, slotted in where space could be found, regardless of the character of the surrounding matter. The result, therefore, often appears to be something of a jumble. But the men who owned and used the book are likely to have known perfectly well what was where; and they will also have known where and when the supplementary prayers, benedictions and exorcisms were to have been pronounced. The principal point to stress, however, is that *A* was not simply put to one side when Plegmund died. His immediate successors evidently felt it worth augmenting. Further study will

---

[220] Ed. Turner, *The Missal of the New Minster*, p. 135; Hughes, *The Portiforium of St Wulfstan* I, 137, no. 1890, with Hohler, 'Books', 73.
[221] See above, p. 167.
[222] See *Le sacramentaire grégorien* II, 40, nos 1811–13.
[223] See *Le sacramentaire grégorien* III, 232–3, nos 4273 and 4277.

probably help determine more precisely who, for example, had the pontifical adapted: Wulfhelm and Oda are both possible.

A's greatest period of expansion came, though, with Dunstan, who had a new calendar and computus added, and so far as one can judge, a selection of masses on new gatherings further on in the book. That the calendar should have been based on the sanctoral of a sacramentary from Glastonbury raises intriguing questions. For as is well known, Dunstan had not only been a monk at the house in his youth, but he served as its abbot from 940 × 6 – 956, and for some undisclosed period after 959. As archbishop, he may simply have had the calendar of one of his own books copied out afresh. That, in turn, raises the possibility that a calendar similar to *A*'s had also been adopted at London and Worcester: for Dunstan was inaugurated as bishop of both sees in 959.[224] On the other hand, Glastonbury may have supplied him with a calendar and computus, or perhaps a sacramentary and calendar, at any time during the 960s. It is hard to say which is the more plausible view of events. However, there can be no doubt that *B*'s calendar is intimately associated with him. There is no reason why this should not also have been the basic calendar of Christ Church in the first decade of the eleventh century. As Alan Thacker has noted, Dunstan seems to have done little to foster cults around the relics possessed by his community, notably SS Blaise (3 Febr.), Austroberta (10 Febr.) and Salvius (26 June), though there are others.[225] Indeed, so far as one can tell, these relics were not promoted in any noticeable way until after the Viking invasions of 1012. We find entries for their feasts in the calendar of London, British Library, Arundel 155, the Christ Church psalter written by Aedui Basan *c.* 1020; episcopal benedictions for use at mass in BL Harley 2892, the mid-eleventh-century 'Canterbury Benedictional'; and invocations in the litanies of a number of indisputably Christ Church books.[226] The post-invasion Christ Church sanctoral, which may be based on that of Winchester, as Bishop saw, is therefore nothing like the one used by St Dunstan. That the post-Conquest sanctoral differs from its forerunner is simply due to the fact that Lanfranc (1070–89) relied on books from Bec, the house from which he had been brought, rather than

---

[224] See N. Brooks, 'The career of St Dunstan', in *St Dunstan*, ed. Ramsay, et al., pp. 1–23.

[225] See A. Thacker, 'Cults at Canterbury: relics and reform under Dunstan and his successors', in *St Dunstan*, ed. Ramsay, et al., 221–45.

[226] See *The Canterbury Benedictional*, ed. Woolley, pp. 85, 86 and 99; *EK*, pp. 171 and 174; and to take two examples, the litanies of CCCC 44 and London, British Library, Cotton Tiberius A. iii, ed. Lapidge, *Anglo-Saxon Litanies*, pp. 98–9 and 174–7.

existing English ones, for the basic structure of his.[227] Lanfranc, Dunstan and Archbishop Lyfing (1013–20) were all liturgical reformers. Whether the same holds true for Plegmund, Wulfhelm and Oda will no doubt be revealed by further study of *A* and *B*.

---

[227] See Heslop, 'The Canterbury calendars and the Norman Conquest', in *Canterbury and the Norman Conquest*, ed. Eales and Sharpe, pp. 53–85; R. W. Pfaff, 'The calendar' in *The Eadwine Psalter*, ed. M. Gibson, T. A. Heslop and R. W. Pfaff, 62–87; and J. Rubinstein, 'Liturgy against history: the competing visions of Lanfranc and Eadmer of Canterbury', *Speculum* 74 (1999), 279–309.

LEOFRIC C

General Introduction

That Bodley 579, more or less as we have it today, was once owned by Leofric, bishop of Crediton (1046–50) and Exeter (1050–72), could not be clearer. A donation inscription in Latin and OE on fol. 1v records that:[1]

> For the use of his successors, Leofric gives this missal to the church of St Peter the Apostle at Exeter.

On fols 2r–3v, we have a series of items relating to the part played by Leofric in founding the new see, transferred from Crediton in 1050. On fols 35v–36r a mass is provided for the express use of the bishop of Exeter. The eleven (or twelve) scribes who participated in the making of *C* all worked in other manuscripts from the cathedral; and the volume is without a shadow of a doubt one of the two *fulle maesse bec* recorded in the list of books procured by Leofric for his cathedral.[2] The evidence for Leofric's ownership, taken as a whole, is therefore conclusive.

The material added to Bodley 579 at Exeter in the mid eleventh century, that is to say, part *C*, was, like the material added to *A* at Canterbury some seventy years earlier, introduced by and large on new gatherings: four at the front of the book; one in the middle (a single sheet and a bifolium); and five at the end. But the volume was brought up to date in other ways too. A series of marginal cues for the Lessons and Gospels to be read at mass were added to the cues for chant already provided; musical notation was supplied for pieces both old and new; prayers were modified and corrected by erasure, marginal annotation and interlinear addition throughout; and entries for a variety of Lotharingian (and other) saints to whom Leofric, born and bred a

---

[1] For the full text of the inscription, see above, p. 1.
[2] See Drage, *Leofric*, p. 48, and M. Lapidge, 'Surviving booklists from Anglo-Saxon England', in *Learning and Literature in Anglo-Saxon England. Studies presented to Peter Clemoes on the Occasion of his Sixty-fifth Birthday*, ed. M. Lapidge and H. Gneuss (Cambridge, 1985), pp. 33–89, at 64–9.

Cornishman, is likely to have become devoted on the continent added to
B's calendar.[3] The book was therefore extensively revamped.

As even the briefest of glances will show, Leofric gathered his
material from a wide variety of sources. He evidently knew books from
Winchester and Canterbury, most likely through the offices of Stigand,
who held the sees in plurality until his expulsion in 1070; some Norman
house, possibly Mont-St-Michel; several houses in southern France; and
at least one major centre in Lotharingia. Indeed, the series of excerpts
from the Romano-German Pontifical added to C were almost certainly
copied from a copy that Leofric had either acquired on the continent
during his time there or sent for on arriving at Crediton or later still,
Exeter. To judge from the inventory drawn up between the years 1069
and 1072, Exeter was pitifully provided for in 1050. The position at
Crediton in 1046 can hardly have been much better.[4]

That Leofric should have looked to Canterbury for a sacramentary is
perfectly understandable. Canterbury was the metropolitan. What better
than to seek its assistance in the setting up of a new see? A and B, in
company with at least two other books acquired by Leofric from Christ
Church, could presumably be parted with because they had become
surplus to requirements.[5] But Leofric does not appear to have looked to
Canterbury alone. BL Cotton Vitellius A. vii, a pontifical, seems to have
been copied from a book from North Elmham (a house ruled over by
Stigand and then Stigand's brother, Aethelmar), and parts of the text of
the model, or that of Vitellius A. vii, were copied again into London,
British Library, Additional 28188, Leofric's select pontifical-cum-
benedictional, though as Prescott has shown, its benedictional was
probably taken over from a Winchester book.[6] Leofric also acquired an
extensive collection of liturgical and canonical texts in the shape of
Cambridge, Trinity College, 241, a mid-tenth-century copy of
Amalarius, *De ecclesiasticis officiis*, from St Augustine's, Canterbury;
and the two manuscripts, probably both from Worcester, that now form
Cambridge, Corpus Christi College, 190. His collectar, on the other

---

[3] See William of Malmesbury, *Gesta Pontificum*, ed. Hamilton, p. 201; and F. Barlow,
Exeter 1046–1184, English Episcopal Acta 9 (Oxford, 1996), pp. xxxii, 1–2.
[4] The inventory is ed. Conner, *Anglo-Saxon Exeter*, pp. 230–3.
[5] On books acquired by and written for Leofric, see Gameson, 'The origin of the Exeter
Book'.
[6] Prescott, 'The structure of English pre-Conquest benedictionals', pp. 130–3.

hand, as has long been recognised, almost certainly descends directly from a model from Liège.[7]

In a sense, the most striking thing about *C* is that it should exist at all. Leofric could easily have had a sacramentary written out anew to suit his particular needs. However, as Drage saw, the making of the manuscript seems to have been an important project, and one with which virtually the whole scriptorium wanted to be associated. Indeed, one of the hands is probably that of Leofric himself. It will be best to turn now to the palaeography and codicology of the additions.

Palaeography

C's palaeography seems first to have attracted serious attention in 1950s. In an article published in the *Transactions of the Cambridge Bibliographical Society* in 1956, T. A. M Bishop traced the work of a number of *C*'s scribes in other books known to have been produced at Exeter, and suggested lines for further study; and in 1957, Neil Ker described, and proposed dates for, the material written in Old English.[8] Bishop and Ker's work is of continuing value. However, the best and most thorough analysis of *C*'s palaeography currently available is the one produced by Eleanor Drage for her D.Phil. thesis in 1978.[9] For the sake of convenience, I reproduce her findings below, retaining the

---

[7] The literature on CCCC 190 is extensive. For general descriptions of its appearance and partial descriptions of its contents, see Ker, *Catalogue of Manuscripts containing Anglo-Saxon*, pp. 170–3, no. 45; Budny, *Insular, Anglo-Saxon and Early Anglo-Norman Manuscript Art*, I, 535–44; M. Bateson, 'A Worcester Cathedral book of ecclesiastical collections', *English Historical Review* 10 (1895), 712–31; P. Wormald, *The Making of English Law*, 2 vols (Oxford: Blackwell's, 1999 and forthcoming) I, 220–4; and J. E. Cross and A. Hamer, *Wulfstan's Canon Law Collection*, Anglo-Saxon Texts 1 (Woodbridge, 1999), esp. pp. 55–61. Most of the liturgical material in CCCC 190, part I, has been printed either in full or in synopsis by B. Fehr, *Die Hirtenbriefe Aelfrics in altenglische und lateinischer Fassung*, Bibliothek der angelsächsischen Prosa 11 (Hamburg, 1914), pp. 234–49 (Anhang III); and C. Jones, 'Two composite texts from Archbishop Wulstan's 'commonplace book': the *De ecclesiastica consuetudine* and the *Institutio beati Amalarii de ecclesiasticis officiis*', *ASE* 27 (1998), 233–71, at 256–71. No-one, however, has yet published a thorough, intelligible, and systematic account of all the individual items contained in the manuscript. On the collectar, which is now BL Harley 2961, see Dewick and Frere, *The Leofric Collectar*, II, xxi–lvii.
[8] T. A. M. Bishop, 'Notes on Cambridge Manuscripts Part III: Manuscripts connected with Exeter', *Transactions of the Cambridge Bibliographical Society* 2 (1954–8), 192–9, esp. 193–4; *idem*, *English Caroline Minuscule*, p. 24; and Ker, *Catalogue of manuscripts containing Anglo-Saxon*, pp. 378–9.
[9] Richard Gameson has a new study of Bodley 579's palaeography in hand.

numbers she assigned to each scribe. An asterisk indicates that her scheme has been corrected by Lapidge.[10]

Gathering 1

Scribe 2. Fol. 1r: Leofric's ex-libris in Old English and Latin (nos 1 and 2). Probably written during his lifetime.[11]

A number of later scribes. Fols 1r–v: a series of manumissions in Old English written in the last decade of the eleventh century (nos 3–7). As Frances Rose-Troup has shown, many of the witnesses mentioned are identifiable in the manumissions attached to Exeter Cathedral Library, 3507, the so-called 'Exeter Book', a late-tenth-century collection of riddles in Old English. The leaves containing these, however, originally belonged to Cambridge, University Library, Ii. 11. 2, a late-eleventh-century copy of the Gospels also from Exeter. Some were written at much the same time as those added to Bodley 579, but by a different set of scribes. The impetus for the inclusion of these manumissions doubtless came from Bishop Osbern FitzOsbern (1072–1103).[12]

Scribe 9. Fols 2r–3r: a report of a letter purportedly sent by Pope Formosus (891–6) to King Edward the Elder (899–924) concerning the revival of the West Saxon dioceses in 905 (no. 8); and a report (fol. 3r) of the circumstances of the promotion of Leofric to the see of Exeter, a later continuation in smaller script (no. 9).[13]

Scribe 10. Fol. 3v: a copy of a letter from Pope Leo IX (d. 1054) to King Edward (1043–65) confirming Leofric in his see, with a preface presumably composed at Exeter (nos 10–11); a report of Leofric's inthronization and installation (no. 12); a report of Leofric's deeds (no. 13); and a report of Leofric's death (no. 14).[14]

Scribe 2.* Fol. 4r lines 1–7: the introit and collect of an 'Eighth-Century Gelasian' set of Ember masses for Easter (nos 15 and 16).

---

[10] Drage, *Leofric,* pp. 71–80, 115–67; M. Lapidge, 'Ealdred of York and MS Cotton Vitellius E. xii', *Yorkshire Archaeological Journal* 55 (1983), 11–25, at 23.

[11] On the other books containing this inscription see Drage, *Leofric,* pp. 29–41; Conner, *Anglo-Saxon Exeter,* pp. 13–17; and Gameson, 'The origin of the Exeter Book', 148–9.

[12] See Rose-Troup, 'Exeter manumissions and quittances of the eleventh and twelfth centuries', 441–5, where plates of fol. 1 are provided.

[13] See Brooks, *The Early History of the Church of Canterbury,* pp. 211–13, and Conner, *Anglo-Saxon Exeter,* pp. 215–25, esp. 215–16.

[14] See Conner, *Anglo-Saxon Exeter,* pp. 215–25.

Scribe 10. Fol. 4r line 8 – fol. 5v: the rest of the Ember mass (nos 17–33).[15] Most of fol. 5v is blank.

Scribe 10. Fols 6r–v: a list of the relics possessed by Exeter, the greater part of which are said to have been donated by King Æthelstan (no. 34).[16] Three similar lists survive in other Exeter books. Fol. 7r seems to have been left blank for the recording of future acquisitions.

Scribe 10. Fol. 7v: a new mass for St Michael (nos 35–8).[17]

Gatherings 4, 5 and 6

Scribe 1. Fols 18r–30r line 10, a single scribe writing increasingly freely: the mass for those tempted to the mass for travellers (nos 141–214).

Scribe 2. Fol. 30r line 11 – fol. 33v: mass for St Nicholas to the mass for the anniversary of the dedication of a church (nos 215–42).

Scribe 3. Fol. 34r: mass for the nativity of St John the Baptist (nos 243–51).

Scribe 12 (not identified by Drage). Fols 34v–36r: mass for the congregation to the mass for the bishop (nos 252–63).

Scribe 2.* Fols 36v–37v: masses for St Egidius, a Queen, and relics possessed of a martyr or confessor (nos 264–74).

Gathering 22

Scribe 1. Fols 155r–156v: exorcism and blessings of incense (nos 1295–8).

Scribe 2. Fols 156v–157v: blessings of church goods (nos 1299–1303).

Gatherings 44–48

Scribe 2. Fols 337r–340v: mass for virtues to the mass of St Mary ad Martyres (nos 2698–2724).

---

[15] See *Liber Sacramentorum Gellonensis,* ed. Dumas and Deshusses, I, 146–8, nos 1096–1115.
[16] For the other early Exeter relic-lists, see Conner, *Anglo-Saxon Exeter*, pp. 171–209, who gives references to a wider literature.
[17] See below, pp. 214–15.

Scribe 10: Fol. 339v. alternative postcommunion for the feast of Mary Magdalene (no. 2713*).

Scribe 11. Fol. 341r lines 1–14: mass for the octave of the Assumption of the Virgin (nos 2725–8).

Scribe 10. Fol. 341r line 15 – fol. 341v: mass for St Margaret (nos 2729–32). Most of fol. 341v and the whole of fol. 342r is blank.

Scribe 4. Fols 342v–344v line 1: masses for SS Alban and Martin (nos 2733–44).

Scribe 2. Fol. 344v lines 2–15: first three prayers of the mass for the twenty-fourth Sunday after the octave of Pentecost (nos 2745–7).

Scribe 3? Fol. 344v lines 16–18: postcommunion of the mass above (no. 2748).

Scribe 2?, but possibly another not identified by Drage. Fols 345r–370v: preface for the vigil of Christmas to the second preface for the dead (nos 2749–2888).

Scribe 2.* Fols 371r–372r: mass to be said by the Bishop of Exeter (nos 2889–98).

Scribe 6. Fols 372v–373r line 15: mass for the Conception of St John the Baptist and the collect of the mass for the Queen (nos 2899–2909).

Scribe 7. Fol. 373r line 16 – fol. 373v: rest of mass for the Queen to the mass for St Gregory (nos. 2910–14).

Scribe 10. Fol. 374r: mass for the Conception of the Virgin (nos 2915–17).

Scribe 4. Fols 374v–375r line 2: mass for a friend in adversity (nos 2918–20).

Scribe 8. Fol. 375r lines 3–18: mass for the octave of St Martin (nos 2921–3).

Scribe 10. Fol. 375r line 19 – fol. 375v: masses for the octave of St Andrew and St Faith (nos 2924–9).

Scribe 9. Fol. 376r: preface for St Peter (no. 2930).

Scribe 10. Fols 376v–377r: masses for SS Augustine and Lazarus (nos 2931–7).

A later scribe. Fol. 377r–v: a manumission in Old English written in the last decade of the eleventh century (no. 2939). Added at much the same time as the manumissions added on gathering 1.[18]

Scribe 1, who wrote in an 'alien' hand, was probably Leofric himself, as Drage has indicated. Minor initials (there is no major decoration) are generally in blue, red, pinkish-red, and occasionally green. The pinkish-red has often faded.

Principal Additions to A and B

(i) Scribe 1, that is to say Leofric, not only added new cues for chant and readings in *A*'s margins throughout, but on occasion noted how certain elements in the existing material should be re-arranged, a case in point being the new 'directions' provided for the Vigils of Easter and Pentecost on fols 112r–113r and 129v–130r.[19]

(ii) Fol. 8r–v: as has already been mentioned, folio 8 is a singleton. On its recto are the remains of a short prayer *ad mensam* (no. 39) and a version of a prayer *super populum* for the first Sunday after Christmas, *Propitiare misericors deus supplicationibus nostris* (no. 40), written by a scribe who wrote elsewhere in *B*. The leaf is therefore likely already to have been in place as a guard when Bodley 579 left Canterbury.[20] Immediately below the prayer we have two badly damaged manumissions in Old English (nos 39–42), now almost unreadable; on the verso, eight more (nos 43–9), better preserved and all concerning people living in south west Devon, principally in the region of Tavistock.[21] As Finberg indicated, the Ordgar whose name appears twice on fol. 8v can only be the Ordgar 'minister' who attests a number of charters in the

---

[18] See Rose-Troup, 'Exeter manumissions and quittances', pp. 442–5.

[19] Drage, *Leofric*, pp. 139–43, 149–50, with Bishop, *English Caroline Minuscule*, p. 24. For the ultimate source of Scribe 1's new directions for the Vigil of Easter and the Vigil of Pentecost, see *Le sacramentaire grégorien* I, 183–5, nos 362–72; and 222–4, nos 507–15. Only certain books, however (noted in the apparatus), give the Cantica. Later we find the same system outlined in the *Regularis Concordia*, ed. Symons, p. 47, and CCCC 190, which Leofric owned. See Fehr, *Die Hirtenbriefe Aelfrics*, pp. 228–9 and 232–3 (Anhang I and II); and Jones, 'Two composite texts', pp. 260–1.

[20] The point was first made by Ker, *Catalogue of Manuscripts containing Anglo-Saxon*, pp. 378–9.

[21] See H. P. R. Finberg, 'The house of Ordgar and the foundation of Tavistock Abbey', *EHR* 58 (1943), 190–200.

second quarter of the eleventh century. In view of their palaeography, the ten entries were presumably copied in at Crediton, less likely early at Exeter, prior to the prefixing of gathering 1. At some point in the middle ages fol. 8 must have become loose, as there is wear on verso as well as recto.[22]

(iii) Fol. 11v: a copy of a surety for land at Stoke Canon between Abbot Leofric (attested *c*. 980 × 993) and Abbess Eadgyfu.[23] Added in the mid eleventh century. The only part of *C* to have been written over an erasure in *A*; no doubt entered when fol. 8v was seen to be full. Copied in either at Crediton, or early at Exeter.

(iv) Fols 38r–44v: various entries throughout *B*'s calendar written, according to Drage, by scribes 1, 2, 7 and 10. However, as we shall, her analysis of these additions requires a certain amount of modification. Scribe 1, for instance, probably played no part in the calendar's augmentation, and scribes 2 and 7 evidently did not write what she thought they had.[24]

(v) Fol. 52v: note concerning the terms of Easter added below a set of verses on the subject (no. 297). Written by scribe 10.

(vi) Fol. 58v lines 23–7: preface for Sundays in Lent (no. 322). Written by scribe 5.

(vii) Fols 59r lines 1–9, and lines 11–22: mass for the octave of St Andrew (nos 323–5), and a copy letter from *Adela, famula dei*, to a certain bishop 'L' (no. 326). As Warren has shown, 'L' cannot be Leofric (a connexion perhaps hoped for by the copyist) as internal evidence suggests that Adela, the fourth daughter of William the Conqueror, wrote this letter sometime in the period 1102–37.[25]

(viii) Fols 59v lines 11–13: termination *Quem laudant* (no. 328). Written by Drage's scribe 4.

(ix) Fol. 59v: a copy of the short version of a spurious decree of Pope

---

[22] *LM*, frontispiece.
[23] For an illustration of fol. 11v, see Rose-Troup, 'The ancient monastery of St Mary and St Peter at Exeter, 680–1050', pp. 179–219. Unfortunately, Rose-Troup, following Warren, 'Manumissions in the Leofric Missal', *Revue Celtique* 5 (1882), 213–17, dates the entry (and those on fol. 8v) much too early.
[24] See below, pp. 221–3.
[25] See *LM*, p. lxii.

Pelagius (578–90) concerning the number of proper prefaces to be adopted for major feasts (no. 329). Written by Drage's scribe 6.[26]

Numerous small additions and corrections were also made in Leofric's time to the main texts given in the manuscript. The most far-reaching of these secondary adaptions was the transformation of the mass for St Timothy on fol. 187v (nos 1657–60) into a mass for SS Timothy and Symphorian. Only the liturgical material on fol. 59r seems to date from Osbern's episcopacy.

Liturgical Material

For the most part, the new masses embodied in *C* are laid out in missal format. In other words, the variable chant and lessons needed for the performance of mass are generally provided in full. The chant, moreover, is often neumed in a distinctively Exeter style, as Susan Rankin has shown.[27] In view of the fact that *C* contains such a variety of new pieces, it seems best to concentrate here solely on the material that is either unusual or unique.

I. Gathering 1 (fols i–7v). The only liturgical matter needing particular comment is the mass for St Michael (nos 35–8) on fol. 7v. The prayer *Deus cuius claritatis fulgore* (no. 35) seems normally to have been reserved for the feast of the saint celebrated on 8 May, as Pierpont Morgan 641, the mid-eleventh-century sacramentary from Mont Saint-Michel, and the mid-eleventh-century manual-cum-collectar from Monte Cassino demonstrate.[28] The collect *Deus qui beatum michahelem archangelum electionis tuae* (no. 36) only otherwise occurs, so far as can be judged, in books from the abbey of Mont Saint-Michel, notably: Avranches, Bibliothèque municipale, 42, a mid-thirteenth-century missal; and Paris, Bibliothèque nationale de France, nouv. acq. lat. 424, a fifteeth-century breviary. The secret is the normal Gregorian formula

---

[26] *Ibid.*, pp. lxii–lxiii. A long version of the decree is to be found as an addition in London, British Library, Add. 17004 (fol. 2), a mid-eleventh-century pontifical from Minden. See further, p. 229, below, on this manuscript. For later copies of the text in its long and short form, see *Regesta Pontificum Romanorum*, ed. P. Jaffé, P. Ewald and S. Loewenfeld, 3 vols (Leipzig, 1885–8) I, 139, no. 1065.

[27] S. Rankin, 'From memory to record: musical notations in manuscripts from Exeter', *ASE* 13 (1984), 97–112.

[28] Pierpont Morgan 641, fol. 111, and *Manuale Casinense*, ed. Rehle, p. 127, no. 358.

Munus populi tui (no. 37). But the postcommunion *Beati archangeli tui michaelis ut omnium angelorum* (no. 38) is respectively the postcommunion of a votive mass for angels in Laon Bibliothèque municipale, 236, an early-eleventh-century sacramentary from Reims; the third alternative prayer for the saint's translation (8 May) in the breviary of Oderisius I, abbot of Monte Cassino (1087–1105); and the postcommunion for the vigil of the feast normally known as *in Monte Tumba* (16 Oct.) in Avranches BM 42.[29] The combination of these prayers is clearly eccentric, and it seems possible that all had their place in books belonging to St Michael's Mount, which, despite the doubts regularly expressed about the genuineness of a number of its charters, certainly looks to have been served by some sort of community in Leofric's time.[30] Unless Leofric dealt with a house with no recorded interest in the saint, it seems reasonable to assume that *C*'s prayers for St Michael came from Mont Saint-Michel by way of Mount's Bay.

II. Gatherings 4, 5 and 6 (fols 18r–37v), probably written by Leofric himself. A number of prayers in this section contain 'invocations'. St Michael, the Virgin and SS Peter and Paul are named in the mass for those tempted; the Virgin, SS Peter and Paul, and St Andrew in the mass for the bishop: the Virgin, St Michael, and SS Peter and Paul in the mass for enemies; and in the mass for a faithful friend the Virgin and St Michael. Most striking of all, however, as has often been noted, are the invocations of the collect of the first *missa generalis uiuorum et mortuorum* (no. 151):[31]

> . . . omnesque congregationes illis commissas, et nos famulos tuos, ac locum nostrum, et familiam beatissimae dei genetricis mariae, necnon et sancti petri apostoli, atque sancti suuithuni confessoris christi.

---

[29] See LeMarie, 'Textes relatifs au culte de l'Archange', 129, 150–1, with *idem*, 'L'office des fêtes de saint Michel dans les bréviaires du Mont', *Millénaire monastique du Mont Saint-Michel* I, 473–87. The Reims book is described by Leroquais, *Les sacramentaires* I, 129–31.

[30] See S. Keynes, 'The Æthelings in Normandy', *Proceedings of the Battle Conference on Anglo-Norman Studies* 13, 1990, ed. M. Chibnall (Woodbridge, 1991), 173–205, at 190–8, with J. J. G. Alexander, *Norman Illumination at Mont Saint-Michel, 966–1100* (Oxford, 1971), p. 83.

[31] *LM*, p. lvii; Barlow, *The English Church 1000–1066*, pp. 213–14, n. 6; Hohler, review of Grant, *Cambridge, Corpus Christi College, 41* in *Medium Aevum* 49 (1980), 276.

That St Swithun's name could remain suggests that Leofric was perfectly happy to adopt prayers containing a litanic element not wholly in
line with local use.[32]

Mass for those tempted (nos 141–50): all four prayers occur together in
Vich 66, the late-tenth-century sacramentary from Vich; in Vich 67, an
eleventh-century sacramentary from Ripoll; and in no other book that
has so far found its way into print.[33] The mass is evidently exceptionally
rare. However, as even the briefest of comparisons will show, the Vich
prayers are substantially longer. I give the secret from Vich 66 on the
left, that of *C* on the right:

Vich.	*C.*
Hostiam domine quam tibi pro me famulo tuo offero clemens adsumme, et benedictionem sancti nominis dignanter perfunde, michique seruo tuo ill. intercedente pro me sancto Michaele archangelo tuo, et beata gloriosa semperque uirgine Maria et beatis apostolis tuis Petro et Paulo, et sanctis confessoribus tuis Hylario, Martino et Gregorio et sancto Benedicto et sancto Germano, et sancto Nicholao, et omni katerua sanctorum, peccatorum meorum omnium indulgenciam tribue, et misericordiam largire, atque haec petenti pro tua inmensa pietate miserere, ut dignus efficiar huius seruitutis sacrique misterii executor, ut quod pro me te, deus clementissime deprecor, tu mihi concedas propicius, qui uiuis.	Hostiam domine quam tibi pro me famulo tuo offero, clemens suscipere digneris, et benedictionem sancti spiritus tui dignanter perfunde mihi seruo tuo, et intercedente pro me sancto michaele archangelo tuo, et beata et gloriosa semperque uirgine maria, et beatis apostolis tuis petro et paulo, et omnium cateruis sanctorum peccatorum meorum omnium indulgentiam tribue, et misericordiam largire mihi famulo tuo, haec petenti pro tua pietate miserere, ut dignus efficiar huius seruitutis sacrique mysterii, ut quod te deus clementissime deprecor, mihi concedas pro tua pietate propitius. Per.

The presence of the invocations of SS Hilary, Martin, Gregory, Benedict, German and Nicholas, a series that does not look particularly
Spanish, suggest that the mass as we have it at Vich originally came
from France, possibly from some monastic house. It may therefore
simply be a matter of chance that copies of the formulae found their way

---

[32] See too the series of litanic prayers in BL Harley 863, Leofric's psalter, ed. Dewick and
Frere, *The Leofric Collectar* I, 443. On the book in general, see now R. W. Pfaff, 'The
sample week in the medieval Latin Divine Office', in *Continuity and Change in Christian
Worship*, ed. R. N. Swanson, Studies in Church History 35 (Woodbridge, 1999), 78–88.
[33] See *El sacramentario di Vich*, ed. Olivar, p. 275, nos 1715–18, and for instance the
Corpus Orationum, ed. Moeller, *et al.*, no. 2941.

to Vich and Exeter, surviving at both places and apparently nowhere else. But it also seems possible that at some point in his career Leofric collected material from some southern French sacramentary.

Mass for peace (nos 195–204). Collects normal. The preface *Cuius potentia aeternalis est in filio* does not appear in any other book that has found its way into print. Dom Moeller thought it 'Gallican' in character.[34]

Mass for travellers (nos 205–14). The collects and preface only otherwise occur together, so far as I have been able to establish, in Rouen BM 274, the early-eleventh-century sacramentary later owned by Robert of Jumièges. As Hohler has pointed out, the book from which Rouen BM 274 ultimately derives is not a book from Peterborough or Ely, but one from Nivelles (in the diocese of Liège), since St Gertrude, patron of the house, is named in the Canon of the Mass. That presents us with two possible paths forward. The first is to presume that Leofric had become familiar with the mass during his sojourn abroad, and brought a copy of it over to England, either in place in a sacramentary or noted down in some commonplace book. We know, for instance, that the model from which his collectar was copied probably came from somewhere close to Liège. The second is to suppose that he had the mass copied from a book either from Canterbury or Winchester.[35] On balance, an English source seems more likely than a Lotharingian, if only because English material figures so strongly elsewhere in *C*.

Mass for St Nicholas (nos 215–17): 6 Dec. Bishop of Myra. Relics translated to Bari in southern Italy by the Normans in 1087. Exeter claimed a portion of his head.[36] The earliest proper masses in the saint's honour surviving in French books seem to be those in: Rouen BM 272, the mid-eleventh-century sacramentary from the abbey of Saint-Wandrille; BNF lat. 10500, the sacramentary of Hughes, archbishop of Besançon; Pierpont Morgan 641, the mid-eleventh-century sacramentary from Mont Saint-Michel; and Paris, Bibliothèque nationale de France, lat. 17306, a mid-eleventh-century sacramentary from Amiens.[37] Leofric's

---

[34] *Corpus Prefationum*, ed. Moeller, no. 179.
[35] Ed. Wilson, *The Missal of Robert of Jumièges*, p. 260; Hohler, 'Les saintes insulaires dans le missel de l'archévêque Robert', pp. 293–303.
[36] See Conner, *Anglo-Saxon Exeter*, pp. 183, 197 and 203.
[37] On these books, see Alexander, *Norman Illumination at Mont St-Michel*, pp. 127–72, and Leroquais, *Les sacramentaires* I, 136, 138 and 141.

mass, as far as masses alone go, is therefore relatively early. However, taking a broader view, it soon becomes clear that the saint's cult was already established in England by Leofric's time, as antiphons for use at office appear as early-eleventh-century additions in Cambridge, Sidney Sussex College, 100, a pontifical probably written for Oswald, bishop of Worcester (961–92) and archbishop of York (972–92); and five votive prayers in St Nicholas's honour occur in BL Cotton Titus D. xxvii, the prayerbook of Ælfwine, dean of Winchester (1023–31). It is well to note too, that, as Charles Jones has indicated, Wulfstan II of Worcester seems to have been specially devoted to the saint: the proper office in London, British Library, Cotton Nero E. i, part of a passional from Worcester seems to have been written for him in the mid to late eleventh century.[38] Leofric's interest in the saint is quite in line with spirit of the day.[39] No blessing for the feast, however, figures in his benedictional, BL Add. 28188.

Mass for enemies (nos 218–22). The collect, secret and postcommunion are relatively common.[40] The preface, on the other hand, seems only otherwise to have been used at Vich, though in a variant form, as the following comparison will show:[41]

Vich.	*C.*
Qui redemptionem hac salute humani generis cruce adfixus pro suis orauit inimicis dicens, pater dimitte illis, non enim sciunt quid faciunt, ipse inimicorum nostrorum absoluat pondera delictorum. Nosque ipsos diligere ac pro persequentibus et calumpnitatibus nobis faciat indesinenter exorare, quia inimicos diligere et pro persequentibus et calumpnitatibus uoluit et iussit pias preces emittere. Nosque, domine,	Qui pro redemptione ac salute humani generis cruci affixus, pro suis orauit inimicis dicens, pater dimitte illis, non enim sciunt quod faciunt. Per ipsum nos quesumus omnipotens pater a cunctis eripe inimicis, eisque

---

[38] Ed. Banting, *Two Anglo-Saxon Pontificals*, p. 170; Günzel, *Ælfwine's Prayerbook*, pp. 195–6. The cult appears to have received its principal liturgical impetus on the continent from the offices composed by Reginold, bishop of Eichstätt, and Isembert, a German monk of the church of Saint-Ouen at Rouen who later became abbot of the abbey of Sainte-Catherine-du-Mont. See Jones, *The St Nicholas Liturgy*, pp. 1–73.

[39] See for instance the material collected by E. M. Treharne, *The Old English Life of St Nicholas with the Old English Life of St Giles*, Leeds Texts and Monographs 15 (Leeds, 1997).

[40] For instance, *Le sacramentaire grégorien* II, nos 2669–71.

[41] Ed. Olivar, *El sacramentario di Vich*, p. 179, nos 1175–8 and p. 190, nos 1250–3.

sancte pater omnipotens aeterne deus, a ueniam tribue delictorum, et cunctis eripe inimicis, eisque ueniam intercedente beata dei genetrice maria tribue delictorum, et ad pacis cum omnibus sanctis, eos ad pacis caritatisque concordiam clementer caritatisque concordiam clementer reuoca, per ipsum, qui karitatis causa reuoca. Per christum. de celis descendit ad terras ut nos qui inimici eramus, reconciliaret, et esset pax nostra iesus christus filius tuus, dominus noster, quem laudant angeli.

In the absence of further versions, it is difficult to say which of these is the 'original', as Moeller noted.[42] It is also difficult to say why the Vich book should have an entirely different set of accompanying collects. Perhaps Leofric simply reset a prayer he had acquired on the continent in an existing mass.

Mass for a faithful friend (nos 223–32): of the books surveyed by Deshusses, only Vienna, Österreichisches Nationalbibliothek, lat. 1815, a mid-ninth-century sacramentary from Reichenau has this mass.[43] However, since a version resurfaces in Rouen BM 274, the 'Missal of Robert of Jumièges', it seems reasonable to suppose that Leofric acquired his copy from some English book.[44]

Proper mass for the bishop of Exeter (nos 261–3): A mass specially composed at Exeter. As Warren noted the collect contains the phrase: *quique me famulum ill. non meis meritis, sed dono tuae gratiae, pontificali cathedra exoniensium sublimasti*; the secret: *me famulum tuum, quem exoniensium uoluisti esse antistitem, et populorum, quem instituendum lege preceptorum tuorum mihi commendasti*; and the postcommunion: *inploro domine deus, ut me famulum tuum quem sancte Exoniensi aecclesiae, preesse uoluisti, et agnos tuos quos tibi ex universali aecclesia specialius electos mihi nutriendos commisisti.*[45] Perhaps composed by Leofric himself.

Mass for St Aegidius (nos 264–8): Better known as St Giles or Gilles. Venerated on 1 Sept. Major relics preserved in Rome and at the pilgrimage church of Saint-Gilles-du-Gard in Provence. Judging by the calendars published by Wormald, the feast did not become popular in

---

[42] *Corpus Prefationum*, ed. Moeller, no. 1178.
[43] *Le sacramentaire grégorien* II, 140, nos 2397–2401. See also Gerbert, *Monumenta* I, 283–4.
[44] *The Missal of Robert of Jumièges*, ed. Wilson, p. 255.
[45] *LM*, p. lvii.

England until after the Conquest.[46] The earliest propers for the day that have come down to us in French sacramentaries are all eleventh century, the books in question being: BNF lat. 818, from Troyes; Paris, Bibliothèque nationale de France, lat. 821, from an abbey in the Limousin; and Montpellier BM 18, from Gellone.[47] In view of the fact that Gellone and Saint-Gilles are only a few miles apart, it seems reasonable to believe that the Montpellier book contains the local relic mass. Whether this is the mass embodied in *C* remains to be seen. That *C* gives a sort of martyrological superscription (no. 264):

> Nemanensi pago, loco qui uocatur uallis flauiana, in prospectu maris, natale sancti egidii abbatis et confessoris; apud athenas greciae urbem, ortus ex patre theodoro, matre uero pelagia.

tends to suggest that the forms acquired by Leofric were relatively 'new', having been drawn up perhaps for non-locals to take home. *C*'s preface derives from a normal 'Eighth-Century Gelasian' preface for a 'confessor', as Moeller demonstrated:[48]

Gellone.	*C.*
Qui in omnium sanctorum tuorum profectione es laude colendus, beati confessoris tui ill. transitu sacro consecrasti. Da aecclesiae tuae quesumus de tanto gaudere patrono, et illam sequi pia deuotionem <doctrinam> qua dilectus tuus tibi gregis pane eruditionis pauit, ut adiuuare nos aput misericordiam tuam <et> exemplis eius sentiamus et meritis. Per christum.	Qui in omnium sanctorum tuorum, es prouectione laude colendum. Maxime in hac die quam beati confessoris tui egidii, sacro transitu consecrasti. Da ergo aecclesiae tuae de tanto gaudere patrono, et illam sequi pia deuotione doctrinam, qua dilectus tuus tuum gregem pane eruditionis pauit, ut adiuuari nos apud misericordiam tuam et exemplis eius sentiamus et meritis. Per christum dominum nostrum.

As can be seen, relatively few changes were made. No blessing for the day figures in BL Add. 28188.

Mass for a Queen (nos 269–71): probably an Exeter composition. The collect is based on a standard Roman daily prayer:[49]

---

[46] For eleventh- and twelfth-century additions, *EK*, pp. 24, 52, 178, 192, 220 and 262. Only BL Cotton Vitellius A. xviii, the sacramentary of Giso of Wells, has an entry in the original hand, *op. cit.*, p. 108.

[47] See Leroquais, *Les sacramentaires* I, 152, 157 and 159.

[48] *Corpus Prefationum*, ed. Moeller, no. 1022; *Liber Sacramentorum Gellonensis*, ed. Dumas and Deshusses, I, 230, no. 1783.

[49] Ed. *Le sacramentaire grégorien* I, 327, no. 931.

Hadrianum.

Guberna domine quesumus plebem tuam et tuis beneficiis semper adcumula, ut et presentis uitae subsidiis gaudeat et aeternae. Per.

C.

Guberna domine famulam tuam et tuis beneficiis semper accumula, ut et presentis uitae subsidiis gaudeat et aeternae. Per.

The secret, however, is unique, and the postcommunion a standard 'Eighth-Century Gelasian'. The Queen in question, if English, is presumably the Conqueror's wife, Mathilda (d. 1086). But the obituary noted in the calendar on the 27th of September is unlikely to be hers, as the woman concerned is not termed *regina*.

III. Additions to the calendar and the computus (fols 39r–44v). The additions made to the calendar at Exeter are:[50]

31 Jan. Obitus Aeglflaed.
10 Feb. Obitus Leofricus episcopus.
13 Feb. Sanctae Eormenhildae. Obitus Godonis iuuenis presbiteri.
16 Feb. Obiit Brihtricus decanus.
1 Mar. Sancti Deuui episcopi confessoris. Albini episcopi confessoris.
18 Mar. Sancti Eadwardi regis et martyris.
19 Mar. Hic obiit Lifingus episcopus.
19 Apr. F. et sancti Aelfheagi archiepiscopi et martyris. Eodem die ordinatus fuit Leofricus episcopus.
28 Apr. et sancti Wynwaloci confessoris.
2 May. Athanasii episcopi et confessoris.
19 May. Depositio Dunstani archiepiscopi.
26 Jun. Obitus Eadrici sacerdotis.
16 Jul. Eustacii, Munulfi, Gundulfi, Servacii et Bertini confessorum.
1 Aug. Ad uincula sancti Petri.
4 Aug. Sanctae Afrae martyris.
29 Aug. Obitus Aelfwini episcopi.
1 Sept. et sancti Egidii abbatis.
3 Sept. Ordinatio beati Gregorii papae.
9 Sept. Obitus Willelmi senioris regis.
12 Sept. Obitus Segiuae.
27 Sept. Obitus Mathildae.
6 Oct. Sanctae Fidis uirginis et martyris.
13 Oct. Sancti Giraldi confessoris.
14 Oct. Sancti Maglorii episcopi. Bartholomei translatio.

---

[50] Warren, *LM*, pp. 23–33, prints all the entries in their proper place in the calendar. Wormald, *EK*, pp. 44–53, gives only the entries for saint's days in the notes to his edition.

2 Nov. Sancti Eustacii cum sociis et Iusti martyris et Aerchi
confessoris. Obitus Aelwoldi monachi.
6 Nov. Sancti Melanii episcopi confessoris.
9 Nov. Obitus Eadulfi episcopi.
12 Nov. Obitus Landberhti piissimi regis.
23 Nov. Obitus Ordlaui laici.
29 Nov. Saturnini martyris.
6 Dec. Sancti Nicholai archiepiscopi.
13 Dec. Hic obiit Ordulfus.
17 Dec. Hic obiit Aelfwerdus sacerdos.
18 Dec. Sancti Lazari episcopi et martyris.

Thanks to Jan Gerchow, we now know that the king named on 11 Nov.
is actually Cnut (1018–35), whose baptismal name had been Lambert; a
good number of the other seculars mentioned are identifiable in the
late-eleventh-century copy of the cathedral's foundation charter still
preserved at Exeter.[51] Two principal scribes seem to have worked on
bringing the calendar up to date. The main scribe, probably Drage's
scribe 10, wrote the entries for:

St Faith (6 Oct.).
St Giraldus (13 Oct.).
St Maglorius, and the translation of St Bartholomew (14 Oct.).
St Melanius (6 Nov.).
Ordlav (23 Nov.).
St Saturninus (29 Nov.).

and perhaps also:

St Edward (18 Mar.).
Lyfingus, bishop of Crediton (19 Mar.).
SS Eustacius, Munulfus, Servacius and Bertinus (16 Jul.).
St Peter's chains (1 Aug.).
Aelfwin, bishop of Winchester (29 Aug.).
St Eustacius, St Iustus, St Aerchus and the obit of Aelwold (2 Nov.).
Ordulfus (13 Dec.).
Aelfwerdus (17 Dec.).

A second, who may have been Drage's scribe 7, added the feasts of St
Giles, the ordination of St Gregory and the obit of Segiva. A third wrote
entries for the feasts of St Nicholas (6 Dec.) and St Lazarus (18 Dec.); a

[51] *LM*, pp. l–li; Drage, *Leofric*, pp. 115–17 and 122–63, and J. Gerchow, *Die
Gedenküberlieferung der Angelsaschen*, Arbeiten zur Fruhmittelalterforschung 20 (Berlin,
1988), pp. 253–7.

222

fourth St Eormenhild and Godo (13 Feb.), St Albinus (1 Mar.), Brihtricus (16 Feb.), St Athanasius (1 May), William the Conqueror (9 Sept.), and perhaps St Afra (4 Aug.) and Eadulf (8 Nov.); and a fifth the obits of Aegflaed (31 Jan.) and Eadric (26 July). All the other additions appear to have been made singly. Drage thought that the obituary notice of Leo IX, which is designated class 'F', had been written by Leofric himself (scribe 1). Although the entry is badly rubbed, this does not seem an unreasonable proposition. As the historical matter at the front of Bodley 579 indicates, Leo approved the foundation of Leofric's see. Drage also suggested that the entry for St Ælfheah and Leofric's ordination had been written by scribe 2, which, again, seems right.

As for the feasts themselves, those of SS Albinus, Maglorius, Melanius and Giraldus, are liable to reflect the direct or indirect influence of some Breton house, perhaps Mont Saint-Michel, or St Michael's Mount. But the abbeys of Landevennec and Quimper are also possible, since Oxford, Bodleian Library, Auct. D. 2. 16, one of Leofric's gospel-books, came from one or other.[52] Most of the other hagiographical entries, on the other hand, are what one might expect: saints of national importance, and those for whom masses were added to *C*. The only feast of a female saint encompassed, besides Faith's, is that of Eormenhild of Ely, presumably to accompany the existing entries for SS Æthelthryth and Sexburh, also of Ely. The additions to the computus by scribe 10 (no. 296 and corrections elsewhere) are slight.

IV. Gathering 22 (fols 155r–157v). Mention has already been made of the renewing of the prayers for the blessing of the incense (*thimiamatum*).[53] That leaves the material added on fols 156r–157v to be considered. First we have the blessing to be said over the ampulles offered by the congregation on Maundy Thursday, *Domine deus omnipotens omnium benedictionum* (no. 1299), which, so far as I have been able to establish, only otherwise occurs in BL Harley 2892, the mid-eleventh-century benedictional from Christ Church, Canterbury. Next we have a blessing each for the episcopal ring and staff (nos 1300–1301), both of which are likely to derive from some copy of the Romano-German Pontifical; and two blessings normally found in

[52] Pierpont Morgan 641 has propers for SS Albinus, Melanius and Giraldus. On the gospel-book see, W. H. Frere, *Studies in Early Roman Liturgy*, 3 vols, Alcuin Club Collections 28, 30 and 32 (Oxford, 1930–5) II, 194–8.
[53] See above, p. 140.

English *ordines* for the dedication of a church: *Deus ad cuius sepulchrum cum aromatibus* (no. 1302) for the thurible; and *Deus qui diversa ad tabernaculum* (no. 1303) for the church goods. *Deus qui diversa* is almost certainly English, only occuring on the continent in books deriving from English models.[54]

V. Gatherings 44–8 (fols 337r–377v). A further supplement of new gatherings, containing an assortment of masses and independent formulae, mainly prefaces, for various occasions and saints' days, and a set of *ordines*, probably adapted from an authoritative copy of the Romano-German Pontifical. Some masses were brought together locally, namely: the mass for 'virgins', which is an assembly of various formulae culled from different sources; and the mass for the dedication of the church of St Mary ad Martyres, which embodies, unexpectedly, a prayer for vespers usually found either in Ambrosian books or books from the diocese of Mainz.[55] However, the most noteworthy items in this section of *C* are the:

Missa de omni caelesti virtute (nos 2698–2701). Probably a tenth or eleventh-century composition. Appears sporadically in books from all over Europe, usually as a mass for the living and dead, but seems particularly at home in England. The collect, secret and postcommunion figure in the sacramentary of Robert of Jumièges, though they may simply have copied from the Lotharingian model; and they are also to be found in the eleventh-century sacramentary from Vich, and in numerous later books.[56] Since mention was originally made in *C* of *episcopus noster*, these prayers will not have been suitable for use by Leofric. The replacing of the words *episcopus noster* by *antistes noster* presumably rectified this. Perhaps the most striking aspect of the mass, however, is its preface, which only otherwise appears in CCCC 422, the so-called 'Red Book of Darley'. That begins to look interesting, for the 'Red Book', as has long been recognised, is essentially a copy of a manual-cum-sacramentary from Winchester written in the mid eleventh century for use in the diocese of Sherborne.[57] Although the Red Book's collects

---

[54] *PRG* I, 220–1 (cap. lxiii, nos 38 and 40). For *Deus ad cuius sepulchrum cum aromatibus* in 'Dunstan' and 'Robert', to take just two examples, see Martene, *AER*, Bk II, cap. xiii, ordo 4, and *The Benedictional of Archbishop Robert*, ed. Wilson, p. 94.

[55] For example, *PRG* I, 175 (cap. xli, no. 6).

[56] Ed. Wilson, *The Missal of Robert of Jumièges*, p. 312; and Olivar, *El sacramentario di Vich*, p. 132, nos 903–5.

[57] CCCC 422, pp. 127–8; *Corpus Prefationum*, ed. Moeller, no. 1356.

are different, its mass is headed *missa in honore omnium celestium et omnium sanctorum*, an intention similar to the one given in *C*. It therefore seems likely that *Quo moriente* somehow became a proper for this type of mass in England, in spite of the fact that its wording seems more suitable for funerals or memorials. Since Sicard did not note its presence in the numerous books he surveyed, further work will have to be undertaken to establish just how unusual it is.

Mass for St Mary Magdalene (nos 2705–13): 22 July. Thanks to Victor Saxer, it seems likely that Leofric acquired his mass from a book akin to BNF lat. 818, the mid-eleventh-century sacramentary from Troyes. BNF lat. 818 has two sets of formulae. The main set consists of the prayers *Largire nobis*, *Hanc nostrae* and *Sanctificet*, and the second has *Sacratissimam* and *Deus qui nos per unigenitum*, as 'spares'. Of these, *C* has *Largire* as its collect (no. 2706), *Deus qui nos per unigenitum* as its first postcommunion (no. 2713), *Sanctificet* in the margins as an alternative (no. 2713*). However, as *C*'s secret is *Offerimus* (no. 2711), a standard 'Eighth-Century Gelasian' for virgins, the Troyes sacramentary, which is probably later than *C* in any case, cannot itself have been the model.[58] But Leofric plainly had access to some cognate text. The only other surviving book to adopt the three three main formulae of *C*'s mass is the late-fourteenth-century missal from Sherborne, now BL Loans 82, which is presumably a sign that Leofric's mass was used at other houses in the west country. Giso of Wells, however, took over a hybrid Norman mass.[59] *C*'s chant is essentially the standard (Vezelay) chant first found in Paris, Bibliothèque nationale de France, lat. 12053, a mid-eleventh-century missal from Lagny.[60] That only the alleluia verse of the mass, *Optimam partem elegit* (no. 2708), should have been fully neumed is probably an indication, as Susan Rankin has suggested, that the notator's object was 'simply to show how [an] old melody, already known in another context, fitted this new text'. In other words, music and text would not have appeared together in the gradual habitually used by Leofric.[61] His strong personal devotion to the Magdalen is evident enough from his collectar, now BL Harley 2961, which embodies proper

---

[58] See V. Saxer, *Le culte de Marie Magdalène en occident*, Cahiers d'archéologie et d'histoire 3 (Paris, 1959), pp. 166–9 and 363–70.

[59] *Missale ad usum ecclesiae Westmonasteriensis,* ed. Legg, III, 1568.

[60] See Saxer, *Le culte de Marie Magdalène*, p. 169, and for a description of the book as a whole, Leroquais, *Les sacramentaires* I, 171–3.

[61] Rankin, 'From memory to record', with a plate of the page in question.

chant, *capitula* and prayers for office on the feast. As Dewick and Frere have shown, these were insertions in the model from which the bulk of the book was copied.[62] Leofric's benedictional, however, makes no proper provision for the feast.

Mass for the feast of St Stephen's invention (nos 2714–24): 3 Aug. As has already been mentioned, *C*'s mass was presumably intended to replace the 'Canterbury' mass provided in *B*, the prayers adopted essentially being those of the mid-eleventh-century missal from the New Minster.[63] However, the picture is less clear when we come to the benediction for the day given in Leofric's benedictional, *Benedictionum omnium uobis copiam*, since this also appears in BL Harley 2892, the so-called 'Canterbury Benedictional', in company with four other English compositions beginning *Benedictionum*. We have *Benedictionum aeternarum copiam* for St Blaise; *Benedictionum omnium auctor christus* for St Luke; *Benedictionum caelestium uos dominus imbre* for the Presentation of the Virgin (21 Nov.); and *Benedictionum omnium largitor* for the ordination of a priest.[64] Few are found elsewhere. Unless one is prepared to suppose that someone at a house other than Canterbury was turning out benedictions based on Canterbury models, a Canterbury origin for this blessing seems certain.

Mass for St Margaret (nos 2729–32): 20 June. Major relics said to have been taken from Antioch to Bolsena, near Rome, in 908. Most of the evidence relating to the cult of the saint in Anglo-Saxon England has been gathered up and printed from all the available pre-Conquest sources by Mary Clayton and Hugh Magennis. They reproduce Leofric's mass in full, giving the text of the preface indicated from *A*, and they publish, usefully, the set of formulae provided in the sacramentary of Giso of Wells.[65] As far as the continent is concerned, a mass of approximately the same date as *C*'s and with the same collect, secret and postcommunion figures in Pierpont Morgan 641, the mid-eleventh-century sacramentary from Mont Saint-Michel. For a French book this is early, for the next in terms of date seems to be Rouen BM 273, the late-eleventh or early-twelfth-century sacramentary of Saint-Évroult, which, as has already been said, is a copy of a book from

---

[62] Ed. Dewick and Frere, *The Leofric Collectar* I, 205–9.
[63] Ed. Turner, *The Missal of the New Minster*, pp. 134–5.
[64] Ed. Woolley, *The Canterbury Benedictional*, pp. 85, 103, 113, 116 and 129.
[65] M. Clayton and H. Magennis, *The Old English Lives of St Margaret* (Cambridge, 1994), pp. 72–83.

Thorney or Crowland taken abroad by Orderic Vitalis.[66] But France and England apart, the place to look for early propers is Italy. Ebner records Bologna, Biblioteca dell'Universita, 2547, a late-eleventh or early-twelfth-century sacramentary from Brescia, but there will presumably be others of a much earlier date.[67] Their prayers are liable to be: *Deus qui beatam uirginam margaretam hodierna die ad celos*; *Haec uictima domine quesumus pro beatae uirginis margaretae*; and *Huius domine sacramenti perceptione*, which are the prayers of the dozen or so Italian books I have consulted.[68] It seems safe to say therefore that *C* contains a 'French' or 'Anglo-Saxon' form of mass. *C*'s mass also re-appears later at Sherborne, but judging by BL Add. 28188, Leofric had no proper benediction.[69]

Mass for St Alban (nos 2733–7), 22 June. The collect, secret and postcommunion are the same as those of the sacramentary of Robert of Jumièges; BNF lat. 819, the late-eleventh-century sacramentary of Saint-Bertin, copied from an English model similar to Robert's book; Laon BM 238, the mid-twelfth-century missal from Bury St Edmunds; and in missals printed for the chapter of Prague Cathedral.[70] The preface is only otherwise preserved in 'Robert', though. *C*'s alternative post-communion is unique. Again, Leofric seems not to have had a proper benediction.

Proper Prefaces (nos 2749–62, 2824–40 and 2855–70). These, together with the series of masses and *ordines* that are interspersed, are arranged as a 'mini temporal and sanctoral', and were presumably introduced with a view to modifying *A*, or at least governing how it was to be used. *C*'s prefaces are therefore Leofric's 'preferred' forms. That he did not make notes, where relevant, in *A*'s margins, may simply indicate that he was reluctant to clutter *A* unduly with supplementary material. Most of his additions are either in the form of cues for chant, or textual correc-tions. The only sizeable insertions of new matter, as we have seen, are those in gathering 22.

---

[66] See Leroquais, *Les sacramentaires* I, 177.

[67] Ebner, *Quellen*, p. 14.

[68] For instance, Oxford, Bodleian Library, Lat. lit. d. 4, a late-eleventh- or early-twelfth-century sacramentary from Como; and the mid-twelfth-century sacramentary from Fonte Avellana, ed. PL 151, col. 894.

[69] For Sherborne, see *Missale ad usum ecclesiae Westmonasteriensis*, ed. Legg, III, 1566–7.

[70] *The Missal of Robert of Jumièges*, ed. Wilson, pp. 5–6; BNF lat. 819, 85v; Laon BM 238, fol. 120.

Ordines for Palm Sunday, Maundy Thursday and Good Friday (nos 2762–2823). The order for Palm Sunday, which appears to be an abrigement of something longer, is not to be found in the form given in *C* elsewhere. The *ordines* for Maundy Thursday and Good Friday, however, run in parallel with the form of *Ordo romanus L* preserved in London, British Library, Additional 17004, an eleventh-century copy of the Romano-German Pontifical written for use at the cathedral of Minden, in the province of Cologne, and later at Amiens. The book is Andrieu's 'J'.[71] According to Andrieu's system of numbering, the order of pieces embodied in *C* is:

> *Feria v*: the penitential order omitted, *C* begins with an abriged form of mass. We then have *Ordo romanus L*, cap. xxv, nos 70–1, 138, 73–87, 88 and note, 90–92, 142, 93–109.
>
> *Feria vi*: runs as *Ordo romanus L*, cap. xxvii, nos 1–14, 32–4, 40, 44.

As Michael Lapidge has indicated, several other manuscripts produced in England, besides *C*, follow the arrangement given in BL Add. 17004:

> Cambridge, Corpus Christi College, 163: copied in the mid eleventh century from a model originally prepared for use at Cologne at some point after 1021, as an invocation of Archbishop Heribert, who died in that year, figures along with those of a number of other Cologne saints in its litany for the dedication of a church.[72] No invocations of English saints were interposed. Indeed, the only local material to have been introduced by CCCC 163's scribe occurs at the end of the book. As Lapidge has demonstrated, this 'supplement', which includes a blessing for a statue of St Swithun, is connectable with Ealdred, archbishop of York (1060–69), who had extensive dealings with Archbishop Herimann II of Cologne on his embassy in Germany. CCCC 163 is therefore likely to be a copy of a book brought back from the continent by Ealdred. However, the pontifical can hardly have been 'copied at or for use in a nunnery', as has been proposed. For the RGP is a book designed for use by bishops or archbishops. That no provision was made in CCCC 163 for the consecra-

---

[71] Ed. *OR* V, 186–260. For an account of the manuscript, see Lapidge, 'The origin of CCCC 163', pp. 19–20. A Cologne provenance must be ruled out, however, even though Archbishop Herimann's name is entered in the *Precamur* clause of the Exultet prayer. Not only is the book's litany not that of Cologne, but St Gorgonius, patron of Minden appears prominently among the confessors. A true Cologne litany is to be found in CCCC 163, ed. Lapidge, *Anglo-Saxon Litanies*, pp. 106–8.
[72] See M. Lapidge, 'The origin of CCCC 163', *Transactions of the Cambridge Bibliographical Society* 8 (1981–5), 18–28.

tion of monks or abbots is simply likely to mean, if the lack of these *ordines* does turn out to be at all significant, that the chapter over which the book's owner presided was secular rather than monastic.

London, British Library, Cotton Vitellius E. xii: a mid-eleventh-century German pontifical that later found its way to Exeter. As Lapidge has demonstrated, a gathering containing a set of *laudes* composed in honour of William the Conqueror between the 11th of May 1068 and the 11th of September 1069, was appended by Drage's scribe 2.[73] It is not certain, however, *pace* Lapidge, that the volume once belonged to Archbishop Ealdred.

and London, British Library, Cotton Tiberius C. i: written in the mid twelfth century, either on the continent, or by a continental scribe in England. Augmented with supplementary material by a number of English and continental scribes at Sherborne. Later transferred to Salisbury, possibly after 1075. Note that the blessings for an episcopal ring and staff, *Creator et conseruator* and *Deus sine quo nihil*, also had to be added, as they were in *C*.[74]

Specimen collation shows that the texts of all five English manuscripts are close. However, *C* has an important variant that sets it somewhat apart. Whereas 'J' and the other four English books have *Subdiaconi autem stent retro altare, vertentes se ad altare, et ibi sicut ceteri flectentes genua* at cap. xxvii, no. 32, *C* gives *Subdiaconi stant retro altare, et ibi sicut ceteri flectentes genua*. The only other manuscript known to omit the words *uertentes se ad altare* is Andrieu's 'Q' (a twin of 'J'): Wolfenbüttel, Landesbibliothek, 164, a twelfth-century copy of the Romano-German Pontifical probably from Verden Cathedral.[75] Leofric presumably had a similar book. That he should have had excerpts from it copied into *C* is striking, but not without parallel. Giso had excerpts from the Wells pontifical copied into his sacramentary, BL Cotton Vitellius A. xviii; and a mid-eleventh-century sacramentary containing extracts from the *RGP*'s prescriptions for Holy Week (though not the same as those in English books) has come down to us from Liège in the shape of Bamberg, Staatliche Bibliothek, Lit. 3.[76] Andrieu sug-

[73] See Lapidge, 'Ealdred of York', pp. 11–25.
[74] Fol. 43r. For a brief comments on the book, see Webber, *Scribes and Scholars*, pp. 10, 12, 143–4 and 145, and N. R. Ker, 'Three Old English Texts in a Salisbury Pontifical, Cotton Tiberius C. i', *The Anglo-Saxons. Studies in some Aspects of their History and Culture Presented to Bruce Dickins*, ed. P. Clemoes (London, 1959), pp. 262–79.
[75] See *OR* I, 419–20.
[76] For a description of this book, see M. Schott, *Zwei Lütticher Sakramentare in Bamberg*

gested that the presence of the *RGP* in England ought to be connected with the arrival of Lotharingian clergy in England during the reign of Edward the Confessor (1042–65). Where Leofric is concerned, he was probably correct.[77] However, as Lapidge has demonstrated, at least one copy came from Cologne in the baggage of Ealdred of York. Quite how Leofric might have squared the *ordines* embodied in *C* with the material provided in his pontifical, BL Cotton Vitellius A. vii, and his benedictional, BL Add. 28188, is hard to say. Perhaps the pontifical and benedictional are slightly later.

Mass for the feast of the Conception of St John the Baptist (nos 2899–2908), 24 Sept. As we have seen, in England, masses for this feast seem only to have been provided in books from the West Country.[78] The prayers adopted in *C* are, however, not to be found elsewhere. No benediction given in BL Add. 28188.

Mass for a King and Queen (nos 2909–11). Probably composed at Exeter. Not found elsewhere.

Mass for the feast of the Ordination of St Gregory (nos 2912–14): 3 Sept. The collect and secret of this mass were evidently once Italian propers for feasts of St Ambrose, a fellow Church Father. At some point, however, probably in France, the formulae seem to have been adapted for St Gregory's ordination. The earliest known books to make provision for the day are: BNF lat. 10500, the sacramentary of Hughes de Salines; Besançon, Bibliothèque municipale, 72, a late-eleventh-century sacramentary from the church of La Madeleine in Besançon; and Rouen BM 273, the late-eleventh or early-twelfth-century sacramentary of Saint-Évroult.[79] It is well to note too that a mass for the day was later copied into CCCC 270, the late-eleventh-century sacramentary from St Augustine's, Canterbury. But this simply consists of a set of commons rather carelessly adapted.[80] Again, no benediction is given in BL Add. 28188.

---

und Paris und ihre Verwandten (Strassburg, 1931); and the catalogue, *Rhein und Maas, Kunst und Kultur 800–1400. Eine Ausstellung des Schnütgen-Museums der Stadt Köln, vom 14 Mai bis 23 Juli, 1972*, ed. A. Legner, 2 vols (Cologne, 1972) I, 229–30.

[77] Leofric was summoned to England by Edward in the 1040s and became his chaplain. Edward later attended Leofric's enthronement at Exeter. See Barlow, *The English Church 1000–1066*, pp. 45–6, 116–17, 154 and 156.

[78] See above, pp. 167–8.

[79] Leroquais, *Les sacramentaires* I, 141, 174 and 177.

[80] Ed. Rule, *The Missal of St Augustine's*, p. 130.

Mass for the feast of the Conception of the Virgin (nos 2915–17). As Edmund Bishop noted in the late 1890s, the feast of the Conception was celebrated before the Conquest at Canterbury, Winchester, Worcester, Exeter and perhaps elsewhere too. Proper formulae are rare, but Leofric's are the same as those given in the New Minster Missal, as has already been mentioned, so Winchester or Canterbury may have been their source.[81] Winchester, however, looks more likely since the Exeter benediction for the day preserved in BL Add. 28188 is not the one used at Christ Church.[82]

Mass for a friend in adversity (nos 2918–20). Probably composed at Exeter. Not found elsewhere.

Mass in honour of St Faith (nos 2927–9): 6 Nov. Relics at the great pilgrimage church of Sainte-Foi, Conques. Proper chant for the feast composed by Ainard (d. 1078), the German abbot of Dives (near Rouen), the house later known as Sainte-Catherine-au-Mont.[83] The earliest books in which proper masses occur, however, are apparently: Rouen BM 272, the early-eleventh-century sacramentary from Saint-Wandrille; BNF lat. 821, the eleventh-century sacramentary from an abbey in the Limousin; and Montpellier BM 18, the eleventh-century sacramentary from the abbey of Gellone. Leofric was therefore pretty well up to date, having a version of the standard 'Norman' mass, not the rarer, later one that found its way into the Sarum Missal.[84] But no proper benediction is embodied in his benedictional.

Mass in honour of St Lazarus (nos 2935–7). Brother of Mary Madgalen and Martha, and venerated principally at the cathedral of Saint-Lazaire at Autun on the 17th of December, which was the day of his martyrdom or *natalis*; and on the 1st of September, the day of his 'sollemnity', as in the fragment of a twelfth-century collectar now preserved at Wells.[85] Marseilles, claiming him as first bishop, celebrated his feast in August.

[81] Ed. Turner, *The Missal of the New Minster*, p. 190.
[82] Gasquet and Bishop, *The Bosworth Psalter*, p. 15, with E. Bishop, 'On the origins of the feast of the Conception of the the Blessed Virgin Mary' in his *Liturgica Historica* (Oxford, 1918), pp. 238–59, where the texts of both benedictions are published. For the calendars, see *EK*, pp. 125, 167 and 223.
[83] Orderic Vitalis, *Historia Ecclesiastica*, ed. M. Chibnall, 6 vols (Oxford, 1969–80) II, 12–13, 352–5.
[84] See Leroquais, *Les sacramentaires* I, 135, 157 and 160, and Legg, *The Sarum Missal*, p. 332.
[85] See Watkin, 'A fragment of a collectar'.

According to Holweck, he was sometimes confused with St Lazarus, bishop of Aix.[86] But in *C* we are presumably dealing with the Biblical figure and an Autun text as the collect reads: *Deus qui per unigenitum <filium> tuum beatum lazarum quatriduanum mortuum resuscitasti a monumento.*[87] As Richard Pfaff has pointed out, the presence of a proper mass is one of the most striking aspects of *C*.[88] That a relic of the saint had been acquired by the community at Exeter by the eleventh century probably counts for little, since no other surviving book from the house gives any indication whatsoever that his cult was at all important or well-established. From a formal standpoint, therefore, it looks as though Leofric formed some sort of personal devotion to the saint, probably acquiring his copy of the mass from some Burgundian book. Leroquais records propers in Paris, BNF lat. 10500, the sacramentary of Hughes de Salines; BNF lat. 821, the mid-eleventh-century sacramentary from an abbey in the Limousin; and Paris, Bibliothèque municipale, lat. 823, an early-twelfth-century missal from the abbey of Remiremont, but only the first seems to have anything further in common with *C*.[89] No benediction figures in BL Add. 28188.

VI. Masses with chant. Thirteen are provided with a full set of pieces, that is to say, an introit, gradual, gradual verse, alleluia verse, offertory and communion. Sometimes these are given in full and neumed, but mostly they appear in the form of cues. The masses concerned are for:

those tempted; the bishop; penitents; familiars; tribulations; peace; journeyers; a faithful friend; the anniversary of the dedication of a church; St John the Baptist; St Mary Magdalene; the feast of the Invention of St Stephen; and the ordination of a bishop.

Presumably these were the feasts for which no suitable parts were provided either in *A*, or in the gradual that Leofric had to hand. As Rankin

[86] F. G. Holweck, *A Biographical Dictionary of the Saints* (St Louis, MO, 1924), pp. 196–7.
[87] See M. Pellechet, *Notes sur les livres liturgiques des diocèses d'Autun, Chalon et Mâcon* (Paris, 1883), p. 231.
[88] R. W. Pfaff, 'Massbooks', *The Liturgical Books of Anglo-Saxon England*, ed. R. W. Pfaff, Old English Newsletter Subsidia 23 (Michigan, 1995), p. 14.
[89] See Leroquais, *Les sacramentaires* I, 141, 157 and 189. On Hughes and Autun, see L. Seidel, *Legends in Limestone. Lazarus, Gislebertus and the Cathedral of Autun* (Chicago, 1999), pp. 56–7.

has indicated, Leofric probably undertook the work of notating select cues in A's margins himself.[90]

VII. At much the same time, Leofric also added short cues in A's margins, in some cases only the first word or two of the passage concerned, for the Epistle and Gospel readings at mass. These have been examined in detail by Ursula Lenker, and appear for the most part to be fairly standard, conforming principally to the lists of readings given in certain pericope lectionaries belonging to Antoine Chavasse's 'Type 3B'.[91] Given that Le Havre BM 330, the 'New Minster Missal', also belongs to this type, it is possible that the book used by Leofric originally issued from Winchester. Surprisingly, however, cues were only entered in A's sanctoral for:

St Stephen.	St Peter.
St John.	St Paul.
The Holy Innocents.	Vigil of St Lawrence.
St Silvester.	St Lawrence.
Conversion of St Paul.	Vigil of the Assumption.
SS Philip and James.	The Assumption.
Invention of the Cross.	Nativity of the Virgin.
Dedication of the church of St Mary Martyr.	St Michael.
	Vigil of All Saints.
Vigil of St John the Baptist.	All Saints.
St John the Baptist.	Vigil of St Andrew.
Vigil of SS Peter and Paul.	Feast of St Andrew.

Drage wondered whether these were the only saints' days much venerated at Exeter under Leofric. But the list of prefaces encompassed towards the end of C shows that this is unlikely to have been the case. Rather, it seems better to suppose that these were the feasts, and all are major feasts of the church year, on which Leofric might have read in his cathedral.

[90] Rankin, 'From memory to record', 100, n. 14.
[91] U. Lenker, *Die westsächsiche Evangelienversion und die Perikopenordnung im angelsächsischen England*, Texte und Untersuchung zur englischen Philologie 20 (Munich, 1997), pp. 118–19, 177, 195–200, 267–8, 481–6.

Conclusion

The material added to Bodley 579 at Exeter falls broadly into two classes: on the one hand, we have the texts that Leofric will have said in private (it is hardly conceivable that the mass for the bishop of Exeter was for any other purpose); on the other, the *ordines*, prayers, blessings, and 'supplementary' formulae reserved for his use in public, that is to say, in the cathedral, on days with special intentions. We see considerably more of Leofric in *C* than we do of Giso of Wells in BL Cotton Vitellius A. xviii. Indeed, in liturgical eclectiscism, Leofric seems to have excelled. He acquired material from Winchester, Canterbury and North Elmham, probably with the assistance of Stigand, or one of Stigand's deputies; he had access to books from Normandy and the south of France; and he had clearly managed either to obtain manuscripts in Lotharingia during his time there or have them sent later. Leofric appears to have been something of a magpie, though one suspects that force of circumstance played its part too: Crediton in 1046 and Exeter in 1050 were in a pitiful state of disarray. But his approach to collecting, wholly admirable as it may have been, evidently had its drawbacks: he ended up with a series of books that were, in many important respects, wholly incompatible with each other. One only has to look to the pontificals to see that; and *C*, too, has its pecularities, not least of which is the absence of any formulae (or entry in the calendar) for the feast of St Olaf (29 July), whose name figures in all Exeter litanies, and whose cult was important enough to warrant an extensive office in Leofric's collectar. Perhaps the prayers necessary for mass were written out in a sacramentary or missal that has not survived.[92] Yet for all that, the general picture is clear enough: Leofric's collection of liturgical texts, as a collection, is without parallel; and it is all the more remarkable that he should have chosen (and preserved) as the basis for his missal a book once owned by St Dunstan.

---

[92] Ed. Dewick and Frere, *The Leofric Collectar* I, cols 209–14.

BIBLIOGRAPHY

I. PRIMARY SOURCES

Manuscripts

Albi, Bibliothèque Rochegude
  34: 60, 119, 121

Angers, Bibliothèque municipale
  80: 149
  90: 168
  91: 126

Arras, Bibliothèque municipale
  271: 128
  297: 128
  309: 128
  339: 127
  391: 128
  444: 7n
  448: 128
  601: 127
  606: 127
  637: 68
  812: 68
  1045: 19

Avranches, Bibliothèque municipale
  42: 214, 215

Baltimore, Walters Art Gallery
  W. 6 ('The Missal of Canosa'): 81

Bamberg, Staatliche Bibliothek
  D. 3: 229

Basel, Universitätsbibliothek
  F. iii. 15e: 42

Bergamo, Biblioteca di San
  Alessandro in Colonna
  s. n.: 81, 109, 163

Berlin, Deutsche Staatsbibliothek
  Phillipps 1667 ('The Phillipps
  Sacramentary'): 63
  Phillipps 1731: 70

Berne, Burgerbibliothek
  289: 54

Besançon, Bibliothèque municipale
  72: 230

Bologna, Biblioteca Universitaria
  2457: 227

Boulogne, Bibliothèque municipale
  637: 68n

Brescia, Biblioteca Queriniana
  G. VI. 7: 82

Brussels, Bibliothèque royale
  7524–55: 69

Cambrai, Bibliothèque municipale
  162–3: 18, 28–9, 38, 51, 53, 56, 60,
  97, 131, 162
  164: 28

Cambridge, Corpus Christi College
  9: 176

41: 197
44: 76–7, 94, 104, 106, 108, 141,
204n
57: 176
146: 75, 78, 87, 90, 91, 95, 104,
106, 108, 142, 151
163: 228–9
190: 207–8
270 ('The St Augustine's Missal'):
59, 169, 170, 172, 173, 175, 196,
230
391 ('The Portiforium of St
Wulfstan'): 90, 163, 164, 165,
202, 218
422 ('The Red Book of Darley'):
122, 176, 224

Cambridge, Pembroke College
308: 12

Cambridge, Sidney Sussex College
100: 218

Cambridge, Trinity College
241: 207
249: 77, 154

Cambridge University Library
Ii. 4. 20: 61
Kk. 5. 32: 54n, 163, 166, 169, 176
Ll. 2. 10: 77

Chartres, Bibliothèque municipale
47: 127
577: 19

Cologne, Dombibliothek
88: 197
106: 40, 68
137: 197

Dijon, Bibliothèque municipale
122: 149

Douai, Bibliothèque municipale
67 ('The Pontifical of Thomas a
Becket'): 77, 106
91: 128
170: 167

Downside Abbey
26536: 78–9

Dublin, Royal Academy
D. II. 3 ('The Stowe Missal'): 111,
114–15

Dublin, Trinity College
98: 77

Durham Cathedral Library
A. IV. 19 ('The Durham Collectar'):
31, 90, 92, 97, 164

Düsseldorf, Universitäts- und
Landesbibliothek
D. 1: 126
D. 2: 118

Florence, Biblioteca Medicea
Laurenziana
Edili 121: 89

Florence, Biblioteca Nazionale
B. R. 231: 201

Freiburg-im-Breisgau,
Universitätsbibliothek
363: 30, 98

Frontale, Chiesa parrochiale di S.
Anna
s. n.: 142

Göttingen, Universitätsbibliothek
theol. 231: 40, 58, 64, 93, 96, 119,
121, 146–7, 174

Heidelburg, Universitäts-Bibliothek
Sal. IXb: 59, 139

Ivrea, Biblioteca Capitolare
10: 28n
31: 28n

Laon, Bibliothèque municipale
226: 7n
236: 215
238: 202, 227

Le Havre, Bibliothèque municipale
330 ('The New Minster Missal'):
170, 171, 172, 175, 197, 202, 233

Le Mans, Bibliothèque municipale
23: 128
77: 17

Lerida, Archivo Capitular
16: 40, 62, 119, 121, 143

Lille, Bibliothèque municipale
23: 127

London, British Library
Add. 7138: 80n
Add. 17004: 214n, 228–9
Add. 26685: 79n
Add. 28188: 76n, 207, 218, 220, 227, 230
Add. 35717 ('The Bosworth Psalter'): 8, 54, 158–84
Add. 36678 ('The Lothar Psalter'): 12–13, 21
Add. 43406: 177
Add. 49598 ('The Benedictional of St Æthelwold'): 171, 175
Add. 57337 ('The Anderson Pontifical'): 75–6, 94, 95–6, 104, 106, 108, 140, 196
Arundel 155: 204
Cotton Claudius A. iii ('The Claudius Pontificals'): 87, 90, 204n
Cotton Galba A. xviii ('The Æthelstan Psalter'): 69–70, 188
Cotton Nero A. ii: 166, 172, 173
Cotton Tiberius B. iii: 83
Cotton Tiberius B. v: 184–94
Cotton Tiberius C. i: 229
Cotton Tiberius C. vi: 188, 189
Cotton Titus D. xxvii and xxviii ('Ælfwine's Prayerbook'): 185, 191, 193, 218
Cotton Vespasian D. xv: 41
Cotton Vitellius A. vii ('The Ramsey Pontifical'): 76n, 77, 90, 140–1, 207, 230
Cotton Vitellius A. xii: 54, 176

Cotton Vitellius A. xviii ('The Sacramentary of Giso of Wells'): 65, 83n, 94–5, 167, 174, 175, 176, 201, 220n, 225, 229, 234
Cotton Vitellius E. xii: 229
Harley 585: 92
Harley 863 ('The Leofric Psalter'): 216n
Harley 2961 ('The Leofric Collectar'): 48, 208, 225
Harley 2892 ('The Canterbury Benedictional'): 87, 94, 167, 170, 171, 175, 183, 198, 203, 204, 223, 226
Harley 2991: 27
Harley 3271: 167, 203
Harley 3667: 189
Harley 5289 ('The Durham Missal'): 41
Lansdowne 451: 79
Loans 36 (14): 26–7, 49
Loans 82 ('The Sherborne Missal'): 167, 168n, 176, 201, 225, 227
Royal 2. A. xx: 69
Royal 2. D. xvii: 111
Stowe 944 ('The Liber Vitae of the New Minster'): 90

Macerata, Biblioteca Comunale, 'Mozzi-Borgetti'
378: 122

Madrid, Academia de la Historia
56: 142

Mainz, Seminarbibliothek
1: 81

Milan, Biblioteca Ambrosiana
A. 24 bis. inf.: 35, 46
DSP 10/27 bis: 33, 65n, 176
M. 12 Sup.: 172

Milan, Biblioteca del Capitolo metropolitano
14: 96, 98
21: 261
D. 3–3: 35, 47

Modena, Biblioteca Capitolare
102: 167

Monte Cassino, Biblioteca
dell'Abbazia
257: 105
451: 106

Montpellier, Bibliothèque municipale
12: 42
18: 220, 231
409: 69

Montpellier, Bibliothèque de la
Faculte de Medecin
314: 138

Monza, Biblioteca Capitolare
f1/101: 53

Munich, Bayerische Hauptstaats-
archiv
Rariten-Selekt 108: 53

Munich, Staatsbibliothek
Clm 3903: 122
Clm 6420: 153
Clm 17027: 111

Nantes, Musée Dobrée
s. n.: 138

New York, Pierpont Morgan Library
641: 214, 217, 226
Glazier 57: 17

Orléans, Bibliothèque municipale
127 ('The Winchcombe
Sacramentary'): 43

Oxford, Bodleian Library
Auct. D. 2. 16: 223
Barlow 7: 41
Bodley 718: 42–3
Bodley 775 ('The Winchester
Troper'): 198
Canon Lit. 320: 48
Canon Lit. 321: 71
Canon Lit. 344: 201

Canon Lit. 345: 48
Canon Lit. 350: 89
Douce 296 ('The Crowland
Psalter'): 141n
Hatton 113: 176, 177
Laud Misc. 482: 122
Rawlinson Lit. g. 10: 197

Oxford, Corpus Christi College
282 ('The Corpus Irish Missal): 198

Oxford, Magdalen College
226 ('The Magdalen College
Pontifical'): 41, 145

Oxford, St John's College
17: 184–94

Padua, Biblioteca Capitolare
D. 47 ('The Padua Sacramentary'):
35, 97

Paris, Bibliothèque de l'Arsenal
227 ('The Pontifical of Poitiers'):
39, 68, 91

Paris, Bibliothèque nationale de France
lat. 816: 52
lat. 817: 168
lat. 818: 120, 220, 225
lat. 819: 54, 101–2, 199, 227
lat. 821: 220, 231, 232
lat. 823: 232
lat. 843: 128
lat. 874: 128
lat. 943 ('The Pontifical of St
Dunstan'): 70, 74, 93, 95, 104,
106, 108, 149, 151, 196
lat. 1095: 128
lat. 1141: 35
lat. 1217: 149
lat. 1218 ('The Pontifical of David
of Bernham'): 95, 145
lat. 1238: 26
lat. 2290: 12, 60, 63
lat. 2291: 24, 126, 162, 202
lat. 2292: 82n
lat. 2297: 164, 168

lat. 2812: 59
lat. 9428 ('The Sacramentary of
    Drogo of Metz'): 24
lat. 9429: 196
lat. 9430: 125, 163
lat. 9432: 19, 32, 34, 47, 119
lat. 9433 ('The Sacramentary of
    Echternach'): 46, 52, 58, 118, 121
lat. 9439: 138
lat. 10062: 171–2
lat. 10500: 11, 164, 217, 230, 232
lat. 10504: 38
lat. 10575 ('The Egbert Pontifical'):
    68, 84, 91, 99–100, 104, 151
lat. 11522: 198
lat. 11532: 12
lat. 12048 ('The Sacramentary of
    Gellone'): 25, 35, 36–7, 47, 62,
    84–5, 86, 91, 92, 93, 113, 151–2,
    153, 154–5, 220
lat. 12050 ('The Sacramentary of
    Hrodradus'): 126
lat. 12051 ('The Missale sancti
    Eligii'): 19, 25–6, 43, 51, 150
lat. 12052 ('The Sacramentary of
    Ratoldus'): 27, 74, 90, 100n, 106,
    112, 126, 149, 150, 195
lat. 12053: 225
lat. 12294: 12
lat. 13258 ('The Bobbio Missal'):
    108, 115
lat. 13764: 45
lat. 14832: 77–8
lat. 17306: 217
nouv. acq. lat. 306
nouv. acq. lat. 424: 214
nouv. acq. lat. 1589: 125, 155

Paris, Bibliothèque S. Genéviève
    111: 126

Prague, Metropolitan Library
    O. 83 ('The Prague Sacramentary'):
    50, 96

Reims, Bibliothèque municipale
    213: 18, 19, 49, 52, 124, 125, 162,
    165, 166

214: 37n, 101–2, 126
225: 128
226: 128
229: 128
231: 128
232: 128
304: 164

Rome, Biblioteca Nazionale
    1565 (Sessorianus 96): 31, 89
    2081 (Sessorianus 95): 40, 120, 121

Rome, Biblioteca Vallicellana
    B. 8: 45
    C. 32: 71, 115–16
    E. 15: 156
    E. 52: 48
    F. 88: 71

Rouen, Bibliothèque municipale
    272: 94, 104, 142, 217, 231
    273: 200, 226, 230
    274 ('The Missal of Robert of
    Jumièges'): 61, 90, 91, 119, 137,
    170, 171, 172, 174, 176, 197, 199,
    217, 219, 224
    298: 200
    368 ('The Lanalet Pontifical'): 76,
    90, 93, 95, 99–100, 122, 140, 151,
    196
    369 ('The Benedictional of
    Archbishop Robert'): 70–1, 75,
    93, 95–6, 104, 140, 143–4, 150,
    151–2, 196
    566: 10–11

St Florian, Bibliothek des
    Chorrenstiftes
    XI. 464: 122
    XI. 467: 120, 121, 122

St Petersburg, Public Library
    Q. v. I. 41: 11, 17, 43

Salerno, Archivio Capitolare
    3: 154

Salisbury Cathedral Library
150 ('The Salisbury Psalter'): 54,
166, 173, 193

Silos Abbey
'Codex Silensis': 152

Solothürn, Zentralbibliothek
U. 1: 172

Stockholm, Kungligla Bibliotheket
Holm A. 136: 18, 24

Toulouse, Bibliothèque municipale
119: 78

Tours, Bibliothèque municipale
184: 125
196: 27

Trent, Museo Diocesano
43: 201

Trent, Museo Provinciale d'Arte
(Castel del Buonconsiglio)
1590 ('The Sacramentary of
Trent'): 57, 114, 124

Troyes, Bibliothèque municipale
2141: 150

Vatican City, Biblioteca Apostolica
Vaticana
Barberini, Gr. 636: 89
Barberini Lat. 560: 89
Chigi C. V. 134: 36, 62, 72
Ottob. lat. 145: 48
Ottob. lat. 313: 69, 126
S. Pietro B. 78: 45
S. Pietro F. 11: 165
S. Pietro F. 12: 44
S. Pietro F. 14: 45, 165
Vat. lat. 290: 190
Vat. lat. 4770: 71, 89, 162, 163
Vat. lat. 4772: 40, 162
Vat. Pal. lat. 485: 91
Vat. Reg. lat. 257 ('The Missale
Francorum'): 74

Vat. Reg. lat. 316 ('The Old or
Vatican Gelasian Sacramentary'):
5, 46–7, 84, 85
Vat. Reg. lat. 317 ('The Missale
Gothicum'): 4, 33
Vat. Reg. lat. 567: 35

Venice, Biblioteca Marciana
lat. III, CXXIV: 154

Vercelli, Biblioteca Capitolare
s. n.: 136

Verona, Biblioteca Comunale
85 ('The Leonine Sacramentary'): 51
86: 139
87 ('The Sacramentary of Wolfgang
of Regensburg'): 28, 172
91: 139

Vich, Museo Episcopal
66 ('The Vich Sacramentary'): 42,
60, 137, 202, 216, 218–19, 224
67: 62, 216

Vienna, Österreichische
Nationalbibliothek
lat. 958: 18
lat. 1815: 219
lat. 1888: 40, 92, 110, 119, 121
Vindob. ser. nov. 2762 ('The
Pontifical of Baturich'): 30, 97–8

Volterra, Biblioteca Guarnacciana
XLVIII. 2. 3: 41

Wolfenbüttel, Herzog August. –
Bibliothek
Helmst 1151 '(The Missal of
Flaccus Illyricus'): 34, 135, 137,
147–8

Wolfenbüttel Landesbibliothek
164: 229

Zurich, Zentralbibliothek
C. 161: 68
Rheinau 43: 124

240

Editions of Sacramentaries and Missals

Das älteste erreichbare Gestalt des Liber sacramentorum anni circuli der romischen Kirche, ed A. Baumstark and K. Mohlberg, Liturgiegeschichtliche Quellen und Forschungen 11–12 (Münster-im-Westfalen, 1927).

Das ambrosianische Sakramentar D. 3–3 aus dem mailändischen Metro-politankapitel, ed. J. Frei, Corpus Ambrosiano-Liturgicum 3, LQF 56 (Münster-im-Westfalen, 1974).

Das ambrosianische Sakramentar von Biasca, ed. O. Heiming, Corpus Ambrosiano Liturgico 2, LQF 51 (Münster-im-Westfalen, 1969).

The Bec Missal, ed. A. Hughes, HBS 94 (London, 1963).

The Bobbio Missal, a Gallican Mass-Book, ed. E. A. Lowe, with J. W. Legg, A. Wilmart and H. A. Wilson, 3 vols, HBS 53, 58 and 61 (London, 1917–24).

Canon Missae Romanae, ed. L. Eizenhöfer, 2 vols, Rerum ecclesiasticarum Documenta, Series minor, Subsidia studiorum 1 and 7 (Rome, 1954–66).

Codice necrologico-liturgico de monasterio di San Salvator o S. Guilia in Brescia, ed. A. Valentini (Brescia, 1887).

Das Drogo-Sakramentar, ed. in facsimile F. Mütherich and W. R. W. Koehler, Codices Selecti phototypice impressi 49 (Graz, 1974), with F. Unterkircher, *Zur Iconographie und Liturgie des Drogo-Sakramentars* (Graz, 1977).

The Gelasian Sacramentary, ed. H. A. Wilson (Oxford, 1894).

Gerbert, M., *Monumenta veteris liturgicae Alemmanicae*, 2 vols (Saint-Blaise, 1777–8).

The Gregorian Sacramentary under Charles the Great, ed. H. A. Wilson, HBS 49 (London, 1915).

Karolingisches Sakramentar-Fragment, ed. F. Unterkircher, Codices Selecti phototypice impressi 25 (Graz, 1971).

The Leofric Missal as used in the Cathedral of Exeter during the episcopate of its first bishop A.D. 1050–1072, together with some account of the Red Book of Derby, the Missal of Robert of Jumièges, and a few other Early Manuscript Service Books of the English Church, ed. F. E. Warren (Oxford, 1883).

Liber Sacramentorum Augustodunensis, ed. O. Heiming, CCSL 159B (Turnhout, 1984).

Liber Sacramentorum Engolismensis, ed. P. Saint-Roch, CCSL 159C (Turnhout, 1987).

Liber Sacramentorum Gellonensis, ed. A. Dumas and J. Deshusses, 2 vols, CCSL 159 and 159A (Turnhout, 1981).

Liber Sacramentorum Romanae ecclesiae ordinis anni circuli, ed. L. C. Mohlberg, Rerum ecclesiasticarum Documenta, Series maior, Fontes 4 (Rome, 1960).

The Manuscript Irish Missal belonging to the President and Fellows of Corpus Christi College, Oxford, ed. F. E. Warren (Oxford, 1888).

'Il messaletto votivo e rituale di Ugo', ed. M. Bocci, *De sancti Hugonis actis liturgicis*, Documenti della Chiesa Volteranna 1 (Florence, 1984), pp. 233–327.

The Missal of the New Minster, Winchester, ed. D. H. Turner, HBS 93 (London, 1962).

The Missal of Robert of Jumièges, ed. H. A. Wilson, HBS 11 (London, 1896).

The Missal of St Augustine's Abbey, Canterbury, ed. M. Rule (Cambridge, 1896).

Missale Beneventanum von Canosa, ed. K. Gamber and S. Rehle, Textus Liturgici et Patristici 9 (Regensburg, 1972).

'Missale sancti Eligii', ed. PL 78, cols 25–582.

Missale Francorum, ed. L. C. Mohlberg, Rerum ecclesiasticarum Documenta, Series maior, Fontes 2 (Rome, 1957).

Missale Gothicum, ed. H. M. Bannister, 2 vols, HBS 52 and 54 (London, 1917–19).

Missale Gothicum, ed. L. C. Mohlberg, Rerum ecclesiasticarum Documenta, Series maior, Fontes 5 (Rome, 1961).

Missale sanctorum Patrum Latinorum, sive Liturgicon Latinum, ed. J. Pamelius, 2 vols (Cologne, 1571).

Missale Pragense (1494).

Missale ad usum ecclesiae Westmonasteriensis, ed. J. W. Legg, 3 vols, HBS 1, 5 and 12 (London, 1891–7).

'Ein oberitaleinisches Plenarmissale des S-Typus', ed. K. Gamber, *Sacris Eruditi* 13 (1962), 353–9.

Das Prager Sakramentar, ed. A. Dold and L. Eizenhöfer, 2 vols, Texte und Arbeiten 38–42 (Beuron, 1944–9).

Sacramentarium Adelpretianum, ed. F. dell'Oro, Monumenta liturgica ecclesiae Tridentinae saeculo XIII antiquiora 2.ii (Trent, 1985), 1039–1237.

Le sacramentaire grégorien: ses principales formes d'après les plus anciennes manuscrits, ed. J. Deshusses, 3 vols, Spicilegium Friburgense 16, 24 and 28, 2nd ed. (Fribourg, 1979–88).

El sacramentario de Vich, ed. A. Olivar, Monumenta Hispaniae Sacra, Serie liturgica 4 (Barcelona, 1953).

Sacramentarium Bergomense, ed. A. Paredi, Monumenta Bergomensiana 6 (Bergamo, 1962).

Sacramentarium Fuldense saeculi X, ed. G. Richter and G. Schönfelder, repr. HBS 101 (London, 1977).

Das Sacramentarium Gregorianum nach dem Aachener Urexemplar, ed. H. Lietzmann, Liturgiewissenschäftliche Quellen und Forschungen 3 (Münster-im-Westfalen, 1921).

Sacramentarium Rivipullense, ed. A. Olivar, Monumenta Hispaniae Sacra, Serie liturgica 7 (Barcelona, 1964).

Sacramentarium Tridentinum, ed. F. dell'Oro, Monumenta liturgica ecclesiae Tridentinae saeculo XIII antiquiora 2.i (Trent, 1984), 75–416.

Sacramentarium Udalricianum, ed. F. dell'Oro, Monumenta liturgica ecclesiae Tridentinae saeculo XIII antiquiora 2.ii (Trent, 1985), 71–874.

Sacramentarium Veronense, ed. L. C. Mohlberg, Rerum ecclesiasticarum Documenta, Series maior, Fontes 1 (Rome, 1960).

Sacramentarium episcopi Warmundi, ed. in facsimile F. dell'Oro (Ivrea, 1990).

The Sacramentary of Echternach, ed. Y. Hen, HBS 110 (London, 1997).

Sakramentar von Metz. Fragment MS Lat. 1141, Bibliothèque Nationale, Paris, F. Müterich, Codices selecti phototypice impressi (Graz, 1972).
Das Sakramentar von Monza, ed. K. Gamber, Texte und Arbeiten 3 (Beuron, 1957).
Das Sakramentar-Pontifikale des Bischofs Wolfgang von Regensburg, ed. K. Gamber and S. Rehle, Textus Patristici et Liturgici 15 (Regensburg, 1985).
The Rites of Durham, ed. J. T. Fowler, Surtees Society 107 (Durham, 1903).
The Sarum Missal, ed. J. W. Legg (Oxford, 1916).
The Stowe Missal, ed. G. F. Warner, 2 vols, HBS 31–2 (London, 1906–15).

Editions of Benedictionals, Collectars, Manuals, Ordinals, Pontificals, Rituals and Prayer-books

Ælfwine's Prayer-book, ed. B. Günzel, HBS 108 (London, 1992).
The Benedictional of Archbishop Robert, ed. H. A. Wilson, HBS 24 (London, 1902).
The Benedictionals of Freising, ed. R. Amiet, HBS 88 (London, 1974).
The Benedictional of St Æthelwold, ed. in facs. G. F. Warner and H. A. Wilson (Oxford, 1910).
The Canterbury Benedictional, ed. R. M. Woolley, HBS 51 (London, 1917).
The Claudius Pontificals, ed. D. H. Turner, HBS 97 (London, 1971).
The Durham Collectar, ed. A. Corrêa, HBS 107 (London, 1992). See also *Rituale ecclesiae Dunelmensis,* ed. Lindelöf.
The Durham Ritual, ed. in facsimile T. J. Brown *et al.,* EEMF 16 (Copenhagen, 1969).
Das Kollektar-Pontificale des Bischofs Baturich von Regensburg (817–48), Spicilegium Friburgense 8 (Fribourg, 1962).
The Leofric Collectar, ed. E. S. Dewick and W. H. Frere, 2 vols, HBS 45 and 56 (London, 1914–21).
The Monastic Ordinal of the Monks of St Vedast's Abbey, Arras, ed. L. Brou, 2 vols, HBS 86–7 (1955–6).
Liber Pontificalis Christopher Bainbridge archiepiscopi Eboracensis, Surtees Society 61 (Durham, 1875).
Liber Pontificalis of Edmund Lacy, Bishop of Exeter, ed. R. Barnes (Exeter, 1847).
Liber tramitis aevi Odilonis abbatis, ed. P. Dinter, Corpus Consuetudinum Monasticarum 10 (Siegburg, 1980).
Manuale Casinense, ed. K. Gamber and S. Rehle, Textus Patristici et Liturgici 13 (Regensburg, 1977).
Manuale Constansiense (1510).
Manuale Hispalense (1494).
Manuale Lincopense, Breviarium Scarense, Manuale Åboense. Katholischer Ritualbucher Swedens und Finlands im Mittelalter, ed. J. Freisen (Paderborn, 1904).
Manuale Lubicense (1485).
Manuale Norwegicum, ed. H. Faehn, Libri Liturgici Provinviae Nidrosiensis Medii Aevi 1 (Oslo, 1962).

Manuale secundum consuetudinem ecclesiae Salmaticensis (1532).

Martene, E., *De antiquis ecclesiae ritibus*, 4 vols, 2nd ed. (Antwerp, 1736–8).

North Italian Services of the Eleventh Century, ed. C. Lambot, HBS 67 (London, 1931).

Officium ecclesiasticum abbatum secundum usum Eveshamensis monasterii, ed. H. A. Wilson, HBS 6 (London, 1893).

Ordinale Exoniense, ed. J. N. Dalton and G. H. Doble, 4 vols, HBS 37, 38, 63 and 79 (London, 1909–40).

Les 'ordines romani' du haut moyen age, ed. M. Andrieu, 5 vols, Spicilegium Sacrum Lovaniense 11, 23, 24, 28 and 29 (Louvain, 1931–65).

Pontificale ecclesiae sancti Andreae. The Pontifical Offices used by David de Bernham, bishop of St Andrew's, ed. C. Wordsworth (Edinburgh, 1885).

Pontificale Lanaletense, ed. G. H. Doble, HBS 74 (London, 1937).

The Pontifical of Magdalen College, ed. H. A. Wilson, HBS 39 (London, 1910).

Pontificale in usum ecclesiae Mediolanesis necnon ordines Ambrosiani ex codicibus saec. IX–XV, ed. M. Magistretti, Monumenta veteris liturgicae Ambrosianae 1 (Milan, 1897).

Le pontifical romano-germanique du dixième siècle, ed. C. Vogel and V. Elze, 3 vols, Studi e Testi 226, 227 and 269 (Vatican City, 1963–72).

Il cosidetto Pontificale di Poitiers, ed. A. Martini, Rerum ecclesiasticarum Documenta, Series maior, Fontes 14 (Rome, 1979).

The Portiforium of St Wulstan, ed. A. Hughes, 2 vols, HBS 89–90 (London, 1959–60).

Precum Libelli Quattuor Aevi Carolini, ed. A. Wilmart (Rome, 1940).

Regularis Concordia Anglicae Nationis Monachorum Sanctimonialiumque. The Monastic Agreement of the Monks and Nuns of the English Nation, ed. T. Symons (Edinburgh, 1953).

Ein Rituale in Beneventanischer Schrift, ed. A. Odermatt, Spicilegium Friburgense 26 (Fribourg, 1980).

Rituale ecclesiae Dunelmensis, ed. A. Lindelöf, Surtees Society 140 (Durham, 1927).

Das Rituale von St Florian aus dem zwölften Jahrhundert, ed. A. Franz (Freiburg-im-Breisgau, 1904).

El sacramentari, ritual i pontifical di Roda, ed. J. Planas (Barcelona, 1975).

Two Anglo-Saxon Pontificals, ed. H. M. J. Banting, HBS 104 (London, 1989).

Zwei karolingische Pontifikalien vom Oberrhein, ed. M. J. Metzger, Freiburger Theologische Studien 17 (Freiburg-im-Breisgau, 1914).

Editions of Calendars, Computistical Collections and Martyrologies

Das altenglische Martyrologium, ed. G. Kotzor, 2 vols, Abhandlungen der Bayerischen Akademie der Wissenschaften, phil.-hist Klasse, nf 88 (Munich, 1988).

Bischoff, B., 'Das karolingische Kalendar der Palimsesthandschrift Ambros. M. 12. Sup.', *Colligere Fragmenta. Festschrift Alban Dold zum 70 Geburstag*, ed. B. Fischer and V. Fiala, Texte und Arbeiten 2 (Beuron, 1962), 469–81.

Bedae Opera de Temporibus, ed. C. W. Jones, Medieval Academy of America Publications 41 (Cambridge, Mass., 1943). *De temporum ratione* is transl. F. E. Wallis, *Bede: The Reckoning of Time* (Liverpool, 1999).

Das Bonifatius-Sakramentar, ed. K. Gamber, Textus Patristici et Liturgici 12 (Regensburg, 1972).

Byrhtferth's Enchiridion, ed. P. Baker and M. Lapidge, Early English Text Society, Supplementary Series 15 (Oxford, 1995).

The Calendar of St Willibrord, ed. H. A. Wilson, HBS 55 (London, 1918).

Édition practique des martyrologes de Bède, de l'Anonyme lyonnais et de Florus, ed. J. Dubois and G. Renaud (Paris, 1976).

English Kalendars before A. D. 1100, ed. F. Wormald, HBS 72 (London, 1939).

Le martyrologe d'Usuard, ed. J. Dubois, Subsidia Hagiographica 40 (Brussels, 1965).

Martyrologium Hieronymianum, ed. G. B. de Rossi and L. Duchesne, *Acta Sanctorum Novembris* II.i (Brussels, 1894).

Wormald, F., 'The liturgical calendar of Glastonbury Abbey', *Festschrift Bernhard Bischoff zu seinem 65 Geburstag*, ed. J. Autenrieth and F. Brunholzl (Stuttgart, 1971), pp. 325–45.

Psalters and Litanies

Anglo-Saxon Litanies of the Saints, ed. M. Lapidge, HBS 106 (London, 1991).

Coens, M., *Recueil d'études Bollandiennes*, Subsidia Hagiographica 37 (Brussels, 1963).

Die Glossen des Psalters von Mondsee, ed. F. Unterkircher, Spicilegium Friburgense 20 (Fribourg, 1974).

The Psalter Collects, ed. L. Brou and A. Wilmart, HBS 83 (London, 1949)

The Salisbury Psalter edited from Salisbury Cathedral MS 150, ed. C. Sisam and K. Sisam, Early English Text Society 242 (Oxford, 1959).

Editions of Antiphoners, Graduals and Hymnals

Analecta Hymnica medii aevi, ed. G. M. Dreves, C. Blume and H. M. Bannister, 55 vols (Leipzig, 1886–1922).

Antiphonale Ambrosianum du Musée Britannique (XII siècle), Codex Additional 24309, ed. A. Mocquereau, Palaéographie musicale 5 (Solesmes, 1896).

Antiphonale missarum sancti Gregorii Xe siècle, Codex 47 de la bibliothèque de Chartres, ed. A. Mocquereau, Palaéographie musicale 11 (Solesmes, 1910).

Antiphonale Missarum sextuplex, ed. J. Hesbert (Brussels, 1935).

The Antiphonary of Bangor: an Early Irish Manuscript in the Ambrosian Library at Milan, ed. F. E. Warren, 2 vols, HBS 4 and 10 (London, 1893–5)

Graduale Sarisburiense, ed. W. H. Frere, Plainsong and Medieval Music Society 1 (London, 1894).

Editions of Chronicles, Histories and Saints' Lives

Annales Elnoneses minores, ed. G. Waitz, MGH SS 5 (Hannover, 1844), pp. 17–19.

Annales Vedastini, ed. B. de Simson, *Annales Xantenses et Annales Vedastini*, MGH Scriptores rerum Germanicarum in usum Scholarum 12 (Hannover, 1909), pp. 40–82.

Bede, *Historia Ecclesiastica Gentis Anglorum*, ed. Bertram Colgrave and R. A. B. Mynors, 2nd ed. (Oxford, 1991).

Byrhtferth of Ramsey, *Vita S. Oswaldi*, ed. J. Raine, *Historians of the Church of York and its Archbishops*, 3 vols, RS 71 (London, 1879–94), I, 399–475.

Felix's Life of Saint Guthlac, ed. B. Colgrave (Cambridge, 1956).

Gervase of Canterbury, *Acta pontificum*, ed. W. Stubbs, RS 73 (London, 1879–80).

Goscelin of Saint-Bertin, *Historia translationis sancti Augustini*, ed. D. Papebroch, *Acta Sanctorum Maii* VI, 408–21.

Vita Edithae, ed. A. Wilmart, 'La légende de Ste Édith en prose et vers par le moine Goscelin', *AB* 56 (1933), 5–101, 265–307.

Gregory of Tours, *Historia Francorum*, ed. W. Arndt, MGH SS rer. Meroving. 1 (Hannover, 1885).

Monumenta Vedastina Minora, ed. O. Holder-Egger, MGH SS 15.i (Hannover, 1887), pp. 402–4.

Orderic Vitalis, *Historia Ecclesiastica*, ed. M. Chibnall, 6 vols (Oxford, 1969–80).

Two Lives of Saint Cuthbert, ed. B. Colgrave (Cambridge, 1940).

Two of the Saxon Chronicles Parallel, ed. C. Plummer, 2 vols (Oxford, 1892–9).

Venerabilis Bedae Opera, ed. C. Plummer, 2 vols (Oxford, 1896).

William of Malmesbury, *De antiquitate Glastoniensis Ecclesiae*, ed. J. Scott, *The Early History of the Church of Glastonbury* (Woodbridge, 1981), with F. Lomax, *The Antiquities of Glastonbury* (repr. Llanerlech, 1992).

De Gestis Pontificum Anglorum, ed. N. E. S. A. Hamilton, RS 52 (London, 1870).

II. SECONDARY SOURCES

Abrams, L., 'St Patrick and Glastonbury: *nihil ex nihilo fit?*', *Saint Patrick*, ed. Dumville, pp. 233–42.

'St Patrick in an Anglo-Saxon Martyrology', *Saint Patrick*, ed. Dumville, pp. 243–4.

Alexander, J. J. G., *Norman Illumination at Mont Saint-Michel, 966–1100* (Oxford, 1971).

Amiet, R., 'Les sacramentaires 88 et 137 du chapitre de Cologne', *Scriptorium* 9 (1955), 76–84.

Le culte liturgique de saint Geneviève (Paris, 1981).

Les manuscrits liturgiques du diocèse de Lyon (Paris, 1998).

Amore, A., 'Il problema dei SS Quattro Coronati', in *Miscellanea Amato Pietro Frutaz*, ed. C. Egger (Rome, 1978), pp. 123–46.

Atchley, E. G. C. F., *A History of the Use of Incense in Divine Worship*, Alcuin Club Collections 13 (London, 1909).

Auda, A., *L'école musicale Liègoise au Xe siècle: Étienne de Liège* (Brussels, 1923).

Barlow, F., *The English Church 1000–1066* (London, 1963).

The English Church 1066–1154 (London, 1979).

Exeter 1046–1184, English Episcopal Acta 9 (Oxford, 1996).

Barré, H., and J. Deshusses, 'A la recherche du missel d'Alcuin', *EL* 82 (1968), 3–44.

Bateson, M., 'A Worcester Cathedral book of ecclesiastical collections', *English Historical Review* 10 (1895), 712–31.

Beer, R., *Kaiserliche Königliche Hof-Bibliothek in Wien. Monumenta palaeographica Vindobonensia. Denkmäler der Schreibkunst aus der Handschriftensammlung des Habsburg-Lothringischen Erzhauses* (Leipzig, 1910).

Batelli, G., 'L'orazionale di Trani', *Benedictina* 19 (1972), 271–87.

Bäumer, S., *Histoire du Bréviaire*, trans. R. Biron, 2 vols (Paris, 1905).

Bernard, E., *Catalogi Librorum Manuscriptorum Angliae et Hiberniae*, 2 vols (Oxford, 1697).

Berschin, W., 'Das Benedictionale Salomons III für Adalbero von Augsburg (Cambridge, Fitzwilliam Museum, MS 27)', in *Churrätisches und St. Gallisches Mittelalter. Feschrift für Otto P. Clavadetscher zu seinem fünfundsechzigsten Geburstag*, ed. H. Maurer (Sigmaringen, 1984), pp. 227–36.

Binns, A., *Dedications of Monastic Houses in England and Wales, 1066–1216* (Woodbridge, 1989).

Bischoff, B., 'Das karolingische Kalendar der Palimsesthandschrift Ambros. M. 12. Sup.', *Colligere Fragmenta. Festschrift Alban Dold zum 70 Geburstag*, ed. B. Fischer and V. Fiala, Texte und Arbeiten 2 (Beuron, 1962), 469–81.

Katalog der festländischen Handschriften des neunten Jahrhunderts (Wiesbaden, 1998–).

and V. Brown and J. John, 'Addenda to *Codices Latini Antiquiores* II', *Medieval Studies* 54 (1992), 286–307.

and M. Lapidge, *Biblical Commentaries from the Canterbury School of Theodore and Hadrian* (Cambridge, 1994).

Bishop, E., 'On some early manuscripts of the Gregorianum', in his *Liturgica Historica* (Oxford, 1918), pp. 62–76.

'On the early texts of the Roman Canon', *ibid.*, pp. 77–115

'On the origins of the feast of the Conception of the Blessed Virgin Mary', *ibid.*, pp. 238–59.

Bishop, T. A. M., 'Notes on Cambridge manuscripts, part III: manuscripts connected with Exeter', *Transactions of the Cambridge Bibliographical Society* 2 (1954–8), 192–9.

'Notes on Cambridge manuscripts, part IV: manuscripts connected with St Augustine's, Canterbury, *ibid.* 2 (1954–8), 323–36.

Bishop, T. A. M., 'Notes on Cambridge manuscripts, part VI: manuscripts connected with St Augustine's, Canterbury, continued', *ibid.* 3 (1959–63), 412–13.

'Notes on Cambridge manuscripts, part VII: manuscripts connected with Christ Church, Canterbury, *ibid.* 3 (1959–63), 413–23.

English Caroline Minuscule (Oxford, 1971).

Boinet, A., *La miniature carolingienne* (Paris, 1913).

Bonner, G., D. Rollason and C. Stancliffe, ed., *St Cuthbert: His Cult and His Community to AD 1200* (Woodbridge, 1989).

Bostock, J. N., *A Handbook of Old High German Literature* (Oxford, 1955).

Bouman, C. A., *Sacring and Crowning*, Bidragen van het Instituut voor middeleeuwe Geschiedenis der Rijks-Universiteit te Utrecht 30 (Groningen, Djakarta, 1957).

Bourque, E., *Étude sur les sacramentaires romaines*, 2 vols in 3 (Rome, 1948–58).

Boutemy, A., 'Le style franco-saxon de Saint-Amand', *Scriptorium* 3 (1949), 260–4.

'Quel fut le foyer du style franco-saxon?', *Miscellanea Touracensia. Mélanges d'archaéologie et d'histoire. Congrés de Tournai 1949*, 2 vols (Brussels, 1951) II, 749–73.

Brooks, N., *The Early History of the Church of Canterbury* (Leicester, 1984).

'The career of St Dunstan', in *St Dunstan*, ed. Ramsay *et al.*, pp. 1–23.

Brückmann, J. 'Latin manuscript pontificals and benedictionals in England and Wales', *Traditio* 29 (1973), 391–458.

Budny, M., *Insular, Anglo-Saxon and Early Anglo-Norman Manuscript Art at Corpus Christi College, Cambridge*, 2 vols (Kalamazoo, 1997).

Bullough, D. A., 'A neglected early-ninth-century manuscript of the Lindisfarne *Vita S. Cuthberti*', *ASE* 27 (1998), 105–37.

Cabrol, F. and H. Leclercq, *Dictionnaire d'archéologie chrétienne et de liturgie*, 30 vols in 15 (Paris, 1907–53).

Capelle, B., *Travaux liturgiques de doctrine et d'histoire,* 3 vols (Louvain, 1955–67).

Catalogus codicum hagiographicorum latinorum qui asservantur in Biblioteca Nationali Parisiensi, {ed. Bollandists}, 3 vols (Brussels, 1889–93).

Chavasse, A., 'Les oraisons pour les dimanches ordinaires', *RB* 93 (1983), 31–70 and 177–244.

Clayton, M., *The Cult of the Virgin in Anglo-Saxon England* (Cambridge, 1990).

and H. Magennis, *The Old English Lives of St Margaret* (Cambridge, 1994).

Clercque, C. de, 'Ordines unctionis infirmi saeculi IX–X', *EL* 44 (1930), 99–123.

Colker, M. L., *Trinity College Library, Dublin. Descriptive Catalogue of the Medieval and Renaissance Latin Manuscripts*, 2 vols (Dublin, 1991).

Combulazier, F., 'Un pontifical du Mont Saint-Michel', *Millénaire monastique*, ed. Laporte *et al.*, I, 383–93.

Conner, P., *Anglo-Saxon Exeter. A Tenth-Century Cultural History* (Woodbridge, 1993).

Cross, J. E., and A. Hamer, *Wulfstan's Canon Law Collection*, Anglo-Saxon Texts 1 (Woodbridge, 1999).

Delaporte, Y., *Les manuscrits enluminés de la Bibliothèque Municipale de Chartres* (Chartres, 1929).

Delehaye, H., 'Hagiographie napolitaine', *AB* 57 (1939), 5–64.

Delisle, L. V., *L'évangeliaire de Saint-Vaast d'Arras et la calligraphie franco-saxonne du IXe siècle* (Paris, 1888).

Deshmann, R., 'The Leofric Missal and tenth-century English art', *ASE* 6 (1977), 145–73.

Deshusses, J., 'Le sacramentaire grégorien pré-Hadrianique', *RB* 80 (1970), 213–37.

'Les messes d'Alcuin', *Archiv für Liturgiewissenschaft* 14.i (1972), 7–44.

'Sur quelques anciens livres liturgiques de Saint-Thierry: les étapes d'une transformation de la liturgie', in *Saint-Thierry, une abbaye du VIe au XXe siècle*, ed. M. Bur (Saint-Thierry, 1979), pp. 122–45.

'Chronologie des grands sacramentaires de Saint-Amand', *RB* 87 (1977), 230–7.

'Les anciens sacramentaires de Tours', *RB* 89 (1979), 281–302.

and H. Barré, 'A la recherche du missel d'Alcuin', *EL* 82 (1968), 3–44.

and J. Hourlier, 'Saint Benoît dans les livres liturgiques', *Studia Monastica* 21 (1979), 143–204.

Delisle, L. V., 'Mémoire sur d'anciens sacramentaires', *Mémories de l'Institut National de France, Académie des Inscriptions et Belles-Lettres* 32.i (Paris, 1886), 57–423.

Dodwell, C. R. and D. H. Turner, *Reichenau Reconsidered*, Warburg Institute Surveys 2 (London, 1965).

Dold, A., *Die Konstanzer Ritualientexte in ihrer Entwicklung von 1482–1721*, Liturgiegeschichte Quellen 5–6 (Münster-im-Westfalen, 1923).

Dorange, A., *Catalogue descriptif et raisonné des manuscrits de la Bibliothèque de Tours* (Tours, 1875).

Dosdat, M., 'Les évêques normands de 985 à 1150', in *Les évêques normands du XIe siècle. Colloque de Cerisy-la-Salle, 30 sept. – 3 oct. 1993*, ed. P. Bouet and F. Neveux (Caen, 1995), pp. 19–35.

Drage, E., 'Bishop Leofric and the Cathedral Chapter: a reassessment of the manuscript evidence' (unpubl. Oxford DPhil. thesis, 1978).

Dubois, M.-M., 'Les rubriques en vieil anglais du missel de Robert de Jumièges', *Jumièges. Congrès scientifique du XIIIe centenaire. Rouen, 10–12 Juin 1954*, 2 vols (Rouen, 1955) I, 305–8.

Duchesne, L., *Fastes épiscopaux de l'ancienne Gaule*, 2nd ed., 3 vols (Paris, 1907–22).

Duine, F., *Bréviaires et missels des églises et abbayes bretonnes de France* (Rennes, 1906).

Inventaire liturgique de l'hagiographie bretonne, La Bretagne et les pays celtiques 16 (Paris, 1922).

Dumville, D. N. (ed.), *Saint Patrick, A.D. 493–1993* (Woodbridge, 1993).

English Caroline Script and Monastic History. Studies in Benedictinism A.D. 950–1030 (Woodbridge, 1993).

Liturgy and the Ecclesiastical History of Late Anglo-Saxon England (Woodbridge, 1995).

Durrieux, A., *Les miniatures des manuscrits de la Bibliothèque de Cambrai*, Mémoires de la Société d'émulation de Cambrai 27.i (Cambrai, 1860).

Eales, R. and R. Sharpe (ed.), *Canterbury and the Norman Conquest: Churches, Saints and Scholars* (London, 1995).

Ebner, A., *Quellen und Forschungen zur Geschichte und Kunstgeschichte des Missale Romanum: Iter Italicum* (Freiburg-im-Breisgau, 1896).

Ellard, G., *Ordination Anointings in the Western Church before 1000 AD* (Cambridge, Mass., 1933).

Fehr, B., *Die Hirtenbriefe Ælfrics in altenglische und lateinischer Fassung*, Bibliothek der angelsächsischen Prosa 11 (Hamburg, 1914).

'Ältenglische Ritualtexte fur Krankenbesuch, heilige Ölung und Begräbnis', *Texte und Forschungen*, ed. Förster and Wildhagen, pp. 20–67.

Finberg, H. P. R., 'The house of Ordgar and the foundation of Tavistock Abbey', *EHR* 58 (1943), 190–200.

Förster, M., 'Zur Liturgik der angelsächsischen Kirke', *Anglia* 66 (1942), 1–51.

Franz, A., *Die kirchliche Benediktionen im Mittelalter*, 2 vols (Freiburg-im-Breisgau, 1909).

Frantzen, A. J., *The Literature of Penance in Anglo-Saxon England* (New Brunswick, New Jersey, 1983).

Frere, W. H., *Pontifical Services*, 2 vols, Alcuin Club Collections 3–4 (Oxford, 1901).

Studies in Early Roman Liturgy, 3 vols, Alcuin Club Collections 28, 30 and 32 (Oxford, 1930–5).

'The Use of Exeter', *Walter Howard Frere. A Collection of his Papers on Liturgical and Historical Subjects*, ed. J. H. Arnold and E. G. P. Wyatt, Alcuin Club Collections 35 (Oxford, 1940), 54–71.

Fryde, E. B., D. E. Greenway, S. Porter and I. Roy (ed.), *Handbook of British Chronology*, 3rd ed. (London, 1986).

Gamber, K., 'Ein oberitaleinisches Plenarmissale des S-Typus', *Sacris Erudiri* 13 (1962), 353–9.

Codices latini liturgici antiquiores, 2 vols, Spicilegii Friburgensis Subsidia 1 and 1A, 2nd ed. (Fribourg, 1969), with the Supplement (Fribourg, 1988).

Gameson, R., *The Role of Art in the Late Anglo-Saxon Church* (Oxford, 1995).

'The origin of the Exeter Book of Old English poetry', *ASE* 25 (1996), 135–85.

Ganz, D., *Corbie in the Carolingian Renaissance*, Beihefte der Francia 20 (Sigmaringen, 1990).

Garrison, E. B., 'Twelfth-century initial styles of central Italy: indices for the dating of MSS. Part II: materials (contd)', in his *Studies in Early Italian Painting*, 4 vols (Florence, 1953–62) IV, 277–307.

'Contributions to the history of twelfth-century Umbro-Roman painting. Part II: Materials, contd. VII. The Italian-Byzantine-Romanesque fusion in the second half of the twelfth century', in his *Studies in Early Italian Painting* IV, 117–78.

Gasquet, F. A. and E. Bishop, *The Bosworth Psalter* (London, 1908).

Gerbert, M., *Monumenta veteris liturgiae Alemmanicae*, 2 vols (St Blasien, 1777–8).

Gerchow, J., *Die Gedenküberlieferung der Angelsachsen*, Arbeiten zur Frühmittelalterforschung 20 (Berlin, 1988).

Gestin, J.-P., and E. Le Bris du Rest (ed.), *Landevennec 485–1485: aux origines de la Bretagne. XVe centenaire de la fondation de l'abbaye de Landevennec*, ed. (Daoulas, 1985).

Gibson, M., T. A. Heslop, and R. W. Pfaff (ed.), *The Eadwine Psalter* (London, 1992).

Giry, A., M. Prou and G. Tessier (ed.), *Recueil des actes de Charles le Chauve*, Chartes et diplômes, 3 vols (Paris, 1943–55).

Gjerløw, L., *Adoratio Crucis* (Oslo, 1961).

Graham, T., 'The Old English prefatory texts in the Corpus Canterbury Pontifical', *Anglia* 113 (1995), 1–15.

Gregoire, R., 'Les prières liturgiques médiévaux en l'hônneur de saint Benoît, sainte Scholastique et saint Maur', *Studia Anselmiana* 54 (Rome, 1965), 1–86.

Gros, R., 'L'ordo pour la dédicace des églises dans la sacramentaire de Nonantola', *RB* 79 (1969), 368–74.

Gulotta, G., and J. Ruysschaert, *Gli antichi cataloghi e i codici della abbazia di Nonantola*, 2 vols, Studi e Testi 182a–b (Vatican City, 1955).

Gwynn, A., 'The Irish Missal of Corpus Christi College, Oxford', *Studies in Church History* 1 (London, 1964), 47–68.

Gy, P.-M., 'Die Segnung von Milch und Honig in der Osternacht', in *Paschatis Sollemnia*, ed. D. Fischer and J. Wagner (Fribourg, 1959), 206–12.

Harrison, O. G., 'The formulas ad virgines sacras. A study of the sources', *EL* 66 (1952), 252–74, 353–7.

Hacke, C. B. von, *Die Palliumverleihungen bis 1143* (Marburg, 1898).

Haddan, A. W. and W. Stubbs, *Councils and Ecclesiastical Documents relating to Great Britain and Ireland*, 3 vols in 4 (Oxford, 1869–78).

Hearne, T., *Remarks and Collections of Thomas Hearne*, ed. C. E. Doble, D. W. Rannie and H. E. Salter, 10 vols, Oxford Historical Society Collections 2, 7, 13, 34, 42, 43, 48, 50, 65 and 67 (Oxford, 1885–1915).

Heiming, O., 'Kleinere Beiträge zur Geschichte der ambrosianische Liturgie', *Archiv für Liturgiewissenshaft* 12 (1970), 130–47.

Henel, H., *Studien zum altenglische Computus*, Beiträge zur englischen Philologie 26 (Leipzig, 1934).

Hesbert, J., *Corpus Antiphonalium Officii*, 6 vols, Rerum ecclesiasticarum Documenta, Series maior, Fontes 7–12 (Rome, 1963–79).

Heslop, T. A., 'De luxe manuscripts and the patronage of King Cnut and Queen Emma', *ASE* 19 (1990), 151–95.

review of D. Dumville, *Early Caroline Script*, in *JTS* 45 (1994), 378–81.

'The Canterbury calendars and the Norman Conquest', in *Canterbury and the Norman Conquest*, ed. Eales and Sharpe, pp. 53–85.

Heyworth, P. L. (ed.), *Letters of Humfrey Wanley, Palaeographer, Anglo-Saxonist, Librarian, 1672–1726* (Oxford, 1989).

Hickes, G., *Thesaurus Grammatico-Criticus et Archaeologicus*, 5 parts (Oxford, 1703–5).

Hoeynck, F. A., *Geschichte der kirchlichen Liturgie des Bistums Augsburg* (Augsburg, 1889).

Hohler, C. E., 'The type of sacramentary used by St Boniface', *Sankt Bonifatius. Gedenkgabe zum zwölfhundertjährigen Todestag* (Fulda, 1954), pp. 89–93.

'Les saintes insulaires dans le missel de l'archévêque Robert', *Jumièges. Congrès scientifique du XIIIe centenaire, Rouen 10–12 juin 1954*, 2 vols (Rouen, 1955) I, 293–303.

'The Durham services in honour of St Cuthbert', *The Relics of St Cuthbert*, ed. C. F. Battiscombe (Oxford, 1956), pp. 155–91.

'The proper office of St Nicholas and related matters with reference to a recent book', *Medium Aevum* 36 (1967), 40–8.

'The Red Book of Darley', *Nordiskt Kollokvium i Latinsk Liturgiforskning* 2 (Oslo, 1972), 39–47.

'Some service-books of the later Saxon Church', *Tenth-century Studies*, ed. D. Parsons (Leicester, 1975), pp. 60–83 and 217–27.

review of R. Grant, *Cambridge Corpus Christi College 41*, in *Medium Aevum* 49 (1980), 275–8.

Hope, W. St John, 'Recent discoveries in the abbey church of St Austin at Canterbury', *Archaeologia Cantiana* 32 (1917), 1–26.

Holweck, F. G., *A Biographical Dictionary of the Saints* (St Louis, MO, 1924).

Hourlier, J., 'La translation de sainte Scholastique au Mans', *Studia Monastica* 21 (1979), 313–33.

Houts, E. M. C. van, 'Historiography and hagiography at Saint-Wandrille: the *inventio et miracula sancti Vulfrani*', *Proceedings of the Battle Conference on Anglo-Norman Studies* 12, 1989, ed. M. Chibnall (Woodbridge, 1990), 233–51

Hull, P. L., 'The foundation of St Michael's Mount in Cornwall, a priory of the abbey of Mont Saint-Michel', *Millénaire monastique*, ed. Laporte *et al.*, I, 703–24.

Irvine, S. E., 'Bones of contention: the context of Ælfric's homily on St Vincent', *ASE* 19 (1990), 117–32.

Jackson, R., *Ordines coronationis Franciae. Texts and ordines for the Coronation of Frankish and French Kings and Queens in the Middle Ages*, 2 vols (Philadelphia, 1995–2000).

Jaffé, P., P. Ewald and S. Loewenfeld, *Regesta Pontificum Romanorum*, 3 vols (Leipzig, 1885–8).

James, M. R., *A Descriptive Catalogue of the Manuscripts in the Library of Pembroke College, Cambridge* (Cambridge, 1905).

A Descriptive Catalogue of the Manuscripts in the Library of Corpus Christi College, Cambridge, 2 vols (Cambridge, 1912).

A Descriptive Catalogue of the Manuscripts in the Library of Trinity College, Cambridge, 4 vols (Cambridge, 1911–12).

Jolly, K. L., *Popular Religion in Late Saxon England: Elf Charms in Context* (Chapel Hill, 1996).

Jones, C. A., *Ælfric's Letter to the Monks of Eynsham* (Cambridge, 1998).

'Two composite texts from Archbishop Wulstan's "commonplace book": the *De ecclesiastica consuetudine* and the *Institutio beati Amalarii de ecclesiasticis officiis*', *ASE* 27 (1998), 233–71.

Jones, C. W., *Bedae Pseudepigrapha* (Ithaca, New York, 1939).

'A legend of St Pachomius', *Speculum* 18 (1943), 198–210.

Jones, C. W., *The St Nicholas Liturgy and its Literary Relationships*, University of California English Studies 27 (Berkeley, 1963).

Jungmann, J. A., *Die lateinischen Bussriten in ihrer Geschichtlichen Entwicklung*, Forschungen zur Geschichte des innerkirchlichen Liebens 3–4 (Innsbruck, 1932).

Keefer, S., 'Margin as archive: the liturgical marginalia of a manuscript of the Old English Bede', *Traditio* 51 (1996), 147–77.

Kelly, T. F., *The Exultet in Southern Italy* (Oxford, 1996).

Ker, N. R., *Catalogue of Manuscripts containing Anglo-Saxon* (Oxford, 1957).

'Three Old English Texts in a Salisbury Pontifical, Cotton Tiberius C. i', *The Anglo-Saxons: Studies in some Aspects of their History and Culture Presented to Bruce Dickins*, ed. P. Clemoes (London, 1959), pp. 262–79.

Medieval Manuscripts in British Libraries, 4 vols (Oxford, 1969–92).

Keynes, S., 'The Æthelings in Normandy', *Proceedings of the Battle Conference on Anglo-Norman Studies* 13, 1990, ed. M. Chibnall (Woodbridge, 1991), pp. 173–205.

(ed.), *Facsimiles of Anglo-Saxon Charters*, Anglo-Saxon Charters, Supplementary Volume 1 (London, 1991).

Kirsch, J. P., 'Die Berner Handschrift des Martyrologium Hieronymianum', *Romische Quartalschrift für christliche Altertumskunde und für Kirchengeschichte* 31 (1923) 113–24.

Kleinheyer, B., 'Studien zur nichtrömisch-westlichen Ordinationsliturgie, Folge 1: Die Ordinationsliturgie gemäss dem Leofric-Missale', *Archiv für Liturgiewissenschaft* 22 (1980), 93–107.

'Studien zur nichtrömisch-westlichen Ordinationsliturgie, Folge 2: Ein spätantik-altgallisches Ordinationsformula', *ibid.* 23 (1981), 313–66

'Studien zur nichtrömisch-westlichen Ordinationsliturgie. Folge 4: Zur Bewertung diverser Gewandüberreichungsriten im Licht ihrer Deuteworte', *ibid.* 33 (1991), 217–74.

Knowles, D., C. N. L. Brooke and V. C. M. London, *The Heads of Religious Houses: England and Wales, 940–1216* (Cambridge, 1972).

Koehler, W., and F. Mütherich, *Die karolingische Miniaturen*, 5 vols in 10 (Berlin, 1930–82).

Korhammer, P. M., 'The origin of the Bosworth Psalter', *ASE* 2 (1973), 178–87.

Kornexl, R., 'The Regularis Concordia and its Old English Gloss', *ASE* 24 (1995), 95–130.

Laborde, A. de, *Les principaux manuscrits à peinture conservés dans l'ancienne bibliothèque impériale publique de Saint-Petersbourg*, 2 vols (Paris, 1936).

Langefeld, B., *'Regula canonicorum* or *Regula monasterialis vitae*? The Rule of Chrodegang and Archbishop Wulfred's reforms at Canterbury', *ASE* 25 (1995), 21–37.

Lapidge, M., 'Some Latin poems as evidence for the reign of Æthelstan', *ASE* 9 (1981), 61–98.

'The origin of CCCC 163', *Transactions of the Cambridge Bibliographical Society* 8 (1981–5), 18–28.

'Ealdred of York and MS Cotton Vitellius E. xii', *Yorkshire Archaeological Journal* 55 (1983), 11–25.

'A tenth-century metrical calendar from Ramsey', *RB* 94 (1984), 326–70.

Lapidge, M., 'Surviving booklists from Anglo-Saxon England', *Learning and Literature in Anglo-Saxon England. Studies presented to Peter Clemoes on the Occasion of his Sixty-Fifth Birthday*, ed. M. Lapidge and H. Gneuss (Cambridge, 1985), pp. 33–89.

and R. Sharpe, *A Bibliography of Celtic-Latin Literature 400–1200*, Royal Academy Dictionary of Medieval Latin from Celtic Sources, Ancillary Publications 1 (Dublin, 1985).

Laporte, J., R. Foreville, M. Baudot and M. Nortier (ed.), *Millénaire monastique du Mont Saint-Michel*, 4 vols (Paris, 1966–7).

Leclercq, J., 'Une série de bénédictions pours les lectures de l'office', *EL* 59 (1945), 318–22.

'Fragmenta Reginensia', *EL* 61 (1947), 289–96.

'Bénédictions pour les leçons de l'office dans un manuscrit de Pistoie', *Sacris Erudiri* 8 (1956), 143–6.

Legg, J. W., 'Liturgical notes on the Sherborne Missal, a manuscript in the possession of the Duke of Northumberland at Alnwick Castle', *Transactions of the St Paul's Ecclesiological Society* 4 (1896), 1–31.

Legner, A. (ed.), *Rhein und Maas, Kunst und Kultur 800–1400. Eine Ausstellung des Schnütgen-Museums der Stadt Köln, vom 14 Mai bis 23 Juli 1972*, 2 vols (Cologne, 1972).

Lemarié, J., 'Textes relatifs au culte de l'Archange et des Anges dans les bréviaires manuscrits de Mont Saint-Michel', *Sacris Erudiri* 13 (1963), 112–52.

'L'office des fêtes de saint Michel dans les bréviaires du Mont', *Millénaire monastique*, ed. Laporte *et al.*, I, 473–87.

'Le pontifical d'Hughes de Salins, son *Ordo Missae* et son *Libellus precum*', *Studi Medievali* 19 (1978), 363–424.

Lemps, M. de and R. Laslier, *Trésors de la Bibliothèque Municipale de Reims* (Reims, 1978).

Lenker, U., *Die westsächische Evangelienversion und die Perikopordnung im angelsächischen England*, Texte und Untersuchung zur englischen Philologie 20 (Munich, 1997).

Leroquais, V., *Les sacramentaires et les missels manuscrits*, 4 vols (Paris, 1924).

Les pontificaux manuscrits, 3 vols (Paris, 1937).

Levison, W., *England and the Continent in the Eighth Century* (Oxford, 1946).

Liebermann, F., *Die Gesetze der Angelsachsen*, 3 vols (Halle, 1903–16).

Lipsius, R. A., *Die apokryphalen Apostelgeschichten und Apostellegenden*, 2 vols in 3 (Brunswick, 1883–90).

Lohier, F., 'Notes sur un ancien sacramentaire de l'abbaye de Saint-Wandrille', in *Mélanges d'histoire offerts à Charles Moeller*, ed. A. Cauchie, 2 vols (Louvain, 1914) I, 407–18.

Lowe, E. A., *Codices Latini Antiquiores*, 11 vols and Supplement (Oxford, 1934–71).

MacGregor, A. J., *Fire and Light in the Western Triduum. Their Use at Tenebrae and at the Paschal Vigil*, Alcuin Club Collections 71 (Minnesota, 1992).

Madan, F. and H. E. Craster, *A Summary Catalogue of the Western Manuscripts in the Bodleian Library at Oxford*, 7 vols in 8 (Oxford, 1895–53).

Magne, J., 'La prière de consécration des vièrges *Deus castorum corporum*', *EL* 72 (1958), 245–67.

Maier, P., *Die Feier der Missa chrismatis; die Reform der Ölweihe des Pontificale Romanum vor dem Hintergrund der Ritusgeschichte*, Studien zur Pastoralliturgie 7 (Regensburg, 1990).

Martène, E., *De antiquis ecclesiae ritibus*, 4 vols, 2nd ed. (Antwerp, 1736–8).

Martimort, A. G., *La documentation liturgique de Dom Edmond Martène*, Studi e Testi 279 (Vatican City, 1978).

Maskell, W., *Monumenta Ritualia Ecclesiae Anglicanae*, 3 vols (Oxford, 1846–7).

McCormick, M., 'A new ninth-century witness to the Carolingian mass against the pagans: Paris BN lat. 2812', *RB* 97 (1987), 68–96

McGurk, P., 'The Computus', *An Anglo-Saxon Illustrated Miscellany: Cotton Tiberius B. v*, ed. P. McGurk, D. N. Dumville, M. R. Godden and Ann Knock, Early English Manuscripts in Facsimile 21 (Copenhagen, 1983), pp. 51–4.

Micheli, G. L., *L'enluminaire du haut moyen âge et les influences irlandaises* (Brussels, 1939).

Moeller, E. (ed.), *Corpus Benedictionum Pontificalium*, 4 vols, CCSL 162, 162A–C (Turnhout, 1971–9).
Corpus Prefationum, 3 vols, CCSL 161A–C (Turnhout, 1980–1).
and B. C. 'T Wallant and J. M. Clement, *Corpus Orationum*, 10 vols, CCSL 160 and 160A–I (Turnhout, 1992–8).

Molin, J. B., 'L'oratio communis fidelium du Xe au XIVe siècle', *Miscellanea liturgica in onore di sua eminenza Cardinale Giacomo Lercaro*, 2 vols (Rome, 1966–7), II, 313–468.

Mollet, G. (ed.), *L'art du moyen âge en Arras. Catalogue de l'exposition, Musée d'Arras, Palais Saint-Vaast, 15 avr. – 30 juin, 1951*, ed. G. Mollet (Arras, 1951).

Moreton, B., *The Eighth-Century Gelasian Sacramentary* (Oxford, 1976).

Morin, G., 'A travers les manuscrits de Bâle', *Basler Zeitschrift für Geschichte und Altertumskunde* 26 (1927), 176–249.

Morin, J., 'Une liste de fêtes chomées à Bologne à l'époque Carolingienne', *RB* 19 (1902), 353–6.

Morinus, J., *Commentarius historicus de disciplina in administratione sacramenti poenitentiae* (Antwerp, 1682).
Commentarius de sacris ecclesiae ordinationibus, 2nd ed. (Antwerp, 1695).

Mutta, R. dalla, 'Un rituel de l'onction des malades du IXe siècle en Flandre, chaînon important entre le rituel Carolingien et les rituels des Xe–Xe', *Mens concordet voci. Mélanges offerts pour Mgr A. G. Martimort*, ed. C. Dagens (Tournai, 1983).

Nelson, J. L., 'The earliest royal *ordo*: some liturgical and historical aspects', in her *Politics and Ritual in Early Medieval Europe* (London, 1986), pp. 341–60.
'The second English *ordo*', *ibid.*, pp. 361–74.

Netzer, V., *L'introduction de la messe romaine en France sous les Carolingiens* (Paris, 1910).

Nicholson, E. W. B., *Early Bodleian Music*, 3 vols (London, 1898–1913).

Nocent, A., 'Un fragment de sacramentaire de Sens au Xe siècle', in *Miscellanea liturgica in onore di sua eminenza il Cardinale Giacomo Lercaro*, 2 vols (Rome, 1966–7), 649–794.

'Les apologies dans la célébration eucharistique', *Liturgie et rémission des péchés. Conférences Saint-Serge XXe semaine d'études liturgiques, Paris, 2–5 juillet*, ed. A. Pistoia, C. M. Triacca and A. M. Triacca, Biblioteca Ephemerides Liturgicae Subsidia 3 (Rome, 1975), 179–96.

Orchard, N. A., 'The Bosworth Psalter and the St Augustine's Missal', *Canterbury and the Norman Conquest: Churches, Saints and Scholars*, ed. Eales and Sharpe, pp. 87–94.

'A note on the masses in honour of St Cuthbert', *RB* 105 (1995), 79–98.

'The English and German masses in honour of St Oswald of Northumbria', *Archiv für Liturgiewissenschaft* 37 (1995), 347–58.

'The medieval masses in honour of St Apollinaris of Ravenna', *RB* (1996), 172–84.

'The English and German masses in honour of St Oswald of Northumbria: a postscript', *Archiv für Liturgiewissenschaft* 40 (1998), 49–57.

'St Willibrord, St Richarius, and Anglo-Saxon symptoms in three mass-books from northern France', *RB* 110 (2000), 261–283.

'Pater sancte: an ordination prayer used by the Anglo-Saxon church', *RB* (forthcoming).

'Some notes on the Sacramentary of Echternach', *Archiv für Liturgiewissenschaft* (forthcoming).

Olivar, A., 'Série de *benedictiones lectionum officii* d'après un document de Montserrat aux environs de 1500', *EL* 63 (1949), 42–56.

Pächt, O. and J. J. G. Alexander, *Survey of Illuminated Manuscripts in the Bodleian Library, Oxford I: The German, Dutch, Flemish and French Schools* (Oxford, 1966).

Palazzo, E., 'Un *libellus missae* du scriptorium de Saint-Amand pour Saint-Denis', *RB* 99 (1989), 286–92.

'Les deux rituels d'un *libellus* de Saint-Amand (Paris, Bibliothèque nationale, lat. 13764)', in *Rituels. Mélanges offerts à Pierre-Marie Gy, O. P.*, ed. P. de Clerck and E. Palazzo (Paris, 1990), pp. 423–36.

Les sacramentaires de Fulda, LQF 77 (Aschendorff Münster, 1994).

Pellechet, P., *Notes sur les livres liturgiques des diocèses d'Autun, Chalon et Macon* (Paris, 1883).

Peressotti, G., 'Le messe votive nel messale Aquileiese', *EL* 113 (1999), 139–55.

Pfaff, R. W., 'Eadui Basan: Scriptorum Princeps?', in *England in the Eleventh Century. Proceedings of the Harlaxton Symposium*, ed. C. Hicks (Stamford, 1992), pp. 267–83.

'The calendar', in *The Eadwine Psalter*, ed. Gibson, *et al.*, pp. 62–87

'Massbooks', in *The Liturgical Books of Anglo-Saxon England*, ed. R. W. Pfaff, Old English Newsletter Subsidia 23 (Michigan, 1995), pp. 7–34.

'The sample week in the medieval Latin Divine Office', in *Continuity and*

Change in Christian Worship, ed. R. N. Swanson, Studies in Church History 35 (Woodbridge, 1999), 78–88.

Pickering, F., *The Calendar Pages of Medieval Service Books*, Reading Medieval Studies 1 (Reading, 1980).

Pirri, P., 'La scuola miniaturistica di S. Eutizio', *Speculum* 3 (1949), 3–10.

Pizarak, M., 'Les bénédictions de la table paschale', *EL* 93 (1979), 202–26.

Plummer, J., *Liturgical Manuscripts for the Mass and Divine Office* (New York, 1964).

The Glazier Collection of Illuminated Manuscripts (New York, 1968).

Porter, A. K., *Lombard Architecture*, 3 vols (New Haven, 1917).

Porter, H. B., 'The origin of the medieval rite for the anointing of the sick and dying', *JTS* ns 8 (1956), 211–25.

'The rites for the dying in the early middle ages I: St Theodulf of Orleans', *JTS* ns 10 (1959), 43–62.

'The rites for the dying in the early middle ages II: the legendary sacramentary of Rheims', *JTS* ns 10 (1959), 299–307.

Ordination Prayers of the Ancient Western Churches, Alcuin Club Collections 49 (London, 1967).

Prescott, A., 'The text of the benedictional of St Æthelwold', *Bishop Æthelwold*, ed. Yorke, pp. 119–47.

'The structure of English pre-Conquest benedictionals', *British Library Journal* 13 (1987), 118–58.

Quentin, H., *Les martyrologes historiques du moyen âge* (Paris, 1908).

Ramsay, N., M. Sparks and T. Tatton-Brown (ed.), *St Dunstan: His Life, Times and Cult* (Woodbridge, 1992).

Rand, E. K., *Studies in the Script of Tours. A Survey of the Manuscripts of Tours*, 2 vols, Medieval Academy of America Publications 3 (Cambridge, Mass., 1929).

Rankin, S., 'From memory to record: musical notations in manuscripts from Exeter', *ASE* 13 (1984), 97–114.

'Some reflections on liturgical music at late Anglo-Saxon Worcester', *St Oswald of Worcester: Life and Influence*, ed. N. Brooks and C. Cubitt (Leicester, 1996), pp. 325–48.

Rasmussen, N. K., 'Unité et diversité des pontificaux latins', *Liturgie de l'église particulière et liturgie universelle. Conférences Saint-Serge XXIIe semaine d'études liturgiques, Paris, 30 juin – 3 juillet, 1975*, ed. A. Pistoia, C. M. Triacca and A. M. Triacca, Biblioteca Ephemerides Liturgicae Subsidia 7 (Rome, 1976), 393–410

Les pontificaux du haut moyen âge. Genèse du livre de l'évêque, Spicilegium Sacrum Lovaniense 49 (Louvain, 1998).

Richter, M., *Canterbury Professions*, Canterbury and York Society 67 (London, 1973).

Rickert, M., *The Reconstructed Carmelite Missal* (London, 1952).

Ridyard, S., *The Royal Saints of Anglo-Saxon England* (Cambridge, 1985).

Robertson, A. W., *The Service Books of the Royal Abbey of Saint-Denis* (Oxford, 1991).

Robinson, J. A., 'The Coronation Order in the tenth century', *JTS* 19 (1917), 56–72.

Robinson, P. R., *A Catalogue of Dated and Datable Manuscripts c. 737–1600 in Cambridge Libraries*, 2 vols (Cambridge, 1988).

Rock, D., *The Church of our Fathers*, 4 vols (London, 1849–50).

Rollason, D., 'Lists of saints' resting-places in Anglo-Saxon England', *ASE* 7 (1978), 61–93.

Rosenthal, J., 'The Pontifical of St Dunstan', *St Dunstan*, ed. Ramsay *et al.*, pp. 143–65.

Rose-Troup, F., 'The ancient monastery of St Mary and St Peter at Exeter 680–1050', *Transactions of the Devonshire Association* 61 (1931), 179–220.
'Exeter manumissions and quittances of the eleventh and twelfth centuries', *Transactions of the Devonshire Association* 69 (1937), 417–45.

Rubenstein, J., 'Liturgy against history: the competing visions of Lanfranc and Eadmer of Canterbury', *Speculum* 74 (1999), 279–309.

Salmon, P., 'Bénédictions de l'office des matins. Nouvelles séries', in his *Analecta Liturgica*, Studi e Testi 273 (Vatican City, 1974), 49–66.

Samaran, C. and R. Marichal, *Catalogue de manuscrits en écriture latine portant des indications de date, de lieu ou de copiste*, 7 vols (Paris, 1959–84).

Santantonio, A., *L'ordinazione episcopale. Storia e teologia dei riti dell'ordinazione nelle antiche liturgie dell'occidente*, Studia Anselmiana 69, Analecta Liturgica 2 (Rome, 1976).

Saxer, V., *Le culte de Marie Magdalène en Occident*, Cahiers d'archaéologie et d'histoire 3 (Paris, 1959).

Schaller, D. and E. Könsgen, *Initia Carminum latinorum saeculo undecimo Antiquiorum* (Göttingen, 1977).

Schmid, T., 'Om Sankt Swithunmassen i Sverige', *Nordisk Tidskrift for Bok- och Bibliotekvasen* 31 (1941), 25–34.

Schmitz, H. J., *Die Bussbücher und die Bussdisciplin der Kirche*, 2 vols (Mainz, 1883–98).

Schott, M., *Zwei lütticher Sakramentare in Bamberg und Paris und ihre Verwandten* (Strassburg, 1931).

Schramm, P. E., 'Die Krönung bei den Westfranken und Angelsachsen von 878 bis um 1000', *Zeitschrift für Rechtsgeschichte* 55, Abt 23 (1934), 117–242.

Scott, K. L., *Later Gothic Manuscripts 1390–1490*, 2 vols, A Survey of Manuscripts Illuminated in the British Isles 6, ed. J. J. G. Alexander (London, 1996).

Seidel, L., *Legends in Limestone. Lazarus, Gislebertus and the Cathedral of Autun* (Chicago, 1999).

Semmler, J., 'Von Sakramentar zum Missale. Bemerkungen zu drei liturgische Handschriften der Universitäts- und Landesbibliothek, Düsseldorf', in *Bucher für die Wissenschaft: Bibliotheken zwischen Tradition und Fortschrift. Festschrift für Günter Gattermann zum 65 Geburstag*, ed. G. Kaiser, H. Finger and E. Niggermann (Munich, 1994), pp. 201–12.

Sharpe, R., 'Goscelin's St Augustine and St Mildreth: hagiography and liturgy in context', *JTS* ns 41 (1990), 502–16.
'The date of St Mildreth's translation from Minster-in-Thanet to Canterbury', *Medieval Studies* 53 (1991), 349–54.

Sicard, D., *La liturgie de la mort dans l'église latine des origines à la réforme carolingienne*, Liturgiewissenschäftliche Quellen und Forschungen 63 (Münster-im-Westfalen, 1978).

Snijders, A., '*Acolytus cum ordinatur*. Eine historische Studie', *Sacris Erudiri* 9 (1957), 163–98.

Staerck, A., *Les manuscrits latins conservés à la bibliothèque impériale de Saint-Petersbourg*, 2 vols (St Petersburg, 1910).

Storms, G., *Anglo-Saxon Magic* (The Hague, 1948).

Stroud, D., 'The provenance of the Salisbury Psalter', *The Library*, 6th ser., 1 (1979), 225–35.

Swarzenski, G., *Das Regensburger Buchmalerei des X und XI Jahrhunderts* (Leipzig, 1901).

Tatlock, R., *An English Benedictional translated and adapted from the Leofric Missal* (London, 1964).

Temple, E., *Anglo-Saxon Manuscripts, 900–1066*, A Survey of Manuscripts Illuminated in the British Isles 2, ed. J. J. G. Alexander (London, 1976).

Thacker, A., 'Æthelwold and Abingdon', *Bishop Æthelwold*, ed. Yorke, pp. 43–64.

'Cults at Canterbury: relics and reform under Dunstan and his successors', in *St Dunstan*, ed. Ramsay, *et al.*, pp. 221–45.

Tirot, P., 'Histoire des prières d'offertoire dans la liturgie romaine du VIIe au XVe siècle', *EL* 98 (1984), 148–97.

Tolhurst, J. B. L., 'Le missel de Robert de Jumièges, sacramentaire d'Ely', *Jumièges. Congrès scientifique du XIIIe centenaire. Rouen, 10–12 Juin 1954*, 2 vols (Rouen, 1955) I, 287–92.

Toswell, M. J., 'St Martial and the dating of late Anglo-Saxon manuscripts', *Scriptorium* 51 (1997), 3–14.

Treharne, E. M., *The Old English Life of St Nicholas with the Old English Life of St Giles*, Leeds Texts and Monographs 15 (Leeds, 1997).

Triacca, A. M., 'Le rite de l'impositio manuum super infirmum', *La maladie et la mort du chrétien dans la liturgie. Conferences Saint-Serge 21e semaine d'études liturgiques, Paris 1974*, ed. A. Pistoia, C. M. Triacca and A. M. Triacca, Biblioteca Ephemerides Liturgicae Subsidia (Rome, 1975).

Tristram, H. L. C., *Sex aetates mundi. Die Weltzeitalter bei den Angelsaschen und den Iren*, Untersuchungen und Texte, Anglistiche Forschungen 165 (Heidelburg, 1985).

Unterkircher, F., 'Interpretatio Canonis Missae in codice Vindobonensi 958', *EL* 91 (1977), 32–50.

Vezin, J., 'Les relieures carolingiennes de cuir', *Bibliothèque de l'École des Chartes* 128 (1970), 81–112.

Voigts, L. E., 'The Latin verse and Middle English prose texts on the Sphere of Life and Death in Harley 3719', *The Chaucer Review* 21 (1986), 291–305.

Vrégille, B. de, 'Le rituel de Saint Prothade et *l'ordo canonicorum* de Saint-Jean de Besançon', *Révue du moyen âge latin* 5 (1949), 97–114.

Wallis, F. E., 'MS Oxford St John's College 17: A Medieval Manuscript in its Context' (unpubl. Ph.D. thesis, University of Toronto, 1984).

Warren, F. E., *Liturgy and Ritual of the Celtic Church*, 2nd ed., repr. with an introduction by J. Stevenson (Woodbridge, 1979).

'Manumissions in the Leofric Missal', *Revue Celtique* 5 (1882), 213–17.

Watkin, A., 'Fragment of a twelfth-century collectarium in the Liber Albus of Wells', *Downside Review* 69 (1950), 85–91.

Watson, A., *Catalogue of Dated and Datable Manuscripts c. 700–1600 in the Dept. of Manuscripts, the British Library*, 2 vols (London, 1979).

Catalogue of Dated and Datable Manuscripts c. 435–1600 in Oxford Libraries, 2 vols (Oxford, 1984).

Webber, T., *Scribes and Scholars at Salisbury Cathedral, c. 1075–c. 1125* (Oxford, 1992).

Werner, M., 'The Liudhard medalet', *ASE* 20 (1991), 27–41.

Whitelock, D., M. Brett and C. N. L. Brooke, *Councils and Synods with other Documents relating to the English Church, A. D. 871–1204*, 2 vols (Oxford, 1981).

Wilmart, A., 'Un sacramentaire à l'usage de Saint-Germain-des-Prés. Mentions nécrologiques relatives à ce monastère', *Revue Mabillon* 17 (1927), 279–94.

'Séries de bénédictions pour l'office dans un recueil de Nonantola', *EL* 45 (1931), 354–61.

'La bénédiction romaine du lait et du miel dans l'eucologe Barberini', *RB* 45 (1933), 10–19.

'Un témoin anglo-saxon du calendrier métrique d'York', *RB* 46 (1934), 41–69.

Wilson, H. A., 'The English coronation order', *JTS* 2 (1901), 481–504.

Wormald, F., 'An English eleventh-century psalter with pictures', *Walpole Society* 38 (London, 1962).

'The liturgical calendar of Glastonbury Abbey', *Festschrift Bernhard Bischoff zu seinem 65 Geburtstag*, ed. J. Autenrieth and F. Brunhölzl (Stuttgart, 1971), pp. 325–45.

Wormald, P., *The Making of English Law*, 2 vols (Oxford, 1999 and forthcoming).

Yorke, B. (ed.), *Bishop Æthelwold: His Career and Influence* (Woodbridge, 1988).

H. Zimmermann, *Papsturkunden 896–1046*, 2 vols, Österreichische Akademie der Wissenschaften, Phil.-hist. Klasse, Denkschriften 174 and 177 (Vienna, 1984–5).

COLLATION TABLE

Since the material embodied in *B* and *C* is so miscellaneous, it has seemed best to draw up a synoptic collation table for *A* alone. Some breaks therefore occur in the numeration. The comparative material cited is:

Add: various additions to the earliest manuscripts of the *Hadrianum* and Supplement, ed. J. Deshusses, *Le sacramentaire grégorien*, 3 vols., Spicilegium Friburgense 16, 24 and 28, 2nd ed. (Fribourg, 1979–89) I, 687–718.

Angoulême: Paris, Bibliothèque nationale de France, lat. 816, an 'Eighth-Century Gelasian' sacramentary probably from Angoulême, ed. P. Saint-Roch, *Liber Sacramentorum Engolismensis*, CCSL 159C (Turnhout, 1987).

AP: Milan, Biblioteca Metropolitana, 14, the late-ninth-century Ambrosian pontifical, ed. M. Magistretti, *Pontificale in usum ecclesiae Mediolanensis*, Monumenta veteris liturgicae Ambrosianae 1 (Milan, 1897).

AP*: the coronation order preserved in Milan, Biblioteca Metropolitana, 21, ed. Magistretti, *Pontificale in usum ecclesiae Mediolanensis*, pp. 111–20.

Bapt: various orders for baptism collected in Deshusses, *Le sacramentaire grégorien* III, 95–112.

Basel: Basel, Universitätsbibliothek F. iii. 15e, a fragmentary tenth-century penitential order from Fulda, ed. F. E. Warren, *The Liturgy and Ritual of the Celtic Church*, 2nd ed., repr. with an introduction by J. Stevenson (Woodbridge, 1979), pp. 151–2.

Bat: Vienna, Österreichisches Nationalbibliotek, Vindob. ser. nov. 2762, the pontifical of Baturich, bishop of Regensburg (817–48), ed. F. Unterkircher, *Das Kollectar-Pontificale des Bischofs Baturich von Regensburg*, Spicilegium Friburgense 8 (Fribourg, 1962).

Be: Bergamo, Biblioteca di S. Alessandro in Colonna, s. n., ed. A. Paredi, *Sacramentarium Bergomense*, Monumenta Bergomensiana 6 (Bergamo, 1962).

Bo: Paris, Bibliothèque nationale de France, lat. 13246, the so-called 'Bobbio Missal', probably written in northern Italy in the mid to late eighth century, ed. E. A. Lowe, with J. W. Legg, A. Wilmart and H. A. Wilson, *The Bobbio Missal*, 3 vols, HBS 53, 58 and 61 (London, 1917–24).

Bv: Rome, Biblioteca Vallicelliana, C. 32, an eleventh-century ritual from a house in central Italy, ed. A. Odermatt, *Ein Rituale in beneventanischer Schrift*, Spicilegium Friburgense 26 (Fribourg, 1980).

Can: Baltimore, Walters Art Gallery, W. 6, an eleventh-century missal from Canosa, ed. S. Rehle, *Missale Beneventanum von Canosa*, Textus Patristici et Liturgici 9 (Regensburg, 1972).

Cant: London, British Library, Harley 2892, an early-eleventh-century benedictional from Christ Church, Canterbury, ed. R. M. Woolley, *The Canterbury Benedictional*, HBS 51 (London, 1917).

DC: Durham Cathedral Library, A. IV. 19, a collectar written somewhere in the south of England in the early tenth century and acquired by the Durham community *c.* 970, ed. U. Lindelöf, *The Durham Ritual*, Surtees Society 140 (Durham, 1927).

Ec: Paris, Bibliothèque nationale de France, lat. 9433, the late-ninth-century sacramentary from Echternach, ed. Y. Hen, *The Sacramentary of Echternach*, HBS 110 (London, 1997).

Eligius: Paris, Bibliothèque nationale de France, lat. 12051, a mid-ninth-century sacramentary probably written at Corbie for Beauvais, ed. PL 78, cols 25–240.

Egbert: Paris, Bibliothèque nationale de France, lat. 10575, the so-called 'Egbert Pontifical', a late-tenth- or early-eleventh-century pontifical written for some house in southern England, ed. H. M. J. Banting, *Two Anglo-Saxon Pontificals*, HBS 104 (London, 1992), pp. 3–153.

F: Göttingen, Universitätsbibliothek, theol. lat. 231, an early-tenth-century sacramentary from Fulda, ed. G. Richter and A. Schönfelder, *Sacramentarium Fuldense saeculi X* (Fulda, 1912), repr. HBS 101 (London, 1977).

Flor: St Florian, Bibliothek des Chorrenstiftes, XI. 467, a twelfth-century ritual, ed. A. Franz, *Das Rituale von St Florian aus dem zwölften Jahrhundert* (Freiburg-im-Breisgau, 1904).

Frei: Freiburg, Universitätsbibliothek, 363, a ninth-century pontifical from Basle, and a ninth-century pontifical probably written at the abbey of St Gallen for the bishop of Konstanz formerly at Donauschingen, ed. M. J. Metzger, *Zwei karolingische Pontifikalien von Oberrhein*, Freiburger Theologische Studien 17 (Freiburg-im-Breisgau, 1914).

G: a collection of southern German books, ed. M. Gerbert, *Monumenta Veteris Liturgiae Alemannicae*, 2 vols (St Blasien, 1777–8).

Ga: the 'Gallican' order for the dead, ed. Deshusses, *Le sacramentaire grégorien* III, 171–5.

Gellone: Paris, Bibliothèque nationale de France, lat. 12048, a late-eighth- or early-ninth-century 'Eighth-Century Gelasian' sacramentary written for Hildoard, bishop of Cambrai, but soon after at the abbey of Gellone, ed. A. Dumas and J. Deshusses, *Liber Sacramentorum Gellonensis*, CCSL 159 (Turnhoult, 1981).

Giso: London, British Library, Cotton Vitellius A. xviii, the sacramentary of Giso, bishop of Wells (1060–88), ed. (in part) F. E. Warren, *The Leofric Missal*, pp. 303–7. Cited by Warren's page number.

Ha. & Sp.: The Hadrianum and Supplement, ed. Deshusses, *Le sacramentaire grégorien* I.

Hes*.: Antiphonale Missarum Sextuplex*, ed. R. J. Hesbert (Brussels, 1935).

Lan: Rouen, Bibliothèque municipale, 368, the late-tenth- or early-eleventh-century 'Lanalet Pontifical', a pontifical from Crediton which probably found its way to Wells soon after it had been written, ed. G. H. Doble, *Pontificale Lanaletense*, HBS 74 (London, 1937).

LC: London, British Library, Harley 2891, a collectar written at Exeter for Bishop Leofric in the mid eleventh century, ed. E. S. Dewick and W. H. Frere, *The Leofric Collectar*, 2 vols, HBS 45 and 56 (London, 1914–21).

Le: Verona, Biblioteca Capitolare, 85, an early-seventh-century sacramentary perhaps from Verona, ed. L. C. Mohlberg, *Sacra-*

mentarium Veronense, Rerum ecclesiasticarum Documenta, Series maior, Fontes 1 (Rome, 1956).

MF: Vatican City, Biblioteca Apostolica Vaticana, Reg. lat. 257, a mid-eighth-century pontifical and sacramentary from a house in northern France, ed. L. C. Mohlberg, *Missale Francorum*, Rerum ecclesiasticarum Documenta, Series maior, Fontes 2 (Rome, 1957).

Milan: Milan, Biblioteca Metropolitana, D. 3–3, an eleventh-century Ambrosian sacramentary from Milan, ed. J. Frei, *Das ambrosianische Sakramentar D. 3–3 aus dem Mailandischen Metropolitankapitel*, LQF 56 (Münster-im-Westfalen, 1974).

Pad: Padua, Biblioteca Capitolare, D. 47, a copy of a pre-Hadrianic Gregorian sacramentary written in Lotharingia in the mid ninth century, ed. Deshusses, *Le sacramentaire grégorien* I, 609–84.

Par: the order for the visitation of the sick in Stockholm, Kungliga Bibliotek, Holm. A. 136, a late-ninth-century sacramentary written at Saint-Amand for the bishop of Sens, ed. Deshusses, *Le sacramentaire grégorien* III, 148–9.

Phillipps: Berlin, Deutsche Staatsbibliothek, 105 (formerly Phillips 1667), an 'Eighth-Century Gelasian' sacramentary from a house in northern France, ed. O. Heiming, *Liber Sacramentorum Augustodunesis*, CCSL 159B (Turnhout, 1987).

Pr: Prague, Metropolitan Library, O. 83, a late-eighth-century sacramentary from Regensburg, later at Prague, ed. A. Dold and L. Eizenhöfer, *Das Prager Sakramentar*, 2 vols, Texte und Arbeiten 38–42 (Beuron, 1944–9).

PRG: the Romano-German Pontifical, generally thought to have been compiled at Mainz in the mid tenth century, ed. C. Vogel and R. Elze, *Le pontifical romano-germanique du dixième siècle*, 3 vols, Studi e Testi 226, 227 and 269 (Vatican City, 1963–72).

Prud: the order for the visitation of the sick in Paris, Bibliothèque nationale de France, lat. 818, a mid-eleventh-century sacramentary from Troyes, known as the 'Pontifical of Prudentius of Troyes', ed. E. Martène, *De antiquis ecclesiae Ritibus*, 4 vols (Antwerp, 1736–8) I, cap. vii, art iii, ordo 3.

Reims: the order for the visitation of the sick from a sacramentary of Reims now lost, partially ed. PL 78, cols 529–37.

Rob: Rouen, Bibliothèque municipale, 369, a pontifical written for Æthelgar, bishop of Selsey (980–8), later owned by an archbishop named Robert, possibly either of Rouen (990–1037) or Jumièges (1052–70), ed. H. A. Wilson, *The Benedictional of Archbishop Robert*, HBS 24 (London, 1902).

Stowe: Dublin, Royal Irish Academy, D. II. 3, the late-eighth-century 'Stowe Missal', ed. G. F. Warner, *The Stowe Missal*, 2 vols, HBS 32 (London, 1915).

TC: Textes complementaires, various supplementary prayers and *ordines* in the manuscripts ed. Deshusses, *Le sacramentaire grégorien* II and III.

Vat. Gel.: Vatican City, Biblioteca Apostolica Vaticana, lat. 316, the so-called 'Vatican Gelasian Sacramentary', copied at the nunnery of Chelles in the mid eighth century, ed. L. C. Mohlberg, *Liber Sacramentorum Romanae aecclesiae ordinis anni circuli*, Rerum ecclesiasticarum Documenta, Series maior, Fontes 4 (Rome, 1960).

COLLATION TABLE

PREFATORY MATERIAL

Leofric A	Ha. & Sp.	TC	Gellone	Durham	Eligius	Others
52				126		
53				126		Bat 288
54				126		Bat 290
55				126		Bat 289
56				126		Bat 294
57				126		Bat 292
58				126		Bat 298
59				126		
60				126		
61				126		
62				127		
63				127		
64				127		
65				127		
66				127		
67				127		
68				127		
69				127		
70				127		
71				127		
72				127		
73				127		
74				127		
75				127		
76				127		
77				127		
78				128		
79				128		
80				128		
81				128		
82				128		Bat 257
83				128		
84				128		
85				128		
86				128		
87				128		

Leofric A	Ha. & Sp.	TC	Gellone	Durham	Eligius	Others
88				128		
89				128		
90				128		
91				128		
92				128		
93				128		
94				128		
95				129		
96						
97		4449	2199			F 2815
98	1467	4448	2198			F 2814
99		4447	2197			
100	1466	4445	2195			F 2812
101		4450	2200			
102		4453	2202			F 2817
103		(4459)	(2208)			(F 2823)
104						
105		(4453)	(2210)			(F 2825)
106						
107						
108						
113						
114						
115						
116						
119		4392				
120		4393				
121		4395				
122		4374				
123						F 2186
127						
128						
129						
130						

267

CANON AND TEMPORAL

Leofric A	Ha. & Sp.	Pad.	Gellone	Angoulême	Eligius	Others
330	3	874				
331	3–4	875				
332	5	876	1933	1755		
333	6	877	1934	1756		
334	7	878	1935	1757		
335	8	879	1936	1758		
336	9–10	880–1	1936–7	1758–9		
337	10–12	881–3	1937–40	1759–61		
338	13	884	1941	1764		
339	13a, 1013	885–6	1942	1765		
340	14	887	1943	1766		
341	15–16	888–9	1944–5	1767		
342	17–18	890–1	1946–7	1768–9		
343	19	892	1948	1770		
344	20	893	1949	1771		
345						Hes. 8
346	33	1	1		29, 1	
347	34	2	2		29, 2	
348	1516				29, 3	
349	1738					
350	35	3	6		29, 4	
351						Hes. 9
352	36	4	8		29, 6	
353	37	5		3	29, 7	
354	1517		11	4	30, 1	
355	39	7		5		
356	40	8	14	6	30, 4	
357	41	9		7	30, 6	
358						Hes. 10
359	42	10	16	12	31, 1	
360	43	11	17	8	31, 3	
361	44	12	10	2	31, 2	
362	45	13	18	9		
363	46	14	22	15	31, 4	
364	47	15	19	10	31, 6	
365	48	16	23	17	31, 5	
366	49	17	26	21	31, 7	
367						Hes. 11
368	50	18	28		31, 8	
369	51				31, 9	

COLLATION TABLE: CANON AND TEMPORAL

Leofric A	Ha. & Sp.	Pad.	Gellone	Angoulême	Eligius	Others
370	52					
371	1738				31, 11	
372	53	19		20, 29	32, 1	
373	54	20	9	1		
374	55	21	32	31	32, 5	
375	56	22	15	11	32, 6	
376	57	23	38	37	32, 2	
377	58	24	25	19	32, 3	
378	59		35	33	32, 7	
379	60		40	38		
380	61		41	39	32, 9	
381						Hes. 17
382	1090	49	67	69	36, 9	
383	1091	50	69	71		
384	1521		70	72		
385	1092	51	71	73		
386			76	82	37, 1	Add. 13*
387			78	84	37, 2	Add. 14*
388						
389	1522		79	85	37, 3	Add. 15*
390	1743				37, 4	
391			80	86	37, 5	Add. 16*
392	1093	52	91	91	37, 6	
393	1094	53	93	93	37, 7	
394	1523		94	94	38, 1	
395	1095	54	95	95	38, 3	
396						
397		55	97	97	38, 5	Add. 20*
398		56	98	98	38, 6	Add. 21*
399		57	100	100	38, 8	Add. 23*
400						Hes. 18
401	87	58	101	101	38, 9	
402	88	59	103	105	39, 1	
403	89	60	117	117	39, 2	
404	90	61	105	107		
405	1744				39, 4	
406	91	62	106	108	39, 5	
407	92	63	108	110	39, 7	
408	94	64	111	111	39, 6	
409	95					
410	96		109	112	39, 8	
411	97		110	113	39, 9	
412	93		121	120	40, 7	Add. 25*

269

Leofric A	Ha. & Sp.	Pad.	Gellone	Angoulême	Eligius	Others
413			115	121	40, 8	Add. 26*
414			124	122	40, 9	Add. 27*
415	98		125	123	39, 10	
416						Hes. 19
417	1096	66	113	114	40, 1	Add. 28*
418	1097	67	116	116	40, 2	Add. 29*
419	1525				40, 3	Add. 30*
420	1098	68	118	118	40, 5	Add. 31*
421	1099		134	129	41, 3	Add. 32*
422	1100	73	136	131		Add. 33*
423	1528		137	132	41, 6	Add. 34*
424	1110	74	138	133	41, 8	Add. 35*
425	912		139	134	41, 9	
426	1102	94	176	171	47, 5	Add. 36*
427						Hes. 21
428	1103	95	178	173	47, 6	Add. 37*
429	1533				47, 7	Add. 38*
430	1104	96	180	175	48, 1	Add. 39*
431	908		181	176	48, 2	
432	1105	100		195	48, 3	Add. 43*
433	1106	101		197	48, 4	Add. 44*
434	1536		179	198	48, 5	Add. 45*
435	1107	102		199	48, 7	Add. 46*
436	918			200		
437						Hes. 26
438	1108			213	48, 8	Add. 47*
439	1109	113	208	215	48, 9	Add. 48*
440	1539		209	216	48, 10	Add. 49*
441	1110		210	217	49, 2	Add. 50*
442	909		211	218		
443	1111		218	225	49, 9	Add. 51*
444	1112		220	227	49, 5	Add. 52*
445	1540		222	228	49, 6	Add. 53*
446	1113		223	229	49, 8	Add. 54*
447	927		224	230		
448						TC 3432, Ec 1644
449						TC 3433, Ec 1645
450						TC 3435, Ec 1647
451	123	103	195	201	46, 1	
452	124	104	196	202	46, 2	
453	125	105	197	204	46, 3	
454	89/1526				46, 4	
455	1746				46, 5	

Leofric A	Ha. & Sp.	Pad.	Gellone	Angoulême	Eligius	Others
456	126	106	199	207	46, 6	
457	127		200		46, 7	
458	140				52, 1	
459	141				52, 2	
460						Hes. 33
461	142				52, 5	
462	1598					
463	143			879	52, 7	
464	(1342)		857	888	52, 6	Add. 337*
465				890	53, 1	
466				891	53, 2	
467						Hes. 34
468	144	118	252	255	53, 8	
469	145	119				
470	1543		250	253	53, 5	
471	146	120	247	250	53, 7	
472			253	256		
473	147	121			53, 9	
474						Hes. 35
475	148		256	260		
476	1544				54, 2	
477	149		258	262		
478			259	263		
479	150	124			54, 6	
480	151	125			54, 7	
481						Hes. 36
482	1545				54, 8	
483	152	126			55, 3	
484			264	264		
485			(265)	(270)		
486	1379		266	271		
487	1380		267	272		
488	1381		268	273		
489	1382		269	274		
490						
491						TC 3969
492						G II 31, F 2378
493						Basel
494	153	127	274	276	55, 4	
495						Hes. 37
496	154	128	275	277	55, 5	
497	155	129	276	278	55, 6	
498	1546		277	279	55, 7	

271

Leofric A	Ha. & Sp.	Pad.	Gellone	Angoulême	Eligius	Others
499	156	130	278	280	55, 8	
500	157	131	283	285	56, 1	
501						Hes. 38
502	158				56, 2	
503	159				56, 3	
504	160				56, 5	
505	161				56, 6	
506						Hes. 39
507	162	132	285	286	56, 7	
508	163	133	261	266	56, 8	
509			288	290	57, 6	
510	165	135	279	281	57, 7	
511						(Hes. 38)
512			291	293		
513			292	294		
514			293	295		
515						
516						Hes. 40
517	166	136	296	297	57, 8	
518	167	137	297	300	57, 9	
519	1547		298	301	57, 10	
520	168	139	299	303	58, 2	
521	170	141	305	306	58, 5	
522	1746				58, 1	
523	169	140	301	305	58, 4	
524	171	142	306	307	58, 8	
525						Hes. 41
526	172					
527	1548		309	311	59, 2	
528	173	144	310	312	59, 3	
529	174	145				
530						Hes. 42
531	175	146	312	315	59, 5	
532	176	147	314	319	59, 6	
533	1549		315	320	59, 7	
534	177	148				
535	178	149	317	322	59, 9	
536						Hes. 43
537	179	150	319	323	59, 10	
538	180	151	325	324	60, 1	
539	181	152				
540	1550		321	326	60, 3	
541	182	153	322	327	60, 4	

Leofric A	Ha. & Sp.	Pad.	Gellone	Angoulême	Eligius	Others
542	183	154			60, 5	
543						Hes. 44
544	184	189	325	324		
545	185	190	320	325	60, 7	
546	1551		327	333	60, 8	
547	186	191		328	60, 9	
548	187	192	323	329	60, 10	
549						Hes. 45
550	188	159	331	336	61, 1	
551	189	160	332	339	61, 2	
552	1552				61, 3	
553	190				61, 4	
554	191	163				
555						Hes. 46a
556	192	164	336	354	61, 6	
557	193	165				
558	194	166	337	355	61, 8	
559	195	167	338	356	61, 9	
560	198	169	339	357	61, 10	
561	199	170			61, 11	
562	200	171	342	359	61, 12	
563	1565					
564	201	173			62, 2	
565	846				62, 3	
566						Hes. 46b
567	202	174	352	363	62, 4	
568	203	175				
569	1554		355	367	62, 6	
570	1747				62, 7	
571	204					
572			357	369	62, 9	Add. 78*
573	205	177	358	370	63, 1	
574						
575	206	178	360	373	63, 2	
576	1555				63, 3	
577	207	179			63, 4	
578	208	180				
579						Hes. 48
580	209	181	364	377	63, 6	
581	210	182	365	378	63, 7	
582	1556				63, 8	
583	211	183			63, 9	
584	212	184				

Leofric A	Ha. & Sp.	Pad.	Gellone	Angoulême	Eligius	Others
585						Hes. 49
586	213	185	372	388	63, 11	
587	214	186	370	385	64, 1	
588	1557				64, 2	
589	215	187			64, 3	
590	216	188			64, 4	
591						Hes. 50
592	217	217	369	384	64, 5	
593	218	218		386		
594	1558				64, 7	
595	219	219	371	387	64, 8	
596	220	220	377	393	64, 9	
597						Hes. 51
598	221	193	379	394	64, 10	
599	222	194	380	397	65, 1	
600	1559				65, 2	
601	223	196	381	399	65, 3	
602	224	197	382	400	65, 4	
603						Hes. 52
604	225	198	384	403	65, 5	
605	226	199	385	406	65, 6	
606	1553		343	360	62, 1	
607	227	200	386	408	65, 8	
608	228	201			65, 9	
609						Hes. 53
610	229	202	389	411	65, 10	
611	230	203				
612	1561		392	414	66, 2	
613	1748				66, 3	
614	231	204	393	415	66, 4	
615			394	416	66, 5	Add. 79*
616	232	205	416	424	66, 6	
617						Hes. 54
618	233	206	413	426	66, 7	
619	1562				66, 8	
620	234	207			66, 9	
621	235	208				
622	236	209	411	429	67, 2	
623	237	210	418	431	67, 3	
624						Hes. 55
625	1563				67, 4	
626	238	211	419	432	67, 5	
627	239	212	470	487		

Leofric A	Ha. & Sp.	Pad.	Gellone	Angoulême	Eligius	Others
628						Hes. 56
629	240	213	421	434	67, 7	
630	241	214	423	436	67, 8	
631	1564				67, 9	
632	242	215	424	437	67, 10	
633	243	216	431	443		
634						Hes. 57
635						
636						
637	1565					
638						
639	247		394	416		
640						Hes. 58
641	248	221	432	444	68, 6	
642	249	222	434	448	68, 7	
643	1566				68, 8	
644	250	224	435	450	68, 9	
645	251	225	455	469		
646	252	226			69, 1	
647	253	227			69, 2	
648						Hes. 59
649	1567				69, 3	
650	254	228			69, 4	
651	255	229	448		69, 5	
652	256		437	458	69, 6	
653						Hes. 60
654	257	231	445	460		
655	1568					
656	258	232	447	462	70, 1	
657	259	230	444	459	70, 2	
658	1749				69, 9	
659						Hes. 61
660	260	233	437	446	70, 3	
661	261				70, 4	
662	1569				70, 5	
663	262					
664	263	236				
665						Hes. 62
666	264	237	459	473	70, 8	
667	265					
668	1570				70, 10	
669	266	239	435	450		
670	267	240	463	478		

COLLATION TABLE: CANON AND TEMPORAL

Leofric A	Ha. & Sp.	Pad.	Gellone	Angoulême	Eligius	Others
671						Hes. 63
672	268	241	464	479		
673	269	242	465	480	71, 4	
674	270	243	466	481	71, 5	
675	1571				71, 6	
676	271	244	467	483	71, 7	
677	272	245	468	484	71, 8	
678						Hes. 64
679	273	273	465	480	71, 9	
680	274	274	461	476	70, 9	
681	1572				72, 2	
682	275	275	462	477	71, 1	
683	276	276	473	490	72, 4	
684						Hes. 65
685	277	250	474	491	72, 5	
686	278	251	485	506	72, 6	
687	1573				72, 7	
688	279	252	477	495	72, 8	
689	280	253			72, 9	
690	281	254	481	525	73, 1	
691						Hes. 66
692	282	255		499	73, 2	
693	1574				73, 3	
694	283	256	482	501	73, 4	
695	284	257	485	505	73, 5	
696	285	258	484	504	73, 6	
697						Hes. 67
698	286	259			73, 7	
699	1575		487	507	73, 8	
700	1750				73, 9	
701	287	260	488	508	73, 10	
702			489	509	74, 1	Add. 91*
703						Hes. 68
704	288	261	495	514	74, 2	
705	289	262	497	518	74, 3	
706	1576				74, 4	
707	290	263	498	519	74, 5	
708	291	264				
709						Hes. 69
710	292	265	500	522	74, 7	
711	293	266	502		74, 8	
712	1577				74, 9	
713	294	267	503	527	74, 10	

Leofric A	Ha. & Sp.	Pad.	Gellone	Angoulême	Eligius	Others
714	295	268	489	509		
715						Hes. 70
716	296	269	506	529	75, 2	
717	297	270	507	531	75, 3	
718	1578				75, 4	
719	298	271	508	533	75, 5	
720	299	272	496	534		
721	300		439	453		
722						Hes. 71
723	301		440	455		
724	1579				75, 9	
725	302			456		
726	303		442	457		
727	304	277	516	542	76, 2	
728						Hes. 72a
729	305	278			76, 3	
730	1580				76, 4	
731	306	279	518	545	76, 5	
732	307		431	443		
733						Hes. 72b
734	308		454	468		
735	309		456	470		
736	1581				76, 9	
737	310		457	471		
738	311		458	472	71, 2	
739						TC 4334, Ec 337
740						Hes. 73
741	312	281	556	558	77,3	
742	313	282			77, 4	
743	1582		568	561	77, 5	
744	314					
745			570	564		Add. 96*
746	1751				77, 6	
747						Hes. 74
748	315	284	572	565	77, 9	
749	316	285			78, 2	
750	1583				78, 3	
751	317	286			78, 4	
752	318	287			78, 5	
753						Hes. 75
754	319	288	577	572	78, 6	
755	320	288a			78, 8	
756	1584				78, 9	

Leofric A	Ha. & Sp.	Pad.	Gellone	Angoulême	Eligius	Others
757	321					
758	322	290			79, 1	
759						Hes. 76
760	323	291	582	580	81, 2	
761	324	292	583	586	81, 4	
762	325	293				
763	1585				81, 7	
764	326	294	586	584	81, 9	
765	327	295	587	590	81, 10	
766			(588)	(598)		
767			594	604		Add. 114*, TC 3963
768			595	605		Add. 115*, TC 3964
769			596	606		Add. 116*, TC 3965
770	1753				83, 9	
771						Hes. 77
772	328	299		642	82, 1	
773	329	300		643	82, 3	
774	1586		614	626		
775	1587				82, 4	
776	330	296		627	83, 2	
777	331	301	(616)	(628)	83, 3	
778	332	302	617	629	83, 5	
779	337	298	639	646	85, 4	
780			(641)	(647)	(85, 5)	
781	328	299	642	648	82, 1	
782			(643)	(649)		
783			644	650		
784			(645)	(651)		
785	338	303	646	652	79, 5	
786	339	304	647	654	79, 6	
787	340	305	648	655	79, 7	
788	341	306	649	657	79, 8	
789	342	307	650	658	79, 9	
790	343	308	651	660	79, 10	
791	344	309	652	661	79, 11	
792	345	310	655		79, 12	
793	346	311	656		80, 1	
794	347	312	657	666	80, 2	
795	348	313	658	667	80, 3	
796	349	314	659	669	80, 4	
797	350	315	660	670	80, 5	
798	351	316	661	672	80, 6	
799	352	317	662	673	80, 7	

Leofric A	Ha. & Sp.	Pad.	Gellone	Angoulême	Eligius	Others
800	353	318	663	675	80, 8	
801	354	319	664	676	80, 9	
802	355	320	665	678	80, 10	
803			666	679	(83, 7)	
804	1021		677	733		
805	1022		678	734		
806	1023		680	741	88, 2	
807	1024		681	742	87, 3	
808	1025			742	87, 4	
809	1026		683	743		
810	1027		682	743		
811	1028		685	744	87, 5	
812	1029		686	744		
813	1030		687	745	87, 9	
814	1031		688	745	87, 10	
815	1032		689	746	87, 11	
816	1033		690	746		
817	1034			747		
818	1035			747	87, 12	
819	1036		691	748		
820	1037		692	748	87, 14	
821	1038		693	749	87, 13	
822	1039		694	749		
823	1040		695	750	87, 7	
824	1041		684	750		
825	1042			751		
826	1043		696	751		
827	1044		697	752		
828	1045		698	752		
829	1046		699	753		
830	1047		700	753		
831						Hes. 831
832	370, (1047)		(700)	(753)	88, 5	
833	1048		701	754	88, 6	
834	(1064)		(702)	(755)		
835	377	327	715	763	91, 1	
836	378	328	719	765	91, 3	
837	379	329	721	767	91, 4	
838	380	330	(722)	(769)	91, 6	
839	381	331	(723)		91, 7	
840	1754				91, 8	
841	382	332				
842	383	333	727	773	92, 2	

Leofric A	Ha. & Sp.	Pad.	Gellone	Angoulême	Eligius	Others
843						Hes. 80
844	384			774	92, 3	
845	385		(730)	(776)	92, 4	
846	386			777	92, 5	
847	387			(769)	92, 6	
848	1755				92, 7	
849	388		732	778	92, 8	
850	389	334	734	780	92, 9	
851	390	335	735	781	92, 10	
852	391	336	736	782	93, 1	
853	392	337	739	784	93, 3	
854						Hes. 81
855	393	328	719	775		
856	394	329	721	767		
857	395		722	768		
858	396	331	723	769		
859	1596				93, 5	
860			743	788	93, 8	
861	398	338	744	789	93, 9	
862	399	339	745	790	93, 10	
863	400	340	746	791	93, 11	
864						Hes. 82
865	401	341	748	792	94, 1	
866	402	342			94, 2	
867	1591			795	94, 3	
868	404	344	753	796	94, 6	
869	405	345	754	797	94, 7	
870	406	346	755	798	94, 8	
871	407	347	756	799	94, 9	
872						Hes. 83
873	408	348		800	94, 10	
874	409	349	759	801	94, 11	
875	1592				94, 12	
876	411	350	763	804	95, 3	
877	412	351	764	805	95, 4	
878	413	352	765	806	95, 5	
879	414	353	766	807	95, 6	
880						Hes. 84
881	415	354	768	808	95, 7	
882	416	355	770	810	95, 8	
883	1593				95, 9	
884	419	356	774	812	95, 12	
885	420	357	775	813	96, 1	

Leofric A	Ha. & Sp.	Pad.	Gellone	Angoulême	Eligius	Others
886	421	358	776	814	96, 2	
887	422	359	777	815	96, 3	
888						Hes. 85
889	423	360	779	816	96, 4	
890	424	361	780	818	96, 5	
891	1594		781	819	96, 6	
892	426	363	784	820	96, 9	
893	427	364	785	821	96, 10	
894	428	365	786	822	96, 11	
895						Hes. 86
896	429	366	788	823	96, 12	
897	430	367	789	825	97, 1	
898	1595				97, 2	
899	432	368	793	827	97, 5	
900	433	369	794	828	97, 6	
901	434	370	795	829	97, 7	
902	435	371	797	830	97, 8	
903	436	372		832	97, 9	
904	1596			833	97, 10	
905	1756				97, 11	
906						Hes. 87
907	437	373			98, 1	
908	438	374	802			
909	439	375	803	836	98, 3	
910	440	376	804	837		
911	441	377	805	383	98, 4	
912	442	378		839	98, 10	
913	443	379		840	98, 5	
914	444	380			98, 6	
915	445		808	841	98, 7	
916	451		806	840	98, 12	
917	452			847	99, 1	
918	456				98, 2	
919	450		819	845		
920	446		834	842	98, 8	
921	447		817		98, 9	
922	448			843	98, 11	
923	449		833	844		
924	453		831	848	105, 8	
925	455		820	850		
926	457		832	851	103, 13	
927	1757					
928	1758					

COLLATION TABLE: CANON AND TEMPORAL

Leofric A	Ha. & Sp.	Pad.	Gellone	Angoulême	Eligius	Others
929		381	837	867		Add. 122*
930		382	839	869		Add. 123*
931	1597	383	840	870		Add. 124*
932		384	842	872		Add. 125*
933						Hes. 88
934	1114	390	861	892	103, 12	
935	1115	391	863	894		
936	1599				104, 1	
937	1116	392	865	896		
938			828	864		
939						Hes. 89
940	1117	396	879	910	104, 5	
941	1118	397	881	912		
942	1602	398			104, 7	
943	1119	399	883	914		
944			880	911		
945	1120	411	925	922	105, 3	
946						Hes. 90
947	1121	412	927	924		
948	1607	413			105, 5	
949	1122	414	929	926		
950			926	923		
951						Hes. 91
952	1123	424	949	944	105, 9	
953	1124	425		946		
954	1610	426			105, 11	
955	1125	427	954	948		
956			951	945		
957	466	400	890	959	106, 3	
958	467	401	891	960	106, 4	
959	468	402	892	961	106, 5	
960	469	403	893	962	106, 6	
961	470	404	894	963	106, 7	
962	471		898	974	106, 8	
963						Hes. 94
964	472	405	895	965	106, 9	
965	473	406	896	966		
966	1604				106, 11	
967	1759				106, 12	
968	474	407	897	968	107, 1	
969	475		899	978	107, 2	
970						
971				2237		

282

Leofric A	Ha. & Sp.	Pad.	Gellone	Angoulême	Eligius	Others
972				2235		
973					107, 10	
974				2224		
975				1949		
976						Hes. 101bis
977			971		108, 4	
978			973			Add. 139*
979			974			Add. 141*
980			975		108, 8	Add. 143*
981			976			Add. 144*
982						Hes. 102
983	497	440	978		108, 10	
984	498	441	979		108, 11	
985	499	442	980		108, 12	
986	500	443	981			
987	1760				110, 1	
988	501	444	982		109, 4	
989	502	446	984		109, 6	
990	503	447	985		109, 8	
991						Hes. 103
992	1126	448	986		109, 9	
993	1127	449	988		109, 10	
994	1613				109, 11	
995	1128	451	990		110, 2	
996			983			
997	1049		996			
998	1050		997			
999	1051		998			
1000	1052		999			
1001	1053		1000			
1002	1054		1001			
1003	1055		1002			
1004	1056		1003		110, 6	
1005	1057		1004			
1006	1058		1005		110, 10	
1007	1059		1006			
1008	1060		1007			
1009	1061		1008		110, 7	
1010	1061a		1009		110, 12	
1011	1062		1010		110, 13	
1012	(1064)		(1012)			
1013	520	460	1014		110, 14	
1014	521	461				

Leofric A	Ha. & Sp.	Pad.	Gellone	Angoulême	Eligius	Others
1015						Hes. 105
1016	1614		1024		111, 2	
1017	523	463	1017		111, 4	
1018	524	464	1018		111, 5	
1019	1761				111, 6	
1020	525	465				
1021			1019		111, 7	
1022	526	466	1028		111, 9	
1023	527		1029		112, 1	
1024						Hes. 106
1025	528		1016		112, 2	
1026	529				112, 4	
1027	530				112, 5	
1028	1762				112, 6	
1029	531		1033		112, 7	
1030			1034			
1031						Hes. 107
1032	532	474	1038		112, 10	
1033	533	475	1039		112, 11	
1034	1615				113, 1	
1035	534	476	1040		113, 2	
1036						Hes. 108
1037	535	477	1041		113, 4	
1038	536	478	1042		113, 5	
1039	1616				113, 6	
1040	537	479	1043		113, 7	
1041						Hes. 109
1042	538	480	1044		113, 8	
1043	539	481	1045		113, 9	
1044	540	482	1046		114, 1	
1045	1617				114, 2	
1046	541	483	1048		114, 3	
1047			1010			Add. 146*
1048						
1049			1015		114, 5	
1050	1618				114, 6	
1051			1026		114, 7	
1052						Hes. 110
1053	542	484	1049		114, 9	
1054	543	485	1050		114, 10	
1055	1619				115, 1	
1056	544	486	1052		115, 2	
1057	545	487	1053		115, 4	

Leofric A	Ha. & Sp.	Pad.	Gellone	Angoulême	Eligius	Others
1058	546	488	1054		114, 4	
1059	547	489	1055		115, 6	
1060	548	490	1056		115, 7	
1061	549	491	1057		115, 8	
1062						Hes. 111
1063	550	492	1058		115, 9	
1064	551	493	1059		(119, 8)	
1065	1620				115, 11	
1066	552	495	1061		116, 2	
1067			1063			Add. 149*
1068			1064			Add. 150*
1069						Hes. 172bis
1070	1621		1065		116, 5	
1071			1066			Add. 151*
1072			1067			
1073						Hes. 173
1074	1129	505	1076		174, 7	
1075	1130	506	1078			
1076	1623		1079		175, 2	
1077	1131	507	1080		175, 4	
1078			1081		175, 5	
1079						Hes. 174
1080	1132		1088	993	175, 6	
1081	1133	509	1090	995	175, 7	
1082	1624		1091	996	175, 6	
1083	1134	510	1092	997	176, 1	
1084			1115			
1085						Hes. 175
1086	1135		1116	998	176, 3	
1087	1136		1118	1000	176, 4	
1088	1626		1119	1001		
1089	1137		1120	1002		
1090			1117	999	176, 8	
1091						Hes. 176
1092	1138	517	1137	1019	176, 9	
1093	1139	518	1139	1021	176, 10	
1094	1628			1022	177, 1	
1095	1140	519	1141	1023	177, 3	
1096			1138	1020	177, 4	
1097						Hes. 177
1098	1141	535	1174	1054	177, 5	
1099	1142	536	1176	1056		
1100	1632		1177	1058	177, 7	

Leofric A	Ha. & Sp.	Pad.	Gellone	Angoulême	Eligius	Others
1101	1143	537	1178	1059	177, 9	
1102			1175	1055	177, 10	
1103						Hes. 178
1104	1144	554	1211	1095	177, 11	
1105	1145	555	1213	1097	178, 1	
1106	1634		1214	1098	178, 2	
1107	1146	556	1215	1099	178, 4	
1108			1212	1096		
1109						Hes. 179
1110	1147		1227	1116	178, 6	
1111	1148		1229	1118	178, 7	
1112	1636		1230	1119	178, 8	
1113	1149		1231	1120	179, 2	
1114			1228	1117	179, 3	
1115						Hes. 180
1116	1150	567	1241	1125	179, 4	
1117	1151		1242	1127	179, 5	
1118	1639				179, 6	
1119	1152	569	1245	1129	179, 8	
1120			1243	1126		
1121						Hes. 181
1122	1153	570	1252	1130	179, 10	
1123	1154	571	1254	1132	179, 11	
1124	1639				180, 1	
1125	1155	572	1256	1134		
1126			1253	1131	180, 3	
1127						Hes. 182
1128	1156		1272	1152		
1129	1157	580	1273	1153	180, 6	
1130	1642		1274	1154	180, 7	
1131	1158	581	1275	1155	180, 9	
1132			1271	1151		
1133						Hes. 183
1134	1159	591	1332	1179	181, 2	
1135	1160	592	1334	1181	181, 3	
1136	1645				181, 4	
1137	1161	593	1336	1183	181, 6	
1138			(349)	(401)		Milan 555
1139						Hes. 184
1140	1162	615	1375	1217	181, 8	
1141	1163	616	1377	1219	181, 9	
1142	1650		1378		181, 10	
1143	1164	617	1379	1221	182, 1	

Leofric A	Ha. & Sp.	Pad.	Gellone	Angoulême	Eligius	Others
1144			1655			
1145						Hes. 185
1146	1165		1371	1248	182, 8	
1147	1166	629	1372	1249		
1148	1655		1373		182, 5	
1149	1167	630	1374	1251	182, 7	
1150			1370	1247	182, 3	
1151						Hes. 186
1152	1168	634	1402	1273	182, 9	
1153	1169	635	1404	1275	182, 10	
1154	1660		1405		182, 11	
1155	1170	636	1406	1277		
1156			1403	1274		
1157						Hes. 187
1158	1171		1423	1293	183, 4	
1159	1172	650	1425	1295		
1160	1663		1426	1296	183, 6	
1161	1173	651	1427	1297		
1162			1424	1294	183, 8	
1163						Hes. 188
1164	1174		1442	1314	183, 10	
1165	1175	660	1444	1316	184, 1	
1166	1666		1445	1317	184, 2	
1167	1176	661	1446	1318	184, 4	
1168			1443	1315	184, 6	
1169						Hes. 189
1170	702	676	1470	1341	184, 7	
1171	703	677	1472	1343	184, 8	
1172	1670		1473	1344		
1173	704	678	1474	1345		
1174			1471	1342	140, 10	
1175						Hes. 190
1176	705	679	1485	1359	140, 11	
1177	706	680	1486	1360		
1178	707	681			141, 2	
1179	1672		1488	1362	141, 3	
1180	708	682	1489	1363	141, 5	
1181						Hes. 191
1182	709	683	1491	1364	141, 6	
1183	710	684	1493	1365	141, 7	
1184	1673		1494	1366	141, 8	
1185	711	685	1496	1367	141, 8	
1186	712	686			141, 9	

Leofric A	Ha. & Sp.	Pad.	Gellone	Angoulême	Eligius	Others
1187	713	687	1499	1369	142, 1	
1188	714	688			142, 2	
1189	715	689				
1190	716	690	1502	1372	142, 4	
1191						Hes. 192
1192	717	691			142, 5	
1193	718	692				
1194	1674		1495	1375	142, 7	
1195	719	693	1506	1376	142, 9	
1196						Hes. 193
1197	720	694	1508	1378	185, 2	
1198			1510	1380	185, 3	
1199	1675		1511	1381	185, 4	
1200			1512	1382	185, 6	
1201			1509	1379		
1202						Hes. 194
1203			1531	1395	185, 8	
1204	1178	706	1533	1397	185, 9	
1205	1678				185, 10	
1206	1179	707	1535	1399	186, 1	
1207	1177		1532	1396		
1208						Hes. 195
1209	1180		1543	1406	186, 3	
1210	1181	718	1545	1408	186, 4	
1211	1679		1546	1409	186, 5	
1212	1182	719	1547	1410		
1213			1544	1407		
1214						Hes. 196
1215	1183		1552	1414	186, 9	
1216	1184	712	1554	1416	186, 10	
1217	1680		1555	1417	186, 11	
1218	1185	713	1556	1418	187, 2	
1219			1553	1415		
1220						Hes. 197
1221	1186	720	1562	1423	187, 4	
1222	1187	721	1564	1425		
1223	1682		1565	1426	187, 6	
1224	1188	722	1566	1427	187, 8	
1225			1563	1424	187, 5	
1226						Hes. 198
1227	1189		1579	1445	188, 2	
1228	1190	724	1581	1447	188, 3	
1229	1685		1582	1448	188, 4	

Leofric A	Ha. & Sp.	Pad.	Gellone	Angoulême	Eligius	Others
1230	1191	725	1583	1449		
1231			1580	1446		
1232						
1233			1589	1458	188, 8	
1234	1193	731	1591	1460	188, 9	
1235	1686		1593	1461	188, 10	
1236	1194	732	1594	1462	189, 2	
1237	1192		1590	1459	189, 3	
1238	1195		1615	1481	189, 4	
1239	1196		1617	1483	189, 5	
1240	1689		1618	1484	189, 6	
1241	1197	747	1619	1485		
1242	1198	748	1621	1487	189, 10	
1243	778	781	1674	1539	190, 8	
1244						Hes. 1
1245	779	782	1676	1541		
1246	1699		1677	1542	190, 10	
1247	780	783	1678	1543	191, 2	
1248			1675	1540		
1249						Hes. 2
1250	781	784	1711	1577	191, 4	
1251	782	785	1713	1579	191, 5	
1252	1703				191, 6	
1253	783	786	1715	1581	192, 1	
1254			1712	1578	196, 11	
1255						Hes. 4
1256	787	790	1720	1586	192, 3	
1257	788	791	1722	1588	192, 4	
1258	1704				192, 5	
1259	789	792	1724	1590	192, 7	
1260			1721	1587	196, 12	
1261						Hes. 5
1262	790	793	1726	1592	192, 8	
1263	791	794	1727	1593	192, 9	
1264	792	795				
1265	1705					
1266	793	796				
1267	794	797	1733	1598	193, 3	
1268	795	798				
1269						Hes. 6
1270	1706				193, 5	
1271	796	799				
1272						Hes. 7

Leofric A	Ha. & Sp.	Pad.	Gellone	Angoulême	Eligius	Others
1273	797	800	1740	1605	193, 7	
1274	798	801		1564	193, 8	
1275	799	802	1743	1607	193, 9	
1276	800	803		1561	193, 10	
1277	801	804		1557	193, 11	
1278	802	805	1746	1610	193, 12	
1279	803	806	1753	1617		
1280	1707				194, 2	
1281	804	807	1749	1613	194, 3	
1282						Hes. 7bis
1283	805	808	1751	1615	194, 4	
1284			1747	1611	194, 1	
1285	1708				194, 6	
1286	807	810	1755	1619		
1287	1768					
1288	1769					
1289	808	811	1733	1598	193, 3	
1290	809		1651	1516	195, 4	
1291	810	813	1734	1599	195, 5	
1292	811	812	1693	1558	195, 6	
1293	812	814	1694	1559	197, 7	
1294	813	815		1560		

SANCTORAL

Leofric A	Ha. & Sp.	Pad.	Gellone	Angoulême	Eligius	Others
1304						Hes. 12
1305	62	25	42	42	33, 1	
1306	63	26			33, 2	
1307	1518		45	44	33, 3	
1308	64	28		45	33, 5	
1309	65	30	53	40	33, 6	
1310	66		49	49	33, 7	
1311	1740				33, 4	
1312						Hes. 14
1313	67	32	51	51	34, 1	
1314	68	33	52	53	34, 2	
1315	1519	34	53	(54)	34, 3	
1316	1741				34, 4	
1317	69	35	54	56	34, 5	
1318	70	36			34, 6	
1319	72	38			35, 1	
1320	71	37			34, 7	

Leofric A	Ha. & Sp.	Pad.	Gellone	Angloulême	Eligius	Others
1321	73		50	50	35, 2	
1322						Hes. 15
1323	75	39	58	60	35, 6	
1324	76	40				
1325	1520	41		63	35, 8	
1326	77	42	62	64	36, 1	
1327	1742				35, 9	
1328	78	43	64	66	36, 2	
1329						Hes. 16
1330	79	46	73	75	36, 5	
1331	80	47	74	78		
1332	81	48	75	77		
1333	99	69	127	124	40, 10	
1334						Hes. 20
1335	100				40, 11	
1336	1527		129	127	41, 1	
1337	101		132		41, 2	
1338						Hes. 22
1339	102	75		135	41, 10	
1340	103	76		137	42, 1	
1341	1529		143	138	42, 2	
1342	104	77	145	139	42, 3	
1343						Hes. 23
1344	105	78	149	144	42, 4	
1345	106	79	150	145	42, 5	
1346	107	80	151	146	42, 6	
1347			152	148		
1348			153	150		
1349			154	151		
1350	108	81	156		42, 7	
1351	109	82		155	42, 8	
1352						Hes. 24
1353	110	83	160	156	42, 9	
1354	111	84	161		42, 10	
1355	112	85		159	42, 11	
1356	1530		165	160	42, 12	
1357	113	86	166		43, 1	
1358						Hes. 25
1359	114	87	169		43, 2	
1360	115	88			43, 3	
1361	1531				43, 4	
1362	116	90				
1363						Hes. 27

Leofric A	Ha. & Sp.	Pad.	Gellone	Angoulême	Eligius	Others
1364	117	91	173	167	43, 6	
1365	118	92				
1366	1532				43, 8	
1367	119	93	175	169	44, 1	
1368						
1369			182	177		
1370			184	179		
1371			185	178		
1372						
1373				181	44, 2	
1374				182	44, 3	
1375				183	44, 4	
1376				184	44, 6	
1377						Hes. 28
1378	120	97	190	190	45, 4	
1379	121	98			45, 5	
1380	122	99			45, 7	
1381						Hes. 30
1382	128	107	202		46, 8	
1383	129	108			47, 1	
1384	1538	109	203	211	47, 2	
1385	130	110				
1386	131	111	201	209	47, 4	
1387	133				47, 3	
1388						Hes. 31
1389	134	115	226		48, 10	
1390	135	116			50, 1	
1391	136	117	228		50, 2	
1392						
1393			230	234		
1394			231	235		
1395			233	237		
1396			234	238	50, 3	Add. 64*
1397						
1398			235	239	50, 4	Add. 65*
1399			236	240	50, 5	
1400			237	241	50, 6	Add. 66*
1401						
1402					50, 8	Add. 68*, TC 3449
1403					50, 9	Add. 69*, TC 3450
1404					51, 3	Add. 70*, TC 3453
1405						Hes. 32
1406	137					

Leofric A	Ha. & Sp.	Pad.	Gellone	Angoulême	Eligius	Others
1407	138					
1408	1542		245	248		
1409						
1410	139					
1411						
1412						TC 3463
1413						TC 3464
1414	1637					
1415			(1240)			TC 3641/3468
1416						Hes. 92
1417	460	393	875	906	99, 6	
1418	461	394			99, 7	
1419	1601		877	908	99, 8	
1420	462	395				
1421						Hes. 93
1422	463				99, 10	
1423	464				100, 1	
1424	1603				100, 2	
1425	465					
1426						Hes. 95
1427	476	408	923	920	100, 9	
1428	477	409			100, 10	
1429	478	410				
1430						Hes.96
1431	479	415	930	927	101, 2	
1432	480	416	932		101, 3	
1433	1608				101, 4	
1434	481	417			101, 5	
1435	482	418	941	936	101, 6	
1436	483		942	937	101, 7	
1437	484					
1438						Hes. 97bis
1439			944	939	101, 10	Add. 129*
1440			946	941		Add. 131*
1441						Add. 132*
1442	1764					
1443			948	943		Add. 134*
1444			945	940		Add. 130*, TC 3500
1445						
1446	485	428	955	949	102, 5	
1447	486	429			102, 6	
1448	487	430			102, 7	
1449						Hes. 98

Leofric A	Ha. & Sp.	Pad.	Gellone	Angoulême	Eligius	Others
1450	488	431			102, 8	
1451	489	432			102, 9	
1452	490	433	960	954	103, 1	
1453						Hes. 99
1454			961	955		Add. 136*
1455			962	956		Add. 137*
1456	1611		963	957		
1457			964	958		Add. 138*
1458						
1459					100, 4	Add. 126*, TC 3493
1460					100, 5	Add. 127*, TC 3494
1461						Add. 128*, TC 3492
1462						Hes. 100
1463	494	437	968		103, 6	
1464	495	438	969		103, 7	
1465	496	439	970		103, 8	
1466						Hes. 104
1467	504	452	993		103, 10	
1468	505	453				
1469	506	454			117, 3	
1470						
1471	556	499	1068		117, 4	
1472	557	500	1069		117, 5	
1473	558	501	1070		117, 6	
1474						Hes. 112
1475	559	502				
1476	560	503			117, 8	
1477	1622					
1478	561	504			118, 1	Add. 158*
1479						Hes. 113
1480			1082	987	118. 2	Add. 159*
1481			1083	988	118, 3	Add. 160*
1482			1084	989	118, 4	Add. 164*
1483			1085	990	118, 5	Add. 165*
1484			1086	991	118, 6	Add. 166*
1485			1087	992		
1486			1122	1003		
1487						
1488			1123	1004		
1489			1125	1006		
1490	562	511			118, 7	
1491						Hes. 115
1492	563	512				

294

Leofric A	Ha. & Sp.	Pad.	Gellone	Angoulême	Eligius	Others
1493	564	513	1128	1009		
1494	565	514				
1495						Hes. 116
1496	566	515				
1497	1627					
1498	567	516				
1499	568	520	1143	1024	120, 12	
1500						Hes. 117
1501	569	521			121, 1	
1502	1629		1146	1027	121, 2	
1503	570	522	1147	1028	121, 3	
1504	571	523	1149	1030	121, 4	
1505	572	524			121, 5	
1506						Hes. 118
1507	573	525	1151	1032	121, 6	
1508	574	526	1152	1033	121, 9	
1509	575	527	1154	1035	121, 10	
1510						Hes. 119
1511	1630		1155	1036	121, 11	
1512	576	528	1156	1037	122, 2	
1513	577	529	1160	1039		
1514	578	530	1161	1040	122, 4	
1515	581	531	1164	1043	122, 7	
1516	579		1162	1041	122, 5	
1517	1763				122, 1	
1518	583	532	1168	1049	123, 1	
1519						Hes. 120
1520	584	533	1170	1050	123, 2	
1521	1631				123, 3	
1522	585	534			123, 4	
1523	586				123, 5	
1524	587				123, 6	
1525	588				123, 7	
1526	589	538	1181	1060		
1527						Hes. 121
1528	590	539				
1529	591	540				
1530	592	541	1184	1063		
1531	592	541	1184	1063		
1532	593	542	1186		124, 5	
1533	594	543	1188		124, 6	
1534	595	544	1190		124, 7	
1535						Hes. 122

Leofric A	Ha. & Sp.	Pad.	Gellone	Angoulême	Eligius	Others
1536	596	(540)	1192		124, 8	
1537	1765				124, 9	
1538	597		1195		125, 1	
1539	599	546	1202		125, 4	
1540	600				125, 2	
1541	602					
1542	601	547	1199	1083	125, 5	
1543						Hes. 123
1544	604	548	1203	1073	125, 7	
1545	605	549		1065	125, 8	
1546	1535					
1547	606	550	1207	1076	125, 11	
1548						Hes. 124
1549	610	551	1208	1092	126, 2	
1550	611	552	1209	1093	126, 3	
1551	612	553	1210	1094	126, 4	
1552	607	557	1217	1106	126, 5	
1553						Hes. 125
1554	608	558	1218	1107		
1555	609	560	1221	1110	126, 8	
1556						Hes. 126
1557	613	561	1223	1112	126, 9	
1558	614	562	1224	1113	126, 10	
1559	1635		1225	1114	127, 1	
1560	615	563	1226	1115	127, 2	
1561			1233	1121		Add. 170*
1562						
1563			1234	1122		Add. 171*, TC 3451
1564			1235	1123		TC 3542
1565			1236	1124		Add. 172*
1566			1247	1135	127, 3	Add. 177*
1567						
1568			1248	1136	127, 4	Add. 178*
1569			1249	1137	127, 5	Add. 179*
1570			1250	1138	127, 6	Add. 180*
1571						Hes. 129
1572			1257	1140		Add. 181*
1573			1258	1141	127, 9	Add. 182*
1574			1259	1142		Add. 183*
1575						Hes. 130
1576	619		1266		127, 11	
1577	620					
1578	621		1268			

Leofric A	Ha. & Sp.	Pad.	Gellone	Angoulême	Eligius	Others
1579	622				128, 4	
1580						
1581	623					
1582	624				128, 6	
1583			1277	1156		Add. 184*
1584			(1279)	(1158)		Add. 186*
1585	1643		1280	1159		
1586			1281	1160		Add. 187*
1587						Hes. 131
1588	625	582	1282	1164	128, 7	
1589	626	583	1283	1165	128, 8	
1590	627	584	1284	1166	128, 9	
1591						Hes. 132
1592	628	585			129, 1	
1593	629	586				
1594	1644		1288	1170	129, 3	
1595	630				129, 4	
1596	631				129, 5	
1597	632	587			129, 6	
1598	633	588	1290	1172	129, 7	
1599	634	589	1291	1173	129, 8	
1600	635	590			129, 9	
1601						
1602			1293	1176		
1603			1295	1177		
1604				1178		
1605						Hes. 134
1606	636	594	1297	1184	129, 10	
1607	637	595				
1608	638	596				
1609						Hes. 135
1610	639	597	1300	1187	130, 1	
1611	640	598	1302	1190	130, 2	
1612	1646				130, 3	
1613	641	599	1306	1192	130, 4	
1614	642	600	1308	1194	130, 7	
1615	643	601			130, 8	
1616	644	602				
1617						Hes. 136
1618	645	603	1311	1199	130, 10	
1619	646	604			130, 11	
1620	1647		1314	1202	131, 1	
1621	647	606				

Leofric A	Ha. & Sp.	Pad.	Gellone	Angoulême	Eligius	Others
1622	648	607	1316	1200	131, 3	
1623						Hes. 137
1624	649	609	1321	1208	131, 7	
1625	650	610		1210	131, 8	
1626	1648		1323	1211	131, 9	
1627	651	611	1324	1212	131, 10	
1628						Hes. 138
1629	652	612				
1630	653	613	1328	1214	132, 2	
1631	1649				132, 3	
1632	654	614	1331	1216	132, 4	
1633	655	618	1338	1222	132, 5	
1634	656	619	1339	1223	132, 6	
1635	657	620				
1636						Hes. 140
1637	658				132, 9	
1638	659				132, 10	
1639	1651					
1640	660				133, 2	
1641	661				133, 4	
1642						
1643	662				133, 5	
1644			1349	1226		Add. 197*
1645	1652				133, 7	
1646	664				134, 1	
1647	1766				133, 9	
1648						Hes. 141
1649			1353	1230		Add. 192*
1650			1355	1232		Add. 194*
1651	1653		1356	1233		Add. 195*
1652			1357	1234		Add. 196*
1653	665	625				
1654						Hes. 142
1655	666	626	1359	1236	134, 4	
1656	667	627				
1657						Hes. 143
1658	668	631	1366	1243	134, 6	
1659	669	632			134, 7	
1660	670	633	1369	1246	134, 8	
1661			1382	1252	134, 9	Add. 202*
1662						
1663			1383	1253	134, 10	Add. 203*
1664	1656		1384	1254	134, 11	

Leofric A	Ha. & Sp.	Pad.	Gellone	Angoulême	Eligius	Others
1665			1385	1255	134, 12	Add. 204*
1666						Hes. 144
1667	671	637				
1668	672	638				
1669	1658		1399	1270	135, 8	
1670	673	639	1400	1271	135, 9	
1671			1412	1282	136, 7	Add. 210*
1672			1413	1283	136, 3	Add. 211*
1673			1414	1284	136, 4	Add. 214*
1674						
1675	1661					
1676					136, 5	
1677	674					
1678	675					
1679	676					
1680						Hes. 146
1681	677	646	1416	1286	136, 8	
1682	678	647	1417	1287	136, 9	
1683	689	648	1418	1288	136, 10	
1684	680		1433		137, 2	
1685						
1686	681		1434		137, 3	
1687	682				137, 4	
1688	1664				137, 5	
1689	683				137, 6	
1690			1435	1307		Add. 221*
1691						Hes. 148
1692			1436	1308		Add. 222*
1693			1438	1310		Add. 224*
1694						Hes. 149
1695	684	656	1439	1211	138, 1	
1696	685	657	1440	1212	138, 2	
1697	1665					Add. 223*
1698	686	658	1441	1313	138, 3	
1699						Hes. 150
1700			1448	1319		Add. 226*
1701			1449	1320	138, 5	Add. 227*
1702						Pr 234, 2
1703	691				138, 7	
1704			1450	1321	138, 8	
1705	687	662				Add. 232*
1706	688	663	1453	1324		
1707	689	664			139, 2	

Leofric A	Ha. & Sp.	Pad.	Gellone	Angoulême	Eligius	Others
1708						Hes. 152
1709	693	666	1461	1332	139, 3	
1710	694	667			139, 4	
1711	695	668	1463	1334	139, 5	
1712	696	669	1464	1335	139, 6	
1713	697	670	1465	1336	139, 7	
1714	698	671	1466	1337	139, 8	
1715						
1716	699	673				
1717	700	675	1468	1339		
1718	701		1469	1340		
1719						Hes. 154
1720			1476	1346	140, 1	Add. 236*
1721			1477	1347	140, 2	Add. 237*
1722			1478	1348	140, 3	Add. 238*
1723			1484	1354		
1724			1479	1349	140, 5	Add. 239*
1725			1480	1350	140, 6	Add. 240*
1726						Hes. 155
1727	1671		1481	1351	140, 7	Add. 241*
1728			1482	1352	140, 8	Add. 242*
1729			1483	1353	140, 4	Add. 243*
1730						
1731				1355		TC 3601
1732				1356		TC 3598
1733				1357		TC 3599
1734				1358		TC 3600
1735	723	697				
1736						Hes. 156
1737	724	698				
1738	1676		1516	1385		
1739	725	699				
1740						Hes. 157
1741	726	700	1518	1387	143, 3	
1742	727	701	1520	1390	143, 4	
1743	1677		1521	1392	143, 5	
1744	728	702	1522	1393	143, 7	
1745			1519	1388		Add. 251*
1746						LC 237
1747	(476)					
1748						
1749	(118)					
1750	(101)					

Leofric A	Ha. & Sp.	Pad.	Gellone	Angoulême	Eligius	Others
1751						Hes. 158
1752	729	708		1400	143, 9	
1753	730	709				
1754	731	710		1402	144, 2	
1755						TC 3636
1756						Hes. 158bis
1757			(1810)	(1677)		(TC 3620)
1758			(1812)	(1679)		(TC 3621)
1759						
1760	732	714	1548	1411	144, 3	
1761	733	715	1549	1412	144, 4	
1762	734	716	1550	1413	144, 5	
1763						
1764			1558	1419	144, 6	Add. 271*
1765			1559	1420	144, 7	Add. 272*
1766	1681		(1560)	1421	144, 8	Add. 273*
1767			1561	1422	144, 9	Add. 274*
1768						Hes. 159
1769			1568	1435	145, 1	Add. 275*
1770			1569	1436	145, 2	Add. 276*
1771	1683		1570	1437	145, 3	Add. 277*
1772			1571	1438	145, 4	Add. 278*
1773						Hes. 160
1774			1572	1439	145, 6	Add. 279*
1775			1574	1441	145, 7	Add. 281*
1776	1685		1575	1442	145, 8	Add. 282*
1777			1576	1443	145, 10	Add. 283*
1778			1578	1444		
1779						
1780					146, 2	Add. 285*, TC 3647
1781					146, 3	Add. 286*, TC 3648
1782						Add. 287*, TC 3649
1783					146, 4	Add. 288*, TC 3650
1784					146, 5	Add. 289*, TC 3651
1785						
1786					146, 9	Add. 290*, TC 3652
1787					146, 10	Add. 291*, TC 3653
1788					146, 11	Add. 292*, TC 3654
1789					147, 3	Add. 293*, TC 3655
1790						Add. 294*, TC 3656
1791	735	726	1585	1450		
1792	736	727	1586	1451	146, 6	
1793	737	728	1587	1452	146, 7	

COLLATION TABLE: SANCTORAL

Leofric A	Ha. & Sp.	Pad.	Gellone	Angoulême	Eligius	Others
1794	738	729			146, 8	
1795					147, 4	Add. 295*
1796	739	733	1596	1463	147, 5	
1797						Hes. 162
1798	740	734			147, 6	
1799	1687		1599	1468	147, 7	
1800	741	735			147, 8	
1801						Hes. 163
1802	742	736	1602		147, 9	
1803	743	737	1603	1469	147, 10	
1804	744	738			147, 11	
1805						
1806	748	742	1608	1474	148, 4	
1807	749	743				
1808	1688				148, 6	
1809	750	744				
1810	745		1605	1471	148, 1	
1811	746					
1812	747					
1813	751	751			148, 9	
1814						Hes. 165
1815	752	752	1633	1499	148, 10	
1816	1692		1634	1500	148, 11	
1817	753					
1818	754					
1819						Hes. 166
1820	755					
1821					149, 4	
1822	756					
1823	757		1641	1507	149, 6	
1824	758					
1825	759		1644		149, 8	
1826						Hes. 167
1827	760		1646		149, 9	
1828	761				150, 1	
1829			1648	1513	150, 2	
1830	762				150, 3	
1831	763				150, 4	
1832	764				150, 5	
1833	765				150, 6	
1834						Hes. 168
1835	766		1659	1523	150, 7	
1836	767		1661	1525	150, 8	

Leofric A	Ha. & Sp.	Pad.	Gellone	Angoulême	Eligius	Others
1837					150, 9	
1838	769		1663	1527	150, 10	
1839			1672	1538		
1840	770		1664	1528	151, 1	
1841						Hes. 169
1842	771	775	1666	1531	151, 2	
1843	772			1532		
1844	773	777			151, 5	
1845	774	778	1670	1537	151, 6	
1846	775	780			150, 12	
1847						Hes. 169bis
1848	784	787			151, 8	
1849	785	788				
1850	786	789				
1851			1757	1621	152, 4	Add. 301*
1852						
1853			1758	1622	152, 5	Add. 302*
1854						Le 282
1855						
1856			1761	1624	152, 8	Add. 303*

COMMUNE SANCTORUM

Leofric A	Ha. & Sp.	TC	Pad.	Angoulême	Eligius	Others
1857	1221	3149				
1858	1222	3150				
1859	1697	3152				
1860	1770					
1861	1223	3151		1630		
1862						
1863	1224	3176				
1864	1225	3177				
1865	1671	3179				
1866	1226	3178				
1867						
1868		3205		1634	163, 5	
1869		3206		1635	163, 6	
1870	1710	3208	820	1636	163, 7	
1871		3207		1637	163, 8	
1872	1227	3212				
1873	1228	3213				
1874	1711	3216			164, 4	
1875	1771	3217			164, 7	

COLLATION TABLE: COMMUNE SANCTORUM

Leofric A	Ha. & Sp.	TC	Pad.	Angoulême	Eligius	Others
1876	1229	3214				
1877						
1878	1230	3254				
1879	1231	3255			166, 6	
1880	1713	3257			166, 7	
1881	1772	3258			166, 8	
1882	1232	3256			166, 9	
1883					167, 3	
1884					167, 4	
1885	1715					
1886						
1887		3308			167, 7	
1888	1233	3309				
1889	1234	3310				
1890	1714	3312			168, 3	
1891	1773				168, 5	
1892	1235	3311			168, 6	
1893						
1894	1235	3350				
1895	1237	3351				
1896	1716	3353			170, 1	
1897	1774	3354			170, 3	
1898	1238	3352				
1899	1239	3387		1655	171, 4	
1900	1240	3389*			172, 5	
1901						
1902	1241	3388	(842)	(1658)		
1903	1718	3398				
1904	1775	3391			172, 2	
1905	1242	3389			172, 4	
1906		3409				
1907		3355		1664	169, 10	
1908		3361		1669		
1909	584		533	1657		
1910		3359		1667	170, 2	
1911		3362		1670	170, 6	
1912		3363		1671	170, 7	
1913	1774				170, 3	

VOTIVES

Leofric A	Ha. & Sp.	TC	Gellone	Angoulême	Eligius	Others
1920		1806				
1921		1807				
1922		1808				
1923		1809				
1924		1810				
1925		1814				
1926		1815				
1927		1816				
1928		1817				
1929		1818				
1930		2302				
1931		2303				
1932						Ec 1706, G I 262
1933		2304				
1934		2305				
1935		2325				
1936		2326				
1937		2327				
1938		2328				
1939		2329				
1940		1856				
1941		1857				
1942		1858				
1943		1859				
1944		1860				
1945		1835				
1946		1836				
1947		1837				
1948		1838				
1949	690		1451	1322		
1950		1841				
1951			1349			
1952		3688				
1953			856			
1954		1844				
1955		1870				
1956		1871				
1957		1872				
1958		1873				
1959		1865				
1960		1866				

Leofric A	Ha. & Sp.	TC	Gellone	Angoulême	Eligius	Others
1961		1867				
1962	1243					
1963	1244					
1964	1245			1642		
1965	1266			2311		
1966	1267			2313		
1967	1268					
1968	1269			2315		
1969	1270				238, 2	
1970	1271				238, 3	
1971	1272				238, 4	
1972	1273					
1973	1276					
1974	1275					
1975	1278					
1976	1720	2042				
1977	1279					
1978	1277					
1979	1280					
1980	1281				237, 3	
1981	1282				237, 4	
1982	1283					
1983	1284				237, 5	
1984	1285					
1985	1286					
1986	1287					
1987	1288					
1988		2078	1867, 1888	2194		
1989		2079	1868, 1889	2195		
1990		2080	1872, 1890	2197		
1991				2198		
1992		2086		2200		
1993		2320		2294		
1994	83			71		
1995		2322		2297		
1996	1308			2204	236, 4	
1997	1309			2207	236, 5	
1998	1310			2210		
1999	1317		2790		211, 4	
2000	1318		2792		211, 5	
2001	1314		2798			
2002	1320		2805			
2003	1321		2806			

COLLATION TABLE: VOTIVES

Leofric A	Ha. & Sp.	TC	Gellone	Angoulême	Eligius	Others
2004	1322		2808			
2005	1343		2764		205, 11	
2006	1344		2766		206, 2	
2007	1345		2767		206, 3	
2008	1323		2716		203, 10	
2009	1324					
2010	1326				204, 2	
2011	1346		2681	2220	238, 8	
2012	1347		2683		238, 9	
2013	1348		2685	2224	238, 10	
2014		2507	2687	2233		
2015		2449				
2016		2509	2688	2235		
2017	1730					
2018		2511	2689	2240	206, 12	
2019		2451				
2020	1360		2731			
2021	1361		2734			
2022	1362		2736			
2023	1352		2738			
2024	1354		2340			
2025	1355		2742			
2026	1357		2723			
2027	1358		2724			
2028	1359		2725			
2029	1330		2744	2326	204, 6	
2030	1332		2745	2327	204, 8	
2031	1333		2746	2328	204, 9	
2032	1334		2748	2330	204, 11	
2033	1336		2757	2333	204, 5	
2034	1335		2756	2332	205, 2	
2035	1337		1215	2334	205, 3	
2036	1338		1374	2335	205, 5	
2037	1339			2341	205, 6	
2038	1340			2342	205, 7	
2039	1341			2344	205, 8	
2040	1342			2345	205, 9	
2041		2564	2687	2233		
2042				2307		
2043		2565	2746	2328		
2044	1729	2560				
2045				2310		
2046		2566	2749			

COLLATION TABLE: VOTIVES

Leofric A	Ha. & Sp.	TC	Gellone	Angoulême	Eligius	Others
2047		2340				
2048		2335				
2049		2336				
2050		2337				
2051		2260				
2052	1309		2509	2207		
2053		2264				
2054	1007	2584	2705	2277	208, 8	
2055	1008		2706	2278	208, 9	
2056		2585	2707	2279	208, 10	
2057	1727	2540				
2058		2586	2709	2281	208, 11	
2059	875		1786	2275		
2060	874		2761	2276		
2061	1349		2711			
2062	1350		2713			
2063	1731	2605				
2064	1351		2715			
2065	1352		2716			
2066		2616	2658			
2067		2617	2659			
2068		2618	2661			
2069	1366		2662		209, 5	
2070	1368		2665		209, 7	
2071	1369		2667		209, 8	
2072	1367		2664		209, 6	
2073	1372		2669		210, 4	
2074	1373		2671		210, 5	
2075	1374		2673		210, 6	
2076	1370				210, 2	
2077	1375		2670		210, 7	
2078	1377		2679			
2079	1378		2680			
2080		2330				
2081						
2082						
2083		2331				
2084		2332				
2085		2333				
2086		2334				
2087	1289		1860			
2088	1290		1853			
2089	1723	2389				

COLLATION TABLE: VOTIVES

Leofric A	Ha. & Sp.	TC	Gellone	Angoulême	Eligius	Others
2090	1291					
2091	1292		1852, 1866	2203		
2092	1293					
2093	1294					
2094	1722	2368				
2095	1325		1851	2180		
2096	1295					
2097	1296					
2098	1297		1847			
2099	1298		1849			
2100		2388				
2101	1299		1853			
2102		2390	1861			
2103		2391	1862			
2104						
2105						
2106		2719				
2107		2720				
2108		2723				
2109		2721				
2110	1304				237, 9	
2111	1305				237, 10	
2112	1725					
2113	1306				238, 1	
2114	1300	2417			237, 6	
2115	1301	2418			237, 7	
2116		2415				
2117	1303	2419			237, 8	
2118		3103				
2119		3104				
2120		3105				
2121		3106				
2122		3107				
2123		3079				
2124		3080				
2125		3081				
2126		3130				
2127		3131				
2128		3132				
2129		3085				
2130		3086				
2131		3087				
2132	1392	2764			238, 11	

Leofric A	Ha. & Sp.	TC	Gellone	Angoulême	Eligius	Others
2133	1393	2765			239, 1	
2134	1732	2769				
2135	1394	2766			240, 1	
2136		2767	2883			
2137	1395		2887			
2138	1396		2888			
2139	1397		2889			
2140		2794				
2141		2795				
2142		2797				
2143		2796				
2144	1010				214, 1	
2145	1011				214, 2	
2146	1012				214, 3	
2147	1013				214, 4	
2148	1014				214, 6	
2149	1015					
2150		2812			214, 7	
2151		2814	2934		215, 11	
2152		2816	2936			
2153		2817	2937			
2154		2813	2933		216, 1	
2155		2870				
2156		2871				
2157						
2158		2872				
2159		2873				
2160	1011					
2161	1416		2968		216, 9	
2162	1417		2969		216, 10	
2163	1418		2971			
2164	1419		2972		216, 11	
2165		3015				
2166		3016				
2167		3017	2978			
2168	1420		2953			
2169	1421		2955			
2170	1423		2957			
2171	1424		2963			
2172	1425		2964			
2173	1426		2965			
2174	1428		2967			
2175	1429		3006		217, 6	

Leofric A	Ha. & Sp.	TC	Gellone	Angoulême	Eligius	Others
2176	1430		3007		217, 7	
2177	1431		3008			
2178	1432		3009		217, 8	
2179	1433		2973		217, 9	
2180	1434		2975			
2181					218, 1	
2182	1435		2977			
2183	1436		2978		218, 2	
2184	1437		2979			
2185	1438		2981			
2186	1440		2982			
2187	1441		2983			
2188		2881	2999		217, 1	
2189		2882	3000		217, 2	
2190		2883	3002		217, 3	
2191			3003		217, 4	
2192		2884	3004			
2193		2885	3005		217, 5	
2194	1444		2988			
2195	1445		2990			
2196	1447		2992			

ORDO DEFUNCTORUM

Leofric A	Ha. & Sp.	TC	Gellone	Phillipps	PRG	Others
2198				1914a	(CLXIX, 1–2)	
2299				1914a	(CXLIX, 3–5)	
2200	1398	4047	2899	1914b	CXLIX, 59	F 2474
2201		4048	2903a	1915		
2202		4050	2896	1916	CLXIX, 63	
2203	1400				CLXIX, 16	F 2464
2204	1401				CXLIX, 17	F 2470
2205	1402				CXLIX, 27	F 2472
2206	1403		2994	2005	CXLIX, 57	F 2473
2207	1404				CXLIX, 81	F 2485
2208	1405				CXLIX, 82	F 2468
2209		4051	2898	1917	CXLIX, 20	
2210	1412	4054	2910	1919	CXLIX, 67	F 2478
2211	1407				CXLIX, 23	F 2479
2212					(CXLIX, 19)	F, p. 303, Ga 172
2213		4052	2900	1918	CXLIX, 21	
2214	1408				CXLIX, 29	F 2480
2215					(CXLIX, 26)	F, p. 303. Ga 173

Leofric A	Ha. & Sp.	TC	Gellone	Phillipps	PRG	Others
2216		4055	2911	1920	CXLIX, 28	
2217						F, p. 304, Ga 173
2218		4056	2912	1921	CXLIX, 55	
2219						Ga 173 (note)
2220		4057	2913	1922	CXLIX, 54	
2221					(CXLIX, 56)	(F, p. 304), Ga 173
2222		4058	2914	1923	CXLIX, 22	
2223					(CXLIX, 64)	F, p. 305, Ga 174
2224		4059	2903	1915	CXLIX, 9	F 2461
2225					CXLIX, 69	F, p. 305, Ga 174
2226	1411	4060	2915	1925	CXLIX, 65	
2227					(CXLIX, 66)	F, p. 305, Ga 174
2228		4061	2906	1926	CXLIX, 70	
2229	1413		2916	1932	(CXLIX, 7)	F 2482
2230		4063	2909	1933		
2231	1410				CXLIX, 62	F 2476
2232	1409				CXLIX, 60	F 2475
2233		4073			CXLIX, 13	
2234	1399		2895	1938	CXLIX, 14	F 2471
2235	1414				CXLIX, 72	F 2481
2236					(CXLIX, 10)	(F, p. 302)
2237		4072			CXLIX, 11	
2238	1404				CXLIX, 81	F 2485
2239	1415				CXLIX, 12	F 2458
2240		4071				F 2459
2241		4065	2921	1936		

ORATIONES IN COMMEMORATIONIBUS SANCTORUM

Leofric A	Ha. & Sp.	Pad.	Gellone	Angoulême	Eligius	Others
2242						Giso (LM, 303)
2243						Be 1090
2244					148, 3	

BIDDING PRAYERS AND LITANY

2277						
2278						
2279						
2280						
2300						

PONTIFICAL

Leofric A	Ha. & Sp.	Gellone	Freiburg	PRG	Egbert	Others
2303	1790	2503–4	7	XV, 9	18	MF 1–2
2304	(1791)	2504	8	XV, 10	(18)	MF 9
2305	1792	2505	9	XV, 11	19	MF 10
2306	1793	2506–7	10, 11	(XV, 12–14)	19	
2307		2508	12	XV, 13	19	MF 12
2308	1794	2509	13	XV, 16	(19)	MF 13
2309	1795	2510–11	14	XV, 17	19	MF 4–5
2310	1796	2512	15	XV, 18	20	MF 14
2311	1797	2513	16	XV, 19	20	MF 15
2312	1798	2514	17	XV, 20	20	MF 3
2313	1799			XV, 24	20	TC 4202
2314		2515	19	XV, 22	21	TC 4203
2315	(1802)	2520	23	XVI, 5	21	
2316	1803	2521	24	XVI, 6	21	MF 17–18
2317	1804	2522	25	XVI, 7	21	MF 19
2318	1805	2523	26	XVI, 8	22	MF 20
2319	30	2525	28	XVI, 12	25	
2320	31		D 29	XVI, 13	25	
2321						Le 950
2322	32	2526	30	XVI, 14	25	MF 23
2323		2538			29	MF 24
2324						Leon 1010
2325						Leon 1011
2326		2541			30	
2327						
2328						
2329		2531	35	XVI, 27	27	MF 28
2330		2532	36	XVI, 28	27	MF 29
2331		2533	37	XVI, 29	27	MF 30
2348		2546		LXIII, 29/33	8	MF 36
2349	21		D 42	LXIII, 32	8	
2350	22	2548	D 43	LXIII, 34	8	Le 946, MF 37

Leofric A	Ha. & Sp.	Gellone	Freiburg	PRG	Egbert	Others
2351						Rob 127
2352	(23)	2549	D 44	LXIII, 35	9	Le 947, MF 40
2353				LXIII, 53	12	Le 943, MF 41
2354	(25)		(D 46)	(XVII, 4)		Le 944, MF 42
2355						Le 945, MF 43
2356						Le 1013, MF 44
2357	815		D 102	XL, 131	35, 50	
2358				(XL, 11–17)		
2359				(XL, 44–55)		
2360	818	2456		XL, 1	53, 55	
2361	819	2457	107	XL, 140	50, 51	
2362				(XL, 47)		
2363			(86)			
2364						
2365				(XL, 134)		Be 1232, (TC 4144)
2366						Can 795
2367						Vat. Gel. 1077
2368	821	2459		XLI, 3	54	
2369						
2370						
2371		(2480)				
2372		2458		(XLI, 5)		
2373	1265	2487	D 136	(XLIX, 5)		
2374	(1256)	(2428)	(92)	(XL, 60)	45	TC 4093, MF 59
2375	1255		90	XL, 59	45	TC 4092, MF 58
2376						
2377				(XL, 66)	51	TC 4145
2378	1257	2431	97	XL, 88	51	TC 4096, MF 62
2379	1258	2432	98	XL, 91	51	TC 4097, MF 63
2380			99	XL, 92	52	TC 4098, MF 64
2381			100	XL, 93	52	TC 4099
2382						
2383						
2384		2429	95	(XL, 74)		TC 4094, MF 60
2385	(1255)	(2427)	(90)	(XL, 59)		(MF 58)
2386		2433	96	XL, 77		TC 4095, MF 66
2387	(376)	(2326)		(CVII, 39)		
2388						
2389				CVII, 41		
2390			122	XL, 86		TC 4100, MF 67
2391			123	XL, 87		TC 4101, MF 68
2392	333					
2393	334		174		128	

Leofric A	Ha. & Sp.	Gellone	Freiburg	PRG	Egbert	Others
2394a & b	335		176		128–9	
2395	336				129–30	
2396				XCIX, 344		Cant 44
2397	1021					
2398						(TC 4358), Cant 44–5
2399	(1022)			(XCIX, 347)		
2400	(1022)			(XCIX, 347)		
2401				(XCIX, 410)	(137)	TC 4355
2402					124	
2403	(1465)		(165)	(CCXXIV, 2)	(124)	
2404	1462	2833	D 237	CCXXVI		TC 4352
2405			D 238	CCXXI, 1	123	TC 4353
2406						DC 129
2407	1463	2832	D 236	CCXXIII		
2408		2842	166	CCXXVII	141	
2409		2448	120	XL, 98	121	
2410		(2447)	(119)	(XL, 97)	(121)	F 2727
2411						
2412						Rob 107
2413	1460	2850		CCXXXIII, 1	133	TC 4366
2414	1461			CCXXXI, 1		TC 4368
2415		2857	D 247	CCXXXII, 1	136	TC 4369
2416		2858		CCXXXII, 2		TC 4370
2417	1457	2818	D 163	CXC, 2	124	TC 4317
2418	1458	2819		CXC, 3		TC 4318
2419	1459	(2674)	D 232	CLXXXV,6	132	
2420			D 267	CLXXIII	107	TC 4473
2421	990	2783	194	CCXXVIII, 1	132	
2422	991			I, 3	125	TC 4182
2423	993	(2499)	D 6	IV, 1	4	TC 4185
2424	1246	2495	D 1	III, 1		TC 4186
2425	1247			III, 2	4	TC 4187
2426	1248–(49)	(2496)	D 2	III, 3		TC 4188
2427	1250	2498	D 4	III, 5	4	TC 4190
2428	994			XXIV, 7	25	
2429	1251	2604	(149)		121	TC 4242
2430	1252	2605–6	150		122, 116	TC 4243
2431	1253	2607	D 153	XX, 14		TC 4244
2432				(XX, 16)	116	(MF 48)
2433				XXIII, 9	117	TC 4250
2434	(1254)	2608–9	(D 154)	(XX, 15)	117	(TC 4245)
2435		2615	D 156	XXV, 8	118	TC 4251
2436		2617		XXIV, 3	119	TC 4253

Leofric A	Ha. & Sp.	Gellone	Freiburg	PRG	Egbert	Others
2437	996	2576	144	XXVI, 5	114	TC 4238
2438		(2577)	(145)	(XXVI, 6)		(TC 4239)
2439						
2440	833	2639		CCLIII, 5		
2441	834			CCLIII, 8		
2442	835	2632		CCLIII, 9		
2443	836			CCLIII, 10		
2444	837	(2629)		CCLIII, 11		
2445	838	2636, 2633		CCLIII, 12		
2446	839	2630		CCLIII, 13		
2447		2651		CCLVIII, 5		
2448		2652		CCLVII, 2		
2449		2396		CXXVI		
2450						
2451		2395	D 273, 371	CXXIV, 2		
2452		2398	D 275	L, 6	(60)	
2453		2399	D 276	L, 7	(60)	
2454		2745			138	
2455					139	MF 72
2456					139	MF 71
2457				CXXXIX, 22	112	Lan 62
2458					109	Lan 60
2459					109	Lan 60
2460					110	Lan 60
2461				LXXII, 10	110	Lan 61
2462					111	Lan 62
2463					112	Lan 62
2464					112	Lan 62
2465					112	Lan 62
2466						Lan 63
2467				LXIV, 1		
2468				LXIV, 2		
2469				LXIV, 3		

EXORCISMS

Leofric A	Ha. & Sp.	Gellone	Freiburg	PRG	Egbert	Others
2470		271		CXXVI, 12	(150)	TC 3960
2471				(CXV, 35)		
2472	(980)			(CIX, 1)		
2473						G II 134
2474	1510	2400		CXIV, 2		

COLLATION TABLE: BAPTISMAL ORDER

Leofric A	Ha. & Sp.	Gellone	Freiburg	PRG	Egbert	Others
2475	1511			CXIV, 3		
2476	1512	2403		CXV, 31		AP 68
2477	1513	2404		CXV, 41		AP 69
2478	1514	2405		CXV, 32–3		AP 69
2479				(CXIV, 7)		G II 132

BAPTISMAL ORDER

Leofric A	Ha. & Sp.	TC	Angoulême	Eligius	PRG	Others
2480	1065		685–6		CVII, 6	
2481	1066		686		CVII, 7	
2482	1067		688		CVII, 8	
2483	1068		689		CVII, 9	
2484	1069		690		CVII, 10	
2485	1070		691		CVII, 11	
2486	373	3939	756	88, 8	CVII, 29	
2487						
2488	374	3940	757	88, 10	CVII, 30	
2489		3942			CVII, 31	
2490	(361, 1082)	(3929)	(727)		CVII, 27	
2491						Bo 233
2492						Bo 232
2493	(1065)	(3901)	(685–6)		(CVII, 6)	Stowe 26, 1
2494						Bv 41
2495	(1069)	3905	690		CVII, 10	
2496						
2497	359, 1080	3916	725		CVII, 23	
2498	1081	3917	726		CVII, 24	
2499		(3936)			CVII, 4	(Bapt 104)
2500		(3936)			CVII, 4	(Bapt 104)
2501	1084	3919		90, 1	CVII, 3	
2502				(90, 1)	(CVII, 33)	(Bapt 102)
2503	(1085)		2004	(90, 1)	CVII, 34	
2504	1086	3921	759	90, 2–3	CVII, 35	
2505		3943			(CVII, 3 & 6)	Add. 119*
2506	376	3944	2007	90, 5	CVII, 39	

ORDER FOR THE VISITATION OF THE SICK

Leofric A	Ha. & Sp.	TC	Eligius	PRG	Reims	Others
2507						F 2378
2508	(1456)	(4014)				
2509						
2510		(4009)	(232, 4)		(530, 2)	Par 149, Prud
2511						
2512				(CXXXIX, 4)	530, 10	
2513		(4027)		CXXXIX, 8	530, 11	
2514				(CXXXIX, 6)	(530, 12)	
2515						Flor 77, Prud
2516		4006			534, 3	
2517			232, 3		530, 1	
2518					538, 3 & 5	Be, p. 330
2519						F 2435, G II 33
2520		3988	234, 4	CXLIII, 3		
2521		3989	234, 7	CXLIII, 5	534, 1	
2522			(235, 1)	CXLIII, 12		Par 149; F, p. 292
2523					536, 2	Lan 138, Prud
2524						F, pp. 292–3
2525		3995		CXLIII, 54	537, 7	
2526				CXLIII, 15	535, 5	F 2418
2527				CXLIII, 23	535, 9	F 2428
2528				CXLIII, 17	535, 7	F 2420
2529				CXLIII, 18	535, 8	F 2422
2530				CXLIII, 21		F 2424
2531				CXLIII, 24	535, 10	F 2430
2532		4002		CXLIII, 14	535, 4	
2533				CXLIII, 25	535, 11	(F 2433)
2534		4012		CXLIII, 30	536, 5	F, p. 294
2535		3972	235, 4	CXLIII, 32	537, 2	
2536	1388		233, 9	CXLIII, 33	534, 7	
2537	1389	3984	234, 1	CXLIII, 34	534, 8	
2538	1390	2772	234, 2	CXLIII, 35	534, 9	
2539	1387		233, 8	CXXXIX, 16	534, 6	
2540	1386		233, 7	CXXXIX, 13	534, 3	
2541	1391	3986	234, 3	CXLIII, 36	534, 10	
2542						
2543				(CXLIII, 41)		Par 149; F, p. 297
2544						

PRAYERS FOR SINS, OCCASIONAL PRAYERS AND BENEDICTIONS

Leofric A	Ha. & Sp.	Pad.	Gellone	Angoulême	Eligius	Others
2545	840	694, 940	509, 1291	535, 1378		
2546	841	280	514	541	196, 13	
2547	842		2176	1943		
2548	843		521	554	197, 1	
2549	844		524	557		
2550	845	941	501	523		
2551	848	942	921	185, 979		
2552	846		2178	1946		
2553	849	943	2700	2262	197, 2	
2554	851	957	900	970, 1945	197, 3	
2555	853		1613, 1738	1479, 1604		
2556	854		394	416		
2557	855		920	969, 1947		
2558	856	946	905	2264	197, 5	
2559	857	947	913	980		
2560	858	948	2702	2266		
2561	859	949	901	97, 2267		
2562	860		2179	1948	197, 6	
2563	862	950	914	981, 2268	197, 8	
2564	866	954	2704	2272	197, 12	
2565	867	955	1955	2273	198, 1	
2566	868		915	983,	198, 2	
2567	869		2180	1949	198, 3	
2568	870	956	917, 2238		197, 11	
2569	871		916	984, 1950	198, 4	
2570	875	958	1786	2275	198, 7	
2571	874	959		982, 2276	198, 6	
2572	873		2181	1951	198, 5	
2573	876	174	352	363		
2574	879	208, 781	1674, 1681	1539, 1546		
2575	878	180, 272	496, 1393	515, 1263		
2576	880		177	172	198, 8	
2577	881	184	390	412	198, 9	
2578	884		1927, 2723	1746		
2579	885		2182	1953	198, 10	
2580	886	374	1497, 1579	1445		
2581	888					
2582	890	898	1337, 1968	1793, 1954		
2583	891		2183	1955	198, 11	

Leofric A	Ha. & Sp.	Pad.	Gellone	Angoulême	Eligius	Others
2584	893	197, 264	382, 1093	401		
2585	895		454, 1115	468		
2586	897		1407, 1926	1745, 1958		
2587	899		504, 1567	528, 1960		
2588	902		2185	1962	198, 12	
2589	904		1595, 1626	1624, 1963		
2590	906		1620	969, 1964		
2591	907		1595, 1626	1624, 1963		
2592	909		211, 918	218		
2593	911	112	219, 2743	226		
2594	913		72, 2715	74		
2595	915		832	851		
2596	914		436			
2597	917		2186	1967	198, 13	
2598	919		1253, 2187	1131, 1968		
2599	921		1679	1970		
2600	922		134	129		
2601	923	72, 141	135, 305	130, 306		
2602	924	253	2188	1971	199, 5	
2603	925		1381	1972		
2604	926	201	1590	213, 1459		
2605	928	939	1776	1973	199, 6	
2606	930		1175	1055		
2607	932		1655	1975		
2608	933		1179	1976		
2609	934	872	899	978		
2610	935	901	2189		202, 6	
2611	936	907		1902	201, 12	
2612	937	905	2116	1882	202, 7	
2613	938	913	2117	1919	202, 8	
2614	939	916	2107	1875	203, 5	
2615	940	928	2143	1905, 1925	202, 1	
2616	941	935	2144	1906	202, 2	
2617	942	922	2118	1883		
2618	943	902	2145	1907	199, 9	
2619	944	903	2146	1908	199, 10	
2620	945	904	2147	1909	199, 11	
2621	946	906	2148	1910	199, 12	
2622	947	908	2149	1911	199, 13	
2623	948	909	2150	1912	199, 14	
2624	949	910	2151	1913	199, 15	
2625	951		2830	1915	199, 17	
2626	953	914	2153	1917	199, 19	

Leofric A	Ha. & Sp.	Pad.	Gellone	Angoulême	Eligius	Others
2627	954	915	2154	1918	199, 20	
2628	955		2155	1920	199, 21	
2629	956		2156	1921	199, 22	
2630	957		2157	1554, 1922	199, 23	
2631	961	919	1580	1446	200, 4	
2632	962	920	2161	1965	200, 5	
2633	964	921	2163	1931	200, 7	
2634	963	149	2162	322, 1930	200, 6	
2635	965	923	2164	1932	200, 8	
2636	967	924	2165	1933	200, 10	
2637	968	925	2166	1934	200, 11	
2638	970	927	2168	1936	200, 13	
2639	969	926	2167	1935	200, 12	
2640	972	930			200, 15	
2641	974	932	860, 1344	891	200, 17	
2642	975	933	2171	1939	200, 18	
2643	976	934	1769	1940	200, 19	
2644	977	936	2172	1941	200, 20	
2645	978	937	2173	1942	200, 21	
2646	979	938	114	115	200, 22	
2647	1504		2134	1899	201, 1	
2648	1509			1906	201, 4	
2649	1502		2138	1897	202, 4	
2650						
2651	1507			1903	201, 3	
2652					203, 5	
2653	1201		1895	1716	198, 5	
2654	1203	850	1897	1718	203, 11	
2655	1204	244, 399	1899	1720		
2656	1205	209	1901	1722		
2657	1206	854	1903	1724		.
2658	1207	856	1905	1726	204, 3	
2659	1208		1907	1728		
2660	1209	858	1909	1730		
2661	1210	860	1912	1732		
2662	1211	861	1914	1734	199, 2	
2663	1212	862	1916	1736		
2664	1213	863	1918	1738		
2665	1214		1920	1740	199, 3	
2666	1215	865	1922	1742		
2667	1216	867	1925	1744		
2668	1217		1928	1747		
2669	1218	869	1929	1748		

COLLATION TABLE: OCCASIONAL PRAYERS

Leofric A	Ha. & Sp.	Pad.	Gellone	Angoulême	Eligius	Others
2670	1219	894	1951	1776		
2671	1220	895	1954			
2672	1777		1963	1862		
2673	1778					
2674	1779					
2675	1780					
2676	1781					
2677	1782					
2678	1783					
2679	1784					
2680	1785					
2681	1786					
2682	1787					
2683	1788					
2684	1789					
2685	1451				231, 2	
2686	1452				231, 3	
2687	1453				231, 4	
2688	1454		2416		232, 1	
2689	1455				232, 2	
2690	1456		2418		232, 3	
2691	1464		2837		233, 2	

INDEX OF BENEDICTIONS, EXORCISMS
AND PRAYERS

Beati proti nos domine et iacinthi foueat pretiosa, 1695
Beati sacerdotis et confessoris tui N. domine precibus adiuuemur, 2913
Beati tyburtii nos domine foueant continuata, 1624
Benedic domine creaturam istam .ill. ut sit remedium, 2691
Benedic domine dona tua quae de tua largitate, 98
Benedic domine et has creaturas fontis lactis et mellis, 2401
Benedic domine et hos fructus nouos uuae, 1596
Benedic domine fortitudinem principis nostrae et opera, 2463
Benedic domine hanc creaturam nouam panis sicut, 2403
Benedic domine hanc crucem tuam ex qua eripuisti, 2410
Benedic domine hos fructus nouos uuae uel fabae, 2404
Benedic domine hunc clementissimum regem cum, 117
Benedic domine hunc praesulem principem qui regna, 2461
Benedicat te deus caeli adiuuet te christe, 124
Benedicat te deus pater sanet te filius illuminet te spiritus, 2525
Benedicat tibi dominus custodiensque te sicut te uoluit, 118, 2684
Benedicat uobis dominus beatorum martyrum suorum, 1881
Benedicat uobis dominus et custodiat uos, 2672
Benedicat uobis dominus qui beatae uirgini .ill. concessit, 1904
Benedicat uobis omnipotens deus beati iohannis baptistae, 1518
Benedicat uobis omnipotens deus cui et ieiunii maceratione, 746
Benedicat uobis omnipotens deus qui per unigeniti, 1442
Benedicat uobis omnipotens deus qui quadragenarium, 522
Benedicat uobis omnipotens deus qui uos beati petri, 1537
Benedicat uos deus omni benedictione caelesti sanctosque, 2301
Benedicat uos deus qui per unigeniti sui passionem, 770, 2791
Benedicat uos omnipotens deus cuius unigenitus hodierna, 987
Benedicat uos omnipotens deus hodierna interueniente, 848
Benedicat uos omnipotens deus ob cuius paraclyti, 1019
Benedicat uos omnipotens deus qui uos gratuiter, 927
Benedicat uos omnipotens deus uestramque ad supernam, 371
Benedico te creatura panis in nomine patris et, 2402
Benedictio tua deus impleat corda fidelium talesque, 2244
Benedictio tua domine larga descendat quae et munera, 1798
Benedictionem domine nobis conferat salutarem, 935
Benedictionem tuam domine populus fidelis accipiat, 2064, 2594
Benedictionibus suis repleat nos dominus, 75
Benedictionis tuae gratiam domine intercedente beato confessore, 1887

Caelestem nobis praebeant haec mysteria quaesumus domine, 1228
Caelesti benedictione omnipotens pater populum tuum sanctifica, 2744
Caelesti lumine quaesumus domine semper et ubique, 414
Caelestia dona capientes quaesumus domine non ad iudicium, 682
Caelestibus domine pasti deliciis quaesumus ut semper, 446
Caelestibus refecti sacramentis et gaudiis supplices, 1734, 1800
Caelestis doni benedictione percepta supplices, 504, 719
Caelestis mensae quaesumus domine sacrosancta libatio, 1200
Caelestis uitae munere uegetati quaesumus domine ut, 514

Da quaesumus omnipotens deus ut qui beatorum martyrum gordiani atque, 1450
Da quaesumus omnipotens deus ut qui in tot aduersis, 748
Da quaesumus omnipotens deus ut qui infirmitatis nostrae conscii, 689, 2602
Da quaesumus omnipotens deus ut sacro nos purificante, 598
De multitudine misericordiae tuae domine populum, 484
De sede sancta sua aspiciat nos, 74
Debitum domine nostrae reddemus seruitutis suppliciter, 1853
Debitum humani corporis sepeliendi officium fidelium, 2229
Defende quaesumus domine intercedente beato benedicto ab omni, 2051*
Dei pater omnipotens misericordiam dilectissimi fratres deprecamur, 2375
Delicta fragilitatis nostrae domine quaesumus miseratus absolue, 2702
Delicta nostra domine quibus aduersa dominantur absterge, 1231, 2631
Depelle domine conscriptum peccati lege cyrographum, 919
Deprecamur domine clementiam pietatis tuae ut, 2414
Deprecationem nostram quaesumus domine benignus exaudi et quibus, 664, 1086
Descendat quaesumus domine deus noster spiritus sanctus tuus super hoc altare, 2694
Det uobis dominus munus suae benedictionis et repleat, 2677
Deum indultorem criminum deus sordium mundatorem, 2452
Deum iudicem uniuersitatis deus caelestium et terrestrium, 2218
Deum patrem omnipotentem supplices deprecamur ut hunc famulum, 2310
Deum patrem omnipotentem suppliciter deprecamur ut hunc famulum, 2304
Deuotas domine humilitatis nostrae preces et hostias misericordiae, 1701
Deuotionem populi tui domine quaesumus benignus, 538, 544
Deuotionem uestram domine dignanter intendat et suae, 2678
Deuotionis nostrae tibi quaesumus domine hostia iugiter, 1257
Deus a quo bona cuncta procedunt largire, 952
Deus a quo et iudas reatus sui poenam, 772, 781, 2777
Deus a quo sancta desideria recta consilia et iusta sunt, 196, 2005
Deus a quo speratur humani corporis omne quod, 2174
Deus ad cuius sepulchrum cum aromatibus, 1302
Deus angelorum deus archangelorum deus prophetarum, 2476
Deus apud quem mortuorum spiritus uiuunt et in quo, 2231
Deus auctor pacis et amator quem nosse, 204, 2007
Deus benedictionis indultor qui ministerium quod salomon, 2383
Deus bonarum uirtutum et omnium benedictionum largus, 2430
Deus caeli terraeque dominator auxilium nobis, 2624
Deus caeli terraeque dominator qui das escam omni, 2262
Deus castitatis amator et continentiae conseruator, 2436
Deus castorum corporum benignus inhabitator et, 2434
Deus celsitudo humilium et fortitudo rectorum, 828
Deus conditor et defensor generis humani qui hominem, 2477
Deus cui cunctae oboediunt creaturae et omnia, 1444
Deus cui omne cor patet et omnis uoluntas loquitur, 1935
Deus cui omnia uiuunt et cui non pereunt moriendo, 2234
Deus cui proprium est misereri semper et parcere, 2155, 2554
Deus cui soli cognitus est numerus electorum in, 2130
Deus cui soli competit medicinam praestare post mortem, 2233
Deus cuius adorandae potentia maiestatis flamma, 33

Fac nos domine quaesumus prompta uoluntate subiectos, 1203
Fac nos domine quaesumus sanctorum tuorum primi et feliciani, 1480
Fac nos quaesumus domine accepto pignore salutis, 601
Fac nos quaesumus domine deus noster in tua deuotione, 2605
Fac nos quaesumus domine deus noster peruigiles atque sollicitos, 1260
Fac omnipotens deus ut qui paschalibus remediis, 925
Fac quaesumus domine hanc cum seruo tuo .ill. misericordiam, 2205
Familiam huius cenobii quaesumus domine intercedente, 2051
Familiam tuam deus suauitas illa contingat et uegetet, 1693
Familiam tuam domine dextera tua perpetuo circumdet, 2595
Familiam tuam quaesumus domine caelesti protectione circumda, 2603
Familiam tuam quaesumus domine continua pietate custodi, 438, 608, 1220*, 1237
Familiam tuam quaesumus domine dextera tua perpetuo, 926
Familiam tuam quaesumus domine propitiatus inlustra, 572
Familiam tuam quaesumus domine propitius intuere et, 1540
Famulis tuis domine caelestis gratiae munus impertire, 1686
Famulorum tuorum domine delictis ignosce ut qui, 1643, 2727
Famulum tuum quaesumus domine tua semper protectione, 2097
Festina quaesumus ne tardaueris domine et auxilium, 1263
Fiat commixtio et consecratio corporis et sanguinis, 2542
Fiat domine quaesumus gratia tua fructuosior, 21
Fiat domine quaesumus hostia sacranda placabilis pretiosi, 1481
Fiat domine quaesumus per gratiam tuam fructuosus noster, 690
Fidelem famulum tuum regem nostrum quem domine, 260
Fideles tui domine perpetuo dono formentur, 471
Fideles tuos domine benedictio desiderata, 1078
Fideles tuos quaesumus domine corpore pariter et mente, 2582
Fidelium deus omnium conditor et redemptor, 2184
Fraterna nos domine martyrum tuorum corona, 1583

Gaudeat domine plebs fidelis ut cum propriae, 924
Gaudeat domine quaesumus plebs tua beneficiis imperatis, 2581
Gaudeat domine quaesumus populus tua semper benedictione, 2596
Gloriam domine sanctorum apostolorum perpetuam uenerantes, 1775
Grata tibi sint domine munera quibus beatus martyr, 449
Grata tibi sit domine haec oblatio famuli tui .ill., 2099
Grata tibi sit domine nostrae seruitutis oblatio pro qua, 1692
Gratia tua nos quaesumus domine non derelinquat quae, 595
Gratiam tuam domine mentibus nostris infunde, 463
Gratias agimus domine multiplicibus largitatibus tuis, 2143
Gratias tibi referat domine, 621*
Gratias tibi referimus domine sacro munere, 150
Guberna domine famulam tuam et tuis beneficiis semper, 269
Guberna quaesumus domine et temporalibus adiumentis quos, 268

Haec commixtio liquorum fiat omnibus perunctis, 2798
Haec domine oblatio salutaris famulum tuum .ill., 1971
Haec domine quae sumpsimus uotiua mysteria festa, 1758

PREFACES

VD per christum dominum nostrum. Per quem pietatem tuam suppliciter petimus, 1050

VD per christum dominum nostrum. Per quem sanctum et benedictum nomen maiestatis tuae, 2747

VD per christum dominum nostrum. Per quem salus mundi per quem uita homninum per quem, 2191, 2887

VD per christum dominum nostrum. Per quem supplices exposcimus ut cuius, 898

VD per christum dominum nostrum. Per quem te inmense deus rogamus ut supplicationes nostras, 1916

VD per christum dominum nostrum. Praecipue in die ista in qua filii tui unigeniti a iudeis, 2270

VD per christum dominum nostrum. Pro cuius amore gloriosi martyres iohannes et paulus, 1522

VD per christum dominum nostrum. Pro cuius caritatis ardore istae et omnes sanctas uirgines, 1903

VD per christum dominum nostrum. Pro cuius nomine gloriosus leuita uincentius, 1366

VD per christum dominum nostrum. Pro cuius nomine poenarum mortisque contemptum, 1384

VD per christum dominum nostrum. Pro cuius nomine ueneranda confessione beatus martyr, 1424

VD per christum dominum nostrum. Pro cuius nominis confessione beatus martyr geruasius, 1498

VD per christum dominum nostrum. Quem in hac nocte inter sacras epulas increpantem, 775, 2778

VD per christum dominum nostrum. Quem iohannes precessit nascendo et in, 1285

VD per christum dominum nostrum. Quem pro salute hominum nasciturum gabrihel, 1265

VD per christum dominum nostrum. Qui ad insinuandum humilitatis suae, 643

VD per christum dominum nostrum. Qui aeternitate sacerdotii sui omnes tibi, 1160

VD per christum dominum nostrum. Qui ascendens super omnes caelos, 1025, 2829, 2830

VD per christum dominum nostrum. Qui beatum augustinum tuum et scientiae, 2933

VD per christum dominum nostrum. Qui continuatis quadraginta diebus et noctibus, 519

VD per christum dominum nostrum. Qui corporali ieiunio uitia comprimis, 19, 498, 2757, 2759

VD per christum dominum nostrum. Qui crucem ascendit sanguinem fudit et omnem, 1702

VD per christum dominum nostrum. Qui de uirgine nasci dignatus per passionem, 942

VD per christum dominum nostrum. Qui ecclesiam tuam in apostolicis tribuisti consistere, 1843, 2834, 2837, 2839, 2864, 2868, 2869, 2870

VD per christum dominum nostrum. Qui est dies aeternus lux indeficiens, 687

VD per christum dominum nostrum. Qui generi humano nascendo subuenit, 994

VD per christum dominum nostrum. Qui inluminatione suae fidei tenebras expulit, 675, 2761

VD per christum dominum nostrum. Qui innocens pro impiis uoluit pati, 763

VD per christum dominum nostrum. Qui nos per paschale mysterium edocuit, 883

VD per christum dominum nostrum. Qui oblatione sui corporis remotis sacrificiorum, 867

INDEX OF CHANT

ALLELUIA VERSES

Adducentur, 388, 1642, 1685, 1903
Adorabo ad templum, 236, 1462, 2362
Adtendite populi, 1109
Amauit, 1888*
Angelus domini descendit, 864, 939
Ascendit deus, 982, 991
Aue maria gratia plena, 452*, 2302
Beatus uir qui timet, 1363, 1421, 1466,
    1470, 1510, 1617, 1648, 1801
Beatus uir qui suffert, 1759, 1872*
Benedictus es domine deus, 1069
Confitebor tibi, 1740
Confitemini domino, 831, 836*, 963, 970,
    1015, 1145
Crucifixus, 888*
De profundis clamaui ad te, 144, 1202
Desiderium, 2344
Deus in dextera, 1073
Deus iudex iustus, 2011*
Dextera domini fecit, 1169
Dextram, 1238*
Dicite in gentibus, 1438
Dies sanctificatus, 367
Diffusa est gratia, 1343, 1377, 1814, 1847
Dilexit andream, 1841
Diligam te domine, 1079
Disposui testamentum, 1334, 2343, 2345
Domine deus salutis meae, 208, 1121
Domine in uirtute, 1085
Domine refugium factus es, 226
Dominus dixit ad me, 351
Dominus in sinai, 982, 991
Dominus regit exultent, 946
Dominus regnauit decorem, 381
Dominus regnauit exultet, 437
Emitte spiritum, 1024, 1031, 1031*,
    1041*, 1048, 1062*
Epulemur, 843
Excita domine potentiam, 1255
Exultabit, 1680
Exultabunt, 1453, 1483, 1605, 1666, 1691

Exultate deo, 1115
Exultauit, 1368
Factus est repente, 1062*
Gaudete iusti, 1372, 1430, 1519, 1543,
    1662
Gauisi sunt, 951*
Gloria et honor, 1338, 1426, 1654, 1708,
    1751, 1824
Haec dies quam, 895, 906
Hic est discipulus, 1312
Hodie maria, 1642**
In conspectu, 1740**
In die resurrectionis, 872, 946
In omnem terram, 1863*
In te domine speraui, 1091, 2081*, 2892
Inter natos mulierum, 246, 2902
Inueni dauid, 1329, 1571, 1587, 1601
Ipse peribit, 1506
Iubilate deo omnis terra, 416, 951, 2293
Iusti epulentur, 1491, 1628, 1736, 1756,
    1785, 1894*
Iustus germinabit, 1748, 1763
Iustus ut palma, 1445, 1458, 1562, 1726,
    1805
Lauda anima mea, 933*, 939, 1208
Lauda hierusalem, 1220
Laudate dominum, 427, 939*, 1163, 1740
Laudate pueri, 895, 1556
Letatus sum, 1249
Mirabilis deus, 1322, 1479, 1548, 1575,
    1623, 1657, 1674, 1694, 1715, 1730,
    1797, 1878*
Nimis honorati, 1430, 1567, 1852
Nonne cor nostrum, 939*
Omnes gentes, 976, 1097
Oportebit, 946*
Optimam partem elegit, 2708
Ostende nobis, 1244
Paraclytus, 1024*, 1062*
Paratum cor meum, 1151
Pascha nostrum, 843, 906

ANTIPHONS

BENEDICTIONS AND VERSES

COMMUNIONS

GRADUALS

GRADUAL VERSES

INTROITS

OFFERTORIES

Exaltabo te domine, 495, 1133
Exaudi deus orationem meam, 146, 617
Expectans expectaui, 665, 1157
Exulta satis filia, 1272
Exultabunt sancti, 1483, 1553, 1666, 1768, 1894*
Factus est dominus, 691, 733
Felix namque es sacra, 2302
Filie regum, 1343
Gloria et honor, 1334, 1363, 1401, 1445, 1458, 1500, 1708, 1719, 1801, 1834, 2343
Gloriabuntur, 1519, 1548, 1694, 1736
Gressus meos, 648
Improperium, 740
In die sollempni, 880
In omnem terram, 1662, 1773, 1863*
In te speraui domine, 530, 1145, 2295
In uirtute tua, 248, 1304, 1388, 1470, 1506, 1623, 1648, 1654, 1759, 1868*, 2719
Inlumina oculos, 603, 1091
Inmittit angelus, 543, 1151
Intende uoci orationis meae, 640, 1073, 2894
Intonuit de celo, 864, 1031
Inueni dauid, 1329, 1587, 1591
Iubilate deo omnis terra, 416, 659
Iubilate deo uniuersa, 427, 946
Iustitiae domini, 609, 1121
Iustus ut palma, 1510, 1674, 2904
Lauda anima mea, 939, 1052
Laudate dominum quia, 653
Letamini, 1352, 1416, 1474, 1495, 1605, 1680, 1715, 1730, 1779, 1878*
Letentur, 351, 396
Leuabo oculos, 525

Meditabor, 536, 1041, 1176
Memor sit dominus, 2342
Mihi autem nimis, 1372, 1527, 1543, 1567, 1580, 1841, 1852
Mirabilis deus, 1368, 1449, 1479, 1487, 1575, 1657, 1756, 1785
Miserere mihi, 579
Offerentur minor, 388, 1358, 1377, 1381, 1392, 1636, 1814, 1847, 1899*, 1903*
Oratio mea, 1609
Oraui deum meum, 1169
Perfice gressus meos, 210, 474, 1103
Populum humilem saluum, 170, 684, 1115
Portas caeli aperuit, 872, 1036
Posuisti domine, 1691, 1726, 1763, 1872*
Precatus est moyses, 591, 1139
Qui posuit fines tuos pacem, 198
Recordare, 1220
Reges Tharsis, 400
Repleti sumus, 1426
Rorate celi, 460*
Sanctificauit moyses, 1196
Scapulis suis, 516
Si ambulauero in medio, 190, 634, 1202
Sicut in holocaustum, 1109
Sperent in te omnes, 137, 180, 709, 1085
Stetit angelus, 1740
Super flumina, 722, 1208, 2011*
Tollite portas, 345
Tremuit terra, 843
Tui sunt celi, 367
Veritas mea, 1338, 1405, 1411, 1466, 1562, 1571, 1748, 1751, 1805, 1819
Vir erat in terra, 1214
Viri galilei, 976, 991

OFFERTORY VERSES

Celi enarrent, 460*
Dirige me, 1244
Et factus est, 843
Fecit salomon, 2364

Letificabimur in salutari, 2342
Notus in iudea, 843
Respice, 1244

PRECES

PSALMS

Diligam te domine, 467
Diligam te domine, 715, 963, 970, 1079
Domine clamaui, 2812
Domine deus salutis, 555, 1062
Domine dominus noster, 1322, 1691
Domine exaudi i, 2512
Domine exaudi ii, 759, 1819, 2512
Domine in uirtute, 1500, 2899
Domine ne in ira i., 2512
Domine ne in ira ii., 490, 2512
Domine ne in tuo, 585
Domine probasti, 843, 1372, 1401, 1535, 1543, 1567, 1580, 1662, 1773, 1841, 1852, 2227
Domini est terra, 345, 2358, 2426
Dominus inluminatio, 579, 709, 991, 1097
Dominus pars hereditatis, 2426
Dominus regnauit decorem, 358, 381, 396, 1462, 2359
Dominus regnauit exultet, 437
Effunde frameam, 747
Ego enim sum deus, 1175
Emitte lucem, 697
Eripe, 2812
Eructauit, 388, 1377, 1381, 1636, 1642, 1685, 1847, 2705
Euntes predicate euangelium, 2344
Exaltabo te deus, 1416
Exaltabo te domine, 506
Exaudi deus orationem cum, 1426, 1654
Exaudi deus orationem meam, 501, 1127, 1363, 1421, 1470, 1708
Exaudi domine iustitiam, 597, 1648
Exaudiat te, 2342, 2343
Exultabunt iusti, 1487, 1894*
Exultate deo, 906, 1031
Exultate iusti, 1430, 1453, 1479, 1548, 1680, 1694, 1736, 1785
Exurgat deus, 1024, 1041, 1048, 1133, 1628, 1715
Exurge deus, 1449
Gaudete iusti, 933

In exitu israel, 2199
In te domine speraui, 481, 628, 728, 1052
Inclina domine, 640, 1163, 2889
Inter natos, 1510**
Iubilate deo uniuersa, 416, 427, 951
Iudica me domine, 574
Laetatus sum, 195, 653, 1196
Laetifica animam serui tui, 141, 1157
Magnificat, 2812
Magnus dominus, 175, 452*, 722, 1115, 1208
Memento domine, 1329, 1466, 1571, 1591, 2225
Miserere i., 490, 2512
Miserere ii., 165, 495, 766, 2358
Miserere mihi, 617, 2212
Misericordias, 1338, 1397, 1805
Noli emulari, 1334, 1368, 1491, 1601, 1657, 1726, 1748, 1759, 1824
Nolite possidere aurum, 2344
Omnes gentes, 982
Pre gaudium matris, 2302
Preoccupemus, 1191
Priusquam fierent montes, 205, 530, 2290
Quam amabilis, 1151
Quam dilecta, 233
Quare fremerunt, 351
Qui habitat, 516
Qui regis israel, 1249, 1272
Qui sedes domine, 460**
Quid gloriaris, 490, 1445, 1458, 1719
Rex meus et deus meus, 648
Saluabit sibi dextera, 946
Si consistant, 1091
Sicut ceruus desiderat, 2223
Sit nomen domini, 1556
Subiecit populos, 976, 1109
Vias tuas domine, 1244
Vitam petiit, 1388, 1801
Voce mea, 2812
Vsquequo domine, 1073
Vt quid deus, 1145

RESPONSORIES AND VERSICLES

R. Domine audiui audiui, 782
R. Heu mihi domine. V. Anima mea turbata, 2219

R. Subuenite sancti dei. V. Requiem aeternam, 2217

SEQUENCES

TRACTS

TRACT VERSES

INDEX OF READINGS

Corde creditur (*Rom. x, 10*), 1841*
Cum appropinquasset ihesus hierusalem (*Luc. xix, 41*), 1127*
Cum audissent apostoli (*Act. App. viii, 14*), 1036*
Cum complerentur (*Act. App. iii, 1*), 1024*
Cum descendisset ihesus (*Matt. viii, 1*), 437*
Cum esset desponsata (*Matt. i, 18*), 345*
Cum esset sero (*Ioh. xx, 19*), 906*
Cum factus esset ihesu (*Luc. ii, 42*), 416*
Cum ieiunatis (*Matt. vi, 16*), 495*
Cum intraret ihesus in domum (*Luc. xiv, 1*), 1169*
Cum intrasset ihesus iherosolimam (*Matt. xxi, 10*), 530*
Cum introisset ihesus capharnum (*Matt. viii, 5*), 501*
Cum multa turba (*Marc. viii, 1*), 1109*
Cum natus esset ihesus (*Matt. ii, 1*), 400*
Cum sero factum esset (*Marc. vi. 47–56*), 511*
Cum subleuasset (*Ioh. vi, 5*), 1238*
Cum turba plurima (*Luc. viii, 4*), 474*
Cum turbae irruerent (*Luc. v, 1*), 1097*
Cum uenerit filius hominis (*Matt. xxv, 31*), 525*, 991*
Cum uideritis nubem orientem (*Luc. xii, 54*), 136
Debitores sumus (*Rom. viii, 12*), 1115*
Defuncto herode (*Matt. ii, 19*), 396*
Deponentes (*I Petr. ii, 1*), 895*
Descendens ihesus de monte (*Luc. vi, 17*), 1779*
Deus caritas est (*I Ioh. iv, 7*), 1073*
Dicebat ihesus ad eos (*Ioh. viii, 31*), 543*
Dicite filie syon (*Is. lxii, 11*), 759*
Dilectus deo et hominibus (*Ecclus. xlv, 1*), 1888*
Dixerunt impii iudei (*Ierem. xviii, 13*), 733*
Dixerunt pharisei ad ihesum (*Luc. iv, 23*), 617*
Dixit dominus ad moysen (*Exod. xii, 1*), 536*, 784, 823, 2818
Dixit hieremias domine demonstrasti (*Ierem. xvii, 13*), 728*, 753*
Dixit ihesus ad quosdam (*Luc. xviii, 9*), 1133*
Dixit ihesus discipulis suis et turbis (*Luc. x, 23*), 1145*
Dixit ihesus discipulis suis et turbis (*Matt. xxv, 31*), 597*

Dixit ihesus petro sequere me (*Ioh. xxi, 19*), 1312*
Dixit ihesus petro, (*Ioh. xxi, 15*), 1527*
Dixit ihesus turbis iudeorum (*Ioh. viii, 21*), 1304*
Dixit ioseph fratribus suis (*Gen. xxxvii, 6*), 597*
Dixit isaias domine deus aperuit mihi (*Is. i, 5*), 747*
Dixit isaias domine quis credidit (*Is. lxii, 11*), 759*
Dixit rebecca filio suo (*Genes. xxviii, 6*), 603*
Domine deus meus (*Ecclus, li, 13*), 412*, 1899*
Dominus deus caeli qui tulit me de domo (*Gen. xxiv, 7*), 207
Dominus mihi astitit (*2 Tim. iv, 17*), 1872*
Ductus est ihesus (*Matt. iv, 1*), 516*
Dum iret ihesus in hierusalem (*Luc. xvii, 11*), 1151*
Duo homines ascenderunt in templum (*Luc. xviii, 9*), 145
Ecce dies ueniunt (*Amos, ix, 13*), 1175*, 1238*
Ecce ego iohannes, 1779*, 1785*
Ecce ego ipse requiram (*Ezech. xxxiv, 11*), 525*
Ecce nos relinquimus (*Matt. xix, 27*), 1372*, 1543*
Ecce sacerdos magnus (*Ecclus. xliv, 16*), 1329*
Ego quasi uitis (*Ecclus. xxiv, 23*), 452**, 1685*
Ego sum lux (*Ioh. viii, 12*), 691*
Ego sum pastor (*Ioh. x, 11*), 933*
Ego uado et queritis me (*Ioh. viii, 21*), 574*
Egressus ihesus perambulabat (*Luc. xix, 1*), 237
Egressus ihesus secessit (*Matt. xv, 21*), 566*
Egrotauit ezechias (*Is. xxxviii, 1*), 501*
Egrotauit filius mulieris (*III Reg. xvii, 17*), 684*
Eleuatis oculis ihesus (*Luc. vi, 20*), 1878*
Elisabeth impletum est (*Luc. i, 57*), 1510*
Erant appropinquantes (*Luc. xv, 1*), 1085*
Erat dies festus iudeorum (*Ioh. v, 1*), 549*
Erat homo ex phariseis (*Ioh. iii, 1*), 928*, 1438*
Erat ihesus eiiciens doemonium (*Luc. xi, 14*), 609*

387